WE[...]
NEW[...]

POCKET
BIOGRAPHICAL
DICTIONARY

Based on
Webster's New World Dictionary®
of American English
Third College Edition

Donald Stewart, Project Editor
Laura Borovac, Biography Editor

Prentice Hall
New York • London • Toronto
Sydney • Tokyo • Singapore

Prentice Hall General Reference
15 Columbus Circle
New York, NY 10023

Copyright © 1994 by Simon & Schuster, Inc.
All rights reserved
including the right of reproduction
in whole or in part in any form

This book is based on and includes material from
Webster's New World Dictionary®, Third College Edition,
copyright © 1994

A Webster's New World™ Book

PRENTICE HALL is a registered trademark of Prentice-Hall, Inc.
WEBSTER'S NEW WORLD DICTIONARY is a registered trademark
of Simon & Schuster, Inc.
Colophon is a trademark of Prentice-Hall, Inc.

Dictionary Editorial Offices:
New World Dictionaries
850 Euclid Avenue
Cleveland, Ohio 44114

Library of Congress Cataloging-in-Publication Data

Webster's New World pocket biographical dictionary/
    Donald Stewart, project editor, Laura Borovac,
    biography editor.
        p. cm.
     "Based on Webster's New World dictionary of
American English, third college edition."
      ISBN 0-671-88349-6
     1. Biography--Dictionaries. I. Stewart, Donald,
1955-. II. Borovac, Laura. III. Webster's New World
dictionary of American English.
CT103. W44 1994   93-32551
920' .003--dc20   CIP

Database service and principal typesetting by
Lexi-Comp, Inc., Hudson, Ohio.
The typefaces used are Century Schoolbook and Athena.

Manufactured in the United States of America

1 2 3 4 5 6 7 8 9 10   94 95 96 97 98

Guide to Use of the Dictionary

The biographical entries in this book are drawn from the computer database of *Webster's New World Dictionary,* Third College Edition. The extraction of entries has not, however, been a purely mechanical one: all entries have been carefully scrutinized, reevaluated, and, where necessary, updated.

Unlike many competing works, this biographical dictionary includes entries from various categories outside the strictly biographical. Here you will find names from the world's religions, mythologies, and folklore; names from the Bible, world literature, and popular culture; and nicknames, pen names, and pseudonyms. In addition, etymologies are given for more than 1,100 entries, including 400 given names.

The typical biographical entry consists of the last name, pronunciation, first name, any titles or other legal names (married or maiden name, for example), birth and death dates, nationality, and occupation or other reason for the person's fame. Boldface entry names are divided into syllables by centered dots; if at all possible, however, written or printed proper names should not be divided at line ends.

Pinyin transcriptions are given for all Chinese names; alternate transcriptions of longstanding convention are also shown.

Entries follow strict alphabetical order. Thus,

MacDowell, Edward Alexander
MacLeish, Archibald
McCormack, John
McKinley, William

When two or more persons with the same family name are entered, they appear in a single entry block, arranged in alphabetical order by first name. Entries for saints are alphabetized by given name, which appears in boldface; the designation "Saint" follows in lightface.

Cross-references are printed in small capitals, for example,

Twain, Mark *pseud. of* Samuel
Langhorne CLEMENS

PRONUNCIATION

Pronunciations are provided in parentheses immediately after the entry word. The complete pronunciation key for English sounds is printed on the inside back cover. A key for foreign sounds is given below. The pronunciations use many of the letters of the alphabet to represent their usual sounds (e.g., (b) for the *b* in *bed* or *rob*, (d) for the *d* in *dog* or *bad*, etc.). A few additional special symbols are used to cover other native sounds of English and foreign sounds. The *key words* that accompany each symbol in the key have been chosen to assist the user in identifying the correct sound associated with that symbol.

Heavy (′) and light (′) stress marks are used to indicate primary and secondary stress, respectively. The stress mark is placed *after* the stressed syllable.

Variant pronunciations are often truncated, as in the following example:

Roo·se·velt (rō′zə vəlt, -velt; rōō′zə-)

Foreign Sounds

The following special symbols are used to represent non-English sounds in various foreign languages:

à   pronounced as intermediate between (a) and (ä).

ë   approximated by rounding the lips as for (ō) and pronouncing (e).

ö   approximated by rounding the lips as for (ō) and pronouncing (ā).

ô̂   any of a range of sounds between (ô) and (u).

ü   approximated by rounding the lips as for (ō) and pronouncing (ē).

kh	approximated by placing the tongue as for (k) but allowing breath to escape in a stream, as in pronouncing (h).
H	formed by placing the tongue as for (sh) but with the tip pointing downward to produce air friction against the forward part of the palate.
n	indicates that the preceding vowel sound is nasalized; that is, the vowel is pronounced with breath passing through both the mouth and the nose; the letter *n* is not pronounced.
r	any of various trilled (r) sounds, produced with rapid vibration of the tongue or uvula.
'	in French, indicates that the preceding consonant, normally voiced, is voiceless; in Russian, used with *y* to indicate an unvoiced (y) sound.

Staff of
Webster's New World Dictionaries

Executive Editor
Michael Agnes

*Editor and
Database Administrator*
Donald Stewart

*Biography and
Geography Editor*
Laura J. Borovac

Citation Readers
Joan Felice
Batya Jundef
Patricia Nash

Senior Editors
Andrew N. Sparks
Jonathan L. Goldman

Editors
Andra I. Kalnins
James E. Naso
Katherine Goidich Soltis
Stephen P. Teresi

*Data Processing and
Administrative Staff*
Alisa Murray Davis
Cynthia M. Sadonick
Betty Dziedzic Thompson

Abbreviations and Symbols
Used in This Book

abbrev.	abbreviation, abbreviated	Ch.	Church
		Chin	Chinese
abl.	ablative	Chron.	Chronicles
acc.	accusative	Class.	Classical
adj.	adjective	Col.	Colossians
adv.	adverb	Colloq.	Colloquial
Afr	African	comb.	combination, combining
Afrik	Afrikaans		
Alb	Albanian	comp.	compound
alt.	alternative	compar.	comparative (grammar)
Am	American		
AmFr	American French	conj.	conjunction
AmInd	Amerindian	contr.	contraction (grammar)
AmSp	American Spanish		
		Cor.	Corinthians
Anglo-Fr	Anglo-French	cu.	cubic
Anglo-Ind	Anglo-Indian	Dan	Danish
Anglo-Ir	Anglo-Irish	Dan.	Daniel (Bible)
Anglo-L	Anglo-Latin	dat.	dative
Anglo-Norm	Anglo-Norman	deriv.	derived, derivative
Ar	Arabic		
Aram	Aramaic	Deut.	Deuteronomy
Arm	Armenian	dial.	dialect, dialectal
art.	article (grammar)	dim.	diminutive
assoc.	associated, association	Du	Dutch
		dupl.	duplicated, duplication
Assyr	Assyrian		
Astrol.	Astrology	E	eastern; English (in etyms)
aug.	augmentative		
Austral	Australian	EC	east central
Bab	Babylonian	Eccl.	Ecclesiastes
back-form.	back-formation	Eccles.	Ecclesiastical
Beng	Bengali	EFris	East Frisian
BrazPort	Brazilian Portuguese	e.g.	for example
		Egypt	Egyptian
Bret	Breton	Eng.	English
Brit	British	Eph.	Ephesians
Bulg	Bulgarian	equiv.	equivalent
c.	circa; century (in etyms)	Esk	Eskimo
		esp.	especially
cap.	capital city	est.	estimated
caus.	causative	etc.	and/or the like
Cdn	Canadian	Etr	Etruscan
CdnFr	Canadian French	etym	etymology
Celt	Celtic	Ex.	example; Exodus
cent.	century, centuries	exc.	except
cf.	compare	Ezek.	Ezekiel

fem.	feminine	interj.	interjection
fig.	figurative, figuratively	Ir	Irish
		Iran	Iranian
Finn	Finnish	irreg.	irregular
Fl	Flemish	Isa.	Isaiah
fl.	flourished; lived (of people)	It	Italian
		Jer.	Jeremiah
fol.	following entry	Josh.	Joshua
Fr	French	Jpn	Japanese
Frank	Frankish	Judg.	Judges
freq.	frequentative	KJV	King James Version
Fris	Frisian		
ft.	foot, feet	km	kilometer(s)
fut.	future	Kor	Korean
Gael	Gaelic	L	classical Latin
Gal.	Galatians	Lam.	Lamentations
Gaul	Gaulish	L(Ec)	Ecclesiastical Latin
Gen.	Genesis		
gen.	genitive	Lev.	Leviticus
Geog.	Geography	LGr	Late Greek
Ger	German	LGr(Ec)	Ecclesiastical Late Greek
ger.	gerund, gerundive	Linguis.	Linguistics
Gmc	Germanic	lit.	literally
Goth	Gothic	Lith	Lithuanian
gov.	governor	LL	Late Latin
gov. gen.	governor general	LL(Ec)	Ecclesiastical Late Latin
Gr	classical Greek	LME	Late Middle English
Gr(Ec)	Ecclesiastical Greek		
Hab.	Habakkuk	LowG	Low German
Hag.	Haggai	LWS	Late West Saxon
Haw	Hawaiian	LXX	Septuagint
Heb	classical Hebrew (language)	m	meter(s)
		Macc.	Maccabees
Heb.	Hebrews	Mal.	Malachi
Heb-Aram	Hebrew-Aramaic	masc.	masculine
Hos.	Hosea	Matt.	Matthew
Hung	Hungarian	MDu	Middle Dutch
Ice	Icelandic	ME	Middle English
IE	Indo-European	met.	metropolitan
i.e.	that is	Mex	Mexican
imper.	imperative	MexSp	Mexican Spanish
imperf.	imperfect	MFl	Middle Flemish
incl.	including	MFr	Middle French
Ind	Indian; Indic (in etyms)	MGr	Medieval Greek
		MHeb	Medieval Hebrew
indic.	indicative		
inf.	infinitive	MHG	Middle High German
infl.	influenced, influence		
		mi.	mile(s)
intens.	intensive	Mic.	Micah

Abbr.	Meaning	Abbr.	Meaning
MIr	Middle Irish	OIt	Old Italian
mistransl.	mistranslation	OL	Old Latin
ML	Medieval Latin	OLowFranc	Old Low Franconian
ML(Ec)	Ecclesiastical Medieval Latin	OLowG	Old Low German
MLowG	Middle Low German	ON	Old Norse
ModE	Modern English	OPers	Old Persian
ModGr	Modern Greek	OProv	Old Provençal
ModHeb	Modern Hebrew	OPrus	Old Prussian
ModL	Modern Latin	orig.	origin, originally
MScot	Middle Scottish	OS	Old Saxon
Myth.	Mythology	Osco-Umb	Osco-Umbrian
N	northern	OSlav	Old Church Slavonic
NAmFr	North American French	OSp	Old Spanish
n.	noun	OSw	Old Swedish
Nah.	Nahum	O.T.	Old Testament
NC	north central	OWelsh	Old Welsh
NE	northeast, northeastern	oz.	ounce(s)
Neh.	Nehemiah	PaGer	Pennsylvania German
Netherl	Netherlandic	part.	participle, participial
neut.	neuter	pass.	passive voice
n.fem.	feminine noun	perf.	perfect tense
NGmc	North Germanic	pers.	person; personal (grammar)
n.masc.	masculine noun	Pers	Persian
nom.	nominative	Pet.	Peter (Bible)
Norm	Norman	PGmc	Proto-Germanic
NormFr	Norman French	Phil.	Philippians
Norw	Norwegian	Philem.	Philemon
n.pl.	plural noun	Phoen	Phoenician
n.sing.	singular noun	phr.	phrase
N.T.	New Testament	PidE	Pidgin English
Num.	Numbers	PIE	Proto-Indo-European
NW	northwest, northwestern	pl.	plural
obj.	object, objective	Poet.	Poetic
OAr	Old Arabic	Pol	Polish
Ob.	Obadiah	pop.	popular; population
Obs., obs.	obsolete	Port	Portuguese
occas.	occasionally	poss.	possessive
OCelt	Old Celtic	pp.	past participle
ODan	Old Danish	prec.	preceding entry
ODu	Old Dutch	prep.	preposition
OE	Old English	pres.	present tense
OFr	Old French	Pres., pres.	President
OFris	Old Frisian	pret.	preterit
OHG	Old High German	prin. pts.	principal parts
OIce	Old Icelandic	priv.	privative
OInd	Old Indic		
OIr	Old Irish		

prob.	probably	transl.	translated, translation
pron.	pronoun		
pronun.	pronunciation	Turk	Turkish
Prov	Provençal	ult.	ultimately
Prov.	Proverbs	UN	United Nations
prp.	present participle	uncert.	uncertain
Prus	Prussian	U.S.	United States
Ps.	Psalms	U.S.S.R.	Union of Soviet Socialist Republics
pseud.	pseudonym		
pt.	past tense		
redupl.	reduplicated, reduplication	v.	verb
		var.	variant; variety
ref.	reference, refer	v.aux.	auxiliary verb
refl.	reflexive	vi.	intransitive verb
Rev.	Revelation	VL	Vulgar Latin
Rom.	Roman	voc.	vocative
Russ	Russian	vt.	transitive verb
S	southern	Vulg.	Vulgate
Sam.	Samuel (Bible)	W	western
SAmSp	South American Spanish	WAfr	West African
		WC	west central
Sans	Sanskrit	WFris	West Frisian
SC	south central	WGmc	West Germanic
Scand	Scandinavian	WInd	West Indian
Scot	Scottish	WS	West Saxon
SE	southeast, southeastern	Yidd	Yiddish
		Zech.	Zechariah
Sem	Semitic	Zeph.	Zephaniah
Serb	Serbian		
sing.	singular		
Sino-Jpn	Sino-Japanese		
Slav	Slavonic, Slavic		
S. of Sol.	Song of Solomon		
Sp	Spanish		
sp.	spelling, spelled		
specif.	specifically		
sq.	square		
S.S.R.	Soviet Socialist Republic		

Note that in etymologies, periods are not used with these abbreviations.

subj.	subject, subjective		**Symbols**
subjunc.	subjunctive	*	not attested (in etyms)
superl.	superlative	+	plus
SW	southwest, southwestern	°	degree
		<	derived from (in etyms)
Swed	Swedish		
TalmudHeb	Talmudic Hebrew	>	from which is derived (in etyms)
Theol.	Theology		
Thess.	Thessalonians	?	uncertain or unknown; perhaps
Tim.	Timothy (Bible)		
Tit.	Titus (Bible)	&	and

Pronunciation Key

English Sounds

Symbol	Key Words	Symbol	Key Words
a	cat	b	bed, dub
ā	ape	d	dip, had
ä	cot	f	fall
		g	get, dog
e	ten	h	help
ē	me	j	joy
		k	kick, quit
i	fit	l	leg, bottle
ī	bite	m	meat
		n	nose, kitten
ō	go	p	put
ô	all, or	r	red
oo	look, pull	s	see
o͞o	tool, rule	t	top, cattle
oi	oil, toy	v	vat
ou	out, plow	w	wish, quick
		y	yard
u	cup	z	zebra
ʉr	turn		
ə	ago, agent, pencil, atom, focus	ŋ	ring, drink
		ch	chin, arch
ər	perhaps, mother	hw	where
		sh	she, motion
		th	thin, truth
'	cattle (kat''l), cotton (kät''n)	*th*	then, father
		zh	measure

The key for foreign sounds can be found
on page iv in the front of the book.

A

Aal·to (äl′tô′), (Hugo) **Al·var** (Henrik) (äl′vär′) 1898-1976; Finn. architect & furniture designer

Aar·on (er′ən, ar′-) ⟦LL < Gr *Aarōn* < Heb *aharon*, lit., the exalted one⟧ **1** a masculine name **2** *Bible* the older brother of Moses and first high priest of the Hebrews: Ex. 4, 40:13-16

A·bad·don (ə bad′′n) ⟦Heb, destruction, abyss⟧ *Bible* in *Revelation*, the angel of the abyss; Apollyon: Rev. 9:11

Ab·ba (ab′ə, ä′bə) *Bible* God: Mark 14:36

Ab·bot (ab′ət), **Charles Greeley** 1872-1973; U.S. astrophysicist

Ab·bott (ab′ət), **Ly·man** (li′mən) 1835-1922; U.S. clergyman, editor, & author

Ab·di·as (ab dī′əs) *Douay Bible name of* OBADIAH

Abd·ul-A·ziz (äb′do̅o̅l ä zēz′) 1830-76; sultan of Turkey (1861-76)

Abd·ul-Ha·mid II (-hä mēd′) 1842-1918; sultan of Turkey (1876-1909)

Abd·ul-Me·djid, Abd·ul-Me·jid (-me jēd′) 1823-61; sultan of Turkey (1839-61)

A·bed·ne·go (ə bed′nə gō′) ⟦Aram *aved nego*, prob., lit., servant of Nego⟧ *Bible* one of the three captives who came out of the fiery furnace unharmed: Dan. 3:12-27

A·bel (ā′bəl) ⟦L < Gr *Abel* < ? Heb *hevel*, lit., breath⟧ **1** a masculine name **2** *Bible* the second son of Adam and Eve, killed by his brother Cain: Gen. 4

A·bé·lard (á bā lär′), **Pierre** 1079-1142; Fr. philosopher, teacher, & theologian: see also HÉLOÏSE: Eng. name **Peter Ab·e·lard** (ab′ə lärd′)

Ab·er·nath·y (ab′ər nath′ē), **Ralph David** 1926-90; U.S. clergyman & civil rights leader

Ab·i·gail (ab′ə gāl′) ⟦Heb *avigayil*, lit., father is rejoicing⟧ a feminine name: dim. *Abby, Gail*

Ab·ner (ab′nər) ⟦L < Heb *avner*, lit., the father is a light⟧ a masculine name

A·bra·ham (ā′brə ham′) ⟦Heb *avraham*, lit., father of many: the original form, *avram*, means "father is exalted": see Gen. 17:5⟧ **1** a masculine name: dim. *Abe* **2** *Bible* the first patriarch and ancestor of the Hebrews: Gen. 12-25

A·bram (ā′brəm) *var. of* ABRAHAM

Ab·sa·lom (ab'sə ləm, -läm') ⟦L < Heb *avshalom*, lit., the father is peace⟧ *Bible* David's favorite son, killed after rebelling against his father: 2 Sam. 18

A·bu al-Qā·sim (ä'bōō' äl kä'sim', ə bōō' əl-) (L. name *Albucasis*) *c.* 936-*c.* 1013; Arab surgeon & medical encyclopedist, in Spain: also **A·bul Ka·sim** (ä'bool kä' sim', ə bool' kä'-)

A·bu–Bakr (ä'bōō bä'kər, ə bōō' bä'-) A.D. 573-634; successor of Mohammed & 1st caliph of Islam (A.D. 632-634): father of Aisha: also **A·bu–Bekr** (-bek'ər)

A·cha·tes (ə kāt'ēz') in Virgil's *Aeneid*, a loyal companion of Aeneas

A·che·be (ä chā'bā), **Chin·ua** (chin'wä') (born *Albert Chinualumgu*) 1930- ; Nigerian critic & writer

A·chil·les (ə kil'ēz') ⟦L < Gr *Achilleus*⟧ *Gr. Myth.* Greek warrior and leader in the Trojan War who kills Hector and is killed by Paris with an arrow that strikes his only vulnerable spot, his heel: he is the hero of Homer's *Iliad*

A·chit·o·phel (ə kit'ə fel') AHITHOPHEL

Ac·tae·on (ak tē'ən) ⟦L < Gr *Aktaiōn*⟧ *Gr. Myth.* a hunter who makes Artemis angry by watching her bathe: she changes him into a stag, and his dogs tear him to pieces

Ac·ton (ak'tən), **1st Baron** (*John Emerick Edward Dalberg-Acton*) 1834-1902; Eng. historian: known as *Lord Acton*

A·cuff (ā'kuf'), **Roy** 1903-92; U.S. composer & country music singer

A·da, A·dah (ā'də) ⟦Heb *ada*, beauty⟧ a feminine name

Ad·am (ad'əm) ⟦Heb < *adam*, a human being⟧ **1** a masculine name **2** *Bible* the first man: Gen. 1-5

Ad·ams (ad'əmz) **1 Charles Francis** 1807-86; U.S. statesman: son of John Quincy **2 Henry (Brooks)** 1838-1918; U.S. historian & writer: son of Charles Francis **3 John** 1735-1826; 2d president of the U.S. (1797-1801) **4 John Quin·cy** (kwin'zē, -sē) 1767-1848; 6th president of the U.S. (1825-29): son of John **5 Samuel** 1722-1803; Am. statesman & Revolutionary leader

Ad·dams (ad'əmz), **Jane** 1860-1935; U.S. social worker & writer: founder of Hull-House in Chicago

Ad·di·son (ad'i sən), **Joseph** 1672-1719; Eng. essayist & poet

Ade (ād), **George** 1866-1944; U.S. humorist

Ad·e·la (ad′lə, ə del′ə) a feminine name: dim. *Della*; var. *Adelia*; Fr. *Adèle*: see ADELAIDE

Ad·e·laide (ad′′l ād′) 〖Fr *Adélaïde* < Ger *Adelheid* < OHG *Adalheidis, Adalheit*, lit., nobility < *adal*, nobility + *-heit*, noun suffix akin to E *-hood* 〗 a feminine name: dim. *Addie*; var. *Adeline, Adela*

Ad·el·bert (ad′′l bʉrt′, ə del′bərt) a masculine name: see ALBERT

A·dele (ə del′) a feminine name: see ADELA

Ad·e·line (ad′′l īn′, -ēn′) a feminine name: var. *Adelina, Aline*: see ADELAIDE

A·de·nau·er (ad′′n our; *Ger* ä′dən ou′ər), **Kon·rad** (kän′rad′; *Ger* kôn′rät′) 1876-1967; Ger. statesman: chancellor of the Federal Republic of Germany (1949-63)

Ad·ler (ad′lər; *for 1, also, Ger* äd′lər) **1 Alfred** 1870-1937; Austrian psychiatrist & psychologist **2 Felix** 1851-1933; U.S. educator & social reformer: founder of the Ethical Cultural Movement **3 Lawrence** (called *Larry*) 1914- ; U.S. musician

Ad·me·tus (ad mēt′əs) 〖L < Gr *Admētos*, lit., wild, unbroken 〗 *Gr. Myth.* a king of Thessaly, husband of Alcestis

Ad·olph (ad′ôlf, ā′dôlf) 〖L *Adolphus* < OHG *Adolf, Adulf*, lit., noble wolf < *adal*, nobility + *wolf*, wolf〗 a masculine name: equiv. L. *Adolphus*, Fr. *Adolphe*, Ger. *Adolf*

Ad·o·na·i (ä′dō nä′ē, -nī′, -noi′; ad′ō nä′ī′) 〖Heb, my Lord < NW Sem *Adōn, Adun*, lord; ? akin to Ar *ʔīdhn*, command 〗 God; Lord: used in Hebrew reading as a substitute for the "ineffable name" JHVH: see JEHOVAH

A·do·nis (ə dän′is, -dōn′-) 〖L < Gr *Adōnis* 〗 *Gr. Myth.* a handsome young man loved by Aphrodite: he is killed by a wild boar

A·dor·no (ə dôr′nō), **Theodore Wie·sen·grund** (vē′zən groont′) 1903-69; Ger. philosopher & music critic

A·dras·tus (ə dras′təs) *Gr. Myth.* a king of Argos who leads the Seven against Thebes

A·dri·an (ā′drē ən) 〖L *Adrianus, Hadrianus* < *Adria, Hadria*, name of two Italian cities 〗 **1** a masculine name: fem. *Adrienne* **2 Adrian IV** (born *Nicholas Breakspear*) c. 1100-59; pope (1154-59): the only Eng. pope **3 E(dgar) D(ouglas)** 1st Baron 1889-1977; Eng.

neurophysiologist

A·dri·enne (ā'drē en'; *Fr* à drē en') a feminine name: see ADRIAN

Adversary, the Satan

Æ, A.E. *see* RUSSELL, George William

Ae·a·cus (ē'ə kəs) 〚L < Gr *Aiakos*〛 *Gr. Myth.* a king of Aegina who, after he dies, becomes one of the three judges of the dead in the lower world, with Minos and Rhadamanthus

Ae·ge·us (ē'jē əs) 〚L < Gr *Aigeus*〛 *Gr. Myth.* a king of Athens who drowns himself when he thinks his son Theseus is dead

Ae·gir (ā'gir'; ē'jir', ā'-) 〚ON〛 *Norse Myth.* the god of the sea

Ae·gis·thus (ē jis'thəs) 〚L < Gr *Aigisthos*〛 *Gr. Myth.* the son of Thyestes and lover of Clytemnestra: he helps her to kill her husband, Agamemnon

Ae·gyp·tus (ē jip'təs) *Gr. Myth.* a king of Egypt whose fifty sons marry the fifty daughters of his brother Danaus: see DANAIDES

Ael·fric (al'frik) *c.* 955-*c.* 1020; Eng. abbot & writer: called *the Grammarian*

Ae·ne·as (i nē'əs) 〚L < Gr *Aineias*〛 *Gr. & Rom. Myth.* a Trojan, son of Anchises and Venus, and hero of Virgil's *Aeneid*: escaping from ruined Troy, Aeneas wanders for years before coming to Latium: he is considered the forefather of the Romans

Ae·o·lus (ē'ə ləs) 〚L < Gr *Aiolos*〛 *Gr. Myth.* **1** the god of the winds **2** a king of Thessaly, the legendary forefather of the Aeolians

Aes·chi·nes (es'ki nēz') 389-314 B.C.; Athenian orator

Aes·chy·lus (es'ki ləs) *c.* 525-456 B.C.; Gr. writer of tragedies

Aes·cu·la·pi·us (es'kyo͞o lā'pē əs) 〚L < Gr *Asklēpios*〛 *Rom. Myth.* the god of medicine and of healing, son of Apollo: identified with the Greek Asclepius

Ae·sop (ē'səp, -säp') real or legendary Gr. author of fables: supposed to have lived 6th cent. B.C.

Aeth·el·stan (ath'əl stan') *var. of* ATHELSTAN

A·ga Khan IV (ä'gə kän') (*Karim al Hussaini Shah*) 1937- ; spiritual leader of the Ismailian sect of Muslims (1957-)

Ag·a·mem·non (ag'ə mem'nän', -nən) 〚Gr〛 *Gr. Myth.* king of Mycenae and commander in chief of the Greek army in the Trojan War, killed by his wife Clytemnestra

Ag·as·siz (ag′ə sē) **1 Alexander** 1835-1910; U.S. zoologist, geologist, & oceanographer, born in Switzerland: son of (Jean) Louis **2 (Jean) Louis (Rodolphe)** 1807-73; U.S. zoologist & geologist, born in Switzerland

Ag·a·tha (ag′ə thə) ⟦L < Gr *Agathē*, lit., good, fem. of *agathos*, good⟧ a feminine name

A·gee (ā′jē′), **James** 1909-55; U.S. writer

A·ges·i·la·us (II) (ə jes′i lā′əs) *c.* 442-*c.* 360 B.C.; king of Sparta during the decline of its supremacy in ancient Greece

Ag·ge·us (a jē′ əs) *Douay Bible name of* HAGGAI

A·gla·ia (ə glā′ə, ə glī′ə) ⟦L < Gr *Aglaia*, lit., brightness⟧ *Gr. Myth.* Brilliance, one of the three Graces

Ag·nes (ag′nis) ⟦Fr *Agnès* < L *Agnes*, *Hagnes* < Gr *hagnē*, fem. of *hagnos*, chaste⟧ **1** a feminine name: dim. *Aggie*; equiv. Sp. *Inez* **2** Saint (died A.D. 304); Rom. virgin martyr: her day is Jan. 21

A·gric·o·la (ə grik′ə lə) **1 (Gnaeus Julius)** A.D. 40-93; Rom. general: governor of Britain (*c.* A.D. 78-*c.* 85) **2 Geor·gi·us** (jôr′jē əs) (L. name of *Georg Bauer*) 1490-1555; Ger. scholar who made the first scientific classification of minerals: called the *Father of Mineralogy*

A·grip·pa (ə grip′ə) **1 (Marcus Vipsanius)** *c.* 63-12 B.C.; Rom. military leader & statesman: commander of Octavian's fleet at Actium **2** *see* HEROD AGRIPPA I

Ag·rip·pi·na (II) (a′gri pī′nə, -pē′-), **(Julia)** *c.* A.D. 15-59; mother of Nero: called *Agrippina the Younger*

A·hab (ā′hab′) ⟦Heb *ach'av*, lit., father's brother⟧ *Bible* a wicked king of Israel of the 9th cent. B.C.: husband of Jezebel: 1 Kings 16:29-22:40

A·has·u·e·rus (ə haz′yōō ir′əs, -has′-) ⟦Heb < OPers *Xxayaršan*⟧ *Bible* either of two kings of the Medes and Persians, esp. the one (often identified as Xerxes I) who was married to Esther: Esth. 1; Ezra 4:6

A·hith·o·phel (ə hith′ə fel′) ⟦Heb *achitofel*, lit., brother is foolishness⟧ *Bible* a counselor of David and associate of Absalom in rebellion against David: 2 Sam. 15-17

Ah·ri·man (ä′ri mən) ⟦MPers *Ahriman*, prob. < Avestan *aṅra mainyu*, the evil (lit., hostile) spirit⟧ *Zoroastrianism* the spirit of evil: see ORMAZD

A·hu·ra Maz·da (ä′hoo rə maz′də) ORMAZD

Ai·ken (ā'kən), **Conrad** (**Potter**) 1889-1973; U.S. poet & fiction writer

Ai·leen (ī lēn', ā-) a feminine name: see EILEEN

A·i·sha (ä'ē shä') *c.* A.D. 614-678; Mohammed's favorite wife; daughter of Abu-Bakr

A·jax (ā'jaks') 〚L < Gr *Aias*〛 *Gr. Myth.* **1** a strong, brave Greek warrior in the Trojan War who kills himself when Achilles' armor is given to Odysseus: called **Ajax Tel·a·mon** (tel'ə män') **2** one of the swiftest runners among the Greek warriors in the Trojan War: called **Ajax the Less**

Ak·bar (ak'bär') 1542-1605; Mogul emperor of Hindustan (1556-1605): called *the Great*

A·khe·na·ten, **A·khe·na·ton** (ä'ke nät''n) *var. of* IKHNA-TON

Akh·ma·to·va (ukh mät'ə və; *E also* äk'mə tō'və), **An·na** (än'ə) (pseud. of *Anna Andreyevna Gorenko*) 1889-1966; Russ. poet

A·ki·hi·to (ä'kē hē'tō) 1933- ; emperor of Japan (1989-)

A·lad·din (ə lad''n) 〚Ar *A'l-ad-dīn*, lit., height of faith < *a'lā*, height + *al*, the + *dīn*, faith〛 a boy in *The Arabian Nights* who finds a magic lamp and a magic ring, with which he can call up a jinni to do his bidding

Al·an (al'ən) 〚ML *Alanus*, of Bret orig.〛 a masculine name: dim. *Al*; var. *Allan, Allen*

A·lar·cón (ä'lär kōn'), **Pe·dro An·to·nio de** (pe'thrô än tô'nyô de) 1833-91; Sp. writer

Al·a·ric (al'ə rik) **1** A.D. 370-410; king of the Visigoths (*c.* 395-410): captured Rome (410) **2 Alaric II** died A.D. 507; king of the Visigoths (*c.* 484-507): issued a code of laws

Al·ba (äl'bä), **Duke of** *var. of* Duke of ALVA

Al·ban (al'bən, ôl'-) 〚L *Albanus*, after *Alba*, name of several Italian cities〛 **1** a masculine name **2** Saint (died *c.* A.D. 304); Brit. martyr: his day is June 22

Al·bee (ôl'bē), **Edward** 1928- ; U.S. playwright

Al·bé·niz (äl bā'nith, -nis), **Isaac** (**Manuel Francisco**) 1860-1909; Sp. composer & pianist

Al·ber·ich (äl'ber iH) 〚Ger < MHG *alb*, elf + *rich* (OHG *rihhi*), leader, king, realm〛 *Gmc. Legend* the king of the dwarfs and leader of the Nibelungs

Al·bers (al'bərz, äl'bərs), **Jo·sef** (yō'zef') 1888-1976; U.S. painter, born in Germany

Al·bert (al'bərt) 〚Fr < OHG *Adalbrecht*, lit., bright through nobility < *adal*, nobility + *beraht*, bright 〛 **1 a** masculine name: dim. *Al, Bert*; var. *Adelbert, Elbert*; fem. *Alberta, Albertine* **2 Albert I** 1875-1934; king of Belgium (1909-34) **3** Prince (*Albert of Saxe-Coburg-Gotha*) 1819-61; husband (Prince Consort) of Queen Victoria of England (1840-61)

Al·ber·ta (al burt'ə) 〚fem. of prec.〛 a feminine name: var. *Albertine*

Al·ber·ti (äl ber'tē), **Le·on Bat·tis·ta** (le ôn' bät tēs'tä) 1404-72; It. architect & painter

Al·ber·tus Mag·nus (al burt'əs mag'nəs), Saint (*Count von Bollstädt*) *c.* 1200-1280; Ger. scholastic philosopher: teacher of Thomas Aquinas

Al·bo·in (al'boin', -bō in') died A.D. 572; king of the Lombards (*c.* 565-572): conqueror of N Italy

Al·bu·ca·sis (al'byoo kā'sis) *Latin name of* ABU AL-QĀSIM

Al·bu·quer·que (äl'boo ker'kə), **Af·fon·so de** (ə fôn'soo də) 1453-1515; Port. navigator: established Port. colonies in the East

Al·cae·us (al sē'əs) fl. 600 B.C.; Gr. lyric poet

Al·ces·tis (al ses'tis) 〚L < Gr *Alkēstis*〛 *Gr. Myth.* the wife of Admetus, king of Thessaly: she offers her life to save that of her husband, but is rescued from Hades by Hercules

Al·ci·bi·a·des (al'sə bī'ə dēz') 450-404 B.C.; Athenian politician & general in the Peloponnesian War

Al·ci·des (al sī'dēz') 〚L < Gr *Alkeidēs*〛 HERCULES

Al·cin·o·üs (al sin'ō əs) *Gr. Myth.* father of NAUSICAÄ

Alc·me·ne (alk mē'nē) 〚L < Gr *Alkmēnē*〛 *Gr. Myth.* the mother of Hercules by Zeus, who seduces her by appearing in the likeness of her husband, Amphitryon

Al·cott (ôl'kət) **1** (Amos) **Bron·son** (brän'sən) 1799-1888; U.S. philosopher and educational reformer **2 Louisa May** 1832-88; U.S. novelist: daughter of (Amos) Bronson

Al·cuin (al'kwin) *c.* A.D. 735-804; Eng. theologian & writer: advisor in the court of Charlemagne

Al·den (ôl'dən), **John** *c.* 1599-1687; Pilgrim settler in Plymouth Colony: character in Henry Wadsworth Longfellow's poem "The Courtship of Miles Standish"

Al·drich (ôl'drich), **Thomas Bailey** 1836-1907; U.S. poet & novelist

Al·drin (ôl′drin), **Edwin Eugene, Jr.** (called *Buzz*) 1930- ; U.S. astronaut: 2d man on the moon

A·lec·to (ə lek′tō) ⟦L < Gr *Alēktō*⟧ *Gr. & Rom. Myth.* one of the three Furies

A·lei·chem (ə lā′kəm), **Sho·lom** (shô′ləm) (pseud. of *Solomon Rabinowitz*) 1859-1916; Russ. writer (also in the U.S.) of humorous stories, drama, etc. in Yiddish

A·le·mán (ä′le män′), **Ma·te·o** (mä tā′ō) 1547-*c.* 1614; Sp. novelist

Alembert, Jean le Rond d' *see* D′ALEMBERT, Jean le Rond

Al·ex·an·der (al′ig zan′dər) ⟦L < Gr *Alexandros*, lit., defender of men < *alexein*, to defend + *anēr* (gen. *andros*), man⟧ **1** a masculine name: dim. *Aleck, Alex, Sandy*; equiv. Fr. *Alexandre*, It. *Alessandro*, Russ. *Aleksandr*, Scot. *Alistair*, Sp. *Alejandro*; fem. *Alexandra, Alexandrina* **2 Alexander I** 1777-1825; czar of Russia (1801-25); grandson of Catherine the Great **3 Alexander I** 1876-1903; king of Serbia (1889-1903): assassinated **4 Alexander I** 1888-1934; king of Yugoslavia (1921-34): assassinated **5 Alexander II** 1818-81; czar of Russia (1855-81): emancipated the serfs: assassinated: son of Nicholas I **6 Alexander III** (born *Orlando Bandinelli*) died 1181; pope (1159-81) **7 Alexander III** 1845-94; czar of Russia (1881-94): son of Alexander II **8 Alexander VI** (born *Rodrigo de Borja y Doms*) 1431-1503; pope (1492-1503): father of Cesare & Lucrezia Borgia **9 Sir Harold R(upert) L(eofric) G(eorge)** 1st Viscount Alexander of Tunis 1891-1969; Brit. general & statesman: governor-general of Canada (1946-52)

Alexander Nev·ski (nef′skē) *c.* 1220-63; Russ. military hero, statesman, & saint

Alexander Se·ve·rus (si vir′əs) *c.* A.D. 208-235; Rom. emperor (A.D. 222-235)

Alexander the Great 356-323 B.C.; king of Macedonia (336-323): military conqueror who helped spread Greek culture from Asia Minor & Egypt to India: also **Alexander III**

Al·ex·an·dra (al′ig zan′drə) ⟦fem. of ALEXANDER⟧ a feminine name: dim. *Sandra, Sandy*; var. *Alexandrina*

A·lex·is (ə leks′is) ⟦Gr, lit., help < *alexein*, to defend⟧ **1** a masculine and feminine name **2 Alexis (I)** 1629-76; czar of Russia (1645-76): father of Peter the Great

A·lex·i·us I (ə leks'ē əs) (*Alexius Comnenus*) 1048-1118; emperor of the Byzantine Empire (1081-1118)

Al·fie·ri (äl fyer'ē), Count **Vit·to·ri·o** (vi tôr'ē ō') 1749-1803; It. dramatist & poet

Al·fon·so XIII (al fän'zō, -sō; *Sp* äl'fôn'sô) 1886-1941; king of Spain (1886-1931); deposed

Al·fred (al'frəd) [[OE *Ælfred*, lit., elf-counsel, hence, wise counselor < *ælf*, elf + *ræd*, counsel]] a masculine name: dim. *Al, Alf, Alfie, Fred*; fem. *Alfreda*

Al·fre·da (al frēd'ə) a feminine name: see ALFRED

Alfred the Great A.D. 849-899; king of Wessex (871-899): put an end to Dan. conquests in England: promoted Eng. culture

Al·ger (al'jər), **Horatio** 1832-99; U.S. writer of boys' stories

Al·ger·non (al'jər nən, -nän') [[apparently < OFr *al grenon*, with a mustache]] a masculine name: dim. *Algie, Algy*

A·li (ä'lē, ä lē') **1** *c.* A.D. 600-661; 4th caliph of Islam (656-661), considered the 1st caliph by the Shiites: son-in-law of Mohammed **2 Mehemet** *see* MEHEMET ALI **3 Muhammad** (born *Cassius Marcellus Clay*) 1942- ; U.S. boxer

A·li Ba·ba (ä'lē bä'bə, al'ē bab'ə) in *The Arabian Nights,* a poor woodcutter who accidentally discovers the treasure of a band of forty thieves in a cave: he makes the door of the cave open by saying "Open sesame!"

Al·ice (al'is) [[ME *Alys, Aeleis* < OFr *Aliz, Aaliz* < *Adaliz* < OHG *Adalheidis*: see ADELAIDE]] a feminine name: dim. *Elsie*; var. *Alicia*

A·li·ci·a (ə lish'ə, -lē'shə; -lish'ē ə, -lē'shē ə) a feminine name: see ALICE

A·li Pa·sha (ä'lē pä shä') 1741-1822; Turk. governor of Albania & part of Greece, including Janina: deposed & assassinated: called the *Lion of Janina*

Al·i·son (al'i sən) [[ME *Alisoun* < OFr *Aliz* (see ALICE) + *-on*, suffix of uncert. meaning]] a feminine name

Al·i·stair (al'i ster') [[< ALEXANDER]] a masculine name

Al·lah (al'ə, ä'lə, ä'lä', ä lä') [[Ar *Allāh* < *al*, the + *ilāh*, god, akin to Heb *eloah*, God]] *the Muslim name for* God

Al·lan (al'ən) a masculine name: see ALAN

Al·len (al'ən) **1** a masculine name: see ALAN **2 Ethan** 1738-89; Am. Revolutionary soldier who led the Green

Mountain Boys in the capture of Fort Ticonderoga

Al·len·by (al'ən bē), **Edmund Henry Hyn·man** (hin'mən) 1st Viscount Allenby 1861-1936; Brit. army officer: commander of Brit. expeditionary forces in Egypt (1917-18)

Al·ma (al'mə) ⟦L, fem. of *almus*, nourishing, bountiful⟧ a feminine name

Al·ma–Tad·e·ma (al'mə tad'i mə), Sir **Lawrence** 1836-1912; Eng. painter, born in the Netherlands

Almighty, the God

Al·o·y·si·us (al'ō ish'əs, -ē əs) ⟦ML *Aloisius*; prob. < OFr *Loeis*: see LOUIS⟧ a masculine name

Al·phe·us (al fē'əs) ⟦L < Gr *Alpheios*⟧ *Gr. Myth.* a river god who pursues Arethusa until she is changed into a stream by Artemis

Al·phon·so (al fän'zō, -sō) ⟦Sp *Alfonso* < Gmc **Athalfuns* < **athal*; akin to OHG *adal*, nobility + *funs*, ready⟧ a masculine name

Al·the·a (al thē'ə) ⟦L *Althaea* < Gr *Althaia*, lit., healer < *althainein*, to heal < IE base **al-*, to grow⟧ a feminine name

Al·va (al'və; *Sp* äl'vä'), Duke of (*Fernando Álvarez de Toledo*) 1508-82; Sp. general who suppressed a revolt in the Low Countries

Al·vah, Al·va (al'və) ⟦Heb *alva, alvan*; often assoc. with L *albus*, white⟧ a masculine name: var. **Al'van** (-vən)

Al·va·ra·do (äl'və rä'dō), **Pe·dro de** (pe'drō dä) 1495-1541; Sp. general with Cortés in the conquest of Mexico

Ál·va·rez Quin·te·ro (äl'vä reth' kēn ter'ō) **1 Joa·quín** (hwä kēn') 1873-1944; Sp. playwright **2 Se·ra·fín** (ser'ə fēn') 1871-1938; Sp. playwright: collaborated with his brother Joaquín

Al·vin (al'vin, -vən) ⟦Ger *Alwin*, lit., noble friend < OHG *adal*, nobility + *wini*, friend⟧ a masculine name

Am·a·dis of Gaul (am'ə dis') ⟦Sp *Amadís*, lit., love of God⟧ the title character of a medieval prose romance in Spanish

A·ma·do (ə mä'dōō), **Jor·ge** (zhôr'zhə) 1912- ; Brazilian writer

Am·a·lek (am'ə lek') *Bible* a grandson of Esau: Gen. 36:9-12

A·man·da (ə man'də) ⟦L, lit., worthy to be loved < the gerund stem of *amare*, to love⟧ a feminine name: dim.

Mandy

A·ma·ti (ä mä′tē; *E* ə mät′ē) 1 name of a family of violin-makers of Cremona, Italy (fl. 16th-17th cent.) 2 **Ni·co·lò** (nē′kô lô′) 1596-1684; violin-maker of this family: teacher of Guarneri & Stradivari

Am·brose (am′brōz′) ⟦L *Ambrosius* < Gr *ambrosios* < *ambrotos*, immortal < *a-*, not + *brotos*, mortal < **mrotos* < IE **mr̥-to*, dead⟧ 1 a masculine name 2 Saint (*c.* A.D. 340-397); bishop of Milan: his day is Dec. 7

A·mel·i·a (ə mēl′yə, -mēl′ē ə) ⟦of Gmc orig.; lit., prob. diligent < base of *amal*, work⟧ a feminine name

A·men (ä′mən) AMON

A·men·ho·tep (ä′mən hō′tep′) 1 name of four pharaohs of Egypt who ruled during the 16th, 15th, & 14th cent. B.C. 2 Amenhotep III (reigned *c.* 1411- *c.* 1375 B.C.) 3 Amenhotep IV IKHNATON Also **A′men·o′phis** (-ō′fis)

A·men-Ra (ä′mən rä′) AMON

Am·herst (am′ərst), Baron Jeffrey 1717-97; Eng. general: led Brit. forces that won control of Canada

A·mis (ā′mis), **Kings·ley** (kiŋz′lē) 1922- ; Brit. writer

Am·mon[1] (am′ən) ⟦L < Gr *Ammōn* < Egypt *Amen*⟧ Gr. & Rom. name for AMON

Am·mon[2] (am′ən) ⟦Heb *amon*, lit., prob., populous⟧ *Bible* a son of Lot: Gen. 19:38

A·mon (ä′mən) ⟦Egypt *ymn Amūn;* ? akin to *ymn*, to hide⟧ *Egypt. Myth.* orig., a local god of fertility and life in Egyptian Thebes: later associated with Re as the chief deity of Egypt (AMON-RE): identified by the Greeks (and Romans) with Zeus (and Jupiter): also sp. **A′mun**

A·mon-Re (ä′mən rä′) ⟦Egypt *ymn-r*ʾ < *Amun* + *r*ʾ, sun⟧ the ancient Egyptian sun god: also **A′mon-Ra′** (-rä′)

A·mos (ā′məs) ⟦Heb *amos*, lit., borne (by God?)⟧ 1 a masculine name 2 *Bible* a Hebrew prophet of the 8th cent. B.C.

Am·père (än per′), **An·dré Ma·rie** (än drā mȧ rē′) 1775-1836; Fr. physicist & mathematician

Am·phi·on (am fī′ən) ⟦L < Gr *Amphiōn*⟧ *Gr. Myth.* the son of Zeus and Antiope: he builds a wall around Thebes by charming the stones into place with a lyre

Am·phi·tri·te (am′fi trīt′ē) ⟦L < Gr *Amphitritē*⟧ *Gr. Myth.* one of the Nereids, goddess of the sea and wife of Poseidon

Am·phi·try·on (am fi′trē ən, -än′) ⟦L < Gr *Amphi-tryōn* ⟧ *Gr. Myth.* a king of Thebes and the husband of ALCMENE

A·mund·sen (ä′mŏon sən), **Ro·ald** (rō′äl) 1872-1928; Norw. explorer: first person to reach the South Pole (1911)

A·my (ā′mē) ⟦ME *Amye* < OFr *Amée*, lit., beloved < fem. pp. of *aimer* to love < L *amare* ⟧ a feminine name

A·nac·re·on (ə nak′rē ən, -rē än′) 6th cent. B.C.; Gr. lyric poet

An·a·ni·as (an′ə nī′əs) ⟦Gr⟧ *Bible* a man who fell dead when Peter rebuked him for withholding from the apostles a part of the proceeds from a sale of his land: Acts 5:1-10

An·a·sta·si·a (an′ə stā′zhə, -shə; -zhē ə, -shē ə) ⟦LL, fem. of *Anastasius* < Gr *Anastasias*, lit., of the resurrection ⟧ a feminine name: dim. *Stacey, Stacy*

An·ax·ag·o·ras (an′aks ag′ə rəs) c. 500-c. 428 B.C.; Gr. philosopher from Ionia who taught in Athens

A·nax·i·man·der (ə naks′ə man′dər) c. 611-c. 547 B.C.; Gr. philosopher, astronomer, & mathematician

An·chi·ses (an kī′sēz′) ⟦L < Gr *Anchisēs*⟧ *Gr. & Rom. Myth.* the father of Aeneas

An·der·sen (an′dər sən), **Hans Christian** 1805-75; Dan. novelist, poet, & writer of fairy tales

An·der·son (an′dər sən) **1** Carl David 1905-91; U.S. physicist; discovered the positron (1932) **2** Dame Judith 1898-1992; U.S. actress, born in Australia **3** Marian 1897?-1993; U.S. contralto **4** Maxwell 1888-1959; U.S. playwright **5** Sherwood 1876-1941; U.S. novelist & short-story writer

An·dré (än′drā′, an′drē′), **Major John** 1750-80; Brit. officer hanged as a spy in the Am. Revolution

An·dre·a (än drā′ə; an′drē ə, än′-) a feminine name: see ANDREW

Andrea del Sarto *see* SARTO, Andrea del

An·drew (an′drōō′) ⟦ME *Andreas* (< LL(Ec) *Andreu*) < OFr *Andrieu* < LL(Ec) *Andreas* < Gr(Ec) < Gr *andreios*, manly < *anēr* (gen. *andros*), man, male < IE base **aner, *ner-*, vital force, man ⟧ **1** a masculine name: dim. *Andy, Drew;* equiv. L *Andreas,* Fr. *André,* It. *Andrea,* Sp. *Andrés;* fem. *Andrea* **2** *Bible* one of the twelve apostles; brother of Simon Peter: his day is

Nov. 30: also **Saint Andrew**

An·drews (an'drōōz'), **Roy Chapman** 1884-1960; U.S. naturalist, explorer, & writer

An·dre·yev (än drā'yef), **Le·o·nid Ni·ko·la·ye·vich** (le'ô nēd' nē'kô lä yā'vich) 1871-1919; Russ. playwright, novelist, & short-story writer

An·dro·cles (an'drə klēz') ⟦L < Gr *Androklēs*⟧ *Rom. Legend* a slave who escapes death when thrown into the arena with a lion because the lion recognizes him as the man who once extracted a thorn from its foot: also **An'dro·clus** (-kləs)

An·drom·a·che (an dräm'ə kē) ⟦L < Gr *Andromachē*⟧ *Gr. Myth.* the wife of Hector

An·drom·e·da (an dräm'ə də) ⟦L < Gr *Andromedē*⟧ *Gr. Myth.* an Ethiopian princess whom Perseus rescues from a sea monster and then marries

An·dro·pov (än drō'pôf'), **Yu·ri V**(**ladimirovich**) (yoor'ē) 1914-84; general secretary of the Communist Party of the U.S.S.R. (1982-84)

An·dros (an'drəs), **Sir Edmund** 1637-1714; Eng. gov. of colonies in America

An·dva·ri (än'dwä rē) *Norse Myth.* a dwarf from whom Loki steals gold and a magic ring

An·ge·la (an'jə lə) ⟦contr. of *Angelica* < ML *angelica*, angelic < LL(Ec) *angelicus* < Gr *angelikos* < *angelos*, messenger⟧ a feminine name: dim. *Angie*; var. *Angelica, Angelina, Angeline*

An·gel·i·co (an jel'i kō'), **Fra** (frä) (born *Guido da Pietro*, also named *Giovanni da Fiesole*) 1387-1455; It. painter

An·ge·li·na (an'jə lē'nə, -li'-) a feminine name: see ANGELA

An·gell (ān'jəl), **Sir Norman** (born *Ralph Norman Angell Lane*) 1874-1967; Brit. economist, writer, & pacifist

Ång·ström (aŋ'strəm, ôŋ'-), **An·ders Jo·nas** (än'dərs yōō' näs'; -dərsh-) 1814-74; Swed. physicist

An·gus (aŋ'gəs) ⟦Gael *Aonghas* & Ir *Aonghus* < *aon*, one⟧ **1** a masculine name **2** *Celt. Myth.* the god of love

A·ni·ta (ə nēt'ə) ⟦Sp dim. of *Ana*: see ANNA⟧ a feminine name: dim. *Nita*

Ann (an) a feminine name: see ANNA

An·na (an'ə) ⟦L *Anna* < Gr < Heb *chana* lit., grace⟧ a feminine name: dim. *Annie, Nan, Nancy;* var. *Ann, Anne, Hannah;* equiv. Fr. *Anne, Annette, Nannette,* Sp. *Ana*

An·na·bel, An·na·belle (an'ə bel') ⟦? altered < *Amabel* < L *amabilis*, lovable < *amare*, to love: now assoc. with prec. & BELLE⟧ a feminine name

Anne (an) **1** a feminine name: see ANNA **2** 1665-1714; queen of Great Britain and Ireland (1702-14): last of the Stuart monarchs **3** Saint according to New Testament Apocrypha, the mother of the Virgin Mary: her day is July 26

Anne Boleyn *see* BOLEYN, Anne

Anne of Aus·tri·a (ôs'trē ə) 1601-66; wife of Louis XIII of France: regent (1643-61) during minority of Louis XIV

Anne of Cleves (klēvz) 1515-57; 4th wife of Henry VIII of England

An·nette (ə net') a feminine name: see ANNA

Annunzio, Gabriele D' *see* D'ANNUNZIO, Gabriele

A·nouilh (à nōō'y'; *E* än wē') , **Jean** (zhän) 1910-87; Fr. playwright

An·selm (an'selm'), Saint (1033-1109); theologian & archbishop of Canterbury (1093-1109), born in Italy: his day is April 21

An·tae·us (an tē'əs) ⟦L < Gr *Antaios*⟧ *Gr. Myth.* a giant wrestler who is invincible as long as he is touching his mother, the earth

An·tho·ny (an'thə nē) ⟦with unhistoric -*h*- < L *Antonius*, name of a Roman gens⟧ **1** a masculine name: dim. *Tony;* var. *Antony;* equiv. L. *Antonius*, It. & Sp. *Antonio*, Fr. *Antoine*, Ger. & Russ. *Anton;* fem. *Antonia* **2** Saint (*c.* A.D. 251-*c.* 356); Egypt. hermit: founder of Christian monasticism: his day is Jan. 17: called *the Great* **3** Saint (1195-1231); Franciscan friar in France & Italy, born in Portugal: his day is June 13: also called Saint **Anthony of Pad·u·a** (paj'ōō ə, pad'yōō ə) **4 Mark** *see* ANTONY, Mark **5 Susan B**(rownell) 1820-1906; U.S. leader in the movement for women's suffrage

An·ti·christ (an'ti krīst', -tĭ-) *Bible* the great antagonist of Christ, expected to spread universal evil before the end of the world but finally to be conquered at Christ's second coming: 1 John 2:18

An·tig·o·ne (an tig'ə nē') ⟦L < Gr *Antigonē*⟧ *Gr. Myth.*

a daughter of Oedipus and Jocasta: she defies her uncle, Creon, by performing funeral rites for her brother, Polynices

An·tig·o·nus (I) (an tig'ə nəs) 382-301 B.C.; Macedonian general under Alexander the Great: king of Macedonia (306-301): called *Cyclops*

An·ti·o·chus (an tī'ə kəs) **1** name of thirteen kings of the Seleucid dynasty of Syria **2 Antiochus III** 242-187 B.C.; king (223-187): called **Antiochus the Great 3 Antiochus IV** died *c.* 163 B.C.; king (*c.* 175-*c.* 163): his suppression of the Jews led to the Maccabean revolt: called **Antiochus E·piph'a·nes'** (ē pif'ə nēz', i pif'-)

An·tip·a·ter (an tip'ə tər) *c.* 397-319 B.C.; Macedonian general under Alexander the Great

An·tis·the·nes (an tis'thə nēz') *c.* 444-*c.* 365 B.C.; Gr. philosopher; founder of Cynicism

An·toi·nette (an'twə net', -tə-; *Fr* än twȧ net') a feminine name: dim. *Nettie, Netty, Toni, Tony:* see ANTONIA

Antoinette, Marie *see* MARIE ANTOINETTE

An·to·ni·a (an tō'nē ə) 〚L, fem. of *Antonius:* see ANTHONY〛 a feminine name: var. *Antoinette, Tonya*

An·to·ni·us (an'tə nī'nəs), **Marcus Aurelius** *see* AURELIUS, Marcus

Antoninus Pius A.D. 86-161; Rom. emperor (138-161)

An·to·ny (an'tə nē) **1** a masculine name: see ANTHONY **2 Mark** (or **Marc**) (Latin name *Marcus Antonius*) *c.* 83-30 B.C.; Rom. general & member of the second triumvirate

A·nu·bis (ə nōō'bis, -nyōō'-) 〚L < Gr *Anoubis* < Egypt *Anpu*〛 *Egypt. Myth.* the god who leads the dead to judgment: usually represented with the head of a jackal

A·pel·les (ə pel'ēz') fl. 4th cent. B.C.; Gr. painter

Aph·ro·di·te (af'rə dīt'ē) 〚? altered < Heb-Phoen *Ashtoreth,* ASHTORETH〛 *Gr. Myth.* the goddess of love and beauty: identified with the Roman Venus

A·pol·li·naire (ȧ pô lē ner'), **Guil·laume** (gē yōm') (born *Wilhelm Apollinaris de Kostrowitzki*) 1880-1918; Fr. poet & essayist

A·pol·lo (ə päl'ō) 〚L < Gr *Apollōn*〛 *Gr. & Rom. Myth.* the god of music, poetry, prophecy, and medicine, represented as exemplifying manly youth and beauty: later identified with Helios

A·pol·lyon (ə päl'yən) 〚Gr *apollyōn*, destroying, ruining < *apollyein*, to destroy < *apo-*, from + *lyein*, to loose〛 *Bible* in *Revelation*, the angel of the abyss; Abaddon: Rev. 9:11

Ap·ple·seed (ap'əl sēd'), **Johnny** (name for *John Chapman*) 1774-1845; U.S. frontiersman who planted apple trees throughout the Midwest

A·pril (ā'prəl) a feminine name: equiv. Fr. *Avril*

A·pu·le·ius (ap'yōō lē'əs), **Lucius** fl. 2d cent. A.D.; Rom. satirist: author of *The Golden Ass*

A·qui·nas (ə kwī'nəs), **Saint Thomas** c. 1225-74; It. theologian & philosopher: called *the Angelic Doctor*

Ar·a·bel·la (ar'ə bel'ə, er'-) 〚? by dissimilation < ANNABEL〛 a feminine name: dim. *Bella*

A·rach·ne (ə rak'nē) 〚L < Gr *Arachnē* < *arachnē*, spider〛 *Gr. Myth.* a girl turned into a spider by Athena for challenging the goddess to a weaving contest

A·ra·gon (à rà gōn'), **Louis** (lwē) 1897-1982; Fr. poet, novelist, & journalist

Ar·buth·not (är buth'nət, är'bəth nät'), **John** 1667-1735; Scot. writer & physician

Arc, Jeanne d' *see* D'ARC, Jeanne

archenemy, the Satan

archfiend, the Satan

Ar·chi·bald (är'chə bôld') 〚of Gmc orig. (akin to OHG *Erchanbald*), prob., nobly bold〛 a masculine name: dim. *Archie, Archy*

Ar·chi·me·des (är'kə mē'dēz') c. 287-212 B.C.; Gr. mathematician & inventor, born in Syracuse (Sicily)

Ar·chi·pen·ko (är'ki peŋ'kō), **Alexander** 1887-1964; U.S. sculptor, born in Russia

Ar·es (er'ēz') 〚L < Gr *Arēs*〛 *Gr. Myth.* the god of war, son of Zeus and Hera: identified with the Roman Mars

Ar·e·thu·sa (ar'ə thōō'zə, er'-; -thyōō'-; -sə) 〚L < Gr *Arethousa*〛 *Gr. Myth.* a woodland nymph, changed into a stream by Artemis so that she might escape her pursuer, Alpheus

A·re·ti·no (ä're tē'nô), **Pie·tro** (pye'trō) 1492-1556; It. satirical writer

Ar·gus (är'gəs) 〚L < Gr *Argos* < *argos*, white < IE base *ar(e)g-*, gleaming, whitish〛 *Gr. Myth.* a giant with a hundred eyes, ordered by Hera to watch Io: after he is killed by Hermes, his eyes are put in the tail of the peacock

Ar·i·ad·ne (ar'ē ad'nē, er'-) ⟦L < Gr *Ariadnē*⟧ *Gr. Myth.* King Minos' daughter, who gives Theseus the thread by which he finds his way out of the labyrinth

Ar·i·el (er'ē əl, ar'-) ⟦< Gr(Ec) *ariēl* < Heb *ariel*, lion of God: a name applied to Jerusalem in the Bible⟧ in Shakespeare's *The Tempest*, an airy spirit who is the servant of Prospero

A·ri·os·to (ä'rē ô'stō'), **Lu·do·vi·co** (lōō'də vē'kō) 1474-1533; It. poet: author of *Orlando Furioso*

Ar·is·tar·chus of Sa·mos (ar'is tär'kəs əv sā'mäs') fl. 3d cent. B.C.; Gr. astronomer

Ar·is·ti·des (ar'is tī'dēz') *c.* 530-*c.* 468 B.C.; Athenian general & statesman: called *the Just*

Ar·is·tip·pus (ar'is tip'əs) *c.* 435-*c.* 365 B.C. Gr. philosopher: founder of the Cyrenaic school

Ar·is·toph·a·nes (ar'i stäf'ə nēz') *c.* 450-*c.* 388 B.C.; Gr. writer of satirical comic dramas

Ar·is·tot·le (ar'is tät''l, er'-) 384-322 B.C.; Gr. philosopher, pupil of Plato: noted for works on logic, metaphysics, ethics, politics, etc.

A·ri·us (ar'ē əs, ə rī'əs) *c.* A.D. 250-336; Alexandrian theologian, born in Libya

Ar·ju·na (är'jōō nə, ur'-) the hero of the Sanskrit epic, the *Mahabharata*

Ark·wright (ärk'rīt'), Sir **Richard** 1732-92; Eng. inventor of a cotton-spinning machine

Ar·lene (är lēn') a feminine name: var. *Arline, Arleen*

Ar·min·i·us (är min'ē əs) **1** (Ger. name *Hermann*) *c.* 17 B.C.-*c.* A.D. 21; Germanic tribal leader **2 Ja·co·bus** (yä kō'bəs) (born *Jacob Harmensen*) 1560-1609; Du. theologian

Arm·strong (ärm'strôŋ') **1 Edwin Howard** 1890-1954; U.S. electrical engineer: developed FM system of radio **2 Louis** (called *Satchmo*) 1901-71; U.S. jazz musician **3 Neil Alden** 1930- ; U.S. astronaut: first man to step onto the moon

Arne (ärn), **Thomas Augustine** 1710-78; Eng. composer

Ar·nold (är'nəld) ⟦Ger < OHG *Aranold* < Gmc *Arnwald*, lit., strong as an eagle < *aran*, eagle + *waltan*, to rule⟧ **1** a masculine name **2 Benedict** 1741-1801; Am. Revolutionary general who became a traitor **3 Matthew** 1822-88; Eng. poet, essayist, & critic **4 Thomas** 1795-1842; Eng. educator: father of Matthew

Arp (ȧrp), **Jean** (zhän) 1887-1966; Fr. painter & sculptor, born in Alsace: also **Hans Arp**

Ar·pad (är'päd) died A.D. 907; Magyar leader: national hero of Hungary

Ar·rhe·ni·us (ä rā'nē ʊos; *E* ə rā'nē əs), **Svan·te Au·gust** (svän'te ou'gʊost) 1859-1927; Swed. physical chemist: first to present the theory of ionization

Ar·row (ar'ō, er'-), **Kenneth Joseph** 1921- ; U.S. economist

Ar·taud (ȧr tō'), **An·to·nin** (an tô nan') 1896-1948; Fr. dramatic theorist, dramatist, & poet

Ar·ta·xer·xes (är'tə zʊrk'sēz) name of three kings of ancient Persia, esp. **Artaxerxes I** (*c.* 465-*c.* 424 B.C.), a son of Xerxes I, and **Artaxerxes II** (*c.* 404-358 B.C.)

Ar·te·mis (är'tə mis) ⟦L < Gr *Artemis*⟧ *Gr. Myth.* the goddess of the moon, wild animals, and hunting, twin sister of Apollo: identified with the Roman Diana

Ar·te·vel·de (är'tə vel'də) **1 Jacob van** *c.* 1290-1345; Fl. statesman **2 Philip van** 1340-81; Fl. leader: son of Jacob

Ar·thur (är'thər) ⟦ML *Arthurus*⟧ **1** a masculine name: dim. *Art;* equiv. It. *Arturo* **2** *Arthurian Legend* a king of Britain and leader of the knights of the Round Table: such a king is supposed to have lived in the 6th cent. **3 Chester Alan** 1829-86; 21st president of the U.S. (1881-85)

A·sa (ā'sə) ⟦Heb *asa*, lit., healer⟧ **1** a masculine name **2** *Bible* a king of Judah, who opposed idolatry: 1 Kings 15:8-24

As·bur·y (az'ber'ē, -bər-), **Francis** 1745-1816; 1st Methodist bishop in U.S.

As·ca·ni·us (as kā'nē əs) ⟦L⟧ *Rom. Myth.* son of Aeneas

Asch (ash), **Sho·lem** (shō'ləm) 1880-1957; U.S. novelist & playwright in Yiddish, born in Poland

As·cham (as'kəm), **Roger** 1515-68; Eng. writer & classical scholar: tutor of Queen Elizabeth I

As·cle·pi·us (as klē'pē əs) ⟦L < Gr *Asklēpios*⟧ *Gr. Myth.* the god of healing and medicine: identified with the Roman Aesculapius

Ash·er (ash'ər) *Bible* Jacob's eighth son, whose mother was Zilpah: Gen. 30:12-13

Ash·ley (ash'lē) a feminine and masculine name

Ash·to·reth (ash'tə reth') ⟦Heb *ashtoret;* akin to Phoen ʃ*shtrt*, Akkadian *Ishtar*, also South Ar ʃ*thtr* (the only manifestation of the deity as a male)] the ancient Phoenician and Syrian goddess of love and fertility: identified with Astarte

A·shur (ä′shoor′) [Akkadian] *Assyr. Myth.* the chief deity, god of war and empire

A·shur·ba·ni·pal (ä′shoor bän′i päl′) died *c.* 626 B.C.; king of Assyria (*c.* 668-*c.* 626)

As·mo·de·us (az′mə dē′əs, as′-) [L *Asmodaeus* < Gr *Asmodaios* < Talmudic Heb *ashmeday* < Avestan *Aēšmā daēva*, Aeshma the deceitful] *Jewish Folklore* an evil spirit or chief demon

A·so·ka (ə sō′kə) died *c.* 232 B.C.; king of India (*c.* 273-*c.* 232): 1st Indian ruler to embrace Buddhism

As·pa·si·a (as pā′zhē ə, -zhə) fl. 5th cent. B.C.; woman of Athens celebrated for her beauty and intellect: mistress of Pericles

As·quith (as′kwith), **Herbert Henry** 1st Earl of Oxford and Asquith 1852-1928; Brit. statesman: prime minister (1908-16)

As·sad (ä säd′), **Ha·fez al–** (hä fez′ al) 1928- ; president of Syria (1971-)

As·sur (ä′soor) *var. of* Ashur

As·sur·ba·ni·pal (ä′soor bän′i päl′) *var. of* ASHURBANI-PAL

A·staire (ə ster′), **Fred** (born *Frederick Austerlitz*) 1899-1987; U.S. dancer, choreographer, & motion-picture actor

As·tar·te (as tär′tē) [L < Gr *Astartē* < Heb *ashtoret*, ASHTORETH] a Semitic goddess of fertility and sexual love, worshiped by the Phoenicians and others: see also ASHTORETH, ISHTAR

As·ton (as′tən), **Francis William** 1877-1945; Eng. chemist & physicist: noted for his work on isotopes

As·tor (as′tər) **1 John Jacob** 1763-1848; U.S. fur merchant & financier, born in Germany **2 Viscountess** (born *Nancy Witcher Langhorne*) 1879-1964; 1st woman member of the Brit. House of Commons (1919-45): born in the U.S.

As·trae·a (as trē′ə) [L < Gr *Astraia* < *astraios*, starry < *astron*, star] *Gr. Myth.* a goddess of justice, later also of innocence and purity: she is the last deity to leave the earth after the Golden Age

As·ty·a·nax (as tī′ə naks′) [L < Gr] *Gr. Myth.* the

young son of Hector and Andromache: he is killed at Troy by the Greek conquerors

A·ta·hual·pa (ä'tə wäl'pə) c. 1502-33; last Inca king of Peru (1525-33)

At·a·lan·ta (at'ə lan'tə) 〚L < Gr *Atalantē*〛 *Gr. Myth.* a beautiful, swift-footed maiden who offers to marry any man able to defeat her in a race: Hippomenes wins by dropping three golden apples, which she stops to pick up, along the way

Ataturk *see* KEMAL ATATÜRK

A·te (ā'tē) 〚Gr *Atē*〛 *Gr. Myth.* the goddess personifying criminal folly or reckless ambition in human beings, which brings on punishment by Nemesis

Ath·a·na·sius (ath'ə nā'shəs), Saint (c. A.D. 296-373); Alexandrian bishop: patriarch of Alexandria (328-373) & opponent of Arianism: his day is May 2: called *the Great*

Ath·el·stan (ath'əl stan') 〚ME < OE *ætheling* < *æthele*, noble〛 c. A.D. 895-940; king of the Mercians & West Saxons (925-940): assumed the title of king of England: grandson of Alfred the Great

A·the·na (ə thē'nə) 〚Gr *Athēnē*〛 *Gr. Myth.* the goddess of wisdom, skills, and warfare: identified with the Roman Minerva: also **A·the'ne** (-nē)

At·kin·son (at'kin sən), (Justin) **Brooks** 1894-1984; U.S. journalist & drama critic

At·las (at'ləs) 〚L < Gr < prothetic *a-* + *tlan*, bearing < IE base **tel-*, **tla-*, to lift, bear〛 *Gr. Myth.* a Titan compelled to support the heavens on his shoulders

At·li (ät'lē) 〚ON < Goth *Attila*, ATTILA〛 *Norse Myth.* a king of the Huns: he is killed by his wife, Gudrun, because he has killed her brothers for Sigurd's treasure

A·tre·us (ā'trē əs) 〚L < Gr〛 *Gr. Myth.* a king of Mycenae and father of Agamemnon and Menelaus: to avenge the treachery of his brother, Thyestes, he kills Thyestes' sons and serves their flesh to him at a banquet

At·ro·pos (a'trə päs') 〚L < Gr lit., not to be turned < *a-*, not + *trepein*, to turn < IE base **trep-*, to turn〛 *Gr. & Rom. Myth.* that one of the three Fates who cuts the thread of life

At·ti·la (at''l ə, ə til'ə) 〚Goth *atta*, father (< baby talk) + *-ila*, dim. suffix〛 c. A.D. 406-453; king of the Huns (c. 433-453): called *the Scourge of God*

Att·lee (at′lē), **Clement Richard** 1st Earl Attlee 1883-1967; Brit. statesman: prime minister (1945-51)

Au·ber (ō be r′), **Da·niel** (François Esprit) (dȧ nyel′) 1782-1871; Fr. composer of operas

Au·brey (ô′brē) 〚Fr *Aubri* < Ger *Alberich* < OHG *alb*, elf (see ALBERICH) + *rihhi*, ruler, realm < IE base **reg̑-*, to put in order, straight 〛 a masculine name

Au·den (ôd′n), **W(ystan) H(ugh)** 1907-73; U.S. poet, born in England

Au·drey (ô′drē) 〚ult. < OE *æthelthryth*, lit., noble might < *æthel*, noble + *thryth*, might, strength 〛 a feminine name

Au·du·bon (ôd′ə bän′), **John James** 1785-1851; U.S. ornithologist, naturalist, & painter, born in Haiti: famed for his paintings of North American birds

Au·gust (ô′gəst) 〚ME < L *Augustus*, after AUGUSTUS Caesar < *augustus*, august < *augere*, to increase < IE base **aweg-*, **aug-* 〛 a masculine name: see AUGUSTUS

Au·gus·ta (ô gus′tə, ə-) 〚L, fem. of AUGUSTUS 〛 a feminine name

Au·gus·tine (ô′gəs tēn′; ə gus′tin, ô-) 〚L *Augustinus*, dim. of fol. 〛 **1** a masculine name: var. *Austin, Augustin;* equiv. Ger. & Fr. *Augustin,* It. *Agostino* **2** Saint (A.D. 354-430); early Christian church father, born in Numidia: bishop of Hippo in N Africa: his day is August 28 **3** Saint (died A.D. 604); Rom. monk sent to convert the English to Christianity: 1st archbishop of Canterbury: his day is May 27

Au·gus·tus (ô gus′təs, ə-) 〚L, AUGUST 〛 **1** a masculine name: dim. *Gus;* fem. *Augusta;* equiv. Fr. *Auguste,* Ger. *August,* It. *Augusto* **2** (*Gaius Julius Caesar Octavianus*) 63 B.C.-A.D. 14; 1st Rom. emperor (27 B.C.-A.D. 14): grandnephew of Julius Caesar: also called *Octavian*

Au·rang·zeb (ôr′əŋ zeb′, ou′rəŋ-) 1618-1707; last influential Mogul emperor of Hindustan (1658-1707): also **Au′rang·zib′** (-zib′)

Au·re·li·a (ô rē′lē ə, -rēl′yə) 〚L, lit., golden < *aurum*, gold < IE base **awes-*, to shine, dawn 〛 a feminine name

Au·re·li·an (ô rē′lē ən, -rēl′yən) (*Lucius Domitius Aurelianus*) c. A.D. 212-275; Rom. emperor (270-275)

Au·re·li·us (ô rē′lē əs, -rēl′yəs), **Marcus** (*Marcus Aurelius Antoninus*) A.D. 121-180; Rom. emperor (161-180)

& Stoic philosopher

Au·ro·ra (ô rôr′ə, ə-) ⟦L, lit., dawn⟧ *Rom. Myth.* the goddess of dawn: identified with the Greek Eos

Au·rung·zeb (ôr′əŋ zeb′) *alt. sp. of* AURANGZEB

Aus·ten (ôs′tən), **Jane** 1775-1817; Eng. novelist

Aus·tin (ôs′tən) **1** a masculine name: see AUGUSTINE **2 Alfred** 1835-1913; Eng. poet: poet laureate (1896-1913) **3 John** 1790-1859; Eng. jurist **4 Stephen** (**Fuller**) 1793-1836; Am. pioneer: founded 1st Am. colony in Tex. in early 1820′s

A·ver·ro·ës, **A·ver·rho·ës** (ə ver′ō ēz′) (Ar. *ibn-Rushd*) 1126-98; Arab philosopher & physician in Spain & Morocco

Av·i·cen·na (av′i sen′ə) (Ar. *ibn-sīnā*) 980-1037; Arab physician & philosopher in Persia

A·vo·ga·dro (ä′vô gä′drô; *E* äv′ə gä′drō), **A·me·de·o** (ä′ me de′ô) (*Conte di Quaregna e Ceretto*) 1776-1856; It. chemist & physicist

Ay·er (ā′ər), **Sir A**(**lfred**) **J**(**ules**) 1910-89; Brit. philosopher

A·ye·sha, **A·ye·shah** (ä′ē shä′) *alt. sp. of* AISHA

A·za·zel (ə zā′zəl, az′ə zel′) ⟦Heb *azazel*, lit., removal: in KJV (Lev 16: 7-10, 21-26) transl. as "scapegoat"⟧ **1** in ancient Hebrew tradition, an evil spirit in the desert to which a scapegoat is to be sent on the Day of Atonement **2** in Milton′s *Paradise Lost*, one of the fallen rebel angels

Az·ra·el (az′rā əl) ⟦Heb *azrael*, lit., help of God⟧ *Jewish Folklore, Muslim Folklore* the angel who parts the soul from the body at death

B

Ba·al (bā′əl) ⟦LL < Heb *baal*⟧ among some ancient Semitic peoples, orig., any of a number of local fertility gods; later, a chief god

Baal Shem Tov (bäl′ shem′ tōv′) (born *Israel ben Eliezer*) *c.* 1700-60; Jewish religious leader in Poland: founder of Hasidism: also **Baal Shem Tob**

Ba·bar (bä′bər) *alt. sp. of* BABUR

Bab·bage (bab′ij), **Charles** 1791-1871; Eng. mathematician & computer pioneer

Bab·bit (bab′it), **Milton Byron** 1916- ; U.S. composer

Ba·bel (bä′bəl), **I·saak** (**Emmanuilovich**) (ē säk′) 1894-

1940; Russ. writer

Ba·bur (bä'bər) (born *Zahir ud-Din Mohammed*) 1483-1530; founder & 1st emperor (1526-30) of the Mogul dynasty of India: also sp. **Ba·ber**

Bac·chus (bak'əs) 〚 L < Gr *Bakchos* 〛 *Gr. & Rom. Myth.* the god of wine and revelry: identified with the Greek Dionysus

Bach (bäkh; *E occas.* bäk) **1 Carl Phi·lipp E·ma·nu·el** (kärl fē'lip ä mä'nōōel') 1714-88; Ger. composer: son of Johann Sebastian **2 Jo·hann Chris·ti·an** (yō'hän' kris' tē än') 1735-82; Ger. organist & composer: son of Johann Sebastian **3 Johann Se·bas·ti·an** (zä bäs'tē än') 1685-1750; Ger. organist & composer

Ba·con (bā'kən) **1 Francis** Baron Verulam, Viscount St. Albans 1561-1626; Eng. philosopher, essayist, & statesman **2 Nathaniel** 1647-76; Am. colonist born in England: leader of a rebellion (1676) which sought social reform **3 Roger** *c.* 1214-94; Eng. philosopher & scientist

Ba·den–Pow·ell (bād'n pō'əl), Sir **Robert Stephenson Smyth** 1st Baron Baden-Powell of Gilwell 1857-1941; Brit. general: founder of Boy Scouts & Girl Guides

Baf·fin (baf'in), **William** 1584-1622; Eng. navigator & explorer

Bage·hot (baj'ət), **Walter** 1826-77; Eng. economist, journalist, & critic

Ba·hā' Al·lah (bä hä' ä lä') (born *Mirzā Ḥoseyn 'Ali Nūrī*) 1817-92; Iranian Muslim religious leader: founder of Bahaism

Bai·ley (bā'lē), **Nathan(iel)** died 1742; Eng. lexicographer

Baird (berd), **John Lo·gie** (lō'gē) 1888-1946; Scot. inventor & television pioneer

Bakst (bäkst), **Lé·on Ni·ko·la·ye·vich** (lā'ôn ni'kô lä'yə vich) (born *Lev Samoylovich Rosenberg*) 1866-1924; Russ. painter and stage designer

Ba·ku·nin (bä kōō'nyin; *E* bə kyōō'nin), **Mi·kha·il A·lek·san·dro·vich** (mē khä ēl'ä'lyik sän'drô vich) 1814-76; Russ. anarchist

Ba·laam (bā'ləm) *Bible* a prophet hired to curse the Israelites: when he beat his donkey, the animal rebuked him: Num. 22-24

Ba·la·ki·rev (bä lä'kē ryef, bä'lä kē'-), **Mi·li A·lek·sey·e·vich** (mē'lē ä'lyik sā'yə vich) 1837-1910; Russ. composer

Bal·an·chine (bal'ən shēn'), **George** (born *Georgy Melitonovich Balanchivadze*) 1904-83; U.S. choreographer, born in Russia

Bal·bo·a (bal bō'ə; *Sp* bäl bô'ä), **Vas·co Nú·ñez de** (väs'kô nōō'nyeth *the*) *c.* 1475-1519; Sp. explorer: 1st European to discover the Pacific Ocean (1513)

Bal·der (bôl'dər, bäl'-) ⟦ ON *Baldr*, lit., bold, dangerous ⟧ *Norse Myth.* the god of light, peace, virtue, and wisdom, son of Odin and Frigg: he is killed by the trickery of Loki: also **Bal·dr** (bäl'drə)

Bald·win (bôld'win') ⟦ ME < OFr *Baldewin, Baudoïn* < MHG *Baldewin,* lit., bold friend < OHG *bald* (akin to OE *beald,* bold) + *wini,* friend ⟧ **1** a masculine name **2 Baldwin I** *c.* 1058-1118; crusader & king of Jerusalem (1100-18) **3 James (Arthur)** 1924-87; U.S. novelist & essayist **4 James Mark** 1861-1934; U.S. psychologist & philosopher **5 Stanley** 1st Earl Baldwin of Bewdley 1867-1947; Brit. statesman: prime minister (1923-24; 1924-29; 1935-37)

Bal·four (bal'foor'), **Arthur James** 1st Earl of Balfour 1848-1930; Brit. statesman & philosopher: prime minister (1902-05)

Ball (bôl), **John** died 1381; Eng. priest: executed as an instigator of the Peasants' Revolt of 1381

Bal·thus (bäl'thəs) (pseud. of *Balthasar Klossowski de Rola*) 1908- ; Fr. painter

Bal·ti·more (bôl'tə môr) **Lord** 1st Baron Baltimore (*George Calvert*) *c.* 1580-1632; Eng. statesman: founder of Maryland

Bal·zac (bal zàk'; *E* bôl'zak), **Ho·no·ré de** (ô nô *r*ä'də) 1799-1850; Fr. novelist

Ban·croft (ban'krôft', baŋ'-; -kräft'), **George** 1800-91; U.S. historian & statesman

Ban·quo (baŋ'kwō) a character in Shakespeare's *Macbeth*: the ghost of Banquo appears to Macbeth, who had ordered his murder

Ban·ting (ban'tiŋ), **Sir Frederick Grant** 1891-1941; Cdn. physiologist: co-discoverer of insulin (1922)

Baptist John the Baptist

Bar·ab·bas (bə rab'əs) ⟦ L(Ec) < Aram < *baraba*, son of Abba ⟧ *Bible* the prisoner whom the people wanted freed rather than Jesus: Matt. 27:16-21

Bar·ba·ra (bär'bə rə, -brə) ⟦ L, fem. of *barbarus*, barbarous < Gr *barbaros*, foreign, strange, ignorant < IE echoic base **barbar-*, used for unintelligible speech of foreigners ‖ a feminine name: dim. *Babs, Barb*; var. *Barbra, Babette*

Bar·ba·ros·sa (bär'bə rôs'ə, -rä'sə), **Frederick** ‖ It < *barba*, beard + *rossa*, red: so named from his beard ‖ *see* FREDERICK I (of the Holy Roman Empire)

Bar·ber (bär'bər), **Samuel** 1910-81; U.S. composer

Bar·deen (bär dēn'), **John** 1908-91; U.S. physicist

Bard of A·von (ā'vän') *name for* William SHAKESPEARE: so called from his birthplace, Stratford-on-Avon

Barleycorn, John *see* JOHN BARLEYCORN

Bar·na·bas (bär'nə bəs) ‖ ME < LL (Vulg.: Acts 4:36) < Gr < Aram *barnebhū'āh*, son of exhortation ‖ **1** a masculine name: dim. *Barney*; var. *Barnaby* **2** *Bible* (original name *Joses* or *Joseph*) a Levite of Cyprus, a Christian apostle & missionary companion of Paul: Acts 4:36

Bar·na·by (bär'nə bē) a masculine name: see BARNABAS

Bar·nard (bär'nərd) **1** a masculine name: see BERNARD **2** George Gray 1863-1938; U.S. sculptor

Bar·ne·veldt (bär'nə velt'), **Jan van Ol·den** (yän'vän ôl'dən) 1547-1619; Du. statesman & patriot

Bar·num (bär'nəm), **P(hineas) T(aylor)** 1810-91; U.S. showman & circus operator

Ba·ro·ja (bä rô'hä), **Pí·o** (pē'ô) 1872-1956; Sp. novelist

Bar·rès (bà res'), **(Auguste) Mau·rice** (mô res') 1862-1923; Fr. novelist, essayist, & politician

Bar·rett (bar'it, ber'-), **Elizabeth** *see* BROWNING, Elizabeth Barrett

Bar·rie (bar'ē, ber'-), **Sir James M(atthew)** 1860-1937; Brit. novelist & playwright, born in Scotland

Bar·ry (bar'ē) a masculine name

Bar·ry·more (bar'ə môr', ber'-) **1** family of U.S. actors **2** Ethel 1879-1959 **3** John 1882-1942 **4** Lionel 1878-1954 **5** Maurice (born *Herbert Blythe*) 1847-1905: father of Ethel, John, & Lionel

Barth (bärt), **Karl** 1886-1968; Swiss theologian

Barthes (bärt), **Roland** 1915-80; Fr. writer & critic

Bar·thol·di (bàr tôl dē'), **Fré·dé·ric Au·guste** (frā dā rēk' ô güst') 1834-1904; Fr. sculptor of the Statue of Liberty

Bar·thol·o·mew (bär thäl'ə myōō') ‖ ME *Bartelmeus* < LL (Vulg.) *Bartholomaeus* < Gr *Bartholomaios* < Aram *bar talmai*, lit., son of Talmai ‖ **1** a masculine name: dim. *Bart*; equiv. Fr. *Bartholomé*, It. *Bartolomeo*, Ger. *Bartholomäus*, Sp. *Bartolomé* **2** *Bible* one of the twelve Apostles: his day is Aug. 24: identified by some authorities with NATHANAEL: also **Saint Bartholomew**

Bart·lett (bärt'lət), **John** 1820-1905; U.S. editor & publisher: compiler of a book of quotations

Bar·tók (bär'tôk'), **Bé·la** (bā'lä) 1881-1945; Hung. composer

Bar·to·lom·me·o (bär'tô lôm mā'ô), **Fra** (born *Bartolommeo di Pagholo del Fattorino*) *c.* 1475-1517; Florentine painter

Bar·ton (bärt'n) **1 Clara** (born *Clarissa Harlowe Barton*) 1821-1912; U.S. philanthropist: founder of the American Red Cross (1881) **2 Sir Derek Harold Richard** 1918- ; Brit. organic chemist

Bar·tram (bär'trəm) **1 John** 1699-1777; Am. botanist **2 William** 1739-1823; Am. naturalist: son of John

Bar·uch (ber'ək) [Heb., lit., blessed] *Bible* Jeremiah's scribe: Jer. 36:4-6

Ba·ruch (bə rook'), **Bernard Man·nes** (man'əs) 1870-1965; U.S. financier & statesman

Ba·sie (bā'sē), **William** (called *Count*) 1904-84; U.S. jazz musician, pianist, & band leader

Bas·il (baz'əl, bā'zəl) [L *Basilius* < Gr *Basileios*, lit., kingly < *basileus*, king] **1** a masculine name **2 Saint** (*c.* A.D. 330-379); Gr. prelate, born in Cappadocia: bishop of Caesarea: his day is Jan. 2: called *the Great*

Bas·ker·ville (bas'kər vil), **John** 1706-75; Eng. printer & type designer

Bath·she·ba (bath shē'bə, bath'shi bə) [Heb *batsheva*, lit., daughter of Sheba, daughter of the oath] *Bible* the mother of Solomon by King David, whom she married after he had sent her first husband, Uriah, to death in battle: 2 Sam. 11

Bau·cis (bô'sis) *Gr. Myth.* a poor old woman who, with her husband, Philemon, shows such hospitality to the disguised Zeus and Hermes that the grateful gods turn their humble cottage into a temple

Bau·de·laire (bōd ler'), **(Pierre) Charles** (shàrl) 1821-67; Fr. poet & essayist

Bau·douin (bō dwan') 1930-93; king of Belgium (1951-93): son of Leopold III

Baum (bôm, bäm), **L(yman) Frank** 1856-1919; U.S. writer of children's books, including the *Oz* books

Ba·yard (bá yàr´; *E* bā´ərd), Chevalier de (born *Pierre Terrail*) *c.* 1473-1524; Fr. military hero: known as *chevalier sans peur et sans reproche* (the fearless & irreproachable knight)

Bayle (bel), **Pierre** 1647-1706; Fr. critic & philosopher

Bea·cons·field (bē´kənz fēld´), Earl of *see* DISRAELI, Benjamin

Beard (bird) **1 Charles Austin** 1874-1948; U.S. historian **2 Daniel Carter** 1850-1941; U.S. author & illustrator: a founder of the Boy Scouts of America **3 Mary** 1876-1958; U.S. historian: collaborated with husband Charles Austin

Beards·ley (birdz´lē), **Aubrey Vincent** 1872-98; Eng. artist & illustrator

Beat·les (bēt´lz), **The** Brit. rock group (1961-70) including John Lennon (1940-80), Ringo Starr (born *Richard Starkey*) (1940-), (James) Paul McCartney (1942-), & George Harrison (1943-)

Bea·ton (bēt´'n), **Sir Cecil (Walter Hardy)** 1904-80; Brit. photographer & theatrical designer

Be·a·trice (bē´ə tris; *for 2, also, It* be´ä trē´che) ⟦It < L *beatrix*, she who makes happy⟧ **1** a feminine name: dim. *Bea*; var. *Beatrix* **2** a Florentine woman (*Beatrice Portinari*, 1266-1290) loved by Dante and immortalized in his *Divine Comedy*

Be·a·trix (bē´ə triks) 1938- ; queen of the Netherlands (1980-)

Beat·ty (bēt´ē), **David** 1st Earl Beatty 1871-1936; Brit. admiral

Beau Brum·mell (bō brum´əl) (name for *George Bryan Brummell*) 1778-1840; Eng. gentleman famous for his fashionable dress and manners

Beau·har·nais (bō àr ne´), **Josephine de** *see* JOSEPHINE; *see also* HORTENSE

Beau·mar·chais (bō màr she´), **Pi·erre Au·gus·tin Ca·ron de** (pyer ō güs tan´ kà rōn´də) 1732-99; Fr. dramatist

Beau·mont (bō´mänt´), **Francis** 1584-1616; Eng. dramatist who collaborated with John Fletcher

Beau·re·gard (bō´rə gärd´, bôr´ə-), **P(ierre) G(ustave) T(outant) de** 1818-93; Confederate general

Beau·voir (bō vwàr´), **Si·mone de** (sē môn´ də) 1908-86; Fr. existentialist writer

Bea·ver·brook (bē'vər brook'), 1st Baron (*William Maxwell Aitkin*) 1879-1964; Brit. newspaper publisher & statesman, born in Canada

Be·bel (bā'bəl), (**Ferdinand**) **Au·gust** (ou goost') 1840-1913; Ger. socialist leader & writer

Be·chet (bə shā'), **Sidney** (**Joseph**) 1897-1959; U.S. jazz musician & composer

Beck·et (bek'ət), **Saint Thomas à** (*c.* 1118-1170); Eng. prelate: archbishop of Canterbury: murdered after opposing Henry II: his day is Dec. 29

Beck·ett (bek'ət), **Samuel** 1906-89; Ir. poet, novelist, & playwright in France, writing mostly in French

Bec·que·rel (be krel'; *E* bek'ə rel') **1 A·lex·an·dre Ed·mond** (à lek sändr' ed mōn') 1820-91; Fr. physicist: father of Antoine Henri **2 An·toine Cé·sar** (än twàn' sä zàr') 1788-1878; Fr. physicist: pioneer in electrochemistry: father of Alexandre **3 Antoine Hen·ri** (än rē') 1852-1908; Fr. physicist: discoverer of radioactivity in uranium

Bede (bēd), **Saint** (A.D. 673-735); Eng. historian & theologian: his day is May 27: called **the Venerable Bede**

Bed·i·vere (bed'ə vir') *Arthurian Legend* the loyal knight who is with the dying King Arthur and sees him off to Avalon

Bee·be (bē'bē), (**Charles**) **William** 1877-1962; U.S. naturalist, explorer, & writer

Bee·cham (bē'chəm), **Sir Thomas** 1879-1961; Eng. orchestral conductor

Bee·cher (bē'chər) **1 Henry Ward** 1813-87; U.S. clergyman & lecturer: brother of Harriet Beecher Stowe **2 Ly·man** (lī'mən) 1775-1863; U.S. clergyman & theologian: father of Henry & of Harriet Beecher Stowe

Be·el·ze·bub (bē el'zə bub') 〚LL(Ec) < Gr(Ec) *Beelzeboub* < Heb *baal-zevuv*, lit., god of flies < *baal* (see BAAL) + *zevuv*, a fly: prob. deliberate pejorative alteration < *Ba'al zebul*; cf. Ugaritic *zbl bˁl ʔrs*, the exalted one, the lord of the earth〛 **1** *Bible* the chief devil; Satan: also **Be·el'ze·bul'** (-bool') **2** in Milton's *Paradise Lost*, Satan's chief lieutenant among the fallen angels

Beer·bohm (bir'bōm'), **Sir** (**Henry**) **Max**(imilian) 1872-1956; Eng. satirist, caricaturist, & critic

Bee·tho·ven (bā'tō'vən), **Lud·wig van** (loot'viH vän) 1770-1827; Ger. composer

Be·gin (bā′gin), **Me·na·chem** (mə näkh′əm) 1913-92; prime minister of Israel (1977-83), born in Poland

Be·han (bē′ən), **Bren·dan** (Francis) (bren′dən) 1923-64; Ir. playwright

Beh·ring (bā′riŋ), **E·mil A·dolf von** (ā′mel ä′dôlf fôn) 1854-1917; Ger. bacteriologist: developed tetanus & diphtheria antitoxins

Behr·man (ber′mən), **S**(amuel) **N**(athaniel) 1893-1973; U.S. playwright

Bei·der·becke (bī′dər bek′), (Leon) **Bix** (biks) 1903-31; U.S. jazz musician

Bel (bāl) ⟦Akkadian form of BAAL⟧ *Bab. Myth.* the god of heaven and earth

Be·las·co (bə las′kō), **David** 1853-1931; U.S. theatrical producer, playwright, & actor

Bel Geddes *see* GEDDES, Norman Bel

Be·li·al (bē′lē əl, bēl′yəl) ⟦ME < LL (Vulg.: Deut. 13:13) < Heb *beliyaal*, worthlessness⟧ **1** *Bible a*) wickedness as an evil force: Deut. 13:13 *b*) Satan: 2 Cor. 6:15 **2** in Milton's *Paradise Lost*, one of the fallen angels

Be·lin·da (bə lin′də) ⟦< Gmc *Betlindis*: *Bet-* (< ?) + *-lindis*, prob. akin to OHG *lind*, gentle < IE base **lento-*, flexible > L *lentus*⟧ a feminine name: dim. *Linda*

Bel·i·sa·ri·us (bel′ə ser′ē əs) *c.* A.D. 505-565; Byzantine general under Justinian I

Bell (bel) **1 Alexander Graham** 1847-1922; U.S. inventor of the telephone, born in Scotland **2** pseudonym for the Brontë sisters: see BRONTË **3 Daniel** 1919- ; U.S. sociologist

Bel·la (bel′ə) a feminine name: see ARABELLA, ISABELLA

Bel·la·my (bel′ə mē), **Edward** 1850-98; U.S. writer & political theoretician: author of *Looking Backward*

Belle (bel) ⟦Fr < adj. *belle*, fem. of *beau*, pretty < L *bellus*, pretty⟧ a feminine name

Bel·ler·o·phon (bə ler′ə fän′) ⟦L < Gr *Bellerephōn*⟧ the hero who kills the monster Chimera, aided by the winged horse Pegasus

Bel·li·ni (bel lē′nē) **1 Gen·ti·le** (jen tē′le) *c.* 1429-1507; Venetian painter: son of Jacopo **2 Gio·van·ni** (jô vän′nē) *c.* 1430-1516: Venetian painter: teacher of Titian: son of Jacopo **3 Ja·co·po** (yä′kô pô) *c.* 1400-*c.* 1470; Venetian painter **4 Vin·cen·zo** (vēn chen′tsô) 1801-35; It. operatic composer

Bel·loc (bel'äk), (**Joseph**) **Hi·laire** (**Pierre**) (hi ler') 1870-1953; Eng. writer, born in France

Bel·lo·na (bə lō'nə) ⟦L < *bellum* < OL *dvellum*, war < IE base *dāu-*, *deu-*, to injure, destroy, burn⟧ *Rom. Myth.* the goddess of war, wife or sister of Mars

Bel·low (bel'ō), **Saul** 1915- ; U.S. novelist, born in Canada

Bel·lows (bel'ōz'), **George** (**Wesley**) 1882-1925; U.S. painter

Bel·shaz·zar (bel shaz'ər) ⟦Heb *belshatsar* < Akkadian *bēl-sharra-uṣur*, lit., "Bel, protect the king"⟧ *Bible* the last king of Babylon, who was warned of defeat by the handwriting on the wall: Dan. 5

Be·na·ven·te (**y Mar·ti·nez**) (be'nä ven'te ē mär tē'neth), **Ja·cin·to** (hä thēn'tô) 1866-1954; Sp. playwright

Bench·ley (bench'lē), **Robert** (**Charles**) 1889-1945; U.S. humorist

Ben·e·dict (ben'ə dikt') ⟦LL(Ec) *Benedictus*, lit., blessed < *benedicere*, to bless < L, to commend < *bene*, well + *dicere*, to speak⟧ **1** a masculine name: var. *Bennet*, *Bennett* **2** Saint (*c*. A.D. 480-*c*. 543); It. monk: founder of the Benedictine order: his day is July 11: also called **St. Benedict of Nur'si·a** (nur'sē ə) **3** **Benedict XIV** (born *Prospero Lambertini*) 1675-1758; pope (1740-58) **4** **Benedict XV** (born *Giacomo della Chiesa*) 1854-1922; pope (1914-22) **5** **Ruth Fulton** 1887-1948; U.S. anthropologist

Be·neš (ben'esh), **E·du·ard** (e'doo ärt) 1884-1948; Czech statesman: president of Czechoslovakia (1935-38; 1946-48): president of government in exile (1939-45)

Be·nét (bi nā', bə-) **1** **Stephen Vincent** 1898-1943; U.S. poet & writer **2** **William Rose** 1886-1950; U.S. poet, novelist, & editor: brother of Stephen

Ben–Gu·ri·on (ben goor'ē ən), **David** 1886-1973; Israeli statesman, born in Poland: prime minister of Israel (1948-53; 1955-63)

Ben·ja·min (ben'jə mən) ⟦Heb *binyamin*, lit., son of the right hand; hence, favorite son⟧ **1** a masculine name: dim. *Ben*, *Benny* **2** *Bible* Jacob's youngest son, whose mother was Rachel: Gen. 35:18 **3** **Judah Philip** 1811-84; U.S. lawyer: Confederate secretary of state (1862-65)

Ben·nett (ben'it) **1** a masculine name: see BENEDICT **2** (**Enoch**) **Arnold** 1867-1931; Eng. novelist **3** **James Gor-**

don 1795-1872; U.S. journalist, born in Scotland: founder of the New York *Herald* **4 Richard Bedford 1st Viscount Bennett** 1870-1947; Cdn. statesman: prime minister of Canada (1930-35)

Ben·ny (ben′ē), **Jack** (born *Benjamin Kubelsky*) 1894-1974; U.S. radio, television, & motion-picture comedian

Ben·tham (ben′thəm, -təm), **Jeremy** 1748-1832; Eng. philosopher, economist, & jurist

Ben·ton (ben′tən) **1 Thomas Hart** 1782-1858; U.S. senator (1821-51) **2 Thomas Hart** 1889-1975; U.S. painter; grandnephew of the senator

Be·o·wulf (bā′ə woolf′) ⟦ < ?; prob. understood in OE as *beo*, bee + *wulf*, wolf, hence as a kenning for "bear" ⟧ hero of the Old English folk epic of that name, an Anglian poem probably composed during the first half of the 8th cent. A.D.

Ber·dya·ev (bir dyä′yif), **Ni·ko·lai** (**Aleksandrovich**) (nē kỗ li′) 1874-1948; Russ. religious philosopher, in France after 1922

Ber·e·ni·ce (bər nēs′, bʉr′nis, ber′ə nī′sē) a feminine name: see BERNICE

Ber·en·son (ber′ən sən), **Bernard** 1865-1959; U.S. art critic, born in Lithuania

Berg (berk; *E* berg), **Al·ban** (äl′bän) 1885-1935; Austrian composer

Bergerac, Cyrano de *see* CYRANO DE BERGERAC, Savinien de

Berg·man (bʉrg′mən; *Swed* bar′y' män) **1** (**Ernst**) **Ing·mar** (iŋ′mär) 1918- ; Swed. motion-picture director **2 Ingrid** 1915-82; U.S. actress, born in Sweden

Berg·son (berk sōn′; *E* berg′sən), **Hen·ri** (äṅ rē′) 1859-1941; Fr. philosopher

Be·ring (bā′riŋ; *E* ber′iŋ, bir′-), **Vi·tus** (vē′toos) *c.* 1680-1741; Dan. navigator & explorer, in the service of Russia

Berke·ley (bärk′lē, bʉrk′-) **1 George** 1685-1753; Ir. philosopher & bishop **2 Sir William** 1606-77; Brit. colonial governor of Virginia (1641-52; 1660-76)

Ber·lin (bər lin′), **Irving** (born *Israel Baline*) 1888-1989; U.S. composer of popular songs, born in Russia

Ber·li·oz (ber′lē ōz′; *Fr* ber lyôz′), (**Louis**) **Hector** 1803-69; Fr. composer

Ber·na·dette (bʉr′nə det′) a feminine name

Ber·na·dotte (bur′nə dät′; *Fr* ber nà dôt′), **Jean Baptiste Jules** (zhäṅ bà tēst zhül′) 1763-1844: Fr. marshal under Napoleon I: as Charles XIV John he was king of Sweden & Norway (1818-44)

Ber·nard (bər närd′, bur′nərd; *for 2* ber nàr′) 〚OFr < OHG *Berinhard*, lit., bold as a bear < *bero*, bear + *hart*, bold, hard〛 **1** a masculine name: dim. *Bernie;* var. *Barnard*; equiv. Ger. *Bernhard* **2 Claude** (klōd) 1813-78; Fr. physiologist

Ber·nar·din de Saint–Pierre (ber nàr dan′ də san pyer′), **Jacques Hen·ri** (zhäk äṅ rē′) 1737-1814; Fr. writer

Bernard of Clair·vaux (kler vō′), **Saint** (c. 1090-1153); Fr. monk & theological writer: founder of Cistercian order: his day is Aug. 20

Bernard of Men·thon (mäṅ tōn′), **Saint** (11th cent.); Fr. monk who founded hospices in the Swiss Alps: his day is May 28

Bern·hardt (burn′härt′; *Fr* ber nàr′), **Sarah** (born *Rosine Bernard*) 1844-1923; Fr. actress

Ber·nice (bər nēs′, bur′nis) 〚L *Berenice* < Gr *Berenikē*, Macedonian var. of *Pherenikē*, lit., bringer of victory < *pherein*, to bear + *nikē*, victory〛 a feminine name: var. *Berenice*

Ber·ni·ni (ber nē′nē), **Gio·van·ni Lo·ren·zo** (jô vän′nē lô ren′tsô) 1598-1680; It. baroque sculptor, architect, & painter

Ber·noul·li, **Ber·nouil·li** (ber nōō′lē; *Fr* ber nōō yē′) **1** family of Swiss mathematicians & scientists **2 Daniel** 1700-82; known for his work on hydrodynamics: son of Jean **3 Jacques** (zhäk) 1654-1705; known for his work on calculus: brother of Jean **4 Jean** (zhäṅ) 1667-1748; known for his work on calculus

Bern·stein (burn′stīn′), **Leonard** 1918-90; U.S. conductor & composer

Ber·tha (bur′thə) 〚Ger < OHG *Berahta*, lit., bright one < *beraht*, bright, shining, akin to OE *beorht, bryht*, bright〛 a feminine name

Ber·tram (bur′trəm) 〚Ger < OHG *Berahtram, Berahthraban < beraht*, bright + *hraban*, raven〛 a masculine name: dim. *Bertie;* var. *Bertrand*

Ber·trand (bur′trənd) a masculine name: see BERTRAM

Beryl (bur′l) 〚< *beryl*, with ref. to gems〛 a feminine name

Ber·ze·li·us (ber sā'lē oos; *E* bər zē'lē əs), **Baron Jöns Ja·kob** (yöns' yä'kôp) 1779-1848; Swed. chemist

Bes (bes) 〚 Egypt *besa* 〛 *Egypt. Myth.* a god of pleasure and a protector of women in childbirth and of children

Bes·ant (bes'ənt), **Annie** (born *Annie Wood*) 1847-1933; Brit. theosophist: leader in India's movement for independence

Bess (bes) a feminine name: see ELIZABETH

Be·the (bā'tē), **Hans Al·brecht** (häns äl'breHt) 1906- ; U.S. theoretical physicist, born in Germany

Beth·mann–Holl·weg (bāt'män hôl'väk), **The·o·bald von** (tā'ô bält' fôn) 1856-1921; chancellor of Germany (1909-17)

Be·thune (bə thyoon'), **Mary** (born *Mary McLeod*) 1875-1955; U.S. educator

Bet·je·man (bech'ə mən), **Sir John** 1906-84; Eng. poet: poet laureate (1972-84)

Bet·sy (bet'sē) a feminine name: see ELIZABETH

Bet·ty (bet'ē) a feminine name: see ELIZABETH

Beu·lah (byoo'lə) 〚 name for Israel (Isa. 62:4) < Heb *beula*, married 〛 a feminine name

Bev·er·ley, Bev·er·ly (bev'ər lē) 〚 < ME *bever*, beaver (animal) + *ley*, lea (meadow) 〛 a feminine name

Beyle (bel), **Ma·rie Hen·ri** (må rē' än rē') *see* STENDHAL

Bid·dle (bid''l) **1 John** 1615-62; Eng. theologian: founder of Eng. Unitarianism **2 Nicholas** 1786-1844; U.S. financier

Bien·ville (byan vēl'), **Sieur de** (born *Jean Baptiste Le Moyne*) 1680-1768; Fr. colonizer & governor of Louisiana: founder of New Orleans

Bierce (birs), **Ambrose** (**Gwinett**) 1842-*c.* 1914; U.S. satirical writer

Bier·stadt (bir'stat), **Albert** 1830-1902; U.S. painter, born in Germany

Bill (bil) a masculine name: see WILLIAM

Bil·lie (bil'ē) 〚 dim. of WILLIAM 〛 a feminine and masculine name

Bil·lings (bil'iŋz), **Josh** (jäsh) (pseud. of *Henry Wheeler Shaw*) 1818-85; U.S. humorist

Bil·ly (bil'ē) a masculine name: see WILLIAM

Billy the Kid (name for *William H. Bonney*) 1859-81; U.S. outlaw

Bing·ham (biŋ'əm), **George Caleb** 1811-79; U.S. painter

Bi·on (bī'än, -ən) fl. 2d cent. B.C.; Gr. pastoral poet

Birds·eye (burdz'ī'), **Clarence** 1886-1956; U.S. inventor of methods of quick-freezing foods

Bish·op (bish'əp), **Elizabeth** 1911-79; U.S. poet

Bis·marck (biz'märk'), **Prince Otto (Eduard Leopold) von** 1815-98; Prus. chancellor of the German Empire (1871-90), which he unified: called the *Iron Chancellor*

Bi·zet (bē zā'), **Georges** (zhôrzh) (born *Alexandre César Léopold Bizet*) 1838-75; Fr. composer

Black (blak), **Hugo (La Fayette)** 1886-1971; U.S. jurist: associate justice, Supreme Court (1937-71)

Black·beard (black'bird') (name for *Edward Teach* or *Thatch*) died 1718; Eng. pirate

Black·ett (blak'it), **Baron P(atrick) M(aynard) S(tuart)** 1897-1974; Eng. nuclear physicist

Black Hawk 1767-1838; chief of the Sauk people: leader in the Black Hawk War against the U.S. (1832)

Black·mun (blak'mən), **Harry Andrew** 1908- ; associate justice, U.S. Supreme Court (1970-)

Black Prince *name for* EDWARD (Prince of Wales)

Black·stone (blak'stōn'; *Brit*, -stən), **Sir William** 1723-80; Eng. jurist & writer on law

Black·well (blak'wəl), **Elizabeth** 1821-1910; 1st woman physician in the U.S., born in England

Blaine (blān), **James G(illespie)** 1830-93; U.S. statesman: secretary of state (1881, 1889-92)

Blake (blāk) **1 Robert** 1599-1657; Eng. admiral **2 William** 1757-1827; Eng. poet & artist

Bla·key (blā'kē), **Art** 1919-90; U.S. jazz musician: Muslim name *Abdullah Ibn Buhaina*

Blanche, Blanch (blanch) [[Fr, lit., white, fem. of *blanc* < Frank *blank*, white, gleaming < IE *bhleg-*, to shine]] a feminine name

Blas·co I·bá·ñez (bläs'kô ē bä'nyeth), **Vi·cen·te** (vē then'te) 1867-1928; Sp. novelist

Bla·vat·sky (blə vät'skē, -vat'-), **Helena Pe·trov·na** (pə trōv'nə) (born *Helena Hahn*) 1831-91; Russ. theosophist in U.S. and elsewhere: called *Madame Blavatsky*

Blé·ri·ot (blā rē ō', bler'ē-), **Louis** 1872-1936; Fr. aeronautical engineer & aviation pioneer

Blessed Virgin the Virgin Mary

Bligh (blī), **William** 1754-1817; Eng. naval officer: commander of the *Bounty*, whose crew mutinied

Bloch (bläk) **1 Ernest** 1880-1959; U.S. composer, born in Switzerland **2 Felix** 1905-83; U.S. physicist, born in

Switzerland **3 Konrad Emil** 1912- ; U.S. biochemist, born in Germany

Blok (blôk; *E* bläk), **A·lek·san·dr A·lek·san·dro·vich** (ä lyik sän′dr′ ä′lyik sän′drô vyich) 1880-1921; Russ. poet

Bloody Mary *name for* MARY I

Bloom·er (bloom′ər), **Amelia Jenks** (jeŋks) 1818-94; U.S. social reformer & feminist

Bloom·field (bloom′fēld′), **Leonard** 1887-1949; U.S. linguist

Blü·cher (blü′Hər; *E* bloo′chər, -kər), **Geb·hard Le·be·recht von** (gep′härt′ lā′bə reHt′ fôn) 1742-1819; Prus. field marshal: helped defeat Napoleon at Waterloo

Blue·beard (bloo′bird′) a character in an old folk tale who married and then murdered one wife after another

Blum (bloom), **Lé·on** (lā ôn′) 1872-1950; Fr. socialist statesman

Bo·ab·dil (bō′əb dēl′) (Ar. name *Abu-Abdullah;* ruled as *Mohammed XI*) died 1538; last Moorish king of Granada

Bo·a·di·ce·a (bō′ad ə sē′ə) died A.D. 62; queen of the Iceni in ancient Britain, who led a vain revolt against the Romans (A.D. 61)

Bo·a·ner·ges (bō′ə nur′jēz′) ⟦LL(Ec) < Gr(Ec) *boaner-ges;* prob. ult. < Heb *b′nāi regesh,* sons of wrath: interpreted in Gr as "sons of thunder"⟧ *Bible* the Apostles John and James: Mark 3:17 An epithet used by Jesus

Bo·as (bō′az′, -as), **Franz** (fränts) 1858-1942; U.S. anthropologist, born in Germany

Bo·az (bō′az′) ⟦Heb *boaz,* lit., swiftness⟧ *Bible* Ruth's second husband: Ruth 4:13

Bob (bäb) *nickname for* ROBERT: dim. *Bobby*

Boc·cac·cio (bō käch′ē ō′; *It* bô kä′chô), **Gio·van·ni** (jô vän′nē) 1313-75; It. author of the *Decameron*

Boc·che·ri·ni (bō′kə rē′nē; *It* bô′kə rē′nē), **Lu·i·gi** (loo ē′ jē) 1743-1805; It. composer

Boc·cio·ni (bô chô′nē), **Um·ber·to** (oom ber′tô) 1882-1916; It. futurist painter & sculptor

Bo·e·thi·us (bō ē′thē əs), (Anicius Manlius Severinus) *c.* A.D. 480-*c.* 524; Rom. philosopher

Bo·gart (bō′gärt′), **Humphrey** (DeForest) 1899-1957; U.S. motion-picture actor

Böh·me (bö′mə; *E* bām), **Ja·kob** 1575-1624; Ger. theosophist & mystic: also **Böhm** (böm; *E* bām)

Bohr (bôr) **1 Aa·ge Niels** (ô′gə nēls′) 1922- ; Dan. physicist: son of Niels **2 Niels (Henrik David)** (nēls) 1885-1962; Dan. nuclear & theoretical physicist

Bo·iar·do (bô yär′dô), **Mat·te·o Ma·ri·a** (mät tā′ô mä rē′ä) *c.* 1434-94; It. poet

Boi·leau (bwä lō′), **Ni·co·las** (nē kô lä′) 1636-1711; Fr. critic & poet: in full **Nicolas Boi·leau–Des·pré·aux** (dā prä ō′)

Bol·eyn (bool′in, bə lin′), **Anne** *c.* 1507-36; 2d wife of Henry VIII of England: mother of Elizabeth I

Bol·ing·broke (bool′iŋ brook′) 1st Viscount (born *Henry St. John*) 1678-1751; Eng. statesman & political writer

Bol·i·var (bäl′ə vər; *Sp* bô lē′vär), **Si·món** (sī′mən; *Sp* sē mōn′) 1783-1830; South American general & revolutionary leader, born in Caracas: hero of South American fight for independence from Spain

Böll (böl), **Hein·rich** (hīn′riH) 1917-85; Ger. novelist

Bo·na·parte (bō′nə pärt′; *Fr* bô nà pàrt′) **1** name of a Corsican family of Italian origin to which belonged Napoleon I and his four brothers **2 Jé·rôme** (zhā rōm′) 1784-1860; king of Westphalia (1807-13) **3 Joseph** 1768-1844; king of Naples (1806-08) & of Spain (1808-13) **4 Louis** 1778-1846; king of Holland (1806-10): father of Louis Napoleon **5 Lu·ci·en** (lü syan′) (*Prince of Canino*) 1775-1840; Fr. government official **6 Na·po·le·on** (nə pō′lē ən, -pōl′yən) 1769-1821; Fr. military leader & emperor of France (1804-15), born in Corsica: in full *Napoleon I* See also NAPOLEON II, LOUIS NAPOLEON

Bon·a·ven·tu·ra (bō′nə ven toor′ə, bän′ə-), Saint (born *Giovanni Fidanza*) (1221-74); It. theologian & scholastic philosopher: his day is July 15: also **Bon·a·ven·ture** (bän′ə ven′chər)

Bon·heur (bỗ nër′), **Ro·sa** (rō zà′) (born *Marie Rosalie Bonheur*) 1822-99; Fr. painter of animal subjects

Bon·i·face (bän′ə fəs, -fās′) **1** Saint (born *Winfrid* or *Wynfrith*) (*c.* A.D. 675-*c.* 754); Eng. monk & missionary in Germany: his day is June 5 **2 Boniface VIII** (born *Benedetto Caetani*) *c.* 1235-1303; pope (1294-1303)

Bon·nard (bỗ nàr′), **Pierre** 1867-1947; Fr. impressionist painter

Bon·nie (bän′e) ‖ < *bonny* (handsome, pretty) < Fr *bon*, good < L *bonus* ‖ a feminine name: var. *Bonny*

Boone (bōōn), **Daniel** 1734-1820; Am. frontiersman

Booth (bōōth) **1 Bal·ling·ton** (bal'iŋ tən) 1859-1940; founder of Volunteers of America (1896): son of William **2 Edwin (Thomas)** 1833-93; U.S. actor: son of Junius Brutus **3 Evangeline Cor·y** (kôr'ē) 1865-1950; U.S. general of Salvation Army, born in England: daughter of William **4 John Wilkes** 1838-65; U.S. actor: assassin of Abraham Lincoln: son of Junius Brutus **5 Junius Brutus** 1796-1852; U.S. actor, born in England **6 William** 1829-1912; Eng. revivalist: founder of the Salvation Army (1865)

Bor·den (bôrd'n), **Liz·zie (Andrew)** (liz'ē) 1860-1927; U.S. woman accused and acquitted of murdering her father & stepmother with an ax (1892)

Bo·re·as (bôr'ē əs) ‖ L < Gr, north wind; ? orig., wind from the mountains < IE base **gwer-*, mountain > OSlav *gora*, mountain ‖ **1** *Gr. Myth.* the god of the north wind **2** [Old Poet.] the north wind personified

Bor·ges (bôr'hes), **Jor·ge Luis** (hôr'he lōō ēs') 1899-1986; Argentine poet, short-story writer, & critic

Bor·gia (bôr'jə, -zhə) **1 Ce·sa·re** (che'zä *re*) c. 1476-1507; It. military leader & cardinal: son of Pope Alexander VI **2 Lu·cre·zia** (lōō kre'tsyä) 1480-1519; duchess of Ferrara: patroness of the arts: sister of Cesare

Bor·glum (bôr'gləm), **(John) Gut·zon** (gut'sən) 1871-1941; U.S. sculptor and painter

Bor·is (bôr'is) ‖ Russ, lit., fight ‖ a masculine name

Born (bôrn), **Max** 1882-1970; Ger. nuclear physicist, in England (1933-53)

Bo·ro·din (bôr'ə dēn', bôr'ə din'; *Russ* bô'rô dyēn'), **A·lek·san·dr Por·fir·e·vich** (ä'lyik sän'dr' pôr fir'yi vich) 1833-87; Russ. composer

Bors (bôrs, bôrz), **Sir** *Arthurian Legend* a knight of the Round Table, nephew of Sir Lancelot

Bosch (bäsh, bôsh; *Du* bôs), **Hi·e·ro·ny·mus** (hē'ə rō'ni məs) (born *Jerome van Aken*) c. 1450-1516; Du. painter

Bose (bōs, bōsh), **Sir Ja·ga·dis Chan·dra** (jə gə dēs' chun'drə) 1858-1937; Ind. physicist & plant physiologist

Bos·suet (bä swā'; *Fr* bô süe'), **Jacques Bé·ni·gne** (zhäk bā nē'ny') 1627-1704; Fr. bishop & orator

Bos·well (bäz'wel', -wəl), **James** 1740-95; Scot. lawyer & writer: biographer of Samuel Johnson

Bo·tha (bō'tə), **Louis** 1862-1919; South African statesman: 1st prime minister (1910-19)

Bot·ti·cel·li (bät'ə chel'ē; *It* bôt'tē chel'ē), **San·dro** (sän'drô) (born *Alessandro di Mariano dei Filipepi*) c. 1445-1510; It. Renaissance painter

Bou·cher (bōō shā'), **Fran·çois** (frän swà') 1703-70; Fr. painter in the rococo style

Bou·ci·cault (bōō'sē kō'), **Di·on** (dē'än) (born *Dionysius Lardner Boursiquot*) c. 1820-90; Brit. playwright & actor, born in Ireland

Bou·gain·ville (bōō gan vēl'), **Louis An·toine de** (lwē än twän' də) 1729-1811; Fr. navigator & explorer

Bou·lan·ger (bōō län zhā'), **Na·dia** (**Juliette**) (nà dyà') 1887-1979; Fr. musician, composer, & teacher of composition

Bou·lez (bōō lez'), **Pierre** 1925- ; Fr. composer & conductor

Bour·bon (boor'bən) name of the ruling family of France (1589-1793; 1814-48, from 1830 to 1848 as the ORLÉANS branch); of Spain (1700-1808; 1813-1931; 1975-); of Naples and Sicily (1734-1806; 1815-60), united as the kingdom of the Two Sicilies, 1815; and of various duchies & principalities in Italy at various times within the periods 1748-1807 & 1815-60, including Parma, Piacenza, Lucca, & Etruria

Bourke–White (bʉrk'hwīt'), **Margaret** 1906-71; U.S. photographer

Bou·tros–Gha·li (bōō'trōs gä'lē), **Bou·tros** (bōō'trōs) 1922- ; Egypt. diplomat: secretary-general of the United Nations (1992-)

Bo·vet (bō vā'), **Daniel** 1907-92; Swiss pharmacologist

Bow·ditch (bou'dich), **Nathaniel** 1773-1838; U.S. mathematician, astronomer, & navigator

Boyle (boil), **Robert** 1627-91; Brit. chemist & physicist, born in Ireland

Boz (bäz; *orig.* bōz) *pseud. of* Charles (John Huffam) DICKENS

Brad·dock (brad'ək), **Edward** 1695-1755; Brit. general, born in Scotland: commander of the Brit. forces in the French & Indian War

Brad·ford (brad'fərd) **1 Gamaliel** 1863-1932; U.S. biographer **2 William** 1590-1657; 2d governor of Plymouth

Colony

Brad·ley (brad'lē) **1** a masculine name **2 Omar Nelson** 1893-1981; U.S. general

Brad·street (brad'strēt), **Anne** (born *Anne Dudley*) *c.* 1612-72; Am. poet, born in England

Bra·dy (brā'dē), **Math·ew B.** (math'yōō) *c.* 1823-96; U.S. photographer, esp. of Lincoln & the Civil War

Bragg (brag) **1 Brax·ton** (brak'stən) 1817-76; Confederate general **2** Sir **William Henry** 1862-1942; Eng. physicist **3** Sir (**William**) **Lawrence** 1890-1971; Eng. physicist, born in Australia: son of William Henry

Bra·gi (brä'gē) *Norse Myth.* the god of poetry and eloquence, son of Odin and Frigg

Bra·he (brä'ə), **Ty·cho** (tü'kō) 1546-1601; Dan. astronomer

Brah·ma (brä'mə) 〚Hindi < Sans *brahman*, worship, prayer〛 *Hinduism* the chief member of the trinity (Brahma, Vishnu, and Siva) and creator of the universe

Brahms (brämz), **Jo·han·nes** (yō hän'əs) 1833-97; Ger. composer

Bra·man·te (brä män'te), **Do·na·to d'A·gno·lo** (dô nä'tô dä nyô'lô) 1444-1514; It. architect

Bran (bran) 〚< ? Ir *bran*, raven〛 *Celt. Myth.* a giant king of Britain

Bran·cuşi (brän'kōōsh), **Con·stan·tin** (kôn'stən tēn') 1876-1957; Romanian sculptor, in Paris after 1904

Bran·deis (bran'dīs', -dīz'), **Louis Dem·bitz** (dem'bits') 1856-1941; U.S. jurist: associate justice, Supreme Court (1916-39)

Bran·des (brän'dəs), **Ge·org Mor·ris** (gē ôr' mô'rēs) (born *Georg Morris Cohen*) 1842-1927; Dan. literary critic

Brant (brant), **Joseph** (born *Thayendanegea*) 1742-1807; Mohawk Indian chief: fought for the British in the French & Indian War and the Revolutionary War

Braque (bràk), **Georges** (zhôrzh) 1882-1963; Fr. painter

Brau·del (brō del'), **Fer·nand Paul** (fer'nän pôl) 1902-85; Fr. historian

Brecht (breHt; *E* brekt), **Ber·tolt** (ber'tôlt) 1898-1956; Ger. playwright

Breck·in·ridge (brek'in rij'), **John Cabell** 1821-75; vice president of the U.S. (1857-61); Confederate general

Bren·da (bren'də) 〚prob. fem. of *Brand* < Ger *brand* or

ON *brandr*, a sword ‖ a feminine name

Bren·nan (bren′ən), **William J(oseph), Jr.** 1906- ; associate justice, U.S. Supreme Court (1956-90)

Bre·ton (brə tōn′), **An·dré** (än drā′) 1896-1966; Fr. poet & art critic: a founder of surrealism

Breu·er (broi′ər), **Marcel (Lajos)** 1902-81; U.S. architect & designer, born in Hungary

Breu·ghel (brü′gəl, broi′-) **1** Jan *alt. sp.* of Jan BRUEGEL **2 Pieter** *alt. sp.* of Pieter BRUEGEL

Brew·ster (brōō′stər), **William** *c.* 1567-1644; Eng. Pilgrim who helped settle Plymouth Colony

Brezh·nev (brezh′nef, -nev), **Le·o·nid I(lyich)** (lā ô nēd′) 1906-82; general secretary of the Communist Party of the U.S.S.R. (1964-82)

Bri·an (brī′ən) ‖ Celt, ? strong ‖ a masculine name

Bri·an Bo·ru (brī′ən bə rōō′) *c.* 926-1014: king of Ireland (1002-14): Ir. name **Brian Bo·ram·he′** (brēn bô rō′)

Bride (brīd) Saint BRIDGET (of Ireland)

Bridg·es (brij′iz), **Robert (Seymour)** 1844-1930; Eng. poet: poet laureate (1913-30)

Bridg·et (brij′it) ‖ Ir *Brighid*, lit., strong, lofty < IE base *bheregh-*, high ‖ **1** a feminine name: equiv. Ger. & Fr. *Brigitte* **2 Saint** (*c.* A.D. 452-*c.* 523); Ir. abbess: a patron saint of Ireland: her day is Feb. 1 **3 Saint** (*c.* 1302-73); Swed. nun: founder of the order of *Bri(d)gittines*: her day is July 23

Bridg·man (brij′mən), **Percy Williams** 1882-1961; U.S. physicist

Bright (brīt), **John** 1811-89; Eng. statesman, political economist, & orator

Brig·id (brij′id) Saint BRIDGET (of Ireland)

Bril·lat-Sa·va·rin (brē yà′ sà và ran′), **An·thelme** (än telm′) 1755-1826; Fr. expert on foods & cooking

Bri·tan·ni·a (bri tan′ē ə, -tan′yə) ‖ L ‖ [Old Poet.] a female figure symbolizing Great Britain or the British Empire

Brit·ten (brit′n), **(Edward) Benjamin** Baron Britten of Aldeburgh 1913-76; Eng. composer

Broch (bräkh), **Her·mann** (her′män) 1886-1951; U.S. novelist, born in Austria

Bro·glie (brô glē′; Fr brô′y′) **1 Achille Charles Léonce Victor** Duc de Broglie 1785-1870; statesman, under Napoleon I & Louis Philippe **2 (Louis César Victor) Maurice** Duc de Broglie 1875-1960; physicist: great-grandson of Achille **3 Louis Victor** Prince de Broglie 1892-1987; physicist: brother of Maurice

Bron·të (brän'të) **1 Anne** (pseud. *Acton Bell*) 1820-49; novelist: sister of Charlotte **2 Charlotte** (Mrs. *Arthur Bell Nicholls;* pseud. *Currer Bell*) 1816-55; novelist: author of *Jane Eyre* **3 Emily Jane** (pseud. *Ellis Bell*) 1818-48; novelist & poet: author of *Wuthering Heights*: sister of Charlotte

Brooke (brook), **Rupert** 1887-1915; Eng. poet

Brooks (brooks) **1 Gwendolyn Elizabeth** 1917- ; U.S. poet **2 Phillips** 1835-93; U.S. clergyman & writer **3 Van Wyck** 1886-1963; U.S. critic & biographer

Brother Jonathan ⟦apparently first applied to New England militia besieging Boston by Brit soldiers evacuating the city (March, 1776)⟧ [Historical] the United States or its people: predecessor of Uncle Sam

Brown (broun) **1 Charles Brock·den** (bräk'dən) 1771-1810; U.S. novelist **2 Herbert Charles** 1912- ; U.S. organic chemist, born in Great Britain **3 John** 1800-59; U.S. abolitionist: as part of a plan for an uprising among slaves, he led a raid on an arsenal at Harpers Ferry: hanged for treason

Browne (broun) **1 Charles Far·rar** (far'ər) *see* WARD, Artemus **2 Sir Thomas** 1605-82; Eng. physician & writer

Brown·ing (broun'iŋ) **1 Elizabeth Barrett** 1806-61; Eng. poet: wife of Robert **2 John Moses** 1855-1926; U.S. inventor of firearms **3 Robert** 1812-89; Eng. poet

Bru·beck (broo'bek), **David Warren** (called *Dave*) 1920- ; U.S. jazz pianist & composer

Bruce (broos) ⟦Scot, after Fr *Brieuse*, locality in France⟧ **1** a masculine name **2 Robert (the)** 1274-1329; king of Scotland (as *Robert I*, 1306-29): won independence of Scotland from England **3 Stanley Melbourne** 1st Viscount Bruce of Melbourne 1883-1967; prime minister of Australia (1923-29)

Bruch (brookh), **Max** 1838-1920; Ger. composer

Bruck·ner (brook'nər), **An·ton** (an'tän) 1824-96; Austrian composer

Brue·gel, Brue·ghel (brü'gəl, broi'-) **1 Jan** (yän) 1568-1625; Fl. painter: son of Pieter **2 Pie·ter** (pē'tər) *c.* 1525-69; Fl. painter of peasant life

Brummell, George Bryan *see* BEAU BRUMMELL

Bru·nel·les·chi (broo'nel les'kē), **Fi·lip·po** (fē lēp'pô)

1377-1446; Florentine architect

Brun·hild (brōōn'hilt', -hild') ⟦MHG *Brünhild* < OHG *brunna*, armor + *hilti* (or OS *hild*), fight; hence, fighter in armor⟧ in the *Nibelungenlied*, a queen of Iceland whom Gunther, king of Burgundy, gets as his bride with the help of Siegfried's magic: see also BRYN-HILD

Bru·no (brōō'nō) ⟦OHG < *brun*, brown⟧ 1 a masculine name 2 **Gior·da·no** (jôr dä'nō) 1548-1600; It. philosopher: burned at the stake by the Inquisition 3 Saint (*c.* 1030-1101); Ger. monk: founder of the Carthusian order: his day is Oct. 6: also Saint **Bruno of Cologne**

Bru·tus (brōōt'əs), (**Marcus Junius**) *c.* 85-42 B.C.; Rom. statesman & general: one of the conspirators who murdered Julius Caesar

Bry·an (brī'ən) 1 a masculine name: see BRIAN 2 **William Jen·nings** (jen'iŋz) 1860-1925; U.S. politician & orator

Bry·ant (brī'ənt), **William Cul·len** (kul'ən) 1794-1878; U.S. poet & journalist

Bryce (brīs), **Viscount James** 1838-1922; Eng. jurist, statesman, & historian, born in Ireland

Bryn·hild (brin'hild') ⟦ON *Brynhildr* < *brynja*, armor + *hildr*, fight⟧ *Norse Myth.* a Valkyrie awakened from an enchanted sleep by Sigurd: deceived by him into marrying Gunnar, she brings about Sigurd's death and then kills herself: see also BRUNHILD

Bu·ber (bōō'bər), **Martin** 1878-1965; Israeli Jewish theologian & philosopher, born in Austria

Bu·chan·an (byōō kan'ən), **James** 1791-1868; 15th president of the U.S. (1857-61)

Büch·ner (bookh'nər) 1 **Eduard** 1860-1917; Ger. biochemist 2 **Georg** 1813-37; Ger. poet & dramatist

Buck (buk), **Pearl** (born *Pearl Sydenstricker*) 1892-1973; U.S. novelist

Buck·ing·ham (buk'iŋ əm) 1 **1st Duke of** (born *George Villiers*) 1592-1628; Eng. statesman 2 **2d Duke of** (born *George Villiers*) 1628-87; Eng. statesman & writer: son of 1st Duke

Bud·dha (bood'ə, bōō'də) ⟦Sans, the enlightened one; pp. of *budh*, to awake, know < IE base **bheudh-*, to be alert, announce⟧ Siddhartha Gautama, religious philosopher and teacher who lived in India *c.* 563-*c.* 483 B.C. and was the founder of Buddhism: the name is a title applied by Buddhists to someone regarded as embodying divine wisdom and virtue

Buffalo Bill *name for* William Frederick CODY

Buf·fon (bü fôn′), Comte de (born *George Louis Leclerc*) 1707-88; Fr. naturalist

Bu·kha·rin (boo khä′rin), **Ni·ko·lai** (Ivanovich) (nĕ′kô lī′) 1888-1938; Russ. Communist leader & editor

Bul·finch (bool′finch′) 1 **Charles** 1763-1844; U.S. architect 2 **Thomas** 1796-1867; U.S. writer & mythologist: son of Charles

Bul·ga·kov (bool gä′kôf), **Mi·kha·il** (Afanasyevich) (mē′ khä ēl′) 1891-1940; Russ. novelist & playwright

Bü·low (bü′lô), Prince **Bern·hard von** (bern′härt fôn) 1849-1929; Ger. statesman: chancellor (1900-09)

Bult·mann (boolt′män), **Rudolf** (**Karl**) 1884-1976; Ger. Protestant theologian

Bul·wer–Lyt·ton (bool′wər lit″n) 1 **Edward George Earle Lytton** 1st Baron Lytton of Knebworth 1803-73; Eng. novelist & playwright: father of Edward Robert Bulwer-Lytton 2 **Edward Robert** *see* MEREDITH, Owen

Bunche (bunch), **Ralph Johnson** 1904-71; U.S. statesman & educator

Bu·nin (boo′nyin), **I·van A·lek·se·ye·vich** (ē vän′ ä′lyik sä′yi vich) 1870-1953; Russ. novelist & poet, in France after 1920

Bun·sen (bun′sən *Ger* boon′zən), **Robert Wilhelm** 1811-99; Ger. chemist: inventor of the spectroscope

Bu·ñu·el (boo′nyoo el′), **Lu·is** (loo ēs′) 1900-83; Sp. film director

Bun·yan (bun′yən) 1 **John** 1628-88; Eng. writer & preacher: wrote *Pilgrim's Progress* 2 **Paul** *see* PAUL BUNYAN

Buo·na·par·te (bwô′nä pär′te) *It. sp. of* BONAPARTE

Buo·nar·ro·ti (bwô′när rô′tē), **Michelangelo** *see* MICHELANGELO

Bur·bage (bʉr′bij), **Richard** *c.* 1567-1619; Eng. actor: associate of Shakespeare

Bur·bank (bʉr′baŋk), **Luther** 1849-1926; U.S. horticulturist: bred numerous varieties of fruits, vegetables, & flowers

Burck·hardt (boork′härt), **Jacob** 1818-97; Swiss art historian & critic

Bur·ger (bʉr′gər), **Warren Earl** 1907- ; U.S. jurist: chief justice of the U.S. (1969-86)

Bur·gess (bur′jəs), (**Frank**) **Ge·lett** (jə let′) 1866-1951; U.S. humorist & illustrator

Burgh·ley (bur′lē), 1st Baron (born *William Cecil*) 1520-98; Eng. statesman: advisor to Elizabeth I

Bur·goyne (bər goin′, bur′goin), **John** 1722-92; Brit. general in the American Revolution: defeated by colonial forces under Gates at Saratoga (1777)

Burke (burk), **Edmund** 1729-97; Brit. statesman, orator, & writer, born in Ireland

Bur·leigh (bur′lē) *alt. sp. of* BURGHLEY

Burne–Jones (burn′jōnz′), Sir **Edward Co·ley** (kō′lē) 1833-98; Eng. painter & designer

Bur·nett (bər net′), **Frances** (**Eliza**) **Hodgson** 1849-1924; U.S. writer, esp. of children's books, born in England

Bur·ney (bur′nē), **Fanny** (born *Frances*; married name *Madame d'Arblay*) 1752-1840; Eng. novelist & diarist

Burns (burnz), **Robert** 1759-96; Scot. poet

Burn·side (burn′sīd′), **Ambrose Everett** 1824-81; Union general in the Civil War

Burr (bur), **Aaron** 1756-1836; U.S. political leader: vice president of the U.S. (1801-05): killed Alexander Hamilton in a duel (1804)

Bur·roughs (bur′ōz) **1 Edgar Rice** 1875-1950; U.S. writer, esp. of the Tarzan stories **2 John** 1837-1921; U.S. naturalist & writer

Bur·ton (burt′'n) **1** Sir **Richard Francis** 1821-90; Eng. writer & explorer **2 Robert** (pseud. *Democritus Junior*) 1577-1640; Eng. writer & clergyman: author of *The Anatomy of Melancholy*

Bush (boosh) **1 George** (**Herbert Walker**) 1924- ; 41st president of the U.S. (1989-93) **2 Van·ne·var** (və nē′vär) 1890-1974; U.S. electrical engineer & administrator

Bu·so·ni (boo zō′nē), **Fer·ruc·cio Ben·ve·nu·to** (fer root′ chō ben′ve noo′tô) 1866-1924; It. composer

Bu·te·nandt (boot′'n änt), **Adolf** (**Frederick Johann**) 1903- ; Ger. chemist

But·ler (but′lər) **1 Benjamin Franklin** 1818-93; U.S. politician & Union general in the Civil War **2 Samuel** 1612-80; Eng. satirical poet **3 Samuel** 1835-1902; Eng. novelist

Bux·te·hu·de (book′stə hoo′də), **Did·er·ik** (dē′də rik) 1637-1707; Dan. (perhaps born in Sweden) organist & composer, later in Germany: also Ger. **Diet′rich** (dēt′

*r*iH)

Byrd (bʉrd) **1 Richard Evelyn** 1888-1957; U.S. naval officer & antarctic explorer **2 William** *c.* 1543-1623; Eng. composer

By·ron (bī′rən) ⟦Fr *Biron*, orig. a family name, after *Biron*, district in Périgord, France⟧ **1** a masculine name **2 George Gordon** 6th Baron Byron 1788-1824; Eng. poet

C

Cab·ell (kab′əl), **James Branch** 1879-1958; U.S. novelist

Ca·be·za de Va·ca (kä be′thä *the* vä′kä), **Ál·var Nú·ñez** (äl′vär nōō′nyeth) *c.* 1490-*c.* 1557; Sp. explorer in the Americas

Ca·ble (kā′bəl), **George Washington** 1844-1925; U.S. novelist

Cab·ot (kab′ət) **1 John** (It. name *Giovanni Caboto*) *c.* 1450-*c.* 1498: It. explorer in the service of England: discovered coast of North America (1497) **2 Sebastian** *c.* 1476-1557; Eng. cartographer & explorer: son of John

Ca·bri·ni (kə brē′nē), **Saint Frances Xavier** (called *Mother Cabrini*) 1850-1917; U.S. nun, born in Italy: first U.S. citizen canonized: her day is Dec. 22

Ca·dil·lac (kȧ dē yȧk′; *E* kad′′l ak′), **Sieur An·toine de la Mothe** (än twȧn də lȧ môt′) *c.* 1658-1730; Fr. explorer in America

Cad·mus (kad′məs) ⟦Gr *Kadmos*⟧ a Phoenician prince and founder of Thebes: he kills a dragon and sows its teeth, from which many armed men rise, fighting each other, until only five are left to help him build the city

Caed·mon (kad′mən) fl. late 7th cent. A.D.; first Eng. poet whose name is known

Cae·sar (sē′zər), **(Gaius) Julius** ⟦L *Caesar*, said to be < *caesus*, pp. of *caedere*, to cut down, but prob. of Etr orig.⟧ *c.* 100-44 B.C.; Rom. general & statesman; dictator (49-44) of the Roman Empire

Cage (kāj), **John** 1912-92; U.S. composer

Ca·glia·ri (käl′yä rē′), **Paolo** *see* VERONESE, Paolo

Ca·glio·stro (käl yôs′trō), **Count A·les·san·dro di** (ä′les sän′drô dē) (born *Giuseppe Balsamo*) 1743-95; Sicilian alchemist & charlatan

Cag·ney (kag′nē), **James** 1899-1987; U.S. motion-picture actor

Cai·a·phas (kā'ə fəs, kī'-) 〚Gr *Kaiaphas*〛 *Bible* the high priest who presided at the trial that led to the condemnation of Jesus: Matt. 26:57-66

Cain (kān) 〚Heb *qayin*, lit., one created〛 *Bible* the oldest son of Adam and Eve: he killed his brother Abel: Gen. 4

Calamity Jane (name for *Martha Jane Burk* or *Burke* or *Martha Jane Canary*) 1852-1903; U.S. frontier figure, noted for her marksmanship

Cal·chas (kal'kəs) 〚L < Gr *Kalchas*〛 *Gr. Myth.* a priest of Apollo with the Greeks during the Trojan War

Cal·der (kôl'dər) **1** Alexander 1898-1976; U.S. abstract sculptor, esp. of mobiles and stabiles **2** Alexander Stir·ling (stʉr'liŋ) 1870-1945; U.S. sculptor: father of Alexander

Cal·de·rón de la Bar·ca (käl'*the* rōn' *the* lä bär'kä), Pe·dro (pe'*thrô*) 1600-81; Sp. playwright

Cald·well (kôld'wel'), Er·skine (ʉr'skən) 1903-87; U.S. novelist

Ca·leb (kā'ləb) 〚Heb *kālēb*, lit., dog: hence, faithful〛 **1** a masculine name **2** *Bible* a leader of the Israelites who, with Joshua, was permitted by God to enter the Promised Land: Num. 26:65; Deut. 1:36

Cal·houn (kal hoon'), **John Caldwell** 1782-1850; U.S. statesman: vice president (1825-32)

Cal·i·ban (kal'i ban', -bən) 〚form of *canibal*, cannibal, with interchanged *n* & *l; canibal* occurs in Hakluyt's *Voyages* (1598)〛 a deformed, brutish creature, the slave of Prospero, in Shakespeare's *The Tempest*

Ca·lig·u·la (kə lig'yŏo lə) (born *Gaius Caesar*) A.D. 12-41; Rom. emperor (A.D. 37-41): noted for his cruelty

Cal·las (kal'əs, kä'läs), **Maria** (born *Maria Anna Sofia Cecilia Kalogeropaulos*) 1923-77; U.S. operatic soprano

Cal·li·o·pe (kə li'ə pē') 〚L < Gr *Kalliopē*, the beautiful-voiced < *kallos*, beauty + *ops*, voice〛 *Gr. Myth.* the Muse of eloquence and epic poetry

Cal·lis·to (kə lis'tō) 〚L < Gr *Kallistō*〛 *Gr. & Rom. Myth.* a nymph loved by Zeus and changed into a bear by Hera

Cal·vert (kal'vərt), **George** *see* BALTIMORE

Cal·vin (kal'vin) 〚ModL *Calvinus* < Fr *Cauvin, Chauvin*, prob. < L *calvus*, bald < IE base **gal-*, bald, naked ‖ **1** a masculine name **2 John** (born *Jean Caulvin, Cauvin,* or *Chauvin*) 1509-64; Fr. Protestant reformer **3 Melvin** 1911- ; U.S. chemist & educator

Ca·lyp·so (kə lip'sō) ‖ L < Gr *Kalypsō* < *kalyptein,* to conceal, cover ‖ in Homer's *Odyssey,* a sea nymph who keeps Odysseus on her island for seven years

Cam·by·ses (II) (kam bī'sēz') died 522 B.C.; king of Persia (529-522): son of Cyrus the Great

Cam·er·on (kam'ər ən), **Richard** c. 1648-80; Scot. minister & Covenanter whose followers formed the Reformed Presbyterian Church (1743)

Ca·mille (kə mēl'; *Fr* kȧ mē'y') ‖ Fr < L *camilla,* virgin of unblemished character ‖ a feminine name: also **Ca·mil·la** (kə mil'ə)

Ca·mões (kə moinsh'), **Lu·iz Vaz de** (loō ēsh' vȧzh də) c. 1524-80; Port. epic poet: Eng. name **Cam·o·ëns** (kam'ō enz')

Camp (kamp), **Walter (Chauncey)** 1859-1925; U.S. football authority and coach

Camp·bell (kam'bəl) **1 Alexander** 1788-1866; U.S. clergyman, born in Ireland: founder of the Disciples of Christ **2 Kim** (born *Avril Phaedra Campbell*) 1947- ; prime minister of Canada (1993) **3 Mrs. Patrick** (born *Beatrice Stella Tanner*) 1865-1940; Eng. actress **4 Thomas** 1777-1844; Scot. poet

Camp·bell–Ban·ner·man (-ban'ər mən), **Sir Henry** 1836-1908; Brit. statesman: prime minister (1905-08)

Cam·pi·on (kam'pē ən), **Thomas** 1567-1620; Eng. poet & composer of songs

Ca·mus (kȧ moō'; *Fr* kȧ mü'), **Albert** 1913-60; Fr. writer, born in Algeria

Ca·na·let·to (kä'nä let'tô), **An·to·nio** (än tô'nyô) (born *Antonio Canal* or *Canale*) 1697-1768; It. painter

Can·ning (kan'iŋ), **George** 1770-1827; Brit. statesman: prime minister (1827)

Can·non (kan'ən), **Joseph Gur·ney** (gur'nē) 1836-1926; U.S. congressman

Ca·no·va (kä nô'vä), **An·to·nio** (än tô'nyô) 1757-1822; It. sculptor

Can·tor (kän'tôr'), **Ge·org (Ferdinand Ludwig Philipp)** (gā'ôrk', gā ôrk') 1845-1918; Ger. mathematician, born in Russia

Ca·nute (kə noōt', -nyoōt') ‖ < Dan *Knut* ‖ c. 994-1035; 1st Dan. king of England (1017-35) & king of Denmark

(1018-35) & of Norway (1028-35): also called **Canute the Great**

Ca·pa·blan·ca (kä′pə bläŋ′kə), **Jo·sé Raul** (hō sä′ rä ool′) 1888-1942; Cuban chess master: called *Capa* or *the Chess Machine*

Ča·pek (chä′pek′), **Ka·rel** (kär′əl) 1890-1938; Czech playwright and novelist

Ca·pet (kā′pit, kap′it; *Fr* kȧ pe′), **Hugh** c. A.D. 938-996; king of France (987-996)

Ca·pone (kə pōn′), **Al(phonse)** 1899-1947; U.S. gangster

Ca·po·te (kə pōt′ē), **Truman** 1924-84; U.S. writer

Cap·ra (kap′rə), **Frank** 1897-1991; U.S. motion-picture director

Cap·u·let (kap′yoo lit, -let′) the family name of Juliet in Shakespeare's *Romeo and Juliet*

Car·a·cal·la (kar′ə kal′ə) (born *Marcus Aurelius Antoninus*) A.D. 188-217; Rom. emperor (211-217)

Ca·ra·vag·gio (kä′rə vä′jō), **Mi·chel·an·ge·lo da** (mē′ke län′je lō dä) (born *Michelangelo Merisi*) 1573-1610; It. painter

Car·do·zo (kär dō′zō), **Benjamin Nathan** 1870-1938; U.S. jurist: associate justice, Supreme Court (1932-38)

Ca·rew (kə roo′), **Thomas** c. 1595-c. 1639; Eng. poet

Carl (kärl) a masculine name: see CHARLES

Car·los (kär′lōs, -ləs), **Don** (born *Carlos Maria Isidro de Borbón*) 1788-1855; Sp. pretender to the throne

Car·lo·ta (kär lō′tä; *E* kär lät′ə) (born *Marie Charlotte Amélie Augustine Victoire Clémentine Léopoldine*) 1840-1927; empress of Mexico (1864-67): wife of Maximilian

Car·lot·ta (kär lät′ə) a feminine name: see CHARLOTTE

Carl·son (kärl′sən), **Chester** 1906-68; U.S. inventor; developed xerography

Car·lyle (kär lïl′, kär′lïl′), **Thomas** 1795-1881; Brit. writer, born in Scotland

Car·ne·gie (kär′nə gē′; kär nā′gē, -neg′ē), **Andrew** 1835-1919; U.S. industrialist & philanthropist, born in Scotland

Car·not (kȧr nō′) **1 La·zare** (Nicolas Marguerite) (lȧ zȧr′) 1753-1823; Fr. soldier & statesman **2 Ni·co·las Lé·o·nard Sa·di** (nē kô lä′ lā ô nȧr′ sȧ dē′) 1796-1832; Fr. physicist: son of Lazare **3** (Marie François) **Sadi** 1837-94; Fr. statesman: president of France (1887-94): grandson of Lazare

Car·ol (kar'əl) **1** a feminine name: see CAROLINE **2** ⟦ML *Carolus*: see CHARLES⟧ a masculine name

Car·o·line (kar'ə lin', -līn) ⟦Ger & Fr < It *Carolina*, fem. < ML *Carolus*, CHARLES⟧ a feminine name: dim. *Car·rie;* var. *Carol*

Car·o·lyn (kar'ə lin') a feminine name: see CAROLINE

Ca·roth·ers (kə ruth'ərz), **Wallace Hume** 1896-1937: U.S. chemist

Car·rel (kar'əl, kə rel'), **Alexis** 1873-1944; Fr. surgeon & biologist in the U.S. (1905-39)

Car·rie (kar'ē) a feminine name: see CAROLINE

Car·roll (kar'əl) **1 Charles** 1737-1832; Am. Revolutionary leader **2 Lewis** (pseud. of *Charles Lutwidge Dodgson*) 1832-98; Eng. writer and mathematician: author of *Alice's Adventures in Wonderland*

Car·son (kär'sən) **1 Kit** (born *Christopher Carson*) 1809-68; U.S. frontiersman **2 Rachel (Louise)** 1907-64; U.S. biologist & science writer

Carte (kärt), **Richard D'Oy·ly** (doi'lē) 1844-1901; Eng. producer of Gilbert & Sullivan operas

Car·ter (kärt'ər) **1 Elliott (Cook, Jr.)** 1908- ; U.S. composer **2 Jimmy** (legal name *James Earl Carter, Jr.*) 1924- ; 39th president of the U.S. (1977-81) **3 Nick** a detective in a popular series of novels, the earliest of which were dime novels of the late 19th cent.

Car·ter·et (kär'tər it), **John** 1st Earl Granville 1690-1763; Brit. statesman & diplomat

Car·tier (kär'tē ā', -tyā'), **Jacques** (zhäk) 1491-1557; Fr. explorer: discovered the St. Lawrence River

Car·tier–Bres·son (kår tyä brä sōn', -bre-), **Hen·ri** (än rē') 1908- ; Fr. photographer

Cart·wright (kärt'rīt) **1 Edmund** 1743-1823; Eng. inventor, esp. of the power loom **2 John** 1740-1824; Eng. political reformer: brother of Edmund

Ca·ru·so (kə rōō'sō; *It* kä rōō'zô), **En·ri·co** (en rē'kô) 1873-1921; It. operatic tenor

Car·ver (kär'vər) **1 George Washington** 1864-1943; U.S. botanist & chemist **2 John** *c.* 1576-1621; Pilgrim leader: 1st governor of Plymouth Colony

Car·y (ker'ē), **(Arthur) Joyce (Lunel)** 1888-1957; Brit. novelist, born in Ireland

Ca·sals (kə sälz', -salz'; *Sp* kä säls'), **Pa·blo** (pä'blô') (born *Pau Carlos Salvador Defillo de Casals*) 1876-1973; Sp. cellist & composer

Ca·sa·no·va (kaz′ə nō′və, kas′ə-; *It* kä′zä nô′vä), **Gio·van·ni Gia·co·mo** (jô vän′nē yä′kô mô) 1725-98; It. adventurer, noted for his *Memoirs*, which include accounts of his many love affairs

Ca·sau·bon (kà zō bōn′; *E* kə sô′bən), **I·sa·ac** (ē zà àk′) 1559-1614; Fr. scholar & theologian, born in Switzerland

Case·ment (kās′mənt), Sir **Roger David** 1864-1916; Ir. nationalist: hanged by the British as a traitor in World War I

Cash (kash), **Johnny** 1932-   ; country music singer & composer

Cas·lon (kaz′lən), **William** 1692-1766; Eng. type designer

Cass (kas), **Lewis** 1782-1866; U.S. statesman

Cas·san·dra (kə san′drə) ⟦L < Gr *Kassandra*⟧ *Gr. Myth.* the daughter of Priam and Hecuba: to win her love, Apollo gives her prophetic power, but when thwarted, decrees that no one should believe her prophecies

Cas·satt (kə sat′), **Mary** 1845-1926; U.S. painter in France

Cas·si·o·pe·ia (kas′ē ō pē′ə, -pē′yə) ⟦L < Gr *Kassiopeia*⟧ *Gr. Myth.* the wife of Cepheus and mother of Andromeda

Cas·si·rer (kə sē′rər), **Ernst** (ernst) 1874-1945; Ger. philosopher in Great Britain, Denmark, & the U.S. after 1933

Cas·si·us (Longinus) (kash′əs, kas′ē əs), **(Gaius)** died 42 B.C.; Rom. general & conspirator against Caesar

Cas·ti·glio·ne (käs′tēl yō′nā), **Conte Bal·das·sa·re** (bäl′ də sä′rä) 1478-1529; It. writer & diplomat

Cas·tle·reagh (kas′əl rā′, käs′-), **Viscount** (*Robert Stewart*) 2d Marquis of Londonderry 1769-1822; Brit. statesman, born in Ireland

Cas·tor (kas′tər) ⟦L < Gr *Kastōr*⟧ *Gr. & Rom. Myth.* the mortal twin of Pollux: see DIOSCURI

Cas·tro (kas′trō; *Sp* käs′trô), **Fi·del** (fē del′) 1926-   ; Cuban revolutionary leader; prime minister (1959-76) & president (1976-): in full **Fidel Castro Ruz** (rōōs)

Cath·er (kath′ər), **Wil·la (Sibert)** (wil′ə) 1873-1947; U.S. writer

Cath·er·ine (kath′ər in) ⟦Fr < L *Catharina, Ecaterina* < Gr *Aikaterinē*; form and meaning infl. by *katharos,* pure, unsullied]] **1** a feminine name: dim. *Cathy, Kate, Kit, Kitty;* var. *Catharine;* equiv. It. *Caterina,* Ir. *Kathleen,* Russ. *Ekaterina,* Scand. *Karen,* Sp. *Catalina, Catarina* **2 Catherine I** c. 1684-1727; wife of Peter the Great; empress of Russia (1725-27) **3 Catherine II** 1729-96; German-born empress of Russia (1762-96): called **Catherine the Great 4** Saint (4th cent. A.D.); Christian martyr of Alexandria: her day is Nov. 25 **5** Saint (1347-80); It. Dominican: her day is April 29: in full Saint **Catherine of Siena**

Catherine de' Medici *see* MEDICI

Catherine of Ar·a·gon (ar'ə gän', er'-) 1485-1536; 1st wife (1509-33) of Henry VIII of England

Cat·i·line (kat''l in') (born *Lucius Sergius Catilina*) c. 108-62 B.C.; Rom. politician & conspirator

Cat·lin (kat'lən), **George** 1796-1872; U.S. ethnologist & artist

Ca·to (kāt'ō) **1** (**Marcus Porcius**) 234-149 B.C.; Rom. statesman: called *the Elder* or *the Censor* **2** (**Marcus Porcius**) 95-46 B.C.; Rom. statesman & Stoic philosopher: great-grandson of Cato (*the Elder*): called *the Younger*

Catt (kat), **Carrie Chapman** 1859-1947; U.S. leader in the movement for women's suffrage

Cat·ton (kat''n), (**Charles**) **Bruce** 1899-1978; U.S. historian

Ca·tul·lus (kə tul'əs), (**Gaius Valerius**) c. 84-c. 54 B.C.; Rom. lyric poet

Ca·va·fy (kə vä'fē), **Constantine** (born *Konstantínos Pétrou Kaváfis*) 1863-1933; Gr. poet, born in Egypt

Cav·ell (kav'əl), **Edith Louisa** 1865-1915; Eng. nurse executed by the Germans in World War I

Cav·en·dish (kav'ən dish'), **Henry** 1731-1810; Eng. chemist & physicist

Ca·vour (kä vōōr'), **Conte Ca·mil·lo Ben·so di** (kä mēl'lô ben'sô dē) 1810-61; It. statesman: a leader in the movement to unify Italy

Cax·ton (kaks'tən), **William** c. 1422-91; 1st Eng. printer

Ce·cil (sēs'əl; *also, and for 2, usually* ses'əl) [[L *Caecilius,* name of a Rom. gens]] **1** a masculine name: fem. *Cecilia, Cecily* **2 William** *see* BURGHLEY, 1st Baron

Ce·cile (sə sēl') a feminine name: see CECILIA

Ce·cil·ia (sə sēl'yə) [[L *Caecilia,* fem. of *Caecilius;* see CECIL]] **1** a feminine name: dim. *Cis, Cissie;* var.

Cecile, Cecily, Cicely, Sheila **2** Saint died c. A.D. 230; Christian martyr: patron saint of music: her day is Nov. 22

Cec·i·ly (ses′ə lē) a feminine name: see CECILIA

Ce·crops (sē′kräps′) ⟦ Gr *Kekrops* ⟧ *Gr. Myth.* the first king of Attica and founder of Athens, represented as half man, half dragon

Ced·ric (sed′rik′, sē′drik′) ⟦ < ? Celt ⟧ a masculine name

Ce·lan (sə län′), **Paul** (pseud. of *Paul Antschel*) 1920-70; Romanian poet, writing in German

Ce·leste (sə lest′) ⟦ Fr *Céleste* < *céleste*, celestial ⟧ a feminine name: var. *Celestine*

Cel·ia (sēl′yə) ⟦ L *Caelia*, fem. of *Caelius*, name of a Roman gens, of Etr orig., lit., prob. "September" ⟧ a feminine name

Cé·line (sā lēn′), **Lou·is–Fer·di·nand** (lwē fer dē nän′) (born *Louis-Ferdinand Destouches*) 1894-1961; Fr. writer

Cel·li·ni (chə lē′nē), **Ben·ve·nu·to** (ben′və nōō′tō) 1500-71; It. sculptor & goldsmith: also known for his autobiography

Ce·phe·us (sē′fē əs, -fyōōs′) ⟦ L < Gr *Kēpheus* ⟧ *Gr. Myth.* the husband of Cassiopeia and father of Andromeda

Ce·res (sir′ēz′) ⟦ L < IE base **ker-*, **krē-*, to grow ⟧ *Rom. Myth.* the goddess of agriculture, daughter of Ops and Saturn: identified with the Greek Demeter

Cer·van·tes (Sa·a·ve·dra) (ther vän′tes sä′ä ved′rä; *E* sər van′tēz′), **Mi·guel de** (mē gel′ *the*) 1547-1616; Sp. novelist, poet, & playwright: author of *Don Quixote*

Cé·zanne (sā zàn′), **Paul** 1839-1906; Fr. painter

Chad (chad) a masculine name

Chad·wick (chad′wik), **Sir James** 1891-1974; Eng. physicist: discovered the neutron

Cha·gall (shə gäl′), **Marc** 1889-1985; Russ. painter in France and the U.S.

Chain (chān), **Ernst Boris** 1906-79; Brit. biochemist, born in Germany

Cha·lia·pin (shä lyä′pin), **Fyo·dor I·va·no·vich** (fyô′dôr ē vä′nô vich) 1873-1938; Russ. operatic basso

Cham·ber·lain (chām′bər lin) **1 Sir (Joseph) Austen** 1863-1937; Brit. statesman **2 Joseph** 1836-1914; Brit. statesman: father of Austen & Neville **3 (Arthur) Nev·ille** 1869-1940; Brit. statesman; prime minister (1937-

40)

Cham·ber·lin (chām'bər lin), **Thomas Chrow·der** (krou'dər) 1843-1928; U.S. geologist

Cham·plain (sham plān'; *Fr* shäⁿ plaⁿ'), **Samuel de** 1567-1635; Fr. explorer: founded Quebec (1608)

Cham·pol·lion (shäⁿ pô lyôⁿ'), **Jean Fran·çois** (zhäⁿ fräⁿ swä') 1790-1832; Fr. Egyptologist

Chan·dler (chand'lər), **Raymond** (**Thornton**) 1888-1959; U.S. detective-story writer

Cha·nel (shə nel'; *Fr* shả nel'), **Ga·bri·elle** (gả brē el') (called *Coco*) 1883-1971; Fr. fashion designer & perfumer

Chan·ning (chan'iŋ), **William El·ler·y** (el'ər ē) 1780-1842; U.S. Unitarian leader & social critic

Chap·lin (chap'lin), **Sir Charles Spencer** (called *Charlie Chaplin*) 1889-1977; Eng. film actor, director, & producer, in the U.S. (1910-52)

Chap·man (chap'mən), **George** *c.* 1559-1634; Eng. poet, playwright, & translator of Homer

Char·cot (shả kō'), **Jean Mar·tin** (zhäⁿ mả taⁿ') 1825-93; Fr. neurologist

Char·din (shả daⁿ') **1** Jean (**Baptiste**) **Si·mé·on** (zhäⁿ sē mä ōⁿ') 1699-1779; Fr. painter **2 Teilhard de** *see* TEILHARD DE CHARDIN

Char·i·ty (char'i tē) ⟦ < ME & OFr *charite* < L *caritas*, costliness, esteem, affection < *carus*, dear, valued < IE **karo-*, < base **ka-*, to like, desire ⟧ a feminine name

Char·le·magne (shär'lə mān') A.D. 742-814; king of the Franks (768-814): emperor of the Holy Roman Empire (800-814): also called **Charles I** or **Charles the Great**

Charles (chärlz) ⟦ Fr < ML *Carolus* or Gmc *Karl*, lit., full-grown; akin to OE *ceorl*, churl ⟧ **1** a masculine name: dim. *Charley, Charlie, Chuck;* var. *Carl;* equiv. L. *Carolus*, Ger. *Carl, Karl*, It. *Carlo*, Sp. *Carlos*, Du. *Karel;* fem. *Charlene, Charlotte, Caroline* **2 Charles** 1948- ; Prince of Wales: son of Elizabeth II **3 Charles I** A.D. 823-877; king of France (843-877) &, as **Charles II**, Holy Roman Emperor (875-877): called *the Bald* **4 Charles I** (born *Charles Stuart*) 1600-49; king of England, Scotland, & Ireland (1625-49): beheaded **5 Charles I** (born *Charles Francis Joseph*) 1887-1922; emperor of Austria &, as **Charles IV**, king of Hungary (1916-18): forced to abdicate **6 Charles I** CHARLEMAGNE **7 Charles II** 1630-85; king of England, Scotland, & Ireland (1660-85) **8 Charles IV** 1294-1328; king of France (1322-28): called *the Fair* **9 Charles IV** 1748-1819; king of Spain (1788-1808): forced to abdicate by Napoleon I **10 Charles V** 1337-80; king of France (1364-80): called *the Wise* **11 Charles V** 1500-58; Holy Roman Emperor (1519-56) &, as **Charles I**, king of Spain (1516-56): abdicated **12 Charles VI** 1368-1422: king of France (1380-1422): called *the Well-Beloved* **13 Charles VII** 1403-61; king of France (1422-61): called *the Victorious* **14 Charles VIII** (born *Charles Albert*) 1697-1745; Holy Roman Emperor (1742-45) **15 Charles XIV** (**John**) *see* BERNADOTTE, Jean Baptiste Jules **16 Ray** (born *Ray Charles Robinson*) 1930- ; U.S. rhythm-and-blues musician, singer, & composer

Charles Edward Stuart *see* STUART, Charles Edward

Charles Martel *see* MARTEL, Charles

Char·lotte (shär′lət) ⟦Fr, fem. of *Charlot*, dim., of *Charles*⟧ a feminine name: dim. *Lotta, Lottie, Lotty*; equiv. It. *Carlotta*

Cha·ron (ker′ən) ⟦L < Gr *Charōn*⟧ *Gr. Myth.* the boatman who ferries souls of the dead across the river Styx to Hades

Char·pen·tier (shȧr pän tyä′), **Gus·tave** (güs tȧv′) 1860-1956; Fr. composer

Chase (chās) **1 Sal·mon Port·land** (sal′mən pôrt′lənd) 1808-73; U.S. jurist; chief justice of the U.S. (1864-73) **2 Samuel** 1741-1811; Am. Revolutionary leader & U.S. jurist: associate justice, Supreme Court (1796-1811)

Cha·teau·bri·and (shȧ tō brē än′), Vicomte **Fran·çois Re·né de** (frän swȧ rə nā′ də) 1768-1848; Fr. statesman & man of letters

Chat·ham (chat′əm), 1st Earl of *see* PITT, William

Chat·ter·ton (chat′ər tən), **Thomas** 1752-70; Eng. poet

Chau·cer (chô′sər), **Geoffrey** *c.* 1340-1400; Eng. poet: author of *The Canterbury Tales*

Chaun·cey (chôn′sē, chän′-) ⟦orig., a surname; prob. of Fr orig.⟧ a masculine name

Chavannes, Puvis de *see* PUVIS DE CHAVANNES, Pierre

Chee·ver (chē′vər), **John** 1912-82; U.S. writer

Che·khov (che′kôf′), **An·ton Pav·lo·vich** (än′tôn päv′lə vich) 1860-1904; Russ. dramatist & short-story writer: also sp. **Che′kov**

Che·ops (kē′äps′) *Gr. name of* KHUFU

Cher·nen·ko (chir nyen′kō), **Kon·stan·tin** (Ustinovich) (kän stən tēn′) 1911-85; general secretary of the Communist Party of the U.S.S.R. (1984-85)

Che·ru·bi·ni (ke′rōō bē′nē), (**Maria**) **Lu·i·gi** (**Carlo Zenobio Salvatore**) (lōō ē′jē) 1760-1842; It. composer

Cher·yl (sher′əl) a feminine name: dim. *Cher, Cheri*

Ches·ter (ches′tər) ⟦ OE *Ceastre,* contr. < L *Legacaestir,* for L *legionum castra,* camp of the legions ⟧ a masculine name: dim. *Chet*

Ches·ter·field (ches′tər fēld′), 4th Earl of (*Philip Dormer Stanhope*) 1694-1773; Eng. statesman & writer on manners

Ches·ter·ton (ches′tər tən), **G**(ilbert) **K**(eith) 1874-1936; Eng. writer

Chiang Kai-shek (chaŋ′ kī shek′; *Chin* jyäŋ′-) (born *Chiang Chung-chen*) 1888-1975; Chin. generalissimo: head of Nationalist government on Taiwan (1950-75)

Chi·ka·mat·su Mon·za·e·mon (chē′kä mät′sōō mōn′zä e mōn′) (born *Sugimori Nobumori*) 1653-1724; Jpn. dramatist: called *the Shakespeare of Japan*

Child (chīld), **Francis James** 1825-96; U.S. scholar and collector of Eng. & Scot. ballads

Chi·ri·co (kē′rē kô), **Gior·gio de** (jôr′jô de) 1888-1978; It. painter, born in Greece

Chi·ron (kī′rän′) ⟦ L < Gr *Cheirōn* ⟧ *Gr. Myth.* the wisest of all centaurs, famous for his knowledge of medicine: he is the teacher of Asclepius, Achilles, and Hercules

Chlo·e, Chlo·ë (klō′ē) ⟦ L < Gr *Chloē,* blooming, verdant ⟧ **1** a feminine name **2** see DAPHNIS AND CHLOE

Choate (chōt), **Rufus** 1799-1859; U.S. lawyer

Chom·sky (chäm′skē), (**Avram**) **No·am** (nō′əm) 1928- ; U.S. linguist & educator

Cho·pin (shō pan′, shô-), **Fré·dé·ric Fran·çois** (frā dā rēk frän swä′) 1810-49; Pol. composer & pianist, in France after 1831

Chou En-lai (jō′en′lī′) 1898-1976; Chin. Communist leader: prime minister (1949-76): Pinyin *Zhou En-lai*

Chré·tien (krā tyan′), **Jean** (**Joseph–Jacques**) 1934- ; prime minister of Canada (1993-)

Chré·tien (or **Chres·tien**) **de Troyes** (krā tyan də trwä′) fl. 12th cent.; Fr. poet

Christ (krīst) ⟦ ME & OE *Crist* < LL(Ec) *Christus* < Gr *christos,* the anointed (in N.T., MESSIAH) < *chriein,* to anoint < IE base **ghrēi-,* to spread over, smear ⟧ **1** the

Messiah whose appearance is prophesied in the Old
Testament **2** Jesus of Nazareth, regarded by Christians as the realization of the Messianic prophecy:
originally a title (*Jesus the Christ*), later used as part
of the name (*Jesus Christ*)

Chris·tian (kris′chən, -tyən) **1** a masculine name: dim.
Chris; fem. *Christina, Christine* **2 Christian X** (born
Carl Frederick Albert Alexander Vilhelm) 1870-1947;
king of Denmark (1912-47)

Chris·tie (kris′tē), Dame **Agatha** (born *Agatha Mary
Clarissa Miller*) 1890-1976; Eng. writer of detective
stories

Chris·ti·na (kris tē′nə) **1** a feminine name: see CHRIS-
TINE **2** 1626-89; queen of Sweden (1632-54)

Chris·tine (kris tēn′) a feminine name: dim. *Chris,
Chrissie, Tina;* var. *Christina, Christy*

Chris·tophe (krēs tôf′), **Hen·ri** (än rē′) 1767-1820; Haitian revolutionary leader: king of Haiti (1811-20)

Chris·to·pher (kris′tə fər) ⟦ME *Christofre* < LL(Ec)
Christophorus < Gr(Ec) *Christophoros,* lit., bearing
Christ < *christos* (see CHRIST) + *pherein,* to bear⟧ **1** a
masculine name: dim. *Chris, Kit, Kris* **2 Saint** (3d
cent. A.D.); Christian martyr of Asia Minor: patron
saint of travelers: his day is July 25

Chris·ty (kris′tē) **1** a feminine name: see CHRISTINE **2**
Howard Chandler 1873-1952; U.S. painter & illustrator

Chrys·os·tom (kris′əs təm, kri säs′təm), **Saint John** (*c.*
A.D. 347-407); Gr. church father: archbishop of Constantinople (398-404): his day is Sept. 13

Church·ill (chur′chil) **1 John** see MARLBOROUGH, 1st
Duke of **2 Lord Randolph (Henry Spencer)** 1849-95;
Brit. statesman **3 Win·ston** (win′stən) 1871-1947; U.S.
novelist **4 Sir Winston (Leonard Spencer)** 1874-1965;
Brit. statesman & writer: prime minister (1940-45;
1951-55): son of Lord Randolph

Cic·e·ly (sis′ə lē) a feminine name: see CECILIA

Cic·e·ro (sis′ər ō′), **(Marcus Tullius)** 106-43 B.C.; Rom.
statesman, orator, & philosopher

Cid (sid; *Sp* thēth), **the** ⟦*Sp* < *Ar sayyid,* a lord⟧ (born
Rodrigo, or *Ruy, Díaz de Bivar*) *c.* 1040-99; Sp. soldier
& celebrated hero, esp. in Sp. literature

Ci·ma·bu·e (chē′mä bōō′ā), **Gio·van·ni** (jô vän′nē) (born
Bencivieni di Pepo) *c.* 1240-*c.* 1302; Florentine painter

Cin·cin·na·tus (sin′sə nāt′əs, -nat′-), **(Lucius Quinctius)** 5th cent. B.C.: Rom. statesman & general: dictator of Rome (458 & 439 B.C.)

Cin·der·el·la (sin′dər el′ə) ⟦ < ModE *cinder* < ME & OE *sinder*, dross of iron, slag < IE base *sendhro-*, coagulating fluid + dim. suffix *-ella*: like Fr *Cendrillon* (dim. < *cendre*, ashes), a partial transl. of Ger *Aschenbrödel*, lit., scullion (< *asche*, ash + *brodeln*, bubble up, brew) ⟧ the title character of a fairy tale, a household drudge who, with the help of a fairy godmother, marries a prince

Cir·ce (sur′sē) ⟦ L < Gr *Kirkē* ⟧ in Homer's *Odyssey*, an enchantress who turns men into swine

Claire (kler) a feminine name: see CLARA

Clar·a (klar′ə) ⟦ < L *clara*, fem. of *clarus*, bright, clear ⟧ a feminine name: var. *Clare, Clarice, Clarissa;* equiv. Fr. *Claire*

Clare (kler) **1** a masculine name: see CLARENCE **2** a feminine name: see CLARA **3** John 1793-1864; Eng. poet

Clar·ence (klar′əns) ⟦ < name of Eng dukedom of *Clarence*, after *Clare*, town in Suffolk ⟧ a masculine name: var. *Clare*

Clar·en·don (klar′ən dən), 1st Earl of (*Edward Hyde*) 1609-74; Eng. statesman & historian

Clar·ice (klar′is, klə rēs′) ⟦ Fr *Clarisse* ⟧ a feminine name: see CLARA

Cla·ris·sa (klə ris′ə) ⟦ It ⟧ a feminine name: see CLARA

Clark (klärk) **1** a masculine name **2 George Rogers** 1752-1818; Am. frontiersman & Revolutionary War leader **3 Tom C**(ampbell) 1899-1977; associate justice, U.S. Supreme Court (1949-67) **4 William** 1770-1838; Am. explorer: see LEWIS, Meriwether

Claude (klôd) ⟦ Fr < L *Claudius*, name of a Roman gens, prob. < *claudus*, lame ⟧ a masculine name: fem. *Claudia*

Clau·del (klō del′), **Paul** (*Louis Charles*) 1868-1955; Fr. poet, playwright, & diplomat

Claude Lor·rain (klōd lô ran′) (born *Claude Gelée*) 1600-82; Fr. painter

Clau·di·a (klô′dē ə) ⟦ L ⟧ a feminine name: see CLAUDE

Clau·di·us (klô′dē əs) name of two Rom. emperors: **Claudius I** (*Tiberius Claudius Drusus Nero Germanicus*), 10 B.C.-A.D. 54, emperor (41-54) and **Claudius II**

(*Marcus Aurelius Claudius Gothicus*), A.D. 214-270, emperor (268-270)

Clau·se·witz (klou′zə vits′), **Karl von** (kärl fôn) 1780-1831; Prus. army officer & writer on military strategy

Clay (klā), **Henry** 1777-1852; U.S. statesman & orator

Cle·ar·chus (klē är′kəs) died *c*. 401 B.C.; Spartan general

Cleis·the·nes (klīs′thə nēz′) fl. *c*. 500 B.C.; Athenian statesman

Cle·men·ceau (klā män sō′; *E* klem′ən sō′), **Georges** (**Benjamin Eugène**) (zhôrzh) 1841-1929; Fr. statesman: premier of France (1906-09; 1917-20)

Clem·ens (klem′ənz), **Samuel Lang·horne** (laŋ′hôrn′) (pseud. *Mark Twain*) 1835-1910; U.S. writer & humorist

Clem·ent (klem′ənt) ⟦L *Clemens* < *clemens*, mild⟧ **1 a** masculine name: dim. *Clem;* fem. **Clementine, Clementina 2 Saint Clement I** died A.D. 97; pope (88-97): martyr & Apostolic Father: his day is Nov. 23 **3 Clement VII** (born *Giulio de' Medici*) 1478-1534; pope (1523-34): excommunicated Henry VIII

Clem·en·tine (klem′ən tīn′, -tēn′) ⟦Fr < L *Clemens* < *clemens*, mild⟧ a feminine name: also **Clem·en·ti·na** (-tē′nə)

Clement of Al·ex·an·dri·a (al′ig zan′drē ə) (*Titus Flavius Clemens*) *c*. A.D. 150-*c*. 215; Gr. Christian theologian

Cle·om·e·nes (klē äm′ə nēz′) name of three Spartan kings of the 6th to the 3d cent. B.C., including **Cleomenes III** (ruled *c*. 235-*c*. 220 B.C.), who sought to institute sweeping social reforms

Cle·on (klē′än′) died *c*. 422 B.C.; Athenian demagogue

Cle·o·pa·tra (klē′ō pa′trə, klē′ə-, -pā′-, -pä′-) *c*. 69-30 B.C.; queen of Egypt (51-49; 48-30): mistress of Julius Caesar & Mark Antony

Cleve·land (klēv′lənd), (**Stephen**) **Gro·ver** (grō′vər) 1837-1908; 22d and 24th president of the U.S. (1885-89; 1893-97)

Clif·ford (klif′ərd) ⟦< family or place name < *cliff* + *ford*, hence, lit., ford at the cliff⟧ a masculine name: dim. *Cliff*

Clif·ton (klif′tən) ⟦< *cliff* + *-ton*, town; hence, lit., town at the cliff⟧ a masculine name

Clin·ton (klint′n) ⟦Eng place name < ? ME *clint*, cliff (< ON) + OE *tun*, enclosure, village⟧ a masculine name: dim. *Clint*

Clinton (klint″n) **1 Bill** (legal name *William Jefferson Clinton;* born *William Jefferson Blythe IV*) 1946- ; 42d president of the U.S. (1993-) **2 De Witt** (də wit′) 1769-1828; U.S. statesman: governor of N.Y. (1817-21; 1825-28) **3 George** 1739-1812; vice president of the U.S. (1805-12): uncle of De Witt **4 Sir Henry** 1738-95; Brit. general: commander of Brit. forces in North America (1778-82)

Cli·o (klī′ō) 〚L < Gr *Kleiō* < *kleiein,* to celebrate < *kleos,* fame, glory 〛 *Gr. Myth.* the Muse of history

Clis·the·nes (klis′thə nēz′) *var. of* CLEISTHENES

Clive (klīv) 〚 < the surname 〛 **1** a masculine name **2 Robert** Baron Clive of Plassey 1725-74; Brit. soldier & statesman: established Brit. control of India

Clo·tho (klō′thō) 〚L < Gr *Klōthō* < *klōthein,* to spin < IE base *klo- > L *colus,* distaff, Gr *klōstēr,* spindle 〛 *Gr. & Rom. Myth.* that one of the three Fates who spins the thread of human life

Clou·et (klōō e′, -ā′) **1 Fran·çois** (frän swä′) c. 1510-c. 1572; Fr. portrait painter: son of Jean **2 Jean** (zhän) c. 1485-c. 1540; Fr. portrait painter of Fl. descent

Clo·vis I (klō′vis) c. A.D. 466-511; founder of Frank. monarchy: king of the Franks (481-511)

Clyde (klīd) a masculine name

Cly·tem·nes·tra, Cly·taem·nes·tra (klī′təm nes′trə) *Gr. Myth.* the wife of Agamemnon: with the aid of her lover Aegisthus she murders her husband and is in turn killed by their son Orestes

Cob·bett (käb′it), **William** (pseud. *Peter Porcupine*) c. 1762-1835; Eng. journalist & political reformer

Cob·den (käb′dən), **Richard** 1804-65; Eng. economist & statesman: advocate of free trade

Cob·ham (käb′əm), Lord *see* OLDCASTLE, Sir John

Co·chise (kō chēs′) c. 1815-74: Apache Indian chief

Cock·croft (käk′krôft′), **Sir John Douglas** 1897-1967; Eng. nuclear physicist

Coc·teau (kôk tō′), **Jean** (zhän) 1889-1963; Fr. poet, novelist, playwright, and film writer and director

Co·dy (kō′dē), **William Frederick** (called *Buffalo Bill*) 1846-1917; U.S. plainsman, frontier scout, & showman

Co·han (kō han′; kō′han), **George M(ichael)** 1878-1942; U.S. actor, playwright, theatrical producer, & writer of popular songs

Cohn (kōn), **Ferdinand Julius** 1828-98; Ger. botanist and early bacteriologist

Coke (kook), **Sir Edward** 1552-1634; Eng. jurist

Col·bert (kôl ber′), **Jean Bap·tiste** (zhän bȧ tēst′) 1619-83; Fr. statesman: minister of finance (1661-83)

Cole·man (kōl′mən), **Or·nette** (ôr net′) 1930- ; U.S. jazz musician & composer

Cole·ridge (kōl′rij, -ər ij), **Samuel Taylor** 1772-1834; Eng. poet & critic

Col·et (käl′it), **John** c. 1467-1519; Eng. theologian & classical scholar

Co·lette (kô let′), **(Sidonie Gabrielle Claudine)** 1873-1954; Fr. novelist

Co·li·gny (kô lē nyē′), **Gas·pard de** (gȧs pȧr′ də) 1519-72; Fr. admiral & Huguenot leader

Co·lin (käl′in, kōl′-) ⟦prob. after Saint COLUMBA (< L *columba*, dove), patron saint of Cornish parishes⟧ a masculine name

Col·leen (käl′ēn′, käl ēn′) ⟦Ir < *cailin*, dim. of *caile*, girl⟧ a feminine name

Col·lins (käl′inz) **1 Michael** 1890-1922; Ir. revolutionary leader **2 (William) Wil·kie** (wil′kē) 1824-89; Eng. novelist **3 William** 1721-59; Eng. poet

Colt (kōlt), **Samuel** 1814-62; U.S. inventor of a type of revolver

Col·trane (kōl′trān′), **John (William)** 1926-67; U.S. jazz musician & composer

Col·um (käl′əm), **Pad·raic** (pô′thrig) 1881-1972; Ir. poet and playwright, in the U.S.

Co·lum·ba (kə lum′bə), **Saint** (A.D. 521-597); Ir. missionary: converted Scotland to Christianity: his day is June 9

Co·lum·bi·a (kə lum′bē ə, -byə) ⟦after Christopher COLUMBUS⟧ [Old Poet.] the U.S. personified as a woman

Co·lum·bus (kə lum′bəs), **Christopher** (It. name *Cristoforo Colombo*; Sp. name *Cristóbal Colón*) c. 1451-1506; It. explorer in the service of Spain: discovered America (1492)

Co·me·ni·us (kō mē′nē əs), **John Amos** (born *Jan Amos Komensky*) 1592-1670; Moravian educational reformer & theologian

Co·mines (kô mēn′), **Phi·lippe de** (fē lēp′ də) c. 1447-c. 1511; Fr. historian & diplomat: also sp. **Com·mines**

Com·mo·dus (käm′ə dəs), **Lu·cius Ae·li·us Au·re·li·us** (lōō′shəs ē′lē əs ô rē′lē əs) A.D. 161-192; emperor of Rome (180-192)

Com·ne·nus (käm nē′nəs) name of a ruling family of the Byzantine Empire (1057-59; 1081-1185) and of the empire of Trebizond (1204-1461)

Comp·ton (kämp′tən) **1 Arthur Hol·ly** (häl′ē) 1892-1962; U.S. physicist **2 Karl Taylor** 1887-1954; U.S. physicist; brother of Arthur

Comte (kōnt; *E* kōmt), **(Isidore) Au·guste** (**Marie François Xavier**) (ô güst′) 1798-1857; Fr. philosopher: founder of positivism

Co·mus (kō′məs) ⟦L < Gr *kōmos*, festival ⟧ *Gr. & Rom. Myth.* a young god of festivity and revelry

Conan Doyle, **Sir Arthur** *see* DOYLE, Sir Arthur Conan

Co·nant (kō′nənt), **James Bryant** 1893-1978; U.S. chemist & educator

Con·dé (kōn dā′), **Prince de** (*Louis II de Bourbon, Duc d'Enghien*) 1621-86; Fr. general: called *the Great Condé*

Con·dil·lac (kōn dē yȧk′), **É·tienne Bon·not de** (ā tyen′ bô nō′ də) 1715-80; Fr. philosopher

Con·don (kän′dən), **Edward U(hler)** 1902-74; U.S. physicist

Con·dor·cet (kōn dôr sā′), **Marquis de** (born *Marie Jean Antoine Nicolas de Caritat*) 1743-94; Fr. social philosopher, mathematician, and political leader

Con·fu·cius (kən fyōō′shəs) (L. name of *K'ung Fu-tzu*) c. 551-c. 479 B.C.; Chin. philosopher & teacher

Con·greve (kän′grēv, kän′-), **William** 1670-1729; Eng. Restoration playwright

Con·rad (kän′rad) ⟦Ger *Konrad* or Fr *Conrade*; both < OHG *Kuonrat, Chuonrat*, lit., bold or wise counselor < *kuon*, bold, wise + *rat*, counsel < *ratan*, to advise ⟧ **1** a masculine name **2 Joseph** (born *Józef Teodor Konrad Nałecz Korzeniowski*) 1857-1924; Eng. novelist, born in Poland

Con·sta·ble (kun′stə bəl, kän′-), **John** 1776-1837; Eng. landscape painter

Con·stance (kän′stəns) ⟦Fr < L *Constantia*, lit., constancy: see CONSTANTINE ⟧ a feminine name: dim. *Connie*

Con·stant (kōn stän′), **Benjamin** (*Henri Benjamin Constant de Rebecque*) 1767-1830; Fr. writer & politician, born in Switzerland

Con·stan·tine (kän′stən tēn′, -tīn′) [[L *Constantinus* < *constans*, prp. of *constare* < *com-*, together + *stare*, to stand < IE base **stā-*, to stand, be placed]] 1 a masculine name 2 **Constantine I** (*Flavius Valerius Aurelius Constantinus*) c. A.D. 280-337; emperor of Rome (306-337): converted to Christianity: called *the Great*

Cook (kook), **James** 1728-79; Eng. naval officer & explorer: explored Australia, New Zealand, Antarctica, etc.

Coo·lidge (kōō′lij), (**John**) **Calvin** 1872-1933; 30th president of the U.S. (1923-29)

Coop·er (kōō′pər, koop′-) 1 **Gary** (born *Frank James Cooper*) 1901-61; U.S. motion-picture actor 2 **James Fen·i·more** (fen′ə môr′) 1789-1851; U.S. novelist 3 **Peter** 1791-1883; U.S. inventor, industrialist, & philanthropist

Co·per·ni·cus (kō pur′ni kəs), **Nic·o·la·us** (nik′ə lā′əs) (L. form of *Mikolaj Kopernik*) 1473-1543; Pol. astronomer

Cop·land (kōp′lənd), **Aaron** 1900-90; U.S. composer

Cop·ley (käp′lē), **John Sin·gle·ton** (siŋ′gəl tən) 1738-1815; Am. painter, in England after 1775

Co·que·lin (kô klan′), **Be·noit Cons·tant** (bə nwä′ kōn stän′) 1841-1909; Fr. actor

Cor·a (kôr′ə) [[L < Gr *Korē*, lit., maiden, name of Proserpina < IE base **ker-*, to grow > CERES, create]] a feminine name

Corbusier, Le *see* LE CORBUSIER

Cor·day (d′Armont) (kôr dā′), (**Marie Anne**) **Charlotte** 1768-93; Fr. Girondist: assassin of Marat

Cor·del·ia (kôr dēl′yə) [[prob. ult. < Celt *Creiryddlydd*, lit., daughter of the sea]] 1 a feminine name 2 in Shakespeare's *King Lear*, the youngest of Lear's three daughters, and the only one faithful to him

Co·rel·li (kô rel′ē; *It* kô rel′lē), **Arc·an·ge·lo** (är kän′je lô) 1653-1713; It. composer & violinist

Co·rinne (kō rin′, -rēn′; kô-, kə-) [[Fr < L *Corinna* < Gr *Korinna*, ? dim. of *Korē*: see CORA]] a feminine name

Cor·mack (kôr′mak), **Allan** (**MacLeod**) 1924- ; U.S. physicist, born in South Africa

Cor·neille (kôr nā′y′), **Pierre** 1606-84; Fr. dramatist

Cor·nel·ia (kôr nēl′yə) [[L, fem. of *Cornelius*]] 1 a feminine name 2 2d cent. B.C.; mother of Gaius & Tiberius

Gracchus

Cor·nel·ius (kôr nēl′yəs) ⟦L, name of a Roman gens⟧ a masculine name: fem. *Cornelia*

Cor·nell (kôr nel′) **1 Ezra** 1807-74; U.S. capitalist & philanthropist **2 Katharine** 1898-1974; U.S. actress

Corn·wal·lis (kôrn wôl′is, -wäl′-), **Charles** 1st Marquis Cornwallis 1738-1805; Eng. general & statesman: commanded Brit. forces during American Revolution

Co·ro·na·do (kôr′ə nä′dō; *Sp* kô′rô̄ nä′*th*ô̄), **Fran·cis·co Vás·quez de** (frän *th*ēs′kô̄ väs′ke*th* *th*e) c. 1510-c. 1554; Sp. explorer of what is now the Southwest in the U.S.

Co·rot (kə rō′; *Fr* kô̄ rō′), **Jean Bap·tiste Ca·mille** (zhän bà tēst′ kà mē′y′) 1796-1875; Fr. painter

Cor·reg·gio (kə rej′ō), (**Antonio Allegri da**) c. 1494-1534; It. painter

Cor·tá·zar (kôr tə zär′; *Sp* kô̄r tä′zər), **Ju·li·o** (hoo′lē ō) 1914-84; Argentine writer

Cor·tés (kôr tez′; *Sp* kô̄r tes′), **Her·nan·do** (hər nan′dō) 1485-1547; Sp. soldier & explorer: conqueror of Mexico: also sp. **Cor·tez: Her·nán** (er nän′) is sometimes used as a variant of *Hernando*

Cot·ton (kät′′n), **John** 1584-1652; Am. Puritan clergyman, born in England: grandfather of Cotton Mather

Cou·perin (koo pran′), **Fran·çois** (frän swä′) 1668-1733; Fr. composer & organist

Cour·bet (koor be′), **Gus·tave** (güs tàv′) 1819-77; Fr. painter

Court·ney (kôrt′nē) a feminine name

Cous·teau (koo stō′), **Jacques** (**Yves**) (zhäk) 1910- ; Fr. marine explorer, writer, & television producer

Cov·er·dale (kuv′ər dāl′), **Miles** 1488-1568; Eng. clergyman & translator of the Bible (1535)

Cow·ard (kou′ərd), **Sir Noel** (**Pierce**) 1899-1973; Eng. playwright, actor, and song writer

Cow·ell (kou′əl), **Henry** (**Dixon**) 1897-1965; U.S. composer

Craig (krāg) **1** a masculine name **2 Edward Henry Gordon** 1872-1966; Brit. theatrical designer & director

Crai·gie (krā′gē), **Sir William Alexander** 1867-1957; Eng. lexicographer, born in Scotland

Cram (kram), **Ralph Adams** 1863-1942; U.S. architect & writer

Cra·nach (krä′näkh), **Lu·cas** (loo′käs) 1472-1553; Ger.

painter & engraver

Crane (krān) **1 (Harold) Hart** (härt) 1899-1932; U.S. poet **2 Stephen** 1871-1900; U.S. novelist & short-story writer

Cran·mer (kran′mər), **Thomas** 1489-1556; Eng. churchman: archbishop of Canterbury (1533-56)

Crash·aw (krash′ô), **Richard** c. 1613-49; Eng. religious poet

Cras·sus (kras′əs), **(Marcus Licinius)** c. 115-53 B.C.; Rom. statesman & general

Crazy Horse (Dakota name *Ta-sunko-witko*) c. 1842-77; Dakota Indian chief

Cre·a·tor (krē āt′ər) God; the Supreme Being

Cre·on (krē′än′) 〚 Gr *Kreōn* 〛 Gr. *Legend* a king of Thebes who has his niece Antigone entombed alive because she defies him: see ANTIGONE

Cres·si·da (kres′i də) *Medieval Legend* a Trojan woman who was unfaithful to her lover, TROILUS

Cre·ü·sa (krē yōō′sə, -ōō′-) *Gr. & Rom. Myth.* **1** the bride of Jason, killed by the sorcery of the jealous Medea **2** the wife of Aeneas and daughter of Priam, lost in the flight from captured Troy

Crève·coeur (krev koor′; *Fr* krev kër′), **Mi·chel Guil·laume Jean de** (mē shel′ gē yōm′ zhän də) (pseud. *J. Hector St. John*) 1735-1813; Am. essayist & agriculturist, born in France

Crick (krik), **Francis H(arry) C(ompton)** 1916- ; Eng. scientist: helped determine the structure of DNA

Crile (krīl), **George Washington** 1864-1943; U.S. surgeon

Cri·sey·de (kri sā′də) *var.* (in Chaucer) *of* CRESSIDA

Cris·pin (kris′pin) 〚 L *Crispinus* < *crispus*, curly < IE base *(s)kreisp-*, to shake 〛 **1** a masculine name **2** Saint (3d cent. A.D.); Rom. Christian martyr: patron saint of shoemakers: his day is Oct. 25

Cro·ce (krō′che; *E* krō′chē), **Be·ne·det·to** (be′ne det′tô) 1866-1952; It. philosopher & critic

Crock·ett (kräk′it), **David** (called *Davy*) 1786-1836; U.S. frontiersman & politician

Croe·sus (krē′səs) fl. 6th cent. B.C.; last king of Lydia (560-546), noted for his great wealth

Cromp·ton (krämp′tən), **Samuel** 1753-1827; Eng. inventor of the spinning mule (1779)

Crom·well (kräm′wel, -wəl; krum′-) **1 Oliver** 1599-

1658; Eng. revolutionary leader & head (Lord Protector) of the Commonwealth (1653-58) **2 Richard** 1626-1712; Lord Protector of the Commonwealth (1658-59): son of Oliver **3 Thomas** Earl of Essex *c.* 1485-1540; Eng. statesman

Cro·nus (krō'nəs) ⟦L < Gr *Kronos*⟧ *Gr. Myth.* a Titan who overthrows his father, Uranus, to become ruler of the universe and is himself overthrown by his son Zeus: identified with the Roman Saturn

Crookes (krooks), Sir **William** 1832-1919; Eng. chemist & physicist

Cros·by (krôz'bē, kräz'-), **Bing** (biŋ) (born *Harry Lillis Crosby*) 1904-77; U.S. popular singer & motion-picture actor

Cruik·shank (krook'shaŋk), **George** 1792-1878; Eng. caricaturist & illustrator

Crusoe, Robinson *see* ROBINSON CRUSOE

Crys·tal (kris'təl) ⟦ < ModE *crystal*, altered (modeled on L) < ME & OFr *cristal*, OE *cristalla* < L *crystallum*, crystal, ice < Gr *krystallos* < *kryos*, frost ⟧ a feminine name

Cu·chul·ain, Cu·chul·lin (koo kul'in) ⟦Ir⟧ *Celt. Legend* a heroic warrior who single-handedly defends his country against invaders

Cul·bert·son (kul'bərt sən), **E·ly** (ē'lē) 1893-1955; U.S. authority on contract bridge, born in Romania

Cul·len (kul'ən), **Coun·tee** (koun'tē) 1903-46; U.S. poet

Cum·mings (kum'iŋz), **E(dward) E(stlin)** 1894-1962; U.S. poet

Cu·pid (kyoo'pid) ⟦ME & OFr *Cupide* < L *Cupido* < *cupido*, desire, passion < *cupidus*, eager, passionate < *cupere*, to desire < IE base **kup-*, to boil, smoke, be disturbed > Gr *kapnos*, smoke ⟧ *Rom. Myth.* the god of love, son of Venus: usually represented as a winged boy with bow and arrow and identified with the Greek Eros

Cu·rie (kyoo rē', kyoor'ē; *Fr* kü rē') **1 Marie** (born *Marie Sklodowska*) 1867-1934; Pol. chemist & physicist in France: discovered polonium & radium (1898) in collaboration with her husband **2 Pierre** 1859-1906; Fr. physicist: husband of Marie

Cur·tis (kʉr'tis) ⟦ < NormFr *curteis* (OFr *corteis*), courteous ⟧ a masculine name

Cur·tiss (kʉr'tis), **Glenn Ham·mond** (ham'ənd) 1878-

1930; U.S. aviator & pioneer in aircraft construction

Cur·zon (kʉr′zən), **George Nathaniel** 1st Marquis Curzon of Kedleston 1859-1925; Eng. statesman: viceroy of India (1899-1905)

Cush (kush) *Bible* the oldest of Ham's sons

Cush·ing (koosh′iŋ) **1 Caleb** 1800-79; U.S. diplomat: negotiated treaty (1845) opening Chin. ports to U.S. trade **2 Harvey (Williams)** 1869-1939; U.S. neurosurgeon

Cus·ter (kus′tər), **George Armstrong** 1839-76; U.S. army officer: killed in a battle with Dakota Indians on the Little Bighorn River

Cuth·bert (kuth′bərt) ⟦OE *Cuthbeorht*, lit., famously splendid < *cuth*, noted + *beorht*, bright⟧ **1** a masculine name **2 Saint** (*c.* A.D. 635-*c.* 687); Eng. bishop: his day is March 20

Cu·vier (kü vyā′; *E* kōō′vē ā′), **Baron Georges (Léopold Chrétien Frédéric Dagobert)** (zhôrzh) 1769-1832; Fr. naturalist

Cuyp (koip), **Ael·bert** or **Aal·bert** (äl′bərt) 1620-91; Du. painter

Cyb·e·le (sib′ə lē′) ⟦L < Gr *Kybelē*⟧ a nature goddess of ancient Asia Minor: identified with the Greek Rhea

Cyg·nus (sig′nəs) ⟦L < *cygnus*, swan < Gr *kyknos*⟧ *Gr. Myth.* a king of the Ligurians who is changed into a swan

Cyn·thi·a (sin′thē ə) ⟦L < Gr *Kynthia*, epithet of Artemis, orig. fem. of *Kynthios*, lit., of or from *Kynthos*, Cynthus, mountain in Delos, celebrated as the birthplace of Apollo and Artemis⟧ **1** a feminine name: dim. *Cindy* **2 ARTEMIS 3** the moon personified

Cyp·ri·an (sip′rē ən), **Saint** (born *Thascius Caecilius Cyprianus*) *c.* A.D. 200-258; Christian martyr: bishop of Carthage (248-258): his day is Sept. 16

Cy·ra·no de Ber·ge·rac (sir′ə nō′də bʉr′zhə rak′; *Fr* sē rà nō′də ber zhə ràk′), **Sa·vi·nien de** (sav′in yen′də; *Fr* sà vē nyan de) 1619-55; Fr. writer & soldier, famous for his large nose: title character of a poetic drama by Edmond Rostand (1897)

Cy·ril (sir′əl) ⟦LL *Cyrillus* < Gr *Kyrillos*, lit., lordly < *kyrios*, a lord⟧ **1** a masculine name **2 Saint** (*c.* A.D. 376-444); Christian theologian: archbishop of Alexandria (412-444): his day is June 27 **3 Saint** (born *Constantine*) *c.* A.D. 827-869; Gr. prelate & missionary;

apostle to the Slavs: his day is February 14

Cy·rus (sī′rəs) 〚L < Gr *Kyros* < OPers *Kūrush*〛 **1** a masculine name: dim. *Cy* **2** *c.* 424-401 B.C.; Pers. prince: called *the Younger* **3 Cyrus II** died *c.* 529 B.C.; king of the Medes & Persians: founder of the Persian Empire: called *the Great*

Cyth·er·e·a (sith′ər ē′ə) 〚L < Gr *Kythereia* < *Kythera*, a Greek island〛 APHRODITE

Czer·ny (cher′nē), **Karl** 1791-1857; Austrian composer

D

Daed·a·lus (ded′′l əs, dēd′-) 〚L < Gr *Daidalos*, lit., the artful craftsman < *daidalos* < *daidallein*, to work artfully < IE base *del*-, to split, carve〛 *Gr. Myth.* the skillful artist and builder of the Labyrinth in Crete, from which, by means of wings he made, he and his son Icarus escaped

da Gam·a (də gam′ə; *Port* dä gä′mä), **Vas·co** (väs′kō) 1460-1524; Port. navigator: discovered the sea route around Africa to India

Dag·mar (dag′mär′) 〚Dan < Gmc *dag*-, day, brightness + *-mar*, akin to OE *mære*, splendid〛 a feminine name

Da·gon (dā′gän′) 〚ME < LL(Ec) < LGr(Ec) < Heb < ? *dāgān*, grain (hence ? god of agriculture)〛 the chief god of the ancient Philistines and later of the Phoenicians, sometimes represented as half man and half fish

Dai·sy (dā′zē) 〚< *daisy*〛 a feminine name

Dalcroze, Émile Jaques *see* JAQUES-DALCROZE, Émile

Dale (dāl) **1** a masculine and feminine name **2 Sir Henry Hallet** 1875-1968: Brit. physiologist **3 Sir Thomas** died 1619; Eng. colonial governor of Va. (1611; 1614-16)

d′A·lem·bert (dà län ber′), **Jean le Rond** (zhän lə rōn′) 1717-83; Fr. philosopher & encyclopedist

Dal·hou·sie (dal hōō′zē, -hou′-) **1 Earl of** (*George Ramsay*) 1770-1838; Brit. general, born in Scotland; governor of the Brit. colonies in Canada (1819-28) **2 Marquis of** (*James Andrew Broun-Ramsay*) 1812-60; Brit. statesman, born in Scotland; governor general of India (1847-59): son of Earl of Dalhousie

Da·li (dä′lē), **Sal·va·dor** (sal′və dôr′) 1904-89; Sp. surrealist painter

Dal·ton (dôlt′'n), **John** 1766-1844; Eng. chemist & physicist

Da·ly (dā′lē), **(John) Au·gus·tin** (ô gus′tin) 1838-99; U.S. playwright & theatrical manager

Da·mi·en (dā′mē ən; *Fr* dà myan′), **Father** (born *Joseph de Veuster*) 1840-89; Belgian Roman Catholic priest & missionary to the leper colony on Molokai

Dam·o·cles (dam′ə klēz′) 〚L < Gr *Damoklēs*〛 *Class. Legend* a courtier of ancient Syracuse who was given a lesson in the perils to a ruler's life when the king seated him at a feast under a sword hanging by a single hair

Da·mon and Pyth·i·as (dā′mən ənd pith′ē əs) *Class. Legend* friends so devoted to each other that when Pythias, who had been condemned to death, wanted time to arrange his affairs, Damon pledged his life that his friend would return: Pythias returned and both were pardoned

Dam·pier (dam′pyer, -pē ər, -pir), **William** 1652-1715; Eng. explorer & pirate

Dam·rosch (dam′räsh), **Walter (Johannes)** 1862-1950; U.S. conductor & composer, born in Germany

Dan (dan) 〚Heb *dān*, a judge〛 *Bible* Jacob's fifth son, whose mother was Bilhah: Gen. 30:1-6

Da·na (dā′nə) **1** a masculine and feminine name **2 Charles Anderson** 1819-97; U.S. newspaper editor **3 James Dwight** 1813-95; U.S. geologist & mineralogist **4 Richard Henry** 1815-82; U.S. writer & lawyer

Dan·a·e, Dan·a·ë (dan′ā ē′) 〚Gr *Danaē*〛 *Gr. Myth.* the mother of Perseus by Zeus, who visits her in the form of a shower of gold

Dan·a·i·des, Da·na·ï·des (də nā′ə dēz′) *Gr. Myth.* the fifty daughters of Danaus, a king of Argos: forty-nine murder their husbands at their father's command and are condemned in Hades to draw water forever with a sieve

Dan·a·us (dan′ā əs) *see* DANAIDES

Dan·iel (dan′yəl) 〚Heb *dāni′ēl*, lit., God is my judge〛 **1** a masculine name: dim. *Dan, Danny*; fem. *Danielle* **2** *Bible* a Hebrew prophet whose faith saved him in the lions' den: Dan. 6:16-23 **3 Samuel** 1562-1619; Eng. poet

Dan·ielle (dan yel′) a feminine name: see DANIEL

Dan·iels (dan′yelz), **Josephus** 1862-1948; U.S. statesman

& journalist: secretary of the navy (1913-21)

D'An·nun·zio (dä nōōn'tsyô̂), **Ga·bri·e·le** (gä'brē e'le) 1863-1938; It. poet, writer, & political adventurer

Dan·te (**Alighieri**) (dän'tā, dan'tē) (born *Durante Alighieri*) 1265-1321; It. poet: wrote *The Divine Comedy*

Dan·ton (dän tōn'), **Georges Jacques** (zhôrzh zhäk) 1759-94; Fr. Revolutionary leader

Daph·ne (daf'nē) ⟦L < Gr *daphnē*, the laurel or bay tree ⟧ 1 a feminine name 2 *Gr. Myth.* a nymph who is changed into a laurel tree to escape Apollo's advances

Daph·nis and Chlo·e (or **Chlo·ë**) (daf'nis ənd klō'ē) two lovers in an old Greek pastoral romance of the same name, attributed to Longus (c. 3d cent. A.D.)

d'Ar·blay (där'blā), **Madame** *see* BURNEY, Fanny

d'Arc (dark), **Jeanne** (zhän) *Fr. name of* JOAN OF ARC

Dare (der), **Virginia** born 1587; 1st child born in America of Eng. parents

Da·ri·us I (də rī'əs) c. 550-c. 486 B.C.; king of Persia (522-486): called *the Great*: also **Darius Hys·tas·pes** (his tasp'əs)

Darn·ley (därn'lē), **Lord** (*Henry Stewart* or *Stuart*) 1545-67; 2d husband of Mary, Queen of Scots: father of James I

Dar·row (dar'ō), **Clarence** (**Seward**) 1857-1938; U.S. lawyer

Dar·win (där'win) 1 **Charles** (**Robert**) 1809-82; Eng. naturalist: originated theory of evolution by natural selection 2 **Erasmus** 1731-1802; Eng. naturalist, physician, & poet: grandfather of Charles Robert Darwin

Dau·bi·gny (dō bē nyē'), **Charles Fran·çois** (shàrl frän swä') 1817-78 Fr. landscape painter

Dau·det (dō dā') 1 **Al·phonse** (à fōns') 1840-97; Fr. novelist 2 **Lé·on** (lā ōn') 1867-1942; Fr. politician & journalist: son of Alphonse

Dau·mier (dō myā'), **Ho·no·ré** (ô nô̂ rā') 1808-79; Fr. painter, lithographer, & caricaturist

D'Av·e·nant, Dav·e·nant (dav'ə nənt), **Sir William** 1606-68; Eng. poet & playwright

Da·vid (dā'vid; *for 5* dà vēd') ⟦Heb *Dāwĭdh*, lit., beloved⟧ 1 a masculine name: dim. *Dave, Davy, Davey*; fem. *Davida, Vida* 2 *Bible* the second king of Israel and Judah, succeeding Saul: reputed to be the writer of many Psalms 3 Saint (6th cent. A.D.); Welsh bishop: patron saint of Wales: his day is March 1 4

David I 1084-1153; king of Scotland (1124-53) **5 Jacques Lou·is** (zhák lwē) 1748-1825; Fr. neoclassic painter

Da·vid d'An·gers (dȧ vēd' dän zhā') (born *Pierre Jean David*) c. 1788-1856; Fr. sculptor

Da·vid·son (dā'vid sən), **Jo(seph)** 1883-1952; U.S. sculptor

da Vin·ci (də vin'chē; *It* dä vēn'chē), **Le·o·nar·do** (lē'ə när'dō; *It* le'ô när'dô) 1452-1519; It. painter, sculptor, architect, engineer, & scientist

Da·vis (dā'vis) **1 Bet·te** (bet'ē) (born *Ruth Elizabeth Davis*) 1908-89; U.S. film actress **2 Jefferson** 1808-89; U.S. statesman; president of the Confederacy (1861-65) **3 Miles** 1926-91; U.S. jazz musician **4 Richard Harding** 1864-1916; U.S. journalist, novelist, & editor

Da·vy (dā'vē), **Sir Humphry** 1778-1829; Eng. chemist

Da·vy Jones (dā'vē jōnz') the spirit of the sea: humorous name given by sailors

Dawn (dôn) 〚ModE *dawn* < ME *daunen*, back-form. < *dauninge*, earlier *dauinge*, daybreak〛 a feminine name

Daw·son (dô'sən), **Sir John William** 1820-99; Cdn. geologist, naturalist, & educator

Day–Lew·is (dā'lōō'is), **C(ecil)** 1904-72; Brit. poet & (under pseud. *Nicholas Blake*) novelist, born in Ireland: poet laureate (1968-72)

Dean (dēn) a masculine name

Deane (dēn), **Silas** 1737-89; Am. Revolutionary patriot & diplomat

Death the personification of death, usually pictured as a skeleton in a black robe, holding a scythe

de Bergerac, Cyrano *see* BERGERAC, Cyrano de

Deb·o·rah (deb'ə rə, deb'rə) 〚Heb *debōrāh*, lit., a bee〛 **1** a feminine name: dim. *Debby, Debbie*; var. *Debra* **2** *Bible* a prophetess and one of the judges of Israel: Judg. 4 & 5

Deb·ra (deb'rə) a feminine name: dim. *Debby*: see DEBORAH

Debs (debz), **Eugene Victor** 1855-1926; U.S. labor leader & Socialist candidate for president

De·bus·sy (də bü sē'; *E* deb'yōō sē', də byōō'sē), **(Achille-)Claude** 1862-1918; Fr. composer

De·bye (də bī'), **Peter J(oseph) W(illiam)** 1884-1966; U.S. physicist & chemist, born in the Netherlands

De·ca·tur (di kāt'ər), **Stephen** 1779-1820; U.S. naval officer

Deck·er (dek′ər), **Thomas** *alt. sp. of* Thomas DEKKER

De·foe (di fō′), **Daniel** *c.* 1660-1731; Eng. writer

De For·est (di fôr′ist, di fär′-), **Lee** 1873-1961; U.S. inventor of telegraphic, telephonic, & radio apparatus

De·gas (də gä′), **(Hilaire Germain) Ed·gar** (ed gàr′) 1834-1917; Fr. painter

de Gaulle (də gôl′; *Fr* gōl′), **Charles (André Joseph Marie)** 1890-1970; Fr. general & statesman: president of France (1959-69)

Deir·dre (dir′drə) 〚OIr *Derdriu*, prob. akin to MIr *der*, young girl〛 **1** a feminine name **2** *Celt. Legend* an Irish heroine who elopes to Scotland with her lover to avoid marrying the king: when the lover is treacherously killed, she commits suicide

De·i·ty (dē′ə tē), **the** God

De Kalb (də kalb′; *G* kälp′), **Jo·hann** (yō′hän) (born *Johann Kalb*) 1721-80; Fr. general, born in Germany, who served in the Am. Revolutionary army: called *Baron de Kalb*

Dek·ker (dek′ər), **Thomas** *c.* 1572-*c.* 1632 Eng. playwright

de Klerk (də klerk′), **F(rederik) W(illem)** 1936- ; president of South Africa (1989-)

de Koon·ing (də kō′niŋ), **Wil·lem** (wil′əm) 1904- ; U.S. painter, born in the Netherlands

de Kruif (də krīf), **Paul (Henry)** 1890-1971; U.S. bacteriologist & writer

De·la·croix (də là krwà′), **(Ferdinand Victor) Eu·gène** (ö zhen′) 1798-1863; Fr. painter

de la Mare (del′ə mer′, -mar′), **Walter (John)** 1873-1956; Eng. poet & novelist

De·la·roche (də là rôsh′), **(Hippolyte) Paul** 1797-1856; Fr. painter

De·la·vigne (də là vēn′y′), **(Jean François) Cas·i·mir** (kà zē mir′) 1793-1843; Fr. poet & playwright

De La Warr (del′ə wer′, -war′), **Baron** (*Thomas West*) 1577-1618; 1st Eng. colonial governor of Va. (1610-11): called *Lord Delaware*

Del·brück (del′brook), **Max** (maks) 1906-81; U.S. biologist, born in Germany

Del·ia (dēl′yə) 〚L, fem of *Delius*, of Delos〛 a feminine name

De·libes (də lēb′), **(Clément Philibert) Lé·o** (lā ō′) 1836-

91; Fr. composer

De·li·lah (di li'lə) 〚Heb *delilāh*, lit., delicate〛 *Bible* the mistress of Samson, who betrayed him to the Philistines: Judg. 16

De·li·us (dē'lē əs, dēl'yəs), **Frederick** 1862-1934; Eng. composer

del·la Rob·bia (del'lä *rôb'*byä; *E* del'ə rō'bē ə), **Lu·ca** (lōō'kä) c. 1400-82; Florentine sculptor & worker in enameled terra cotta: member of a family of artists

De·lorme, de l'Orme (də lôrm'), **Phi·li·bert** (fē lē ber') 1515-70; Fr. Renaissance architect

De·me·ter (di mēt'ər) 〚Gr *Dēmētēr* < Gr(Doric) *Damatēr* < *da-* (? name for the earth) + *matēr*, mother〛 *Gr. Myth.* the goddess of agriculture and fertility: identified with the Roman Ceres

De Mille (də mil') **1 Agnes (George)** 1905-93; U.S. dancer & choreographer: niece of Cecil **2 Cecil B(lount)** 1881-1959; U.S. film producer & director

De·moc·ri·tus (di mäk'rə təs) c. 460-c. 370 B.C.; Gr. philosopher: exponent of atomism

De·mo·gor·gon (dē'mō gôr'gən, dem'ō-) 〚LL〛 a terrifying and mysterious god or demon of the underworld in ancient mythology

De·mos·the·nes (di mäs'thə nēz') 384-322 B.C.; Athenian orator & statesman

Demp·sey (demp'sē), **Jack** (born *William Harrison Dempsey*) 1895-1983; U.S. professional boxer

Deng Xiao·ping (duŋ' shou'piŋ) 1904- ; Chin. Communist leader; member of the Central Committee of the Communist Party (resigned 1987); held various official titles (1967-89), including deputy prime minister; China's de facto ruler (c. 1981-)

Den·is (den'is) 〚Fr < L *Dionysius*〛 **1** a masculine name: var. *Dennis*; fem. *Denise* **2** Saint (3d cent. A.D.); patron saint of France: his day is Oct. 9

De·nise (də nēs') a feminine name: see DENIS

Den·nis (den'is) a masculine name: see DENIS

De·nys (den'is; *Fr* də nē'), Saint *see* DENIS, Saint

De Quin·cey (də kwin'sē), **Thomas** 1785-1859; Eng. essayist & critic

De·rain (də ran'), **An·dré** (än drā') 1880-1954; Fr. painter

Der·ek (der'ik) a masculine name: var. *Derrick*; equiv. Du. *Dirk*

Der·ri·da (də rē′də; *Fr* de rē̄ dà′), **Jacques** (zhàk) 1930- ; Fr. philosopher, born in Algeria

Des·cartes (dā kärt′), **Re·né** (rə nā′) 1596-1650; Fr. philosopher & mathematician

Des·de·mo·na (dez′də mō′nə) *see* OTHELLO

de Se·ver·sky (də sə ver′skē), **Alexander P**(rocofieff) 1894-1974; U.S. aeronautical engineer, born in Russia

De Si·ca (də sē′kə; *It* de sē′kä), **Vit·to·rio** (vi tôr′ē ō; *It* vēt tô′ryô) 1901-74; It. motion-picture actor & director

Des·mou·lins (dā mōō lan′), (**Lucie Simplice**) **Ca·mille** (**Benoît**) (kà mē′y′) 1760-94; Fr. Revolutionary journalist & pamphleteer

De So·to, de So·to (di sōt′ō), **Her·nan·do** (hər nan′dō) *c.* 1500-42; Sp. explorer in America: discovered the Mississippi River (1541)

de Staël, Madame *see* STAËL

Deu·ca·li·on (dōō kāl′ē ən, dyōō-) 〚L < Gr *Deukaliōn*〛 *Gr. Myth.* a son of Prometheus: he and his wife, Pyrrha, were the only survivors of a great flood sent by Zeus

De Va·ler·a (dev′ə ler′ə, -lir′-), **Ea·mon** (ā′mən) 1882-1975; Ir. statesman, born in U.S.: prime minister of Ireland (1937-48; 1951-54; 1957-59): president (1959-73)

Dev·e·reux (dev′ə rōō′, -rōōks′), **Robert** *see* ESSEX, 2d Earl of

De·vi (dā′vē) 〚Sans, fem. of *deva*, god < IE base **dei-*, to gleam, shine〛 a Hindu goddess, the consort of Siva

De Vries (də vrēs′), **Hugo** 1848-1935; Du. botanist

Dew·ey (dōō′ē, dyōō′-) **1 George** 1837-1917; U.S. admiral in the Spanish-American War **2 John** 1859-1952; U.S. philosopher & educator: exponent of pragmatism **3 Mel·vil** (mel′vil) (born *Melville Louis Kossuth Dewey*) 1851-1931; U.S. librarian & educator: originator of a system (*Dewey Decimal System*) for book classification in libraries, using three-digit numbers, further extended beyond a decimal point for subclasses

Dia·ghi·lev (dyä′gi lyef; -lef), **Ser·gei Pav·lo·vich** (syer gyā′i päv lô′vich) 1872-1929; Russ. ballet producer

Di·an·a (dī an′ə) 〚ML < L < **Diviana* < *divus, dius*, divine〛 **1** a feminine name: dim. *Di*; Fr. *Diane* **2** *Rom. Myth.* the virgin goddess of the moon and of hunting: identified with the Greek Artemis

Di·ane (dī an′) a feminine name: dim. *Di*; var. *Dianne*: see DIANA

Di·as (dē′əsh; *E* dē′əs), **Bar·tho·lo·me·u** (bär′too loo me′ oo) *c.* 1450-1500; Port. navigator & explorer: 1st European to round Cape of Good Hope (1486)

Dí·az (dē′äs), (**José de la Cruz**) **Por·fi·ri·o** (pôr fē′rē ô) 1830-1915; Mex. general & statesman: president of Mexico (1877-80; 1884-1911)

Dí·az (dē′äth), **Ber·nal** (ber näl′) *c.* 1492-*c.* 1581; Sp. historian & soldier with Cortés: in full **Bernal Díaz del Cas·til·lo** (del käs tēl′yô)

d'I·ber·ville (dē ber vēl′), **Sieur** (born *Pierre Le Moyne*) 1661-1706; Fr. explorer in North America

Dick (dik) *nickname for* RICHARD

Dick·ens (dik′ənz), **Charles** (**John Huffam**) (pseud. *Boz*) 1812-70; Eng. novelist

Dick·in·son (dik′in sən) **1 Emily** (**Elizabeth**) 1830-86; U.S. poet **2 John** 1732-1808; Am. statesman

Di·de·rot (dē′də rō′; *Fr* dē drō′), **Denis** 1713-84; Fr. encyclopedist & philosopher

Di·do (dī′dō) 〚L < Gr *Didō*〛 *Rom. Myth.* founder and queen of Carthage: in the *Aeneid* she falls in love with Aeneas and kills herself when he leaves her

Did·rik·son (did′rik sən), **Mildred** (**Babe**) (married name *Zaharias*) 1913-56; U.S. athlete in many sports

Did·y·mus (did′ə məs) *see* THOMAS (the Apostle)

Diels (dēlz; *Ger* dēls), **Otto** (**Paul Hermann**) 1876-1954; Ger. organic chemist

Die·trich (dē′trik, -triH), **Mar·le·ne** (mär lā′nə, -lē′nə) (adoptive name *Maria Magdalena von Losch*, born *Maria Magdalena Dietrich*) *c.* 1901-92: U.S. motion-picture actress, born in Germany

Dil·they (dil′tā), **Wilhelm** 1833-1911; Ger. philosopher

Di·Mag·gi·o (də mä′jē ō′, -maj′ē ō′), **Joseph** (**Paul**) (called *Joe*) 1914- ; U.S. baseball player

Di·nah (dī′nə) 〚Heb *dīnāh*, lit., judged〛 a feminine name

d'In·dy (dan dē′), (**Paul Marie Théodore**) **Vin·cent** (van sän′) 1851-1931; Fr. composer

Din·e·sen (dē′nə sən, din′ə-), **I·sak** (ē′säk) (pseud. of *Karen Christence Dinesen, Baroness Blixen-Finecke*) 1885-1962; Dan. author

Din·wid·die (din wid′ē, din′wid ē), **Robert** 1693-1770;

Brit. lieutenant governor of Va. (1751-58)

Di·o·cle·tian (dī′ə klē′shən) (L. name *Gaius Aurelius Valerius Diocletianus*) A.D. 245-313; Rom. emperor (284-305)

Di·og·e·nes (dī äj′ə nēz′) *c.* 412-*c.* 323 B.C.; Gr. Cynic philosopher: noted for his asceticism

Di·o·me·des (dī′ə mē′dēz′) *Gr. Legend* a Greek warrior at the siege of Troy, who helps Odysseus steal the statue of Athena: also **Di′o·med′** (-med′) or **Di′o·mede′** (-mēd′)

Di·o·ny·si·us (dī′ə nish′əs, -nis′ē əs, -nī′sē əs) **1** *c.* 430-367 B.C.; Gr. tyrant of ancient Syracuse (405-367): called *the Elder* **2** *c.* 395-*c.* 340 B.C.; Gr. tyrant of Syracuse (367-356; 347-343): son of Dionysius the Elder: called *the Younger*

Dionysius Ex·ig·u·us (ig zig′yŏŏ əs, -sig′-) 6th cent. A.D.; Rom. monk & Christian theologian, born in Scythia: believed to have introduced the current system of numbering years on the basis of the Christian Era

Dionysius of Hal·i·car·nas·sus (hal′ə kär nas′əs) fl. 1st cent. B.C.; Gr. critic & historian in Rome

Di·o·ny·sus, Di·o·ny·sos (dī′ə nī′səs) 〖L < Gr *Dionysos* 〗 *Gr. Myth.* the god of wine and revelry: identified with the Roman Bacchus

Di·or (dē ôr′; *Fr* dē ôr′), **Chris·tian** (kris′chən; *Fr* krēs tyän′) 1905-57; Fr. couturier

Di·os·cu·ri (dī′äs kyoor′ī′) 〖Gr *Dioskouroi* < *Dios* (gen. of *Zeus*) + *kouroi*, pl. of *kouros*, boy, son 〗 *Gr. Myth.* Castor and Pollux, twin sons of LEDA

Di·rac (di rak′), **Paul Adrien Maurice** 1902-84; Eng. mathematician & nuclear physicist

Dis (dis) 〖L, contr. < *dives*, rich, transl. of Gr *Ploutōn*, PLUTO 〗 the god of the lower world; Pluto

Dis·ney (diz′nē), **Walt(er Elias)** 1901-66; U.S. motion-picture producer, esp. of animated cartoons

Dis·rae·li (diz rā′lē), **Benjamin** 1st Earl of Beaconsfield 1804-81; Brit. statesman & writer: prime minister (1868; 1874-80)

Dit·mars (dit′märz), **Raymond Lee** 1876-1942; U.S. naturalist & zoo curator

Di·ves (dī′vēz′) 〖ME: so named < use of L *dives*, rich, in the parable in the Vulg. 〗 *traditional name of* the rich man in a parable: cf. Luke 16:19-31

Divinity, the God

Do·bie (dō′bē), **J**(ames) **Frank** 1888-1964; U.S. writer, esp. on the folklore of the Southwest

Dodg·son (däj′s′n), **Charles Lut·widge** (lut′wij) *see* CAR-ROLL, Lewis

Doe (dō) a name (*John Doe, Jane Doe*) used in law courts, legal papers, etc. to refer to any person whose name is unknown

Doh·ná·nyi (dô′nän yē), **Er·nö** (er′në) (Ger. name *Ernst von Dohnanyi*) 1877-1960; Hung. composer & pianist

Do·lor·es (də lôr′is) 〚Sp < *Maria de los Dolores*, lit., Mary of the sorrows 〛 a feminine name: dim. *Lolita*

Do·min·go (də miŋ′gō), **Pla·ci·do** (plä′si dō′) 1941- ; Sp. operatic tenor

Dom·i·nic (däm′ə nik) 〚ML *Dominicus*, lit., of the Lord < L, belonging to a master < *dominus*, a master < *domonos* < base of *domus*, house < IE *domu-* < base *dem-*, to build 〛 **1** a masculine name: dim. *Dom*; var. *Dominick* **2** Saint (1170-1221); Sp. priest: founder of the Dominican order: his day is Aug. 8

Dom·i·nick (däm′ə nik) a masculine name: see DOMINIC

Dom·i·no (däm′ə nō′), **An·toine, Jr.** (an′twän) (called *Fats*) 1928- ; U.S. rock-and-roll pianist & composer

Do·mi·nus (dō′mē noͻs) 〚L〛 the Lord

Do·mi·tian (də mish′ən) (L. name *Titus Flavius Domitianus Augustus*), A.D. 51-96; Rom. emperor (81-96)

Don·ald (dän′əld) 〚Ir *Donghal*, lit., brown stranger (or ? Gael *Domhnall*, lit., world ruler) 〛 a masculine name: dim. *Don*

Do·nar (dō′när′) 〚OHG〛 the god of thunder: identified with the Norse Thor

Do·na·tel·lo (dô′nä tel′lô; *E* dän′ə tel′ō) (born *Donato di Niccolò di Betto Bardi*) c. 1386-1466; It. sculptor

Do·ni·zet·ti (dän′ə zet′ē; *It* dô′nē dzet′tē), **Ga·e·ta·no** (gä′e tä′nô) 1797-1848; It. composer

Don Ju·an (dän′wän′, -hwän′; *also,* dän′jōō′ən) Sp. *Legend* a dissolute nobleman and seducer of women: he is the hero of many poems, plays, and operas

Don·na (dän′ə) 〚It < L *domina*, fem. of *dominus*: see DOMINIC 〛 a feminine name

Donne (dun), **John** 1572-1631; Eng. metaphysical poet

Don Qui·xo·te (dän′kē hōt′ē, -ā; *also,* dän′kwik′sət) the title character of a novel by Cervantes: he tries in a chivalrous but unrealistic way to rescue the oppressed and fight evil

Dor·a (dôr′ə) a feminine name: see DOROTHEA, THEO-
DORA

Dor·cas (dôr′kəs) 〚 L < Gr *Dorkas*, lit., gazelle 〛 *Bible* a
woman who spent her life making clothes for the poor:
Acts 9:36-41

Do·ré (dô̊ rā′), **(Paul) Gus·tave** (güs tȧv′) 1832-83; Fr.
book illustrator & painter

Dor·is (dôr′is) 〚 L < Gr *Dōris* 〛 a feminine name

Dor·o·the·a (dôr′ə thē′ə, där′-) 〚 L < Gr *Dōrothea*, lit.,
gift of God < *dōron*, gift (< IE base *do-, to give) +
theos, God 〛 a feminine name: var. *Dorothy*; dim.
Dolly, Doll, Dora, Dot, Dotty

Dor·o·thy (dôr′ə thē, där′-; dôr′thē) a feminine name:
see DOROTHEA

Dos Pas·sos (dəs pas′əs), **John** (Roderigo) 1896-1970;
U.S. writer

Dos·to·ev·ski, Dos·to·yev·sky (dôs′tô̊ yef′skē), **Feo·dor
Mi·khai·lo·vich** (fyô̊′dôr mi khī′lô̊ vich) 1821-81; Russ.
novelist

Dou (dou), **Ge·rard** (gā′rärt) 1613-75; Du. painter

Dou·ble·day (dub′əl dā′), **Abner** 1819-93; U.S. army
officer: traditional inventor of baseball

Dough·ty (dout′ē), **C(harles) M(ontagu)** 1843-1926; Eng.
travel writer & poet

Doug·las (dug′ləs) 〚 < Gael, lit., black stream 〛 **1** a masculine name: dim. *Doug* **2** Sir **James** *c.* 1286-1330;
Scottish military leader: called *Black Douglas* **3** Sir
James *c.* 1358-88; Scottish military leader **4** (George)
Norman 1868-1952; Brit. novelist & essayist **5** Stephen A(rnold) 1813-61; U.S. politician: noted for his
debates with Lincoln in Illinois senatorial campaign
(1858) **6** William O(rville) 1898-1980; associate justice, U.S. Supreme Court (1939-75)

Doug·lass (dug′ləs), **Frederick** (born *Frederick Augustus
Washington Bailey*) *c.* 1817-95; U.S. black leader, journalist, & statesman

Dow (dou), **Gerard** *alt. sp. of* Gerard DOU

Dow·den (dou′dən), **Edward** 1843-1913; Ir. critic, biographer, & Shakespearean scholar

Doyle (doil), Sir **Arthur Co·nan** (kō′nən) 1859-1930;
Eng. writer of popular fiction: known for his *Sherlock
Holmes* stories

D'Oyly Carte, Richard *see* CARTE, Richard D'Oyly

Dra·co (drā'kō) 7th cent. B.C.; Athenian statesman & lawgiver: also **Dra'con'** (-kän')

Drake (drāk), Sir Francis c. 1540-96; Eng. admiral & buccaneer: 1st Englishman to sail around the world

Dra·per (drā'pər) **1** Henry 1837-82; U.S. astronomer **2** John William 1811-82; U.S. historian & scientist, born in England: father of Henry

Dray·ton (drāt'ʼn), Michael 1563-1631; Eng. poet

Drei·ser (drī'sər, -zər), Theodore (Herman Albert) 1871-1945; U.S. novelist

Drey·fus (drā'fəs, drī'-; *Fr*, dre füs'), Alfred 1859-1935; Fr. army officer convicted of treason & imprisoned but later exonerated when proved to be the victim of anti-semitism & conspiracy

Dry·den (drīd'ʼn), John 1631-1700; Eng. poet, critic, & playwright: poet laureate (1670-88)

du Bar·ry (do͞o bar'ē; *Fr* dü bà rē'), Comtesse (born *Marie Jeanne Bécu*) c. 1743-93; mistress of Louis XV of France

du Bois (dü bwä'), Guy Pène (gē pen) 1884-1958; U.S. painter & art critic

Du Bois (do͞o bois'), W(illiam) E(dward) B(urghardt) 1868-1963; U.S. historian, educator, & civil rights leader

Du·buf·fet (do͞o'bo͞o fā'), Jean(–Philippe–Arthur) (zhän) 1901-85; Fr. painter

Du·champ (dü shän'), Mar·cel (màr sel') 1887-1968; U.S. painter, born in France

Dude·vant (düd vän'), Baronne *see* SAND, George

Dud·ley (dud'lē) ⟦ < the family (earlier place) name, orig. "Dudda's lea" ⟧ **1** a masculine name **2** Robert *see* LEICESTER, Earl of

Du·fy (dü fē'), Ra·oul (Ernest Joseph) (rä o͞ol') 1877-1953; Fr. painter

Du·ha·mel (dü à mel'), Georges (zhôrzh) 1884-1966; Fr. novelist, poet, & dramatist

Dul·ci·ne·a (dul'sə nē'ə, -nā'-) ⟦ Sp < *dulce*, sweet < L *dulcis* ⟧ the name given by Don Quixote to a coarse peasant girl whom he imagines to be a beautiful lady and falls in love with

Dul·les (dul'əs), John Foster 1888-1959; U.S. diplomat: secretary of state (1953-59)

Du·mas (dü mà'; *E* do͞o'mä) **1** Alexandre 1802-70; Fr. novelist & playwright: called *Dumas père* **2** Alexandre

1824-95; Fr. playwright & novelist: called *Dumas fils*: son of *Dumas père*

du Mau·ri·er (dōō môr′ē ā′, dyōō-), **George** (**Louis Palmella Busson**) 1834-96; Eng. illustrator & novelist, born in France

Du·nant (dü nän′), **Jean Hen·ri** (zhän än rē′) 1828-1910; Swiss philanthropist: founder of the Red Cross

Dun·bar (dun′bär) **1 Paul Laurence** 1872-1906; U.S. poet **2 William** 1460-1520; Scot. poet

Dun·can (duŋ′kən) 〖Gael *Donnchadh*, lit., brown warrior〗 **1** a masculine name **2 Isadora** 1878-1927; U.S. dancer

Duns Sco·tus (dunz skōt′əs), **John** (or **Johannes**) *c.* 1265-1308; Scot. scholastic philosopher and theologian

Duns·tan (dun′stən), **Saint** (*c.* A.D. 924-988); Eng. prelate: archbishop of Canterbury (959-988): his day is May 19

Du·ples·sis–Mor·nay (dü ple sē′môr nā′) *see* MORNAY

du Pont (dōō pänt′, dōō′pänt; dyōō-; *Fr* dü pōn′), **É·leu·thère I·ré·née** (*Fr* ā lë ter′ ē rā nā′) 1771-1834; U.S. industrialist, born in France

Dü·rer (dü′rər; *E* dyōōr′ər), **Al·brecht** (äl′breHt) 1471-1528; Ger. painter & wood engraver

Durk·heim (dʉr′kem, dʉrk′hīm), **Émile** 1858-1917; Fr. sociologist

Dur·rell (dʉr′əl, dʉr el′), **Lawrence** (**George**) 1912-90; Brit. writer

Dür·ren·matt (door′ən mät), **Fried·rich** (frēd′rik) 1921-90; Swiss playwright & novelist

Du·se (dōō′ze), **E·le·o·no·ra** (e′le ô nô′rä) 1859-1924; It. actress

du Vi·gneaud (dōō vēn′yō, dyōō-), **Vincent** 1901-78; U.S. chemist

Dvo·řák (dvôr′zhäk, -zhak), **An·to·nín** (än′tô nin) 1841-1904; Czech composer

Dwayne (dwān) a masculine name

Dwight (dwīt) 〖orig. a surname < ?〗 a masculine name

Dy·lan (dil′ən), **Bob** (born *Robert Allen Zimmerman*) 1941- ; U.S. folk-rock singer & composer

E

Eads (ēdz), **James Buchanan** 1820-87; U.S. engineer: noted for bridge construction & river control

Ea·kins (ā′kinz), **Thomas** 1844-1916; U.S. painter & sculptor

Ear·hart (er′härt′), **Amelia** 1898-1937; U.S. pioneer aviator

Earl (url) ⟦ModE *earl* < ME *erl*, nobleman, count < OE *eorl*, warrior⟧ a masculine name

Ear·ly (ur′lē), **Jubal Anderson** 1816-94; Confederate general in the Civil War

Earp (urp), **Wyatt (Berry Stapp)** 1848-1929; U.S. lawman

East·man (ēst′mən), **George** 1854-1932; U.S. industrialist & inventor of photographic equipment

Ea·ton (ēt′'n), **Cyrus S(tephen)** 1883-1979; U.S. industrialist & financier, born in Canada

Eb·en·e·zer (eb′ə nē′zər) ⟦Heb *even-haezer*, lit., stone of the help: see 1 Sam. 7:12⟧ a masculine name

Eb·lis (eb′lis) ⟦Ar *Iblīs*⟧ *Muslim Myth.* Satan

Ec·cles (ek′əlz), **John Ca·rew** (kə rōō′) 1903- ; Brit. neurobiologist, born in Australia

Ech·o (ek′ō) *Gr. Myth.* a nymph who, because of her unreturned love for Narcissus, pines away until only her voice remains

Eck (ek), **Jo·hann Mai·er von** (yō′hän′ mī′ər fôn) 1486-1543; German Catholic theologian

Eck·hart (ek′härt′), **Jo·han·nes** (yō̂ hän′əs) *c.* 1260-*c.* 1327; German theologian & mystic: called *Meister Eckhart·*

Ed·ding·ton (ed′iŋ tən), **Sir Arthur Stanley** 1882-1944; Eng. astronomer & astrophysicist

Ed·dy (ed′ē), **Mary Bak·er** (bā′kər) (born *Mary Morse Baker*) 1821-1910; U.S. founder of Christian Science (*c.* 1866)

E·den (ēd′'n), **(Robert) Anthony Earl of Avon** 1897-1977; Brit. statesman: prime minister (1955-57)

Ed·gar (ed′gər) ⟦OE *Eadgar* < *ead*, riches, prosperity, happiness + *gar*, a spear⟧ a masculine name: dim. *Ed, Ned*

Edge·worth (ej′wərth), **Maria** 1767-1849; Ir. novelist, born in England

Ed·i·son (ed′i sən), **Thomas Alva** 1847-1931; U.S. inventor, esp. of electrical & communication devices, including the incandescent lamp, phonograph, & microphone

E·dith (ē′dith) ⟦OE *Eadgyth* < *ead* (see EDGAR) + *guth*, combat, battle, war⟧ a feminine name: dim. *Edie*

Ed·mund, Ed·mond (ed′mənd) ⟦OE *Eadmund* < *ead* (see EDGAR) + *mund*, hand, protection⟧ a masculine name: dim. *Ed, Ned*

Ed·na (ed′nə) ⟦Gr < Heb, delight⟧ a feminine name

E·dom (ē′dəm) *Bible* Esau, Jacob's brother: Gen. 25:30

Ed·ward (ed′wərd) ⟦OE *Eadweard* < *ead* (see EDGAR) + *weard*, guardian, protector: hence, wealthy (or fortunate) guardian⟧ **1** a masculine name: dim. *Ed, Eddie, Ned, Ted, Teddy*; equiv. Fr. *Édouard*, Ger. *Eduard*, It. & Sp. *Eduardo*, Scand. *Edvard* **2** 1330-76; Prince of Wales: son of Edward III: called the *Black Prince* **3 Edward I** 1239-1307; king of England (1272-1307): son of Henry III **4 Edward II** 1284-1327; king of England (1307-27): son of Edward I **5 Edward III** 1312-77; king of England (1327-77): son of Edward II **6 Edward IV** 1442-83; king of England (1461-70; 1471-83): son of Richard, duke of York **7 Edward V** 1470-83; king of England (1483): son of Edward IV: reputed to have been murdered by order of Richard III **8 Edward VI** 1537-53; king of England & Ireland (1547-53): son of Henry VIII & Jane Seymour **9 Edward VII** 1841-1910; king of Great Britain & Ireland (1901-10): son of Queen Victoria **10 Edward VIII** *see* WINDSOR, Duke of

Ed·wards (ed′wərdz), **Jonathan** 1703-58; Am. theologian

Edward the Confessor *c.* 1004-66; king of England (1042-66): canonized: his day is Oct. 13

Ed·win (ed′win) ⟦OE *Eadwine* < *ead* (see EDGAR) + *wine*, friend < Gmc **weniz* < IE base **wen-*, to strive, desire, love: lit., rich friend⟧ a masculine name: dim. *Ed, Eddie*; fem. *Edwina*

Ed·wi·na (ed wē′nə, -win′ə) ⟦fem. of prec.⟧ a feminine name: dim. *Winnie*: see EDWIN

Eg·bert (eg′bərt) ⟦OE *Ecgbeorht* < *ecg* < IE base **ak-*, sharp + *beorht* < IE base **bhereg-*, to gleam, white: hence, bright sword⟧ **1** a masculine name: dim. *Bert* **2** died A.D. 839; king of the West Saxons (802-839) & first king of the English (829-839)

E·ge·ri·a (ē jir′ē ə) ⟦L < Gr *Ēgeria*⟧ *Rom. Myth.* a nymph who advised Numa, second king of Rome

Eg·gles·ton (eg′əl stən), **Edward** 1837-1902; U.S. writer

Eg·mont (eg′mänt′; *Du* ekh′mônt), Count of (born *Lamoral Egmont*) 1522-68: Fl. statesman & general

Ehr·en·burg (er′ən burg′), **Il·ya** (**Grigoryevich**) (ēl′yä′) 1891-1967; Soviet writer

Ehr·lich (er'lik) **1 Paul** 1854-1915; Ger. bacteriologist: pioneer in immunology & chemotherapy **2 Paul Ralph** 1932- ; U.S. biologist

Ei·gen (i'gən), **Man·fred** (män'frāt') 1927- ; Ger. chemist

Ei·leen (ī lēn', ā-) ⟦Ir *Eibhlin*⟧ a feminine name; var. *Aileen*

Ein·stein (īn'stīn'), **Albert** 1879-1955; U.S. physicist, born in Germany: formulated theory of relativity

Ei·sen·how·er (ī'zen hou'ər), **Dwight David** 1890-1969; U.S. general & 34th president of the U.S. (1953-61): commander of Allied forces in Europe (1943-45; 1951-52)

Ei·sen·staedt (ī'zən stat'), **Alfred** 1898- ; U.S. photographer, born in Germany

Ei·sen·stein (ī'zən stīn'), **Ser·gei Mik·hai·lo·vich** (syer gyä' mē khī'lô vich') 1898-1948; Russ. motion-picture director & producer

El·a·gab·a·lus (el'ə gab'ə ləs) (born *Varius Avitus Bassianus*) *c.* A.D. 205-222; Rom. emperor (218-222)

E·laine (ē lān', i-) ⟦OFr⟧ **1** a feminine name: see HELEN **2** *Arthurian Legend a)* a woman of Astolat, who loves Lancelot *b)* the mother of Galahad

El·ea·nor (el'ə nər, -nôr') ⟦OFr *Elienor*: see HELEN⟧ a feminine name: dim. *Ella, Nell, Nora*; var. *Leonora*

Eleanor of Aq·ui·taine (ak'wə tān') *c.* 1122-1204; queen of France (1137-52) as the wife of Louis VII & queen of England (1154-89) as the wife of Henry II

El·e·a·zar (el'ē ā'zər) ⟦LL(Ec) *Eleazar* < Gr(Ec) < Heb *elazar*, lit., God has helped⟧ *Bible* Aaron's son and successor as high priest: Num. 20:28

E·lec·tra (ē lek'trə, i-) ⟦L < Gr *Elektra*, lit., shining one⟧ *Gr. Myth.* a daughter of Agamemnon and Clytemnestra: she encourages her brother, Orestes, to kill their mother and their mother's lover, who together murdered Agamemnon

El·gar (el'gər, -gär'), **Sir Edward (William)** 1857-1934; Eng. composer

El Gre·co (el grek'ō) (born *Domenikos Theotokopoulos*) *c.* 1541-*c.* 1614; painter in Italy (*c.* 1560-75) & Spain, born in Crete

E·li (ē'lī') ⟦Heb, lit., high⟧ **1** a masculine name **2** *Bible* a high priest of Israel and teacher of Samuel: 1 Sam. 3

E·li·a (ē'lē ə) *pseud. of* Charles LAMB

E·li·as (ē lī'əs, i-) ⟦L < Gr *Elias* < Heb: see ELIJAH⟧

Bible var. of ELIJAH

E·li·hu (ē li′hyōō′, i-; el′i hyōō′) [Heb, lit., my God is he] *Bible* one of Job's visitors in his affliction: Job 32-37

E·li·jah (ē li′jə, i-) [Heb *eliyahu*, lit., Jehovah is God] **1** a masculine name: dim. *Lige*; var. *Elias, Ellis, Eliot* **2** *Bible* a prophet of Israel in the 9th century B.C.: 1 Kings 17-19; 2 Kings 2:1-11

El·i·nor (el′ə nər, -nôr′) a feminine name: see ELEANOR

El·i·ot (el′ē ət, el′yət) [dim. of ELLIS] **1** a masculine name: see ELLIS **2 Charles William** 1834-1926; U.S. educator: president of Harvard University (1869-1909) **3 George** (pseud. of *Mary Ann Evans*) 1819-80; Eng. novelist **4 John** 1604-90; Am. clergyman, born in England: known for missionary work among the Am. Indians **5 T(homas) S(tearns)** 1888-1965; Brit. poet & critic, born in the U.S.

E·lis·a·beth (ē liz′ə bəth, i-) a feminine name: see ELIZABETH

E·li·sha (ē li′shə, i-) [Heb, lit., God is salvation] **1** a masculine name: var. *Ellis* **2** *Bible* a prophet of Israel, ordained by Elijah as his successor: 1 Kings 19:16, 19; 2 Kings 2

E·li·za (ē li′zə, i-) a feminine name: dim. *Liza*: see ELIZABETH

E·liz·a·beth (ē liz′ə bəth, i-) [LL(Ec) *Elizabetha* < Gr(Ec) *Elisabet* < Heb *elisheva*, lit., God is (my) oath] **1** a feminine name: dim. *Bess, Bessie, Beth, Betsy, Betty, Elsie, Libby, Lisa, Lizzie*; var. *Elisabeth, Eliza* **2** *Bible* the mother of John the Baptist and a kinswoman of Mary: Luke 1 **3** *see* ELIZABETH PETROVNA **4 Elizabeth I** 1533-1603; queen of England (1558-1603): daughter of Henry VIII & Anne Boleyn **5 Elizabeth II** (born *Elizabeth Alexandra Mary*) 1926- ; queen of Great Britain & Northern Ireland: head of the Commonwealth of Nations (1952-): daughter of George VI

Elizabeth Pe·trov·na (pə trōv′nə) 1709-62; empress of Russia (1741-62): daughter of Peter I

El·la (el′ə) a feminine name: see ELEANOR

El·len (el′ən) a feminine name: dim. *Ellie*: see HELEN

El·ling·ton (el′iŋ tən), **Duke** (born *Edward Kennedy Ellington*) 1899-1974; U.S. jazz musician & composer

El·li·ot, El·li·ott (el′ē ət) a masculine name: see ELIOT

El·lis (el'is) **1** a masculine name: dim. *Eliot*: see ELIJAH, ELISHA **2 (Henry) Have·lock** (hav'läk, -lək) 1859-1939; Eng. psychologist & writer, esp. on human sexual behavior

El·li·son (el'i sən), **Ralph Waldo** 1914- ; U.S. writer

Ells·worth (elz'wurth') **1 Lincoln** 1880-1951; U.S. polar explorer **2 Oliver** 1745-1807; U.S. jurist: chief justice of the U.S. (1796-1800)

El·man (el'mən), **Mi·scha** (mish'ə) 1891-1967; U.S. violinist, born in Russia

El·mer (el'mər) ⟦ult. < ? OE *Æthelmær* (< *æthel*, noble + *mære* famous), or < ? *Egilmær* (< *egil-* < *ege*, awe, dread + *mære*) ⟧ a masculine name

E·lo·him (e'lō him', -hēm'; e lō'him', -hēm') ⟦Heb *elohim*, pl. of *eloah*, God ⟧ God: name used in parts of the Jewish scriptures: see JEHOVAH

E·lo·hist (e'lō hist', e lō'-) the unknown author of those parts of the Hebrew scriptures in which the name *Elohim*, instead of *Yahweh* (Jehovah), is used for God: see YAHWIST

El·o·ise (el'ō ēz', el'ō ēz') a feminine name: equiv. Fr. *Héloïse*: see LOUISE

El·sa (el'sə) ⟦Ger < ? ⟧ a feminine name

El·sie (el'sē) a feminine name: see ALICE, ELIZABETH

É·lu·ard (ā lü är'), **Paul** (pôl) (pseud. of *Eugène Grindel*) 1895-1952; Fr. poet

El·vi·ra (el vī'rə, -vir'ə) ⟦Sp, prob. < Goth ⟧ a feminine name

El·ze·vir (el'zə vir') **1** name of a family of Du. printers & publishers of the 16th & 17th cent. **2 Bon·a·ven·ture** (bän'ə ven'chər) 1583-1652: son of Louis **3 Louis** *c.* 1540-1617; founder of his family's printing tradition

E·man·u·el (i man'yoo el', -əl) *var. of* EMMANUEL

Em·er·son (em'ər sən), **Ralph Waldo** 1803-82; U.S. essayist, philosopher, & poet

E·mil (ē'məl, ā'-; em'əl; ā mēl') ⟦Ger < Fr *Émile* < L *Aemilius*, name of a Roman gens < L *aemulus*, trying to equal or excel < IE base *ai-*, to give, accept, take ⟧ a masculine name: fem. *Emily*: also **É·mile** (ā mēl')

Em·i·ly (em'ə lē) ⟦Fr *Émilie* < L *Aemilia*, fem. of *Aemilius*: see prec. ⟧ a feminine name: var. *Emilia, Emeline, Emmeline*

Em·ma (em'ə) ⟦Ger < *Erma* < names beginning with *Erm-* (e.g., *Ermenhilde*): see IRMA ⟧ a feminine name

Em·man·u·el (i man'yōō el', -əl) ⟦Gr *Emmanouēl* < Heb *imanuel*, lit., God with us⟧ **1** a masculine name: dim. *Manny*; var. *Emanuel, Immanuel, Manuel* **2** the Messiah: see IMMANUEL

Em·or·y (em'ər ē) ⟦prob. via OFr *Aimeri* < OHG *Amalrich*, lit., work ruler < **amal-*, work (in battle) + **rich*, ruler⟧ a masculine name: var. *Emery*; equiv. Ger. *Emmerich*, It. *Amerigo*

Em·ped·o·cles (em ped'ə klēz') c. 495-c. 435 B.C.; Gr. philosopher & poet

En·ders (en'dərz), **John** F(ranklin) 1897-1985; U.S. bacteriologist

En·dym·i·on (en dim'ē ən) ⟦L < Gr *Endymiōn*⟧ Gr. *Myth.* a beautiful young shepherd loved by Selene

E·nes·co (i nes'kō), **Georges** (zhôrzh) 1881-1955; Romanian violinist, composer, & conductor

En·gels (eŋ'gəlz; Ger eŋ'əls), **Frie·drich** (frē'driH) 1820-95; Ger. socialist leader & writer, in England after 1850: close associate of Karl Marx

E·nid (ē'nid) ⟦prob. < OWelsh *enaid*, soul, used as term of endearment⟧ **1** a feminine name **2** *Arthurian Legend* the wife of Geraint: she is a model of constancy

E·noch (ē'nək) ⟦Gr *Enōch* < Heb *chanoch*, lit., dedicated⟧ **1** a masculine name **2** *Bible a*) the eldest son of Cain: Gen. 4:17 *b*) the father of Methuselah: Gen. 5:21

E·nos (ē'nəs) ⟦Gr *Enōs* < Heb *enosh*, lit., man, mankind⟧ **1** a masculine name **2** *Bible* a son of Seth: Gen. 4:26

En·sor (en'sôr'), **James Sydney** 1860-1949; Belgian painter

E·os (ē'äs') ⟦L < Gr *Ēos* < *ēōs*, dawn < IE base **awes-*, to shine⟧ Gr. *Myth.* the goddess of dawn: identified with the Roman goddess Aurora

E·pam·i·non·das (i pam'ə nän'dəs) c. 418-362 B.C.; Theban (Gr.) general & statesman

E·phra·im (ē'frā im, -frē əm) ⟦LL(Ec) < Gr(Ec) < Heb *efrayim*, lit., very fruitful⟧ **1** a masculine name **2** *Bible* the younger son of Joseph: Gen. 41:51

Ep·ic·te·tus (ep'ik tēt'əs) c. A.D. 50-c. 135; Gr. Stoic philosopher in Rome & Epirus

Ep·i·cu·rus (ep'ə kyoor'əs) 341-270 B.C.; Gr. philosopher: founder of the Epicurean school, which held that the goal of man should be a life characterized by serenity of mind and the enjoyment of moderate pleasure

Ep·stein (ep'stīn), Sir **Jacob** 1880-1959; Brit. sculptor, born in the U.S.

E·ras·mus (i raz'məs), **Des·i·der·i·us** (des'ə dir'ē əs) (born *Gerhard Gerhards*) *c.* 1466-1536; Du. humanist, scholar, & theologian

E·ras·tus (i ras'təs), **Thomas** (born *Thomas Liebler* or *Lieber*) 1524-83; Ger. theologian & physician

Er·a·to (er'ə tō') 〚L < Gr *Eratō* < *eratos*, beloved < *eran*, to love〛 *Gr. Myth.* the Muse of erotic lyric poetry

Er·a·tos·the·nes (er'ə täs'thə nēz') *c.* 275-*c.* 195 B.C.; Gr. geographer, astronomer, & mathematician

Er·ic (er'ik) 〚Scand < ON *Eirìkr*, lit., honorable ruler〛 a masculine name: var. *Erik*; fem. *Erica, Erika*

Er·i·ca (er'i kə) a feminine name: var. *Erika*: see ERIC

Er·ic·son, Er·ics·son (er'ik sən), **Leif** fl. 1000; Norw. explorer & adventurer: discovered Vinland, believed to be part of North America: son of Eric the Red

Er·ics·son (er'ik sən), **John** 1803-89; U.S. naval engineer & inventor, born in Sweden: builder of the *Monitor*

Eric the Red fl. 10th cent.; Norw. explorer & adventurer: discovered & colonized Greenland

E·rig·e·na (i rij'ə nə), **Jo·han·nes Sco·tus** (jō hän'əs skōt' əs) A.D. 810-877; Ir. theologian & philosopher in France

Er·in (er'in) 〚OIr *Ērinn*, dat. of *Ēriu*, Eire〛 a feminine name

E·rin·y·es (ē rin'i ēz', er in'-) 〚L < Gr *Erinys*〛 *Gr. Myth.* FURIES

E·ris (ē'ris, er'is) 〚L < Gr *Eris*, lit., strife < IE *erei- < base *er-*, to set in motion〛 *Gr. Myth.* the goddess of strife and discord

Er·nest (ʉr'nist) 〚Ger *Ernst* < OHG *Ernust, Ernost*, lit., resolute < *ernust*: see EARNEST〛 a masculine name: dim. *Ernie*; var. *Earnest*; equiv. It. & Sp. *Ernesto*, Ger. *Ernst*; fem. *Ernestine*

Er·nes·tine (ʉr'nis tēn') 〚Ger, fem. < *Ernst*: see prec.〛 a feminine name: dim. *Tina*

Ernst (ernst), **Max** (mäks) 1891-1976; Ger. surrealist painter, in France & the U.S.

E·ros (er'äs', ir'-) 〚L < Gr *Erōs* < *erōs*, love〛 *Gr. Myth.* the god of love, son of Aphrodite: identified with the Roman god Cupid

Er·rol (er′əl) a masculine name

Er·skine (ur′skin) **1** John 1509-91; Scot. religious
reformer: called **Erskine of Dun 2** John 1695-1768;
Scot. jurist: called **Erskine of Carnock 3** John 1879-
1951; U.S. educator & writer

Er·win (ur′win) ⟦Ger *Erwin*, earlier *Herwin* < OHG
hari, host, crowd (akin to OE *here*: see HARRY) + *wini*,
wine (see EDWIN)⟧ a masculine name: var. *Irwin*

E·sau (ē′sô′) ⟦L < Gr *Ēsau* < Heb *esav*, lit., hairy⟧ *Bible*
the son of Isaac and Rebecca, who sold his birthright
to his younger twin brother, Jacob: Gen. 25:21-34, 27

Es·cof·fier (es kô fyā′), **Au·guste** (ô güst′) 1847-1935;
Fr. chef & writer on cooking

Es·sex (es′iks), 2d Earl of (*Robert Devereux*) 1566-1601;
Eng. soldier & courtier: executed for treason

Es·telle (e stel′, i-) ⟦Fr⟧ a feminine name; var. *Estella,
Stella*

Es·ther (es′tər) ⟦LL(Ec) *Esthera* < Gr(Ec) *Esthēr* <
Heb *ester*, prob. < Pers *sitareh*, star < IE base **ster-*,
star⟧ **1** a feminine name: var. *Hester* **2** *Bible* the Jewish wife of the Persian king Ahasuerus: she saved her
people from slaughter by Haman

E·te·o·cles (ē tē′ə klēz′, -tē′ō-) ⟦L < Gr *Eteoklēs*⟧ *Gr.
Myth.* a son of Oedipus and Jocasta

Eternal, the *name for* God

E·than (ē′thən) ⟦LL(Ec) < Heb *etan*, lit., strength, firm-
ness⟧ a masculine name

Eth·el (eth′əl) ⟦short for *Ethelinda, Etheldred*, and
other names compounded < OE *Æthelu* < *æthele*,
noble⟧ a feminine name: var. *Ethyl*

Eth·el·bert (eth′əl bərt) ⟦OE *Æthelbryht*, lit., noble
bright < *æthele*, noble + *beorht*, bright: see ALBERT⟧
1 a masculine name **2** *c.* A.D. 552-616; king of Kent
(560-616)

Eth·el·red II (eth′əl red′) A.D. 968-1016; king of England
(978-1016): called *the Unready*

Eth·er·ege (eth′ər ij), Sir **George** *c.* 1635-91; Eng. playwright of the Restoration

Eu·clid (yoo′klid) ⟦L *Euclides* < Gr *Eukleidēs*⟧ fl. 300
B.C.; Gr. mathematician: author of a basic work in
geometry

Eu·gene (yoo jēn′, yoo′jēn; *for 2, Fr* ö zhen′) ⟦Fr
Eugène < L *Eugenius* < Gr *Eugenios* < *eugenēs*, well-
born⟧ **1** a masculine name: dim. *Gene*; fem. *Eugenia*

2 Prince (*François Eugène de Savoie-Carignan*) 1663-1736; Austrian general, born in France

Eu·ge·ni·a (yo͞o jē′nē ə, -jēn′yə) 〚L < Gr *Eugenia*: see prec. (the masculine name) 〛 a feminine name: dim. *Genie*

Eu·gé·nie (yo͞o jē′nē; *Fr* ö zhä nē′), Empress (born *Eugenia Maria de Montijo de Guzmán*) 1826-1920; wife of Louis Napoleon & empress of France (1853-71), born in Spain

Eu·ler (oi′lər), **Le·on·hard** (lā′ôn härt′) 1707-83; Swiss mathematician

Eu·nice (yo͞o′nis) 〚LL(Ec) < Gr *Eunikē*, lit., good victory < *eu-*, good, well (< IE base **esu-*, good) + *nikē*, victory 〛 a feminine name

Eu·phros·y·ne (yo͞o fräs′i nē′) 〚L < Gr *Euphrosynē* < *euphrōn*, cheerful < *eu-*, good, well (< IE base **esu-*, good) + *phrēn*, mind 〛 *Gr. Myth.* Joy, one of the three Graces

Eu·rip·i·des (yo͞o rip′ə dēz′) 480-406 B.C.; Gr. writer of tragedies

Eu·ro·pa (yo͞o rō′pə) 〚L < Gr *Eurōpē* 〛 *Gr. Myth.* a Phoenician princess loved by Zeus: he, disguised as a white bull, carries her off across the sea to Crete

Eu·rus (yo͞o′rəs) 〚ME < L < Gr *euros*, prob. ult. < IE base **eus-*, to burn > L *urere*, to burn 〛 *Gr. Myth.* the god of the east wind or southeast wind

Eu·ryd·i·ce (yo͞o rid′i sē′) 〚L < Gr *Eurydikē* 〛 *Gr. Myth.* the wife of ORPHEUS

Eu·se·bi·us (Pam·phi·li) (yo͞o sē′bē əs pam′fə li′) c. A.D. 264-340; Gr. ecclesiastical historian

Eu·ter·pe (yo͞o tʉr′pē) 〚L < Gr *Euterpē* < *euterpēs*, charming < *eu-*, good, well (< IE base **esu-*, good) + *terpein*, to delight, charm < IE base **terp-*, enjoy 〛 *Gr. Myth.* the Muse of music and lyric poetry

E·va (ē′və) a feminine name: see EVE

Ev·an (ev′ən) 〚Welsh, var. of JOHN 〛 a masculine name

E·van·ge·line (ē van′jə lēn′, -lin′, -lin) 〚Fr *Évangeline* < LL(Ec) *evangelium*, good news (in LL(Ec), gospel) < Gr *euangelion*, good news (in N.T., gospel) < *euangelos*, bringing good news < *eu-*, well + *angelos*, messenger 〛 a feminine name

Ev·ans (ev′ənz) **1** Sir **Arthur John** 1851-1941; Eng. archaeologist **2 Herbert Mc·Lean** (mə klän′) 1882-1971; U.S. anatomist & biologist **3 Mary Ann** *see*

ELIOT, George **4 Maurice** 1901-89; U.S. actor, born in England **5 Walker** 1903-75; U.S. photographer

Eve (ēv) ⟦ ME < LL(Ec) *Eva, Heva* < Heb Ḥawwāh, lit., life, living being ⟧ **1** a feminine name: var. *Eva* **2** *Bible* the first woman, Adam's wife: Gen. 3:20

Ev·e·lyn (ev'ə lin; *Brit usually*, ēv'lin) **1** a feminine and masculine name: fem. var. *Evelina, Eveline* **2 John** 1620-1706; Eng. diarist

Ev·er·ett (ev'ər it, ev'rit) ⟦ Du *Evert, Everhart* < OFr *Everart* < OHG *Eburhart* < *ebur*, wild boar + *harto*, strong: hence, lit., strong (as a) wild boar ⟧ **1** a masculine name **2 Edward** 1794-1865; U.S. statesman, orator, & clergyman

Everlasting, the *name for* God

Evil One, the the Devil; Satan

Ew·ell (yōō'əl), **Richard Stod·dert** (städ'ərt) 1817-72; Confederate general in the Civil War

E·ze·ki·el (ē zē'kē əl, i-) ⟦ LL(Ec) *Ezechiel* < Gr *Iezekiēl* < Heb *yechezkel*, lit., God strengthens ⟧ **1** a masculine name: dim. *Zeke* **2** *Bible* a Hebrew prophet of the 6th cent. B.C. **3 Moses Jacob** 1844-1917; U.S. sculptor

Ez·ra (ez'rə) ⟦ LL(Ec) < Heb *ezra*, lit., help ⟧ **1** a masculine name **2** *Bible* a Hebrew scribe, prophet, and religious reformer of the 5th cent. B.C.

F

Fa·bi·us (fā'bē əs) (full name *Quintus Fabius Maximus Verrucosus*) died 203 B.C.; Rom. general & statesman: defeated Hannibal in the second Punic War by a cautious strategy of delay and avoidance of direct encounter: called *Cunctator* (the Delayer)

Faf·nir (fäv'nir') ⟦ ON *Fāfnir* ⟧ *Norse Myth.* a giant who, in the form of a dragon, guards the Nibelung treasure: he is killed by Sigurd

Fahd (fäd) (born *Fahd ibn Abdul Aziz*) 1922- ; king of Saudi Arabia (1982-)

Fair·banks (fer'baŋks'), **Douglas (Elton)** 1883-1939; U.S. motion-picture actor

Faith (fāth) ⟦ ModE *faith* < ME *feith* < OFr *feid, fei* < L *fides*, confidence, belief (in LL(Ec), the Christian religion) < *fidere*, to trust < IE base *bheidh- to urge, be convinced ⟧ a feminine name

Fa·lla (fä'lyä), **Ma·nuel de** (mä nwel' thə) 1876-1946; Sp.

composer

Fal·staff (fôl'staf'), Sir **John** in Shakespeare's *Henry IV* and *The Merry Wives of Windsor*, a fat, witty, boastful knight, convivial but dissolute

Fan·nie, Fan·ny (fan'ē) a feminine name: see FRANCES

Far·a·day (far'ə dā'), **Michael** 1791-1867; Eng. scientist: noted esp. for his work in electricity & magnetism

Far·mer (fär'mər), **Fannie** (**Merritt**) 1857-1915; U.S. teacher & writer on cooking

Far·quhar (fär'kwər, -kər), **George** 1678-1707; Brit. playwright, born in Ireland

Far·ra·gut (far'ə gət), **David Glas·gow** (glas'kō, glaz'gō) (born *James Glasgow Farragut*) 1801-70; U.S. admiral: Union naval commander in the Civil War

Far·rell (far'əl), **James T**(homas) 1904-79; U.S. novelist

Fates *Gr. & Rom. Myth.* the three goddesses who control human destiny and life: see CLOTHO, LACHESIS, ATROPOS

Father God, or God as the first person in the Trinity

Father Time time personified as a very old man carrying a scythe and an hourglass

Fat·i·ma (fat'i mə, fät'-; fə tē'mə) *c.* A.D. 606-632; daughter of Mohammed

Faulk·ner (fôk'nər), **William** 1897-1962; U.S. novelist

Fau·nus (fô'nəs) ⟦L < ? IE **dhaunos*, wolf, strangler < base **dhau-*, to strangle > Gr *Daunos*; infl. by Roman folk-etym. assoc. with L *favere*, to favor⟧ *Rom. Myth.* a god of nature, the patron of farming and animals: identified with the Greek Pan

Fau·ré (fō rā'), **Gabriel** (**Urbain**) 1845-1924; Fr. composer

Faust (foust) ⟦Ger < L *faustus*, fortunate < base of *favere*, to favor < IE base **ghow-*, to perceive⟧ the hero of several medieval legends, and later literary and operatic works, an old philosopher who sells his soul to the devil in exchange for knowledge and power: also **Faus'tus** (fôs'təs, fous'-)

Fawkes (fôks), **Guy** 1570-1606; Eng. conspirator: executed for participating in the Gunpowder Plot

Fay, Faye (fā) ⟦< ?⟧ a feminine name

Fei·ning·er (fī'niŋ ər), **Ly·o·nel** (**Charles Adrian**) (lī'ə nəl) 1871-1956; U.S. painter

Fe·li·ci·a (fə lish'ə, -ē ə; -lē'shə, -shē ə; -lis'ē ə) a feminine name: see FELIX

Fe·lix (fē′liks) ⟦L, lit., happy, orig., fertile, fruitful, nourishing⟧ a masculine name: fem. *Felicia*

Fel·li·ni (fə lē′nē; *It* fel lē′nē), **Fe·de·ri·co** (fe′də rē′kō; *It* fe′de rē′kô) 1920-93; It. motion-picture director

Fé·ne·lon (fān lōn′; *E* fen′ə län′), **Fran·çois de Sa·li·gnac de La Mothe** (frän swä′ də sà lē nyàk′ də là mōt′) 1651-1715; Fr. clergyman & writer

Fer·di·nand (furd′n and) ⟦Fr⟧ **1** a masculine name **2** Ferdinand I *c.* 1000-65; king of Castile (1035-65) & of León (1037-65): called *the Great* **3** Ferdinand I 1503-64; emperor of the Holy Roman Empire (1558-64), born in Spain **4** Ferdinand I (born *Maximilian Karl Leopold Maria*) 1861-1948; king of Bulgaria (1908-18): abdicated: father of *Boris III* **5** Ferdinand II 1578-1637; emperor of the Holy Roman Empire (1619-37) **6** Ferdinand V 1452-1516; king of Castile (1474-1504); (as **Ferdinand II**) king of Aragon & Sicily (1479-1516); (as **Ferdinand III**) king of Naples (1504-16): husband of Isabella I of Castile: called *the Catholic*

Fer·mi (fer′mē), **En·ri·co** (en rē′kō) 1901-54; U.S. nuclear physicist, born in Italy

Fey·deau (fā dō′), **Georges** (zhôrzh) 1862-1921; Fr. playwright

Feyn·man (fīn′mən), **Richard Phillips** 1918-88; U.S. physicist

Fich·te (fiH′tə), **Jo·hann Gott·lieb** (yō′hän gôt′lēp) 1762-1814; Ger. philosopher

Field (fēld) **1** Cyrus West 1819-92; U.S. industrialist: promoted the first transatlantic cable **2** Eugene 1850-95; U.S. journalist & poet

Field·ing (fēl′diŋ), **Henry** 1707-54; Eng. novelist

Fields (fēldz), **W.C.** (born *Claude William Dukenfield*) 1880-1946; U.S. actor & comedian

Fiend, the Satan

Fie·so·le (fye′zō le), **Gio·van·ni da** (jô vän′nē dä) *see* ANGELICO, Fra

Fill·more (fil′môr), **Mill·ard** (mil′ərd) 1800-74; 13th president of the U.S. (1850-53)

Fi·o·na (fē ō′nə) a feminine name

Fir·dau·si (fir dou′sē) (born *Abul Kasim Mansur*) *c.* 940-1020; Pers. epic poet: also **Fir·du·si** (-dōō′-)

Fisch·er (fish′ər) **1** Emil 1852-1919; Ger. organic chemist **2** Hans 1881-1945; Ger. organic chemist

Fish (fish), **Hamilton** 1808-93; U.S. statesman

Fiske (fisk), **John** (born *Edmund Fisk Green*) 1842-1901; U.S. historian & philosopher

Fitch (fich) **1 (William) Clyde** 1865-1909; U.S. playwright **2 John** 1743-98; U.S. inventor of a steamboat

Fitz·ger·ald (fits jer'əld) **1 Ella** 1918- ; U.S. jazz singer **2 F(rancis) Scott (Key)** 1896-1940; U.S. author

FitzGerald, Edward (born *Edward Purcell*) 1809-83; Eng. poet & translator of *The Rubáiyát*: also written **Fitzgerald**

Flag·stad (flag'stad'; *Norw* fläg'stä'), **Kir·sten** (kir'sten; *Norw* kish'tən) 1895-1962; Norw. soprano

Fla·her·ty (fla'ər tē), **Robert (Joseph)** 1884-1951; U.S. motion-picture director, esp. of documentaries

Flam·ma·rion (flȧ ma ryōn'), **Camille** 1842-1925; Fr. astronomer

Flan·a·gan (flan'ə gən), **E(dward) J(oseph)** 1886-1948; U.S. Rom. Catholic clergyman; founder of Boys Town

Flau·bert (flō ber'), **Gus·tave** (güs tȧv') 1821-80; Fr. novelist

Flem·ing (flem'iŋ) **1 Sir Alexander** 1881-1955; Brit. bacteriologist: discovered penicillin together with Sir Howard Walter Florey **2 Ian (Lancaster)** 1908-64; Brit. writer

Fletch·er (flech'ər), **John** 1579-1625; Eng. playwright: collaborated with Francis Beaumont

Fleu·ry (flë rē') **1 An·dré Her·cule de** (än drā er kül' də) 1653-1743; Fr. cardinal & statesman: prime minister (1726-43) under Louis XV **2 Claude** (klōd) 1640-1723; Fr. ecclesiastical historian

Flo·ra (flôr'ə, flō'rə) 〚L < *flos*, flower: adopted by Carolus LINNAEUS (1745) as term for the plants of a region〛 **1** a feminine name **2** *Rom. Myth.* the goddess of flowers

Flor·ence (flôr'əns, flär'-) 〚Fr < L *Florentia*, lit., a blooming < *florens*, prp. of *florere*, to bloom < *flos* < IE *bhlō-*, var. of base *bhel-*, to swell, sprout〛 a feminine name: dim. *Flo, Flossie*; equiv. Ger. *Florenz*, It. *Fiorenza*, Sp. *Florencia*

Flo·rey (flôr'ē), **Sir Howard Walter** 1898-1968; Brit. pathologist, born in Australia: developed penicillin together with Sir Alexander Fleming

Flo·ri·o (flôr'ē ō'), **John** c. 1553-1625; Eng. writer & lexicographer: translator of Montaigne

Flo·ry (flôr'ē), **Paul John** 1910-85; U.S. chemist

Flo·tow (flō′tō), Baron **Frie·drich von** (frē′driH fôn) 1812-83; Ger. operatic composer

Floyd (floid) ⟦var. of LLOYD: *Fl-* for Welsh *Ll-*⟧ a masculine name

Flying Dutchman a fabled Dutch sailor condemned to sail the seas off the Cape of Good Hope until Judgment Day

Foch (fôsh), **Fer·di·nand** (fer dē nän′) 1851-1929; Fr. marshal: commander in chief of Allied forces (1918)

Fo·kine (fô kēn′), **Mi·chel** (mē shel′) (born *Mikhail Mikhailovich Fokin*) 1880-1942; U.S. choreographer, born in Russia

Fok·ker (fäk′ər), **Anthony Herman Gerard** 1890-1939; U.S. aircraft designer, born in Dutch East Indies: built airplanes for Germany & the Netherlands, 1911-21

Fon·tanne (fän tan′), **Lynn** *c.* 1887-1983; U.S. actress: wife of Alfred Lunt

Fon·teyn (fän tān′), **Dame Margot** (born *Margaret Hookham*) 1919-91; Eng. ballerina

Ford (fôrd) **1 Ford Ma·dox** (mad′əks) (born *Ford Madox Hueffer*) 1873-1939; Eng. writer & editor **2 Gerald R(udolph), Jr.** (born *Leslie Lynch King, Jr.*) 1913- ; 38th president of the U.S. (1974-77) **3 Henry** 1863-1947; U.S. automobile manufacturer **4 John** 1586-*c.* 1639; Eng. dramatist **5 John** (born *Sean O'Feeney*) 1895-1973; U.S. motion-picture director

For·es·ter (fôr′is tər, fär′-), **C(ecil) S(cott)** 1899-1966; Eng. novelist

For·ster (fôr′stər), **E(dward) M(organ)** 1879-1970; Eng. novelist

For·tu·na (fôr tōō′nə, -tyōō′-) ⟦L < *fortuna*⟧ Rom. *Myth.* the goddess of fortune

Fos·ter (fôs′tər, fäs′-) **1 Stephen Collins** 1826-64; U.S. composer of songs **2 William Z(ebulon)** 1881-1964; U.S. Communist Party leader

Fou·cault (fōō kō′) **1 Jean Ber·nard Lé·on** (zhän ber när′ lā ōn′) 1819-68; Fr. physicist **2 Mi·chel** (mē shel′) 1926-84; Fr. philosopher

Fou·rier (fōō ryā′; *E* foor′ē ər) **1 Fran·çois Ma·rie Charles** (frän swä′ må rē′ shårl) 1772-1837; Fr. socialist & reformer **2 Baron Jean Bap·tiste Jo·seph** (zhän bå tēst′ zhō zef′) 1768-1830; Fr. mathematician & physicist

Fow·ler (fou′lər), **H(enry) W(atson)** 1858-1933; Eng. lexicographer & arbiter of linguistic usage

Fox (fäks) **1 Charles James** 1749-1806; Eng. statesman & orator **2 George** 1624-91; Eng. religious leader: founder of the Society of Friends

Fra·go·nard (frá gồ nár′), **Jean Ho·no·ré** (zhän ồ nồ rä′) 1732-1806; Fr. painter

France (frans, fräns), **A·na·tole** (an′ə tōl′) (pseud. of *Jacques Anatole François Thibault*) 1844-1924; Fr. novelist & literary critic

Fran·ces (fran′sis, frän′-) ⟦OFr fem. form of *Franceis*: see Francis⟧ a feminine name: dim. *Fran, Fannie, Fanny*

Fran·ces·ca (frän ches′kä), **Pie·ro del·la** (pye′rồ del′lä) *c.* 1420-92; It. painter

Francesca da Ri·mi·ni (dä *rē*′mē nē′) 13th-cent. It. woman famous for her adulterous love affair with her brother-in-law, Paolo

Fran·cis (fran′sis) ⟦OFr *Franceis* < ML *Franciscus*⟧ **1** a masculine name: dim *Frank*; equiv. Fr. *Françqis*, Ger. *Franz*, It. *Francesco, Franco*, Sp. *Francisco*; fem. *Frances, Francine* **2 Francis I** 1494-1547; king of France (1515-47) **3 Francis II** 1768-1835; last emperor of the Holy Roman Empire (1792-1806) &, as **Francis I**, first emperor of Austria (1804-35)

Francis Ferdinand 1863-1914; archduke of Austria: his assassination led to the outbreak of World War I

Francis Joseph I 1830-1916; emperor of Austria (1848-1916) and king of Hungary (1867-1916): uncle of Francis Ferdinand

Francis of As·si·si (ə sē′zē), **Saint** (born *Giovanni di Bernardone*) *c.* 1181-1226; It. friar: founder of the Franciscan Order: his day is Oct. 4

Francis of Sales (sälz), **Saint** (1567-1622); Fr. bishop & writer: his day is Jan. 29

Francis Xavier, Saint *see* Xavier, Saint Francis

Franck (fränk), **Cé·sar** (**Auguste**) (sä zàr′) 1822-90; Fr. composer & organist, born in Belgium

Fran·co (fraŋ′kồ; *Sp* fräŋ′kồ), **Fran·cis·co** (fran sis′kồ; *Sp* frän thēs′kồ) (born *Francisco Paulino Hermenegildo Teódulo Franco Bahamonde*) 1892-1975; Sp. general: dictator of Spain (1939-75)

Frank (fraŋk) **1** a masculine name: dim. *Frankie*: see Francis **2 Robert** 1924-   ; U.S. photographer, born in Switzerland

Frank·en·stein (fraŋk'ən stīn') **1** the title character in a novel (1818) by Mary Wollstonecraft SHELLEY: he is a young medical student who creates a monster that destroys him **2** popularly, Frankenstein's monster

Frank·furt·er (fraŋk'fər tər), **Felix** 1882-1965; associate justice, U.S. Supreme Court (1939-62), born in Austria

Frank·lin (fraŋk'lin) [[ModE *franklin*, a freeholder < ME *frankelein* < Anglo-Fr *fraunkelain* < ML *france-lengus* < *francus* < LL *Frankus*, a Frank, hence free man (i.e., member of the ruling group in Gaul)]] **1** a masculine name **2 Benjamin** 1706-90; Am. statesman, scientist, inventor, & writer **3 Sir John** 1786-1847; Eng. arctic explorer

Franz Jo·sef I (fränts yō'zef; *E* fränts jō'zəf) *Ger. name of* FRANCIS JOSEPH I

Fra·zer (frā'zər), **Sir James (George)** 1854-1941; Scot. anthropologist

Fre·da (frē'də) a feminine name: see FRIEDA

Fred·er·i·ca (fred'ər ē'kə) [[see fol.]] a feminine name

Fred·er·ick (fred'rik, -ər ik) [[Fr *Frédéric* < Ger *Friedrich* < OHG *Fridurih* < Gmc **frithu-*, peace (< *fri-*, to love, protect + *-thu-*, substantive particle) + **rik-*, king, ruler]] **1** a masculine name: dim. *Fred, Freddy, Freddie*; equiv. Fr. *Frédéric*, Ger. *Friedrich, Fritz*, It. & Sp. *Federico*; fem. *Frederica*: also **Frederic, Fredric,** or **Fredrick 2 Frederick I** *c.* 1123-90; king of Germany (1152-90) & emperor of the Holy Roman Empire (1155-90): called *Frederick Barbarossa* **3 Frederick I** 1657-1713; 1st king of Prussia (1701-13) &, as **Frederick III**, elector of Brandenburg (1688-1701): son of Frederick William, the Great Elector **4 Frederick II** 1194-1250; emperor of the Holy Roman Empire (1215-50): king of Sicily (1197-1250) **5 Frederick II** FREDERICK THE GREAT **6 Frederick III** 1463-1525; elector of Saxony (1486-1525): protector of Luther after the diet at Worms **7 Frederick IX** 1899-1972; king of Denmark (1947-72)

Frederick the Great 1712-86; king of Prussia (1740-86): son of Frederick William I

Frederick William 1 1620-88; elector of Brandenburg (1640-88): called *the Great Elector* **2 Frederick William I** 1688-1740; king of Prussia (1713-40) **3 Frederick William II** 1744-97; king of Prussia (1786-97) **4 Frederick William III** 1770-1840; king of Prussia (1797-

1840)

Fre·ge (frā′gə), **Gott·lob** (gôt′lôp) 1848-1925; Ger. philosopher & mathematician

Fré·mont (frē′mänt), **John Charles** 1813-90; U.S. politician, general, & explorer, esp. in the West

French (french), **Daniel Chester** 1850-1931; U.S. sculptor

Fre·neau (fri nō′), **Philip** (**Morin**) 1752-1832; U.S. poet & journalist

Fres·nel (frā nel′), **Au·gus·tin Jean** (ō güs tan′zhän) 1788-1827; Fr. physicist

Freud (froid), **Sigmund** 1856-1939; Austrian physician & neurologist: founder of psychoanalysis

Frey (frā) *Norse Myth.* the god of crops, fruitfulness, love, peace, and prosperity: also **Freyr** (frār)

Frey·a (frā′ə, -ä′) *Norse Myth.* the goddess of love and beauty, sister of Frey: also **Frey′ja′** (-yä′)

Frick (frik), **Henry Clay** 1849-1919; U.S. industrialist & philanthropist

Fri·day (frī′dā; *also,* -dē) *n.* ⟦after the devoted servant of ROBINSON CRUSOE⟧ a faithful follower or efficient helper

Frie·da (frē′də) ⟦Ger < OHG *fridu*, peace: see FREDERICK⟧ a feminine name: var. *Freda*

Fried·man (frēd′mən), **Milton** 1912- ; U.S. economist

Frie·drich (frē′driH), **Caspar David** (käs′pär′ dä′vēt′) 1774-1840; Ger. painter

Frigg (frig) ⟦ON, akin to OHG *Fria* & Sans *priyā*, beloved⟧ the wife of Odin and goddess of the skies, presiding over marriage and the home: also **Frig′ga** (frig′ə)

Friml (frim′əl), (**Charles**) **Rudolf** 1879-1972; U.S. composer, born in Bohemia

Fro·bish·er (frō′bi shər), **Sir Martin** *c.* 1535-94; Eng. navigator & explorer

Froe·bel, Frö·bel (frō′bəl; *E* frā′bəl), **Frie·drich** (**Wilhelm August**) (frē′driH) 1782-1852; Ger. educator: originated the kindergarten system

Froh·man (frō′mən), **Charles** 1860-1915; U.S. theatrical manager & producer

Frois·sart (frwȧ sȧr′; *E* froi′särt), **Jean** (zhän) 1337-*c.* 1410; Fr. chronicler & poet

Fromm (främ), **Er·ich** (er′ik) 1900-80; U.S. psychoanalyst, born in Germany

Fron·te·nac (frōnt nàk′; *E* frän′tə nak′), Comte **de (Frontenac et de Palluau)** (born *Louis de Buade*) 1620-98; Fr. colonial governor in North America (1672-82; 1689-98)

Frost (frôst, fräst), **Robert** (**Lee**) 1874-1963; U.S. poet

Froude (frōōd), **James Anthony** 1818-94; Eng. historian

Fry (frī), **Christopher** (born *Christopher Hammond*) 1907- ; Eng. playwright

Fuen·tes (fwen′tās, -tes), **Carlos** 1928- ; Mex. novelist

Fu·gard (fōō′gärd, fyōō′-), **Ath·ol** (ath′ôl, -əl) 1932- ; South African playwright

Full·er (fool′ər) **1** (**Richard**) **Buck·min·ster** (buk′min stər) 1895-1983; U.S. engineer, inventor, & philosopher **2** (**Sarah**) **Margaret** (*Marchioness Ossoli*) 1810-50; U.S. writer, critic, & social reformer **3 Melville Wes·ton** (wes′tən) 1833-1910; U.S. jurist: chief justice of the U.S. (1888-1910)

Ful·ton (foolt′'n), **Robert** 1765-1815; U.S. inventor & engineer: designer of the 1st commercially successful U.S. steamboat, the *Clermont* (launched 1807)

Fu·ries (fyoor′ēz) ⟦ME < L *Furiae*, pl. of *furia*, fury⟧ *Gr. & Rom. Myth.* the three terrible female spirits with snaky hair (Alecto, Tisiphone, and Megaera) who punish the doers of unavenged crimes

Fur·ness (fʉr′nis), **Horace Howard** 1833-1912; U.S. Shakespearean scholar

Fur·ni·vall (fʉr′ni vəl), **Frederick James** 1825-1910; Eng. philologist & editor

Furt·wäng·ler (fōōrt′veŋ′lər), **Wilhelm** 1886-1954; Ger. conductor

G

Ga·ble (gā′bəl), (**William**) **Clark** 1901-60; U.S. motion-picture actor

Ga·bo (gä′bō), **Na·um** (nä′ōōm) (born *Naum Pevsner*) 1890-1977; U.S. sculptor, born in Russia

Ga·bor (gä′bôr, gə bôr′), **Dennis** 1900-79; Brit. physicist, born in Hungary

Ga·bri·el (gā′brē əl) ⟦Heb *gavriel*, lit. ? man of God < *gever*, man + *el*, God⟧ **1** a masculine name; dim. *Gabe*; fem. *Gabriella, Gabrielle* **2** *Bible* one of the archangels, the herald of good news: Dan. 8:16; Luke 1:26

Ga·bri·elle (gāb′rē el′, ga′brē-) ⟦It & Sp⟧ a feminine

name: equiv. It. & Sp. *Gabriella*: see GABRIEL

Gad (gad) 〖Heb *gad*, lit., good fortune〗 *Bible* Jacob's seventh son, whose mother was Zilpah: Gen. 30:11

Gad·da·fi (gə dä′fē) *see* QADDAFI, Muammar al-

Gads·den (gadz′dən), **James** 1788-1858; U.S. diplomat: negotiated (1853) a purchase of land (Gadsden Purchase) from Mexico, which became part of N.Mex. & Ariz.

Gae·a (jē′ə) 〖Gr *Gaia* < *gē*, earth〗 *Gr. Myth.* a goddess who is the personification of the earth, the mother of the Titans: identified with the Roman Tellus

Ga·ga·rin (gä gär′in), **Yu·ri A·lek·se·ye·vich** (yōō′rē ä′ lyek sā′yə vich) 1934-68; Soviet cosmonaut: 1st man to orbit the earth in a space flight (1961)

Gage (gāj), **Thomas** 1721-87; Brit. general in the American Revolution

Gai·a (gā′ə, gī′ə) *var. of* GAEA

Gail (gāl) a feminine name: var. *Gayle*: see ABIGAIL

Gains·bor·ough (gānz′bʉr ō, -bər ə), **Thomas** 1727-88; Eng. painter

Gai·ser·ic (gī′zə rik) *var. of* GENSERIC

Ga·ius (gā′əs) c. A.D. 110-c. 180; Rom. jurist

Gaj·du·sek (gī′doo shek′, -də-), **D(aniel) Carle·ton** (kärl′ tən) 1923- ; U.S. pediatrician & virologist

Gal·a·had (gal′ə had′) *Arthurian Legend* a knight who is successful in the quest for the Holy Grail because of his purity and nobility of spirit: he is the son of Lancelot and Elaine

Gal·a·te·a (gal′ə tē′ə) a statue of a maiden which is given life by Aphrodite after its sculptor, Pygmalion, falls in love with it: name applied in post-classical times

Gal·ba (gal′bə, gôl′-), (**Servius Sulpicius**) c. 3 B.C.-A.D. 69; Rom. emperor (68-69)

Ga·len (gā′lən) (L. name *Claudius Galenus*) c. A.D. 130-c. 200; Gr. physician & writer on medicine & philosophy

Gal·i·le·an (gal′ə lē′ən), **the** Jesus

Gal·i·le·o (gal′ə lē′ō, -lā′-) (born *Galileo Galilei*) 1564-1642; It. astronomer, mathematician, & physicist: with the telescope, which he improved, he demonstrated the truth of the Copernican theory: condemned for heresy by the Inquisition

Gal·la·tin (gal′ə tin), (**Abraham Alfonse**) **Albert** 1761-1849; U.S. statesman & financier, born in Switzerland; secretary of the treasury (1801-13)

Gal·lau·det (gal′ə det′), **Thomas Hopkins** 1787-1851;
U.S. educator: noted for his work with deaf-mutes

Gal·lup (gal′əp), **George Horace** 1901-84; U.S. statisti-
cian

Gals·wor·thy (gôlz′wʉr′thē, galz′-), **John** 1867-1933; Eng.
novelist & playwright

Gal·ton (gôlt″n), **Sir Francis** 1822-1911; Eng. scientist &
writer: pioneer in eugenics

Gal·va·ni (gal vä′nē), **Lu·i·gi** (lōō wē′jē) 1737-98; It.
physiologist & physicist

Gama, Vasco da see DA GAMA, Vasco

Ga·ma·li·el (gə mā′lē əl, -māl′yəl) ⟦LL < Gr *Gamaliēl* <
Heb *gamliel*, lit., reward of God⟧ *Bible* a teacher of
Saul of Tarsus; Acts 22:3

Ga·mow (gam′ôf, -äf), **George Antony** 1904-68; U.S.
astrophysicist, born in Russia

Gan·dhi (gän′dē, gan′-) **1 Mrs. In·di·ra (Nehru)** (in dir′
ə) 1917-84; Indian statesman: prime minister of India
(1966-77; 1980-84): assassinated: daughter of
Jawaharlal Nehru **2 Mo·han·das K(aramchand)** (mō
hän′dəs) 1869-1948; Hindu nationalist leader & social
reformer: assassinated: called *Mahatma Gandhi*

Gan·y·mede (gan′i mēd′) ⟦Gr *Ganymēdēs*⟧ *Gr. Myth.* a
beautiful youth carried off by Zeus to be the cupbearer
to the gods

Gar·bo (gär′bō), **Greta** (born *Greta Lovisa Gustafsson*)
1905-90; U.S. motion-picture actress, born in Sweden

Gar·ci·a Lor·ca (gär thē′ä lôr′kä; *E* gär sē′ə lôr′kə), **Fe·
de·ri·co** (fe′de rē′kô) 1899-1936; Sp. poet & playwright

Gar·ci·a Már·quez (gär sē′ä mär′kes; *E* gär sē′ə mär′
kez), **Ga·bri·el** (gä′vrē el′; *E* gä′brē əl, gä′brē el′)
1928- ; Colombian writer

Gar·di·ner (gärd′nər), **Samuel Raw·son** (rô′sən) 1829-
1902; Eng. historian

Gard·ner (gärd′nər), **Erle Stanley** (ʉrl) 1889-1970; U.S.
writer

Gar·eth (gar′ith) *Arthurian Legend* a knight of the
Round Table, nephew of King Arthur

Gar·field (gär′fēld), **James Abram** 1831-81; 20th president of the U.S. (1881): assassinated

Gar·gan·tu·a (gär gan′chōō ə, -tyōō ə) ⟦Fr < Sp *gar-
ganta*, throat, gullet < echoic base **garg-*⟧ a giant
king, noted for his size and prodigious feats and appe-
tite, in *Gargantua and Pantagruel*, a satire by Rabelais

(1552)

Gar·i·bal·di (gar′ə bôl′dē; *It* gä′rē bäl′dē), **Giu·sep·pe** (jōō zep′pe) 1807-82; It. patriot & general: leader in the movement to unify Italy

Gar·land (gär′lənd) 1 (**Hannibal**) **Ham·lin** (ham′lin) 1860-1940; U.S. novelist & short-story writer 2 **Judy** (born *Frances Gumm*) 1922-69; U.S. motion-picture actress, singer, & dancer

Gar·rick (gar′ik), **David** 1717-79; Eng. actor & theater manager

Gar·ri·son (gar′ə sən), **William Lloyd** 1805-79; U.S. editor, lecturer, & abolitionist leader

Gar·vey (gär′vē), **Marcus** 1887-1940; Jamaican black nationalist leader in the U.S.

Gar·y (ger′ē, gar′-) ⟦< OE **Garwig*, lit., spear (of) battle < *gar*, a spear + *wig* < Gmc **wiga-*, battle < IE base **wĭk-*, to be bold > L *vincere*, to conquer ⟧ a masculine name: var. *Garry*

Gas·kell (gas′kəl), **Mrs.** (**Elizabeth Cleghorn**) (born *Elizabeth Cleghorn Stevenson*) 1810-65; Eng. novelist

Gasset, **José Ortega y** *see* ORTEGA Y GASSET, José

Gates (gāts), **Horatio** *c.* 1728-1806; Am. general in the Revolutionary War

Gau·di (i Cor·net) (gou dē′ē kôr′net), **An·to·nio** (än tô′nyô) 1852-1926; Sp. architect

Gau·guin (gō gan′), (**Eugène Henri**) **Paul** (pôl) 1848-1903; Fr. painter, in Tahiti after 1891

Gau·ta·ma (gout′ə mə, gôt′-) *see* BUDDHA

Gau·tier (gō tyā′), **Thé·o·phile** (tā ô fēl′) 1811-72; Fr. poet, novelist, & critic

Ga·wain (gə wān′; gä′wän′, -win) ⟦Fr *Gauvain* < ? Gmc **Gawin* ⟧ *Arthurian Legend* a knight of the Round Table, nephew of King Arthur

Gay (gā), **John** 1685-1732; Eng. poet & playwright

Gayle (gāl) a feminine name: see GAIL

Gay–Lus·sac (gā lü såk′), **Jo·seph Louis** (zhô zef′ lwē) 1778-1850; Fr. chemist & physicist

Ge (jē; gā) ⟦Gr *gē*, earth ⟧ var. of GAEA

Ged·des (ged′ēz), **Norman Bel** (bel) 1893-1958; U.S. theatrical & industrial designer

Gei·sel (gī′zəl), **Theodor Seuss** (sōōs) (pseud. *Dr. Seuss*) 1904-91; U.S. writer & illustrator, esp. of children's books

Gell–Mann (gel män′, -man′), **Murray** 1929- ; U.S.

physicist

Gene (jēn) a masculine name: see EUGENE

Ge·nêt (zhə nā′) **1** Ed·mond Charles É·douard (ed mōn′ shàrl ā dwàr′) 1763-1834; Fr. diplomat, in the U.S. after 1793: called *Citizen Genêt* **2** Jean 1910-86; Fr. playwright & novelist

Gen·e·vieve (jen′ə vēv′) ⟦Fr *Geneviève* < LL *Genovefa* < ? Celt⟧ **1** a feminine name **2** Saint (*c.* A.D. 422-*c.* 512); Fr. nun; patron saint of Paris: her day is Jan. 3

Gen·ghis Khan (geŋ′gis kän′, jeŋ′gis) (born *Temuchin*) *c.* 1162-1227; Mongol conqueror of central Asia

Gen·ser·ic (jen′sər ik, gen′-) *c.* A.D. 400-477; king of the Vandals (427-477): conqueror in N Africa & of Rome

Geof·frey (jef′rē) ⟦ME *Geffrey* < OFr *Geoffroi* < Gmc *Walafrid* < *wala-, traveler + *frithu, peace (> Ger *friede*)⟧ a masculine name: dim. *Jeff*; var. *Jeffrey*

Geoffrey of Mon·mouth (män′məth) *c.* 1100-54; Brit. bishop & chronicler: preserver of the Arthurian legend

George (jôrj) ⟦< Fr & L; Fr *Georges* < LL *Georgius* < Gr *Geōrgios* < *geōrgos*, husbandman, lit., earthworker < *gaia*, *gē*, earth + base of *ergon*, work⟧ **1** a masculine name: dim. *Georgie*; equiv. Fr. *Georges*, Ger. & Scand. *Georg*, It. *Giorgio*, Sp. *Jorge*; fem. *Georgia*, *Georgiana*, *Georgina* **2** George I 1660-1727; king of Great Britain & Ireland (1714-27), born in Germany: great-grandson of James I **3** George II 1683-1760; king of Great Britain & Ireland (1727-60), born in Germany: son of George I **4** George III 1738-1820; king of Great Britain & Ireland (1760-1820): grandson of George II **5** George IV 1762-1830; king of Great Britain & Ireland (1820-30); regent (1811-20): son of George III **6** George V 1865-1936; king of Great Britain & Ireland (1910-36): son of Edward VII **7** George VI 1895-1952; king of Great Britain & Northern Ireland (1936-52): son of George V **8** Saint (died *c.* A.D. 303); Christian martyr, possibly from Cappadocia: patron saint of England: his day is April 23 **9** David Lloyd *see* LLOYD GEORGE, David **10** Henry 1839-97; U.S. political economist: advocate of the single tax

Geor·gia (jôr′jə) a feminine name; dim. *Georgie*: see GEORGE

Ge·raint (jə rānt′) ⟦< Celt⟧ *Arthurian Legend* a knight of the Round Table, husband of Enid

Ger·ald (jer′əld) ⟦< OFr or OHG; OFr *Giraut*, *Giralt* <

OHG *Gerald, Gerwald* < *ger*, spear + base of *waldan*,
to rule ‖ a masculine name: dim. *Jerry*; fem. *Geraldine*

Ge·rard (jə rärd′) ⟦OFr *Girart* < OHG *Gerhart* < *ger*
(see prec.) + *hart*, hard ‖ a masculine name: dim. *Jerry*

Gé·ri·cault (zhā rē kō′), (**Jean–Louis–André–**)**Thé·o·
dore** (tā ô dôr′) 1791-1824; Fr. painter

Ger·man·i·cus Caesar (jər man′i kəs) 15 B.C.-A.D. 19;
Rom. general: father of Caligula

Ge·ron·i·mo (jə rän′ə mō′) ⟦Sp, Jerome, used as a nickname by the Mexicans ‖ *c.* 1829-1909; Apache Indian
chief

Ger·ry (ger′ē), **El·bridge** (el′brij) 1744-1814; Am. statesman: signer of the Declaration of Independence: vice
president of the U.S. (1813-14)

Gersh·win (gursh′win), **George** (born *Jacob Gershvin*)
1898-1937; U.S. composer

Ger·trude (gur′trŏŏd′) ⟦ < Fr & Ger: Fr *Gertrude* < Ger
Gertrud < OHG *Geretrudis* < *ger*, spear + *trut*, dear ‖
a feminine name: dim. *Gert, Gertie, Trudy*

Ge·sell (gə zel′), **Arnold L(ucius)** 1880-1961; U.S. psychologist: authority on child behavior

Ghi·ber·ti (gē ber′tē), **Lo·ren·zo** (lô ren′tsô) (born
Lorenzo di Cione di Ser Buonaccorso) 1378-1455; Florentine sculptor, painter, & worker in metals

Ghir·lan·da·io (gir′län dä′yô), **Do·men·i·co** (dô mā′nē
kô) (born *Domenico di Tommaso Bigordi*) 1449-94;
Florentine painter: also sp. **Ghir′lan·da′jo**

Gia·co·met·ti (jä′kô met′tē), **Al·ber·to** (äl ber′tô) 1901-
66; Swiss sculptor & painter, mainly in France

Gi·auque (jē ōk′), **William Francis** 1895-1982; U.S.
chemist

Gib·bon (gib′ən), **Edward** 1737-94; Eng. historian

Gib·bons (gib′ənz), **Orlando** 1583-1625; Eng. organist &
composer

Gibbs (gibz), **J(osiah) Willard** 1839-1903; U.S. mathematician & physicist

Gib·ran (ji brän′), **Kha·lil** (kä lēl′) (Ar. name *Jubrān
Khalil Jubrān*) 1883-1931; Lebanese novelist, poet, &
artist, in the U.S. (after 1910)

Gide (zhēd), **An·dré** (**Paul Guillaume**) (än drā′) 1869-
1951; Fr. writer

Gid·e·on (gid′ē ən) ⟦Heb *gidon*, lit., hewer < *gada*, to
hew ‖ **1** a masculine name **2** *Bible* a judge of Israel
and a leader in the defeat of the Midianites: Judg. 6-8

Giel·gud (gēl'good'), Sir (**Arthur**) **John** 1904- ; Eng. actor

Gil·bert (gil'bərt) ⟦OFr *Guillebert* < OHG *Williberht* < *willo*, will + *beraht*, bright⟧ 1 a masculine name: dim. *Gil* 2 **Cass** (kas) 1859-1934; U.S. architect 3 Sir **Humphrey** *c.* 1539-83; Eng. navigator and colonizer in North America 4 Sir **William Schwenck** (shwenk) 1836-1911; Eng. humorous poet & librettist: collaborated with Sir Arthur Sullivan in writing comic operas

Gil·da (gil'də) a feminine name

Giles (jīlz) ⟦OFr *Gilles* < L *Aegidius* < *aegis*, the shield of Zeus < Gr *aigis*⟧ 1 a masculine name 2 Saint (*c.* 7th cent. A.D.); semilegendary Athenian hermit in S Gaul: his day is Sept. 1

Gil·ga·mesh (gil'gə mesh') ⟦< Bab⟧ *Bab. Legend* an ancient king and hero of an epic (*Gilgamesh Epic*) completed about 2000 B.C. containing an account of a flood like the Biblical Flood: also **Gil'ga·mish'** (-mish')

Gil·les·pie (gi les'pē), **Dizzy** (born *John Birks Gillespie*) 1917-93; U.S. jazz musician

Gil·lette (ji let'), **King Camp** 1855-1932; U.S. inventor of the safety razor

Gil·li·an (jil'ē ən) a feminine name

Gi·na (jē'nə) a feminine name: see REGINA

Gin·ger (jin'jər) a feminine name: see VIRGINIA

Gin·ie (jin'ē) a feminine name: see VIRGINIA

Gins·berg (ginz'bʉrg), **Allen** 1926- ; U.S. poet

Gins·burg (ginz'bʉrg'), **Ruth Ba·der** (bā'dər) 1933- ; associate justice, U.S. Supreme Court (1993-)

Gior·gio·ne (jôr jō'ne), **Il** (ēl) (born *Giorgio Barbarelli*) *c.* 1478-1510; Venetian painter

Giot·to (**di Bon·do·ne**) (jōt'tô dē bôn dô'ne; *E* jät'ō) *c.* 1266-1337; Florentine painter & architect

Gi·rard (jə rärd'), **Stephen** 1750-1831; Am. financier & philanthropist, born in France

Gi·rau·doux (zhē rō doō'), (**Hippolyte**) **Jean** 1882-1944; Fr. playwright & novelist

Gis·sing (gis'iŋ), **George** (**Robert**) 1857-1903; Eng. novelist

Glad·stone (glad'stōn; *Brit*, -stən), **William Ew·art** (yoō' ərt) 1809-98; Brit. statesman: prime minister (1868-74; 1880-85; 1886; 1892-94)

Glad·ys (glad'is) ⟦Welsh *Gwladys*, prob. < L *Claudia*: see CLAUDIA⟧ a feminine name

Gla·ser (glä′zər), **Donald Arthur** 1926- ; U.S. physicist

Glas·gow (glas′kō, glaz′gō), **Ellen (Anderson Gholson)** 1873-1945; U.S. novelist

Gla·show (gla′shō), **Sheldon Lee** 1932- ; U.S. physicist

Glass (glas), **Philip** 1937- ; U.S. composer

Gla·zu·nov (glä zōō nôf′), **A·lek·san·dr Kon·stan·ti·no·vich** (à lyek sän′dr' kôn′stän tē′nô vich) 1865-1936; Russ. composer

Glen·da (glen′də) a feminine name

Glen·dow·er (glen′dou ər, glen dou′ər), **Owen** c. 1359-c. 1416; Welsh chieftain: rebelled against Henry IV

Glenn, Glen (glen) 〚Celt, mountain valley〛 a masculine name

Glenn (glen), **John (Herschel, Jr.)** 1921- ; U.S. astronaut & senator: 1st American to orbit the earth (1962)

Glin·ka (glin′kä; E gliŋ′kə), **Mi·kha·il I·va·no·vich** (mē khä ēl′ i vä′nô vich) 1804-57; Russ. composer

Glo·ri·a (glôr′ē ə, glô′rē ə) 〚L, glory〛 a feminine name

Gluck (glook), **Chris·toph Wil·li·bald** (kris′tôf vil′i bält′) 1714-87; Ger. composer

God in monotheistic religions, the creator and ruler of the universe, regarded as eternal, infinite, all-powerful, and all-knowing; Supreme Being; the Almighty

Go·dard (gô dàr′: E gō där′), **Jean–Luc** (zhän lük′; E zhän lōōk′) 1930- ; Fr. motion-picture director

God·dard (gäd′ərd), **Robert Hutchings** 1882-1945; U.S. physicist

Gö·del (gō′dəl), **Kurt** (koort) 1906-78; U.S. mathematician, born in Czechoslovakia

God·frey (gäd′frē) 〚OFr *Godefrei* < OHG *Godafrid* < *god*, GOD + *fridu*, peace: hence, lit., peace (of) God〛 a masculine name: equiv. Ger. *Gottfried*

Godhead God: usually with *the*

Go·di·va (gə dī′və) *Eng. Legend* an 11th-cent. noblewoman of Coventry who, on the dare of her husband, rides naked through the streets on horseback so that he will abolish a heavy tax

Go·du·nov (gô′doo nôf′), **Bo·ris Feo·do·ro·vich** (bô rēs′ fyô′dô rô′vich) c. 1551-1605; czar of Russia (1598-1605)

God·win (gäd′win) 〚OE *Godewine*, friend (of) God: see EDWIN〛 **1** a masculine name **2 Mary Wollstonecraft** *see* WOLLSTONECRAFT, Mary **3 William** 1756-1836; Eng. political philosopher & writer

Goeb·bels (gö'bəls), **Joseph** (**Paul**) 1897-1945; Ger. Nazi propagandist

Goe·ring, Gö·ring (gö'riŋ), **Her·mann** (**Wilhelm**) (her'män) 1893-1946; Ger. Nazi field marshal

Goe·thals (gō'thəlz), **George Washington** 1858-1928; U.S. army officer & engineer: in charge of building the Panama Canal (1907-14)

Goe·the (gö'tə; *also Anglicized to* gʉr'tə, gāt'ə), **Jo·hann Wolf·gang von** (yō'hän vôlf'gäŋ fôn) 1749-1832; Ger. poet & dramatist

Gogh, Vincent van *see* VAN GOGH, Vincent

Go·gol (gô'gôl; *E* gō'gəl), **Ni·ko·lai Va·sil·ie·vich** (nē'kô li' vä sēl'yə vich) 1809-52; Russ. novelist & dramatist

Gold·i·locks (gōl'dē läks') a little girl in a folk tale who visits the home of three bears

Gol·ding (gōl' diŋ), **William Gerald** 1911-93; Brit. writer

Gol·do·ni (gôl dô'nē), **Car·lo** (kär'lô) 1707-93; It. dramatist

Gold·smith (gōld'smith), **Oliver** *c.* 1730-74; Brit. poet, playwright, & novelist, born in Ireland

Gold·wyn (gōld'win'), **Samuel** (born *Samuel Goldfish*) 1882-1974; U.S. motion-picture producer, born in Poland

Go·li·ath (gə lī'əth) ⟦LL(Ec) < Heb *golyat*⟧ *Bible* the Philistine giant killed by David with a stone shot from a sling: 1 Sam. 17:4, 49

Gom·pers (gäm'pərz), **Samuel** 1850-1924; U.S. labor leader, born in England

Gon·court (gōn kōōr') **1 Ed·mond Louis An·toine Hu·ot de** (ed môn' lwē' än twän' ü ō'də) 1822-96; Fr. novelist & art critic **2 Jules Al·fred Huot de** (zhül' ăl fred') 1830-70; Fr. novelist & art critic: brother of Edmond, with whom he collaborated

Gon·er·il (gän'ər il) in Shakespeare's *King Lear*, the elder of Lear's two cruel and disloyal daughters

Good·man (good'mən), **Ben·ny** (ben'ē) (born *Benjamin David Goodman*) 1909-86; U.S. clarinetist, jazz musician, & band leader

Good Shepherd *name for* JESUS: John 10:11

Good·year (good'yir'), **Charles** 1800-60; U.S. inventor: originated the process for vulcanizing rubber

Gor·ba·chev (gôr'bə chôf', gôr'bə chôf'), **Mi·kha·il S(ergeyevich)** (mē'khä ēl') 1931- ; general secretary of the Communist Party of the U.S.S.R. (1985-91)

Gor·don (gôrd″n) 〚Scot < surname *Gordon*〛 1 a masculine name 2 **Charles George** 1833-85; Brit. general in China, Egypt, & Sudan: called *Chinese Gordon*

Gore (gôr), **Albert** (**Arnold, Jr.**) 1948- ; vice president of the U.S. (1993-)

Gor·gas (gôr′gəs), **William Craw·ford** (krô′fərd) 1854-1920; U.S. army medical officer: chief sanitary officer in the Canal Zone during construction of the Panama Canal

Gor·gon (gôr′gən) 〚ME < L *Gorgo* (gen. *Gorgonis*) < Gr *Gorgō* < *gorgos*, terrible, fierce〛 *Gr. Myth.* any of three sisters with snakes for hair, so horrible that the beholder is turned to stone

Gor·ki, Gor·ky (gôr′kē), **Max·im** (mak′sim) (pseud. of *Aleksei Maximovich Peshkov*) 1868-1936; Russ. novelist & playwright

Gor·ky (gôr′kē), **Ar·shile** (är′shēl) (born *Vosdanig Manoog Adoian*) 1904-48: U.S. artist, born in Turkish Armenia

Go·ta·ma (gô′tə mə) *alt. sp. of* GAUTAMA: see BUDDHA

Gott·schalk (gät′shôk′), **Louis Mo·reau** (mô rō′) 1829-69; U.S. composer

Gou·dy (gou′dē), **Frederic William** 1865-1946; U.S. printer & designer of printing types

Gould (gōōld), **Jay** (born *Jason Gould*) 1836-92; U.S. financier

Gou·nod (gōō nō′; *E* gōō′nō), **Charles** (**François**) (shȧrl) 1818-93; Fr. composer

Gour·mont (gōōr mōn′), **Ré·my de** (rə mē′ də) 1858-1915; Fr. poet, novelist, & literary critic

Gow·er (gou′ər, gō′ər), **John** 1330-1408; Eng. poet

Go·ya (**y Lu·cien·tes**) (gô′yä ē lōō thyen′tās), **Fran·cis·co Jo·sé de** (frän thēs′kô hô se′ the) 1746-1828; Sp. painter

Grac·chus (grak′əs) 1 **Ga·ius Sem·pro·ni·us** (gā′əs sem prō′nē əs) 153-121 B.C.; Rom. statesman & social reformer 2 **Ti·ber·i·us Sempronius** (tī bir′ē əs) 163-133 B.C.; Rom. statesman and social reformer: brother of Gaius The two brothers are called **the Grac′chi** (-ī)

Grace (grās) 〚ModE *grace* < ME < OFr < L *gratia*, pleasing quality, favor, thanks < *gratus*, pleasing < IE base *gwer-*, to lift up the voice, praise〛 a feminine name: dim. *Gracie*

Grac·es (grās′iz) 〚transl. of L *Gratiae* (see prec.), transl.

of Gr *Charites*, pl. of *Charis* < *charis*, grace, beauty, kindness < *chairein*, to rejoice at < IE base **g̑her-*, to desire, like] *Gr. Myth.* the three sister goddesses who have control over pleasure, charm, and beauty in human life and in nature: Aglaia, Euphrosyne, and Thalia

Grae·ae (grē'ē') [[L < Gr *Graiai*, pl. of *graia*, old woman < *grais*, old, akin to *gēras*, old age]] *Gr. Myth.* the three old sisters who act as guards for the Gorgons and have only one eye and one tooth to share among them

Gra·ham (grā'əm) **1 Billy** (legal name *William Franklin Graham*) 1918- ; U.S. evangelist **2 Martha** *c.* 1893-1991; U.S. dancer & choreographer

Gra·hame (grā'əm), **Kenneth** 1859-1932; Brit. writer

Grai·ae (grī'ē', grā'ē') *var. of* GRAEAE

Gram·sci (gräm'shē), **An·to·nio** (än tô'nyô) 1891-1937; It. Communist leader & Marxist theoretician

Gra·na·dos (grə nä'dōs), **En·rique** (en rē'kä) 1867-1916; Sp. composer

Grant (grant) **1 Cary** (born *Archibald Leach*) 1904-86; U.S. motion-picture actor, born in England **2 Ulysses Simp·son** (simp'sən) (born *Hiram Ulysses Grant*) 1822-85; 18th president of the U.S. (1869-77): commander in chief of Union forces in the Civil War

Gran·ville–Bar·ker (gran'vil bär'kər), **Har·ley** (här'lē) 1877-1946; Eng. playwright, critic, & actor

Grass (gräs; *E* gräs), **Gün·ter** (**Wilhelm**) (gün'ter; *E* gōōn'tər) 1927- ; Ger. writer

Gra·tian (grā'shən) (L. name *Flavius Gratianus*) A.D. 359-383; Rom. emperor (375-383)

Grat·tan (grat''n), **Henry** 1746-1820; Ir. statesman

Graves (grāvz), **Robert** (**Ranke**) 1895-1985; Eng. poet, novelist, & critic

Gray (grā) **1 Asa** 1810-88; U.S. botanist **2 Thomas** 1716-71; Eng. poet

Greco, El *see* EL GRECO

Gree·ley (grē'lē), **Horace** 1811-72; U.S. journalist & political leader

Green (grēn) **1 John Richard** 1837-83; Eng. historian **2 Paul** (**Eliot**) 1894-1981; U.S. playwright **3 William** 1873-1952; U.S. labor leader

Green·a·way (grēn'ə wā'), **Kate** 1846-1901; Eng. painter & illustrator, esp. of children's books

Greene (grēn) **1 Graham** 1904-91; Eng. writer, esp. of novels **2 Nathanael** 1742-86; Am. general in the Revolutionary War **3 Robert** *c.* 1558-92; Eng. poet, dramatist, & pamphleteer

Gree·nough (grē′nō), **Horatio** 1805-52; U.S. sculptor

Greer (grir), **Ger·maine** (jər mān′) 1939- ; Austral. journalist, writer, & feminist

Greg·o·ry (greg′ər ē) ⟦LL *Gregorius* < Gr *Grēgorios*, lit., vigilant, hence, watchman < dial. form of *egeirein*, to awaken < IE base **ger-*, to grow, awaken ⟧ 1 a masculine name: dim. *Greg*; var. *Gregg*; equiv. Fr. *Gregoire*, Ger. & Scand. *Gregor*, It. & Sp. *Gregorio* **2 Gregory I** (*c.* A.D. 540-604); pope (590-604): his day is Sept. 3: called *the Great*: also called **St. Gregory I 3 Gregory VII** (born *Hildebrand*) *c.* 1020-85; pope (1073-85): his day is May 25: also called **St. Gregory VII 4 Gregory XIII** (born *Ugo Buoncompagni*) 1502-85; pope (1572-85) **5 Lady Augusta** (born *Isabella Augusta Persse*) 1852-1932; Ir. playwright

Gregory of Nys·sa (nis′ə), **Saint** (*c.* A.D. 335-*c.* 394); Gr. theologian & bishop in Cappadocia: his day is March 9: brother of Saint Basil

Gregory of Tours (toor), **Saint** (*c.* A.D. 538-*c.* 594); Frank. historian & bishop: his day is Nov. 17

Gren·del (gren′dəl) the male monster slain by BEOWULF

Gren·fell (gren′fel′), **Sir Wilfred Thom·a·son** (täm′ə sən) 1865-1940; Eng. physician, writer, & medical missionary to Labrador

Gret·a (gret′ə, grāt′ə) ⟦Swed or < Ger *Grete*⟧ a feminine name: see MARGARET

Gretch·en (grech′ən) ⟦Ger, dim. of *Margarete*⟧ a feminine name: see MARGARET

Greuze (grēz), **Jean Bap·tiste** (zhän bả tēst′) 1725-1805; Fr. painter

Grey (grā) **1 Charles** 2d Earl Grey, 1764-1845; Eng. statesman; prime minister (1830-34) **2 Lady Jane** Lady Jane Dudley, 1537-54; queen of England (July 10-19, 1553): beheaded **3 Zane** (zān) 1875-1939; U.S. novelist

Grieg (grēg; *Norw* grig), **Ed·vard** (**Hagerup**) (ed′värd; *Norw* ed′värt) 1843-1907; Norw. composer

Grif·fith (grif′ith) ⟦Welsh *Gruffydd* < ? L *Rufus*: see RUFUS⟧ 1 a masculine name **2 D(avid) (Lewelyn) W(ark)** 1875-1948; U.S. motion-picture producer & director

Grimm (grim) **1 Ja·kob** (**Ludwig Karl**) (yä′kôp) 1785-1863; Ger. philologist **2 Wil·helm** (**Karl**) (vil′helm) 1786-1859; Ger. philologist: brother of Jakob, with whom he collaborated in the collection of fairy tales

Grim Reaper, the death: often personified as a shrouded skeleton bearing a scythe

Gris (grēs), **Juan** (hwän) (born *José Victoriano González*) 1887-1927; Sp. painter, in France after 1906

Gri·sel·da (gri zel′də, -sel′-) ⟦Fr or It < Ger *Griseldis, Grishilda*⟧ **1** a feminine name **2** the heroine of various medieval tales, famous for her meek, long-suffering patience

Gro·my·ko (grō̂ mē′kō̂; *E* grə mē′kō) **An·drei An·dre·ye·vich** (än drā′ än drā′yi vich) 1909-89: Soviet diplomat

Gro·pi·us (grō′pē əs), **Walter** 1883-1969; U.S. architect, born in Germany: founder of the Bauhaus

Grosz (grōs), **George** 1893-1959; U.S. painter & caricaturist, born in Germany

Gro·ti·us (grō′shē əs), **Hugo** (born *Huigh de Groot*) 1583-1645; Du. scholar, jurist, & statesman

Grun·dy (grun′dē), **Mrs.** ⟦a neighbor repeatedly referred to (but never appearing) in Tom Morton's play *Speed the Plough* (1798) with the question "What will Mrs. Grundy say?"⟧ *personification of* conventional social disapproval, prudishness, narrow-mindedness, etc.

Grü·ne·wald (grü′nə vält′), **Mat·thi·as** (mä tē′äs) (born *Mathis Gothardt*) c. 1470-1528; Ger. painter

Guar·ne·ri (gwär ne′rē) **1** (L. name *Guarnerius*) name of a family of violin-makers of Cremona, Italy (fl. 17th-18th cent.) **2 Giu·sep·pe An·to·nio** (jōō zep′pe än tô′nyô) c. 1687-1745; It. violin-maker

Gud·run (gōōd′rōōn′) ⟦ON *Guthrūn* < *guthr*, war, battle + *runa*, close friend (secret-sharer) < ON *rūn*, secret, mystery, runic character < IE echoic base *reu-*, hoarse sound, roar, grumble⟧ the daughter of the Nibelung king: she lures Sigurd away from the Valkyrie Brynhild and marries him

Gue·va·ra (gä vär′ə), **Che** (chā) (born *Ernesto Guevara*) 1928-67; Cuban revolutionary leader, born in Argentina

Gui·do d'A·rez·zo (gwē′dô dä ret′tsô) c. 990-c. 1050; It. monk & musical theoretician: also called **Guido Aretino**

Guin·e·vere (gwin'ə vir') 〚< Celt; first element < Welsh *gwen*, white 〛 **1** a feminine name **2** *Arthurian Legend* the wife of King Arthur and mistress of Lancelot Also sp. **Guin'e·ver**

Guin·ness (gin'əs), Sir Al·ec (al'ik) 1914- ; Eng. actor

Guise (gēz) **1** name of a Fr. ducal family of the 16th & 17th cent. **2 Fran·çois de Lor·raine** (frän swå' də lô ren') 2d Duc de Guise 1519-63; statesman **3 Hen·ri de Lorraine** (än rē') 3d Duc de Guise 1550-88; statesman: son of François

Gun·nar (goon'när') 〚ON *Gunnarr* < *gunnr*, older form of *guthr*, war 〛 the brother of Gudrun and husband of Brynhild

Gun·ther (goon'tər) 〚Ger < Gmc **gund-*, **gunt-*, war (> ON *gunnr, guthr*) + **har-* (> OE *here*), army 〛 in the *Nibelungenlied*, a king of Burgundy and husband of Brunhild

Gus·taf V (goos'täf) 1858-1950; king of Sweden (1907-50): also called **Gustav** (or **Gustavus**)

Gustaf VI (Adolf) 1882-1973; king of Sweden (1950-73): also called **Gustav** (or **Gustavus**) **VI**

Gus·ta·vus (gəs tā'vəs, gəs tä'vəs) **1** name of six kings of Sweden **2 Gustavus I** (born *Gustavus Eriksson Vasa*) 1496-1560; king of Sweden (1523-60) **3 Gustavus II** (born *Gustavus Adolphus*) 1594-1632; king of Sweden (1611-32): grandson of Gustavus I **4 Gustavus III** 1746-92; king of Sweden (1711-92) **5 Gustavus IV** 1778-1837; king of Sweden (1792-1809); deposed: son of Gustavus III See also GUSTAF V & GUSTAF VI (ADOLF)

Gu·ten·berg (goot''n burg'), **Jo·hann** (yō'hän) (born *Johannes Gensfleisch*) c. 1400-68; Ger. printer: reputedly the first European to print with movable type

Guth·rie (guth'rē), **Woodrow Wilson** (called *Woody*) 1912-67; U.S. folk singer, guitarist, & composer

Guy (gī; Fr gē) 〚Fr *Gui, Guy*, lit., leader 〛 a masculine name: equiv. It. & Sp. *Guido*

Gwen·do·line (gwen'də lən) 〚< Celt: see GUINEVERE 〛 a feminine name: dim. *Gwen*; var. *Gwendolyn*

Gwin·nett (gwi net'), **But·ton** (but''n) c. 1735-77; Am. patriot, born in England: signer of the Declaration of Independence

Gwyn, Gwynne (gwin), **Nell** (born *Eleanor Gwyn*) 1650-87; Eng. actress: mistress of Charles II

H

Haa·kon VII (hô'koon) 1872-1957; king of Norway (1905-57)

Ha·bak·kuk (hab'ə kuk', hə bak'ək) ⟦Heb Ḥabhaqqūq, prob. < ḥābaq, to embrace⟧ *Bible* a Hebrew prophet of *c*. 7th cent. B.C.

Ha·ber (hä'bər), **Fritz** (frits) 1868-1934; Ger. chemist

Ha·ber·mas (hä'bər mäs), **Jur·gen** (yür'gən) 1929- ; Ger. philosopher & sociologist

Habs·burg (haps'bʉrg'; *Ger* häps'boͦorkh) *alt. sp.* of HAPSBURG

Ha·des (hā'dēz') ⟦Gr *Haidēs*⟧ *Gr. Myth.* the god of the underworld

Ha·dri·an (hā'drē ən) (L. name *Publius Aelius Hadrianus*) A.D. 76-138; Rom. emperor (117-138)

Haeck·el (hek'əl), **Ernst Hein·rich** (ernst hīn'riH) 1834-1919; Ger. biologist & philosopher

Ha·fiz (hä fiz') (born *Shams-ud-Din Mohammed*) *c.* 1325-*c.* 1390; Pers. lyric poet

Ha·gar (*for 1* hā'gär', -gər; *for 2* hā'gär') ⟦Heb *Hāghār*, lit., prob. fugitive⟧ **1** a feminine and masculine name **2** *Bible* a concubine of Abraham and slave of Abraham's wife Sarah: see ISHMAEL

Ha·gen (hä'gən) ⟦Ger⟧ in the *Nibelungenlied*, Gunther's uncle, who murders Siegfried at Brunhild's bidding

Hag·ga·i (hag'ā ī', hag'ī') ⟦Heb *Ḥaggai*, lit., festal⟧ *Bible* a Hebrew prophet of *c.* 6th cent. B.C.

Hag·gard (hag'ərd), **Sir H(enry) Rid·er** (rīd'ər) 1856-1925; Eng. novelist

Hahn (hän), **Otto** 1879-1968; Ger. nuclear physicist

Hah·ne·mann (hä'nə mən), **(Christian Friedrich) Samuel** 1755-1843; Ger. physician: founder of homeopathy

Haig (hāg), **Douglas** 1st Earl Haig 1861-1928; Brit. commander in chief, World War I

Hai·le Se·las·sie (hī'lē sə las'ē, -läs'ē) (born *Tafari Makonnen*) 1892-1975; emperor of Ethiopia (1930-36; 1941-74): deposed

Hak·luyt (hak'loͦot), **Richard** *c.* 1552-1616; Eng. geographer & chronicler of explorations & discoveries

Hal·dane (hôl'dān) **1** J(ohn) B(urdon) S(anderson) 1892-

1964; Eng. biologist & writer **2 Richard Bur·don** (bûr´dən) 1st Viscount Haldane of Cloan 1856-1928; Scot. statesman & philosopher: uncle of J. B. S. Haldane

Hale (hāl) **1 Edward Everett** 1822-1909; U.S. clergyman & writer **2 George El·ler·y** (el´ər ē) 1868-1938; U.S. astronomer **3 Nathan** 1755-76; Am. soldier in the Revolutionary War: hanged by the British as a spy

Ha·lé·vy (à lā vē´), **Jacques** (zhȧk) (born *Jacques François Fromental Élie Lévy*) 1799-1862; Fr. composer

Hall (hôl) **1 Charles Martin** 1863-1914; U.S. chemist: discovered electrolytic process for reducing aluminum from bauxite **2 G(ranville) Stanley** 1844-1924; U.S. psychologist & educator

Hal·lam (hal´əm), **Henry** 1777-1859; Eng. historian

Hals (häls), **Frans** (fräns) 1580-1666; Du. painter

Hal·sey (hôl´zē), **William Frederick** 1882-1959; U.S. admiral

Ham (ham) *Bible* Noah's second son: Gen. 6:10

Ha·man (hā´mən) *Bible* a Persian official who sought the destruction of the Jews and was hanged when his plot was exposed to Ahasuerus by Esther: Esth. 7

Ha·mil·car Bar·ca (hə mil´kär bär´kə; ham´əl kär´) *c.* 270-*c.* 228 B.C.; Carthaginian general: father of Hannibal

Ham·il·ton (ham´əl tən) **1 Alexander** *c.* 1755-1804; Am. statesman: 1st secretary of the U.S. treasury (1789-95) **2 Edith** 1867-1963; U.S. educator, writer, & classical scholar **3 Emma Lady** (born *Amy Lyon*) *c.* 1765-1815; mistress of Lord Nelson

Ham·let (ham´lit) the title character of a play by Shakespeare: Hamlet is a Danish prince who avenges the murder of his father, the king, by killing his uncle Claudius, the murderer

Ham·mar·skjöld (häm´àr shüld´), **Dag (Hjalmar Agne Carl)** (dȧg) 1905-61; Swed. statesman: secretary-general of the United Nations (1953-61)

Ham·mer·stein II (ham´ər stīn´), **Oscar** 1895-1960; U.S. librettist & lyricist of musical comedies

Ham·mu·ra·bi (hä´moo rä´bē, ham´ə-) fl. 18th cent. B.C.; king of Babylon: a famous code of laws is attributed to him

Hamp·ton (hamp´tən, ham´-), **Wade** 1818-1902; U.S. politician & Confederate general

Ham·sun (häm´soon; *E* ham´sən), **Knut** (knōōt) (born

Knut Pedersen) 1859-1952; Norw. novelist

Han·cock (han′käk) **1 John** 1737-93; Am. statesman: president of the Continental Congress (1775-77) & 1st signer of the Declaration of Independence **2 Win·field Scott** (win′fēld) 1824-86; Union general in the Civil War

Hand (hand), **(Billings) Lear·ned** (lʉr′nid) 1872-1961; U.S. jurist

Han·del (han′dəl), **George Fri·der·ic** (frē′dər ik, -drik) (born *Georg Friedrich Händel*) 1685-1759; Eng. composer, born in Germany

Han·dy (han′dē), **W(illiam) C(hristopher)** 1873-1958; U.S. jazz musician & composer

Han·na (han′ə), **Mark** (born *Marcus Alonzo Hanna*) 1837-1904; U.S. financier & politician

Han·nah, Han·na (han′ə) ‖ Heb *Ḥannáh*, lit., graciousness ‖ **1** a feminine name: see ANNA, JOAN **2** *Bible* the mother of Samuel: 1 Sam. 1:20

Han·ni·bal (han′ə bəl) 247-*c.* 183 B.C.; Carthaginian general: crossed the Alps to invade Italy in 218 B.C.

Han·o·ver (han′ō vər) name of the ruling family of England (1714-1901), founded by George I, orig. Elector of Hanover

Hans (hans, hanz; *Ger* häns) ‖ *Ger* abbrev. of *Johannes*: equivalent to JACK ‖ a masculine name

Han·son (han′sən), **Howard** 1896-1981; U.S. composer

Haps·burg (haps′bʉrg′; *Ger* häps′bōōrkh) name of a ruling family of Austria & Austria-Hungary (1278-1918), of Spain (1516-1700), & of the Holy Roman Empire (1438-1806)

Har·ald (har′əld; *Norw* hä′rəld) 1937- ; king of Norway (1991-)

Har·ding (här′diŋ), **Warren Gamaliel** 1865-1923; 29th president of the U.S. (1921-23)

Har·dy (här′dē) **1 Oliver** 1892-1957; U.S. motion-picture comedian **2 Thomas** 1840-1928; Eng. novelist & poet

Har·greaves (här′grēvz, -grāvz), **James** died 1778; Eng. inventor of the spinning jenny

Har·lan (här′lən) **1** ‖ < the surname *Harlan* ‖ a masculine name **2 John Marshall** 1899-1971; U.S. jurist; associate justice, Supreme Court (1955-71)

Har·le·quin (här′li kwin, -kin) ‖ Fr *harlequin*, *arlequin* < OFr *hierlekin*, *hellequin*, demon: Fr sense & form infl. by It *arlecchino* < same OFr source ‖ a traditional comic character in pantomime, who wears a mask and gay, spangled, diamond-patterned tights of many colors, and sometimes carries a wooden wand or sword

Har·mo·ni·a (här mō'nē ə) ‖ L < Gr < *harmos*, a fitting < IE base **ar-*, to fit (together) ‖ *Gr. Myth.* **1** the daughter of Aphrodite and Ares, and wife of Cadmus **2** *personification of* harmony and order

Harms·worth (härmz'wurth'), **Alfred Charles William** *see* NORTHCLIFFE, Viscount

Har·old (har'əld) ‖ OE *Hereweald* & *Harald* < ON *Haraldr*, both < Gmc **Hariwald*, lit., army chief < **harja-*, army (OE *here*, OHG *heri*) + **waldan*, to rule ‖ **1** a masculine name: dim. *Hal* **2 Harold I** died 1040; king of England (1035-40): son of Canute: called **Harold Harefoot 3 Harold II** *c.* 1022-66; last Saxon king of England (1066): killed in the Battle of Hastings

Har·ri·et (har'ē it) ‖ fem. dim. of HARRY ‖ a feminine name: dim. *Hattie*: see HARRY

Har·ri·man (har'ə mən) **1 Edward Henry** 1849-1909; U.S. financier & railroad magnate **2 W(illiam) Averell** 1891-1986; U.S. diplomat, politician, & businessman: son of Edward Henry

Har·ris (har'is) **1 Joel Chandler** 1848-1908; U.S. writer: author of the *Uncle Remus* stories **2 Roy (Ellsworth)** 1898-1979; U.S. composer

Har·ri·son (har'ə sən) **1 Benjamin** *c.* 1726-91; Am. Revolutionary patriot: signer of the Declaration of Independence: father of William Henry **2 Benjamin** 1833-1901; 23d president of the U.S. (1889-93): grandson of William Henry **3 William Henry** 1773-1841: U.S. general; 9th president of the U.S. (1841): called *Tippecanoe*

Har·ry (har'ē) ‖ ME *Herry* < HENRY ‖ a masculine name: fem. *Harriet*

Harte (härt), **Bret** (bret) (born *Francis Brett Hart*) 1836-1902; U.S. writer, esp. of short stories

Ha·run ar–Ra·shid (hä rōōn' är rä shēd') *c.* A.D. 764-809; caliph of Baghdad (786-809): given popular fame as a hero of the *Arabian Nights*

Har·vard (här'vərd), **John** 1607-38; Eng. clergyman, in America: 1st benefactor of Harvard College

Har·vey (här'vē) ‖ Fr *Hervé* < OHG *Herewig*, lit., army battle < Gmc **harja*, army + **wig-*, fight, akin to OE *wig* < IE base **weik-* ‖ **1** a masculine name **2 William** 1578-1657; Eng. physician: discovered the circulation of the blood

Has·dru·bal (haz'droŏ bəl) **1** died 221 B.C.; Carthaginian general: brother-in-law of Hannibal **2** died 207 B.C.; Carthaginian general: crossed the Alps (207) to aid Hannibal, his brother: son of Hamilcar Barca

Ha·šek (hä'shek), **Ja·ro·slav** (yä'rō släf') 1883-1923; Czech writer

Has·sam (has'əm), **(Frederick) Childe** (child) 1859-1935; U.S. painter & etcher

Has·sel (häs'əl), **Odd** (ôd) 1897-1981; Norw. chemist

Has·tings (hās'tiŋz), **Warren** 1732-1818; Eng. statesman: 1st governor general of India (1773-84)

Hath·a·way (hath'ə wā'), **Anne** *c.* 1557-1623; maiden name of the wife of William Shakespeare

Hath·or (hath'ôr') ‖ Gr *Hathōr* < Egypt. *Ḥet-Ḥert*, lit., the house above ‖ *Egypt. Myth.* the goddess of love, mirth, and joy, usually represented as having the head or ears of a cow

Hat·tie (hat'ē) a feminine name: see HARRIET

Haupt·mann (houpt'män), **Ger·hart** (ger'härt) 1862-1946; Ger. dramatist, novelist, & poet

Haw·kins (hô'kinz), **Coleman** 1907-69; U.S. jazz musician

Ha·worth (härth, hou'ərth), **Sir (Walter) Norman** 1883-1950; Brit. organic chemist

Haw·thorne (hô'thôrn'), **Nathaniel** 1804-64; U.S. novelist & short-story writer

Hay (hā), **John (Milton)** 1838-1905; U.S. statesman & writer: secretary of state (1898-1905)

Hay·dn (hīd'n), **(Franz) Jo·seph** (yō'zef) 1732-1809; Austrian composer

Ha·yek (hī'ək, hä'yek), **Friedrich August von** 1899-1992; Brit. economist, born in Austria

Hayes (hāz) **1 Helen** (born *Helen Hayes Brown*) 1900-93; U.S. actress **2 Ruth·er·ford B(irchard)** (ruth'ər fərd) 1822-93; 19th president of the U.S. (1877-81)

Hays (hāz), **Arthur Garfield** 1881-1954; U.S. lawyer & civil libertarian

Ha·zel (hā'zəl) ‖ Heb *Hazā'el*, lit., God sees ‖ a feminine name

Haz·litt (haz'lit), **William** 1778-1830; Eng. essayist

Hearn (hurn), **Laf·cad·i·o** (laf kad'ē ō) (born *Patricio*

Lafcadio Tessima Carlos Hearn; Jpn. name *Yakumo Koizumi*) 1850-1904; U.S. writer, born in Greece: became a citizen of Japan (*c.* 1890)

Hearst (hurst), **William Randolph** 1863-1951; U.S. newspaper & magazine publisher

Heath (hēth), **Edward** (**Richard George**) 1916- ; Eng. politician: prime minister (1970-74)

Heath·er (he*th*′ər) a feminine name

He·be (hē′bē) ⟦L < Gr *Hēbē* < *hēbē*, youth⟧ *Gr. Myth.* the goddess of youth, daughter of Hera and Zeus: she is a cupbearer to the gods

Hec·a·te (hek′ə tē, hek′it) ⟦L < Gr *Hekatē*⟧ *Gr. Myth.* a goddess of the moon, earth, and underground realm of the dead, later regarded as the goddess of sorcery and witchcraft

Hec·tor (hek′tər) ⟦L < Gr *Hektōr*, lit., holding fast < *echein*, to hold, have⟧ **1** a masculine name **2** in Homer's *Iliad*, the greatest Trojan hero, killed by Achilles to avenge the death of Patroclus: he is Priam's oldest son

Hec·u·ba (hek′yōō bə) ⟦L < Gr *Hekabē*⟧ in Homer's *Iliad*, wife of Priam and mother of Hector, Troilus, Paris, and Cassandra

He·gel (hā′gəl), **Ge·org Wil·helm Frie·drich** (gā ôrkh′ vil′helm frē′driH) 1770-1831; Ger. philosopher

Hei·deg·ger (hī′di gər), **Martin** 1889-1976; Ger. existentialist philosopher

Hei·di (hī′dē) a feminine name

Hei·fetz (hī′fits), **Ja·scha** (yä′shə) 1901-87; U.S. violinist, born in Russia

Heim·dall (hām′däl′) ⟦ON *Heimdallr*⟧ *Norse Myth.* the watchman of Asgard, home of the gods

Hei·ne (hī′nə), **Hein·rich** (hīn′riH) 1797-1856; Ger. poet & essayist

Hei·sen·berg (hī′zən berkh), **Wer·ner** (**Karl**) (ver′nər) 1901-76; Ger. theoretical & nuclear physicist

Hek·a·te (hek′ə tē) HECATE

Hel (hel) ⟦ON⟧ *Norse Myth.* Loki's daughter, goddess of death and the underworld

Hel·en (hel′ən) ⟦< Fr or L: Fr *Hélène* < L *Helena* < Gr *Helenē*, lit., torch⟧ a feminine name: dim. *Nell, Nelly, Lena;* var. *Helena, Ellen, Eleanor;* equiv. Fr. *Hélène, Elaine,* It. & Sp. *Elena*

Hel·e·na (hel′i nə, hə lē′nə) a feminine name: see

HELEN

Helen of Troy (troi) *Gr. Legend* the beautiful wife of Menelaus, king of Sparta: the Trojan War is started because of her abduction by Paris to Troy

He·li·o·gab·a·lus (hē'lē ə gab'ə ləs) *var. of* ELAGABALUS

He·li·os (hē'lē äs') 〚Gr *hēlios*, the sun < IE base **sāwel-, *swel-, *sun-*, sun > L *sol*, ON *sol*〛 *Gr. Myth.* the sun god, son of Hyperion: later identified with Apollo

Hel·le (hel'ē) 〚L < Gr *Hellē*〛 *Gr. Legend* a girl who, while fleeing with her brother on a ram with golden fleece, falls off and drowns in the Hellespont

Hel·len (hel'ən) 〚L < Gr *Hellēn*〛 *Gr. Legend* the ancestor of the Hellenes, a son of Deucalion and Pyrrha

Hell·man (hel'mən), **Lillian** 1905-84; U.S. playwright

Helm·holtz (helm'hōlts'), **Her·mann Lud·wig Fer·di·nand von** (her'män lŏŏt'vikh fer'di nänt' fôn) 1821-94; Ger. physiologist & physicist

Hel·o·ise (hel'ō ēz', hel'ō ēz') a feminine name: see ELO-ISE

Hé·lo·ïse (ā lô ēz'; *E* hel'ō ēz') 1101-64; mistress &, later, wife of her teacher, Pierre Abélard

Hel·vé·tius (el vā syüs'; *E* hel vē'shē əs), **Claude A·dri·en** (klōd á drē an') 1715-71; Fr. philosopher

Hem·ing·way (hem'iŋ wā'), **Ernest** 1899-1961; U.S. novelist & short-story writer

Hen·drix (hen'driks), **Jim·i** (jim'ē) (born *Johnny Allen Hendrix*) 1942-70; U.S. rock singer, composer, & guitarist

Hen·gist (heŋ'gist) 〚OE < *hengest*, stallion, akin to Ger *hengst* < IE base **kak-*, to leap, spurt forth〛 died A.D. 488; Jute chief; with his brother Horsa (died 455), he is reputed to have led the first Germanic invasion of England & to have founded the kingdom of Kent

Hen·ri·et·ta (hen'rē et'ə) 〚Fr *Henriette*, dim. of *Henri*: see fol.〛 a feminine name: dim. *Etta, Hetty, Nettie, Netty*

Hen·ry (hen'rē) 〚Fr *Henri* < Ger *Heinrich* < OHG *Haganrih*, lit., ruler of an enclosure & also altered < OHG *Heimerich*, lit., home ruler (< *heim*, home)〛 **1** a masculine name: dim. *Hal, Hank, Henny*; var. *Harry*; equiv. L. *Henricus*, Du. *Hendrik*, Fr. *Henri*, Ger. *Heinrich*, It. *Enrico*, Sp. *Enrique*; fem. *Henrietta* **2** 1394-1460; prince of Portugal: called *Henry the Navi-*

gator **3 Henry I** 1068-1135; king of England (1100-35): son of William the Conqueror **4 Henry II** 1133-89; king of England (1154-89): 1st Plantagenet king **5 Henry III** 1207-72; king of England (1216-72) **6 Henry III** 1551-89; king of France (1574-89) **7 Henry IV** 1050-1106; king of Germany (1056-1105) & Holy Roman Emperor (1084-1105): dethroned **8 Henry IV** 1367-1413; king of England (1399-1413): 1st Lancastrian king: son of John of Gaunt: called *Bolingbroke* **9 Henry IV** 1553-1610; king of France (1589-1610): 1st Bourbon king: called *Henry of Navarre* **10 Henry V** 1387-1422; king of England (1413-22): defeated the French at Agincourt **11 Henry VI** 1421-71; king of England (1422-61; 1470-71) **12 Henry VII** 1457-1509; king of England (1485-1509): 1st Tudor king **13 Henry VIII** 1491-1547; king of England (1509-47): broke with the papacy and established the Church of England **14 O.** (pseud. of *William Sydney Porter*) 1862-1910; U.S. short-story writer **15 Patrick** 1736-99; Am. patriot, statesman, & orator

Hen·ze (hent′sə), **Hans Wer·ner** (häns ver′nər) 1926- ; Ger. composer

Hep·burn (hep′burn′), **Katharine** 1909- ; U.S. actress

He·phaes·tus (hē fes′təs) ⟦ Gr *Hēphaistos* ⟧ *Gr. Myth.* the god of fire and the forge, son of Zeus and Hera: see VULCAN

Hep·worth (hep′wurth), Dame **Barbara** 1903-75; Brit. sculptor

He·ra (hir′ə, hē′rə) ⟦ L < Gr *Hēra, Hērē*, lit., protectress, akin to *hērōs*, hero ⟧ *Gr. Myth.* the sister and wife of Zeus, queen of the gods, and goddess of women and marriage: identified with the Roman Juno

Her·a·cli·tus (her′ə klīt′əs) fl. about 500 B.C.; Gr. philosopher

Her·a·cli·us (her′ə klī′əs, hi rak′lē əs) *c.* A.D. 575-641; Byzantine emperor (610-641)

Her·a·kles, Her·a·cles (her′ə klēz′) HERCULES

Her·bart (her′bärt; *E* hur′bärt), **Jo·hann Frie·drich** (yō′hän frē′driH) 1776-1841; Ger. philosopher & educator

Her·bert (hur′bərt) ⟦ OE *Herebeorht*, lit., bright army < *here* (see HAROLD) + *beorht*, bright ⟧ **1** a masculine name: dim. **Herb, Bert 2 George** 1593-1633; Eng. poet & clergyman **3 Victor** 1859-1924; U.S. composer & conductor, born in Ireland

Her·cu·les (hur′kyōō lēz′) ⟦L < Gr *Hērakleēs* < *Hēra*, HERA + *kleos*, glory⟧ *Gr. & Rom. Myth.* the son of Zeus and Alcmene, renowned for his strength and courage, esp. as shown in his performance of twelve labors imposed on him

Her·man (hur′mən) ⟦Ger *Hermann* < OHG *Hariman* < *heri*, army (see HAROLD) + *man*, man⟧ a masculine name: equiv. Fr. *Armand*, Ger. *Hermann*, It. *Ermanno*

Her·maph·ro·di·tus (hər maf′rō dīt′əs) ⟦L < Gr *Hermaphroditos*⟧ *Gr. Myth.* the son of Hermes and Aphrodite: while bathing, he becomes united in a single body with a nymph

Her·mes (hur′mēz′) ⟦L < Gr *Hermēs*⟧ *Gr. Myth.* the god who serves as herald and messenger of the other gods, generally pictured with winged shoes and hat, carrying a caduceus: he is also the god of science, commerce, eloquence, and cunning, and guide of departed souls to Hades: identified with the Roman Mercury

Hermes Tris·me·gis·tus (tris′mə jis′təs) ⟦Gr *Hermēs trismegistos*, lit., Hermes the thrice greatest⟧ *Gr. name for* THOTH

Her·mi·o·ne (hər mī′ə nē) *Gr. Legend* the daughter of Menelaus and Helen of Troy

He·ro (hē′rō′, hir′ō) ⟦L < Gr *Hērō*⟧ **1** *Gr. Legend* a priestess of Aphrodite at Sestos: her lover, Leander, swims the Hellespont from Abydos every night to be with her; when he drowns in a storm, Hero throws herself into the sea **2** HERON

Her·od (her′əd) ⟦L *Herodes* < Gr *Hērōdēs*⟧ *c.* 73-4 B.C.; Idumaean king of Judea (37-4): called *Herod the Great*

Herod Agrippa I *c.* 10 B.C.-A.D. 44; king of Judea (A.D. 37-44): grandson of Herod (the Great)

Herod An·ti·pas (an′ti pas′) died *c.* A.D. 40; tetrarch of Galilee (*c.* 4 B.C.-A.D. 39): son of Herod (the Great)

He·ro·di·as (hə rō′dē əs) *Bible* the second wife of Herod Antipas & mother of Salome: Mark 6:17-28

He·rod·o·tus (hə räd′ə təs) *c.* 484-*c.* 425 B.C.; Gr. historian: called the *Father of History*

Her·on (hir′än) fl. 3d cent. A.D.; Gr. mathematician & inventor: also called **Heron of Al·ex·an·dri·a** (al′ig zan′ drē ə)

Her·re·ra (e re′rä), **Fran·cis·co de** (frän thēs′kô *the*) *c.* 1576-*c.* 1656; Sp. painter: called *El Viejo* (the Elder)

Her·rick (her′ik), **Robert** 1591-1674; Eng. poet

Her·schel (hur'shəl) **1** Sir **John Frederick William** 1792-1871; Eng. astronomer, chemist, & physicist: son of Sir William **2** Sir **William** (born *Friedrich Wilhelm Herschel*) 1738-1822; Eng. astronomer, born in Germany

Hertz (herts; *E* hurts), **Hein·rich Ru·dolf** (hīn'riH rōō'dôlf) 1857-94; Ger. physicist

Herz·berg (hurts'bərg), **Ger·hard** (ger'härt) 1904- ; Cdn. physicist, born in Germany

Herzl (her'ts'l), **The·o·dor** (tā'ô dôr') 1860-1904; Austrian writer, born in Hungary: founder of Zionism

He·si·od (hē'sē əd, hes'ē-) fl. 8th cent. B.C.; Gr. poet

Hess (hes), **(Walther Richard) Ru·dolf** (rōō'dôlf) 1894-1987; Ger. Nazi leader

Hesse (hes'ə), **Her·mann** (her'män) 1877-1962; Ger. novelist in Switzerland

Hes·ter (hes'tər) a feminine name: see ESTHER

Hes·ti·a (hes'tē ə) ⟦Gr⟧ *Gr. Myth.* the goddess of the hearth: identified with the Roman Vesta

Hey·rov·ský (hā'rôf'skē), **Ja·ro·slav** (yä'rō släf') 1890-1967; Czech chemist

Hez·e·ki·ah (hez'i kī'ə) ⟦Heb *ḥizqīyāh*, lit., God strengthens⟧ *Bible* a king of Judah in the time of Isaiah: 2 Kings 18-20

Hi·a·wa·tha (hī'ə wä'thə) the Indian hero of *The Song of Hiawatha*, a long narrative poem (1855) by Henry Wadsworth Longfellow: named for an Indian chief thought to have lived in the 16th cent.

Hick·ok (hik'äk), **James Butler** 1837-76; U.S. frontier scout & marshal: called *Wild Bill Hickok*

Hi·er·on·y·mus (hī'ə rän'ə məs) *see* JEROME, Saint

Hig·gin·son (hig'in sən), **Thomas Went·worth Stor·row** (went'wurth' stär'ō) 1823-1911; U.S. writer & social reformer

Hil·a·ry (hil'ə rē) ⟦L *Hilarius*, lit., cheerful < *hilaris*, *hilarus* < Gr *hilaros*, cheerful < IE base **sel-*, favorable, in good spirits⟧ a masculine and feminine name: var. *Hillary*: equiv. Fr. *Hilaire*

Hil·bert (hil'bərt; *Ger*, -bərt), **Da·vid** (*Ger* dä'vit) 1862-1943; Ger. mathematician

Hil·da (hil'də) ⟦Ger < Gmc **hild-*, battle, war < IE base **kel-*, to strike, split: often contr. of names containing base (e.g., *Hilde*gunde, Brun*hilde*)⟧ a feminine name

Hil·de·garde (hil'də gärd') ⟦Ger < Gmc **hild-*, battle (see prec.) + *gard-*, to protect < IE *gherdh-*, to enclose, surround < base *ĝher-*, to grasp, contain; hence, lit., battle protector ‖ a feminine name: see HILDA

Hill (hil), **James Jerome** 1838-1916; U.S. railroad magnate & financier, born in Canada

Hil·la·ry (hil′ər ē), Sir **Edmund Percival** 1919- ; New Zealand mountain climber & explorer

Hil·lel (hil′el, -əl) *c.* 60 B.C.-*c.* A.D. 10; Jewish rabbi & scholar in Jerusalem

Him·a·vat (him′ə vat′) ‖ Hindi ‖ *Hindu Myth.* the personification of the Himalayas and father of Devi

Himm·ler (him′lər), **Hein·rich** (hīn′riH) 1900-45; Ger. Nazi leader: head of the SS & the Gestapo

Hin·de·mith (hin′də məth; -mit), **Paul** 1895-1963; U.S. composer, born in Germany

Hin·den·burg (hin′dən burg′; *Ger,* -boorkh′), **Paul** (**Ludwig Hans Anton von Beneckendorff und**) **von** 1847-1934; Ger. field marshal: president of the Weimar Republic (1925-34)

Hines (hīnz), **Earl** (**Kenneth**) (called *Fatha*) 1905-83; U.S. jazz pianist & composer

Hin·shel·wood (hin′shəl wood′), Sir **Cyril Norman** 1897-1967; Brit. chemist

Hip·par·chus (hi pär′kəs) 2d cent. B.C.; Gr. astronomer

Hip·poc·ra·tes (hi päk′rə tēz′) *c.* 460-*c.* 377 B.C.; Gr. physician: called the *Father of Medicine*

Hip·pol·y·ta (hi päl′i tə) *Gr. Myth.* a queen of the Amazons, whose magic girdle is obtained by Hercules as one of his twelve labors: also **Hip·pol′y·te′** (-tē′)

Hip·pol·y·tus (hi päl′i təs) *Gr. Myth.* a son of Theseus: when he rejects the love of his stepmother, Phaedra, she turns Theseus against him by false accusations, and at Theseus' request, Poseidon brings about his death

Hip·pom·e·nes (hi päm′i nēz′) *Gr. Myth.* the youth who wins the race against ATALANTA

Hi·ram (hī′rəm) ‖ Heb *ḥirām*, prob. < *a'ḥīrām*, exalted brother ‖ a masculine name: dim. *Hi*

Hi·ro·hi·to (hir′ō hē′tō) 1901-89; emperor of Japan (1926-89)

Hi·ro·shi·ge (hir′ō shē′gā), **An·do** (än′dō) 1797-1858; Jpn. painter

Hiss (his), **Al·ger** (al′jər) 1904- ; U.S. public official: convicted of perjury

Hitch·cock (hich′käk), **Alfred** (**Joseph**) 1899-1980; Brit. film director

Hit·ler (hit′lər), **Adolf** 1889-1945; Nazi dictator of Germany (1933-45), born in Austria

Hob (häb) Robin Goodfellow, or Puck

Hob·be·ma (häb′ə mä), **Mein·dert** (mīn′dərt) 1638-1709; Du. painter

Hobbes (häbz), **Thomas** 1588-1679; Eng. social philosopher: author of *Leviathan*

Hob·gob·lin (häb′gäb′lin) Robin Goodfellow; Puck

Hob·son (häb′sən), **John Atkinson** 1858-1940; Eng. economist

Ho Chi Minh (hō′chē′min′) (born *Nguyen That Thanh*) 1890-1969; president of North Vietnam (1954-69)

Hock·ney (häk′nē), **David** 1937- ; Brit. painter

Hodg·kin (häj′kin) **1** Sir **Allan Lloyd** 1914- ; Brit. biophysicist **2 Dorothy Crow·foot** (krō′foot′) 1910- ; Brit. chemist

Hoff·mann (hôf′män), **Ernst The·o·dor Am·a·de·us** (ernst tā′ô dôr ä′mä dā′oos) 1776-1822; Ger. writer & composer

Hof·mann (häf′mən, hôf′-) **1 Hans** 1880-1966; U.S. painter, born in Germany **2 Ro·ald** (rō′äl) 1937- ; U.S. chemist, born in Poland

Hof·manns·thal (hôf′mäns täl′), **Hu·go von** (hoo′gô fôn) 1874-1929; Austrian playwright & poet

Hof·stadt·er (häf′stat′ər), **Richard** 1916-70; U.S. historian

Ho·gan (hō′gən), **Ben** (born *William Benjamin Hogan*) 1912- ; U.S. golfer

Ho·garth (hō′gärth), **William** 1697-1764; Eng. painter & engraver: known for his satirical pictures of 18th-cent. English life

Hogg (hôg, häg), **James** 1770-1835; Scot. poet

Hoh·en·stau·fen (hō′ən shtou′fən) name of the ruling family of Germany (1138-1208; 1215-54) & of Sicily (1194-1268)

Hoh·en·zol·lern (hō′ən tsôl′ərn; *E*, -zäl′ərn) name of the ruling family of Brandenburg (1415-1918), of Prussia (1701-1918), & of Germany (1871-1918)

Ho·ku·sai (hō′koo sī′), **Ka·tsu·shi·ka** (kä′tsoo shē′kä) 1760-1849; Jpn. painter & wood engraver

Hol·bein (hōl′bīn) **1 Hans** *c.* 1465-1524; Ger. painter:

called *the Elder* **2 Hans** *c.* 1497-1543; Ger. portrait painter in England: son of Hans Holbein (the Elder): called *the Younger*

Hol·i·day (häl'ə dā'), **Billie** (born *Eleonora Fagan Holiday*) 1915-59; U.S. jazz singer: called *Lady Day*

Ho·lins·hed (häl'inz hed', -in shed'), **Raphael** died *c.* 1580; Eng. chronicler: also **Hol·lings·head** (häl'iŋz hed')

Hol·land (häl'ənd), **John Philip** 1840-1914; U.S. inventor, born in Ireland: developed U.S. Navy's 1st submarine

Hol·ly (häl'ē) a feminine name

Holmes (hōmz, hōlmz) **1 John Haynes** (hānz) 1879-1964; U.S. clergyman & reformer **2 Oliver Wen·dell** (wen'dəl) 1809-94; U.S. writer & physician **3 Oliver Wendell** 1841-1935; associate justice, U.S. Supreme Court (1902-32): son of the writer **4 Sherlock** *see* SHERLOCK HOLMES

Hol·o·fer·nes (häl'ə fur'nēz') a general of Nebuchadnezzar's army, killed by Judith: see JUDITH

Holst (hōlst), **Gus·tav** (**Theodore**) (goos'täv) 1874-1934; Eng. composer

Ho·mer (hō'mər) ⟦L *Homerus* < Gr *Homēros* < *homēros*, a pledge, hostage, one led, hence blind⟧ **1** a masculine name **2** semilegendary Gr. epic poet of *c.* 8th cent. B.C.: the *Iliad* & the *Odyssey* are both attributed to him **3 Winslow** 1836-1910; U.S. painter

Ho·neg·ger (hän'ə gər, hō'neg ər; *Fr* ô ne ger'), **Arthur** 1892-1955; Fr. composer

Hooch (hōkh), **Pie·ter de** (pē'tər də) *c.* 1629-*c.* 1684; Du. painter

Hood (hood) **1 John Bell** 1831-79; Confederate general **2 Robin** *see* ROBIN HOOD **3 Thomas** 1799-1845; Eng. poet & humorist

Hoogh (hōkh), **Pieter de** *var. of* Pieter de HOOCH

Hooke (hook), **Robert** 1635-1703; Eng. physicist, mathematician, & inventor

Hook·er (hook'ər) **1 Joseph** 1814-79; Union general in the Civil War **2 Richard** 1554-1600; Eng. clergyman & writer **3 Thomas** *c.* 1586-1647; Eng. Puritan clergyman, in America after 1633

Hoo·ver (hoo'vər) **1 Herbert Clark** 1874-1964; 31st president of the U.S. (1929-33) **2 J(ohn) Edgar** 1895-1972; U.S. government official: director of the FBI

(1924-72)

Hope (hōp) **1** ‖ < ModE *hope* < OE *hopa* ‖ a feminine name **2 Anthony** (pseud. of *Sir Anthony Hope Hawkins*) 1863-1933; Eng. novelist

Hopkins (häp′kinz) **1** Sir Frederick Gow·land (gou′lənd) 1861-1947; Eng. biochemist **2 Gerard Man·ley** (man′lē) 1844-89; Eng. poet & Jesuit priest **3 Johns** 1795-1873; U.S. financier & philanthropist **4 Mark** 1802-87; U.S. educator

Hop·kin·son (häp′kin sən), **Francis** 1737-91; Am. jurist & poet: signer of the Declaration of Independence

Hop·per (häp′ər), **Edward** 1882-1967; U.S. painter

Hor·ace (hôr′is, här′-) ‖ < L *Horatius* ‖ **1** a masculine name: see HORATIO **2** (L. name *Quintus Horatius Flaccus*) 65-8 B.C.; Rom. poet: known for his odes

Ho·ra·ti·o (hō rā′shō, -shē ō′; hə-) ‖ altered (modeled on L) < It *Orazio* < L *Horatius*, name of a Roman gens ‖ a masculine name: var. *Horace*

Ho·ra·ti·us (hō rā′shəs, -shē əs; hə-) *Rom. Legend* a hero who defends a bridge over the Tiber against the Etruscans

Hor·o·witz (hôr′ə wits, här′-), **Vlad·i·mir** (vlad′ə mir′) 1904-89; U.S. pianist, born in Russia

Hor·sa (hôr′sə) ‖ OE ‖ see HENGIST

Hor·tense (hôr tens′, hôr′tens; *Fr* ôr täns′) ‖ Fr < L *Hortensia*, fem. of *Hortensius*, name of a Roman gens ‖ **1** a feminine name **2** (born *Hortense de Beauharnais*) 1783-1837; queen of Holland (1806-10): wife of Louis Bonaparte

Ho·rus (hō′rəs) ‖ L < Gr *Hōros* < Egypt. *Ḥeru*, hawk ‖ *Egypt. Myth.* the sun god, represented as having the head of a hawk: the son of Osiris and Isis

Ho·se·a (hō zē′ə, -zā′ə) ‖ Heb *hōshēa‘*, lit., salvation ‖ *Bible* a Hebrew prophet of the 8th cent. B.C.

Hou·din·i (hoo dē′nē), **Harry** (born *Ehrich Weiss*) 1874-1926; U.S. stage magician & escape artist

Hou·don (oo dōn′; *E* hoo′dän), **Jean An·toine** (zhän än twän′) 1741-1828; Fr. sculptor

Houns·field (hounz′fēld′), **Godfrey New·bold** (noo′bōld′) 1919- ; Brit. engineer & inventor: developed the CAT scanner

Hours (ourz) ‖ ult. < Gr *hōra*, hour, time, period, season < IE base **yē-*, year, summer (< **ei-*, to go) ‖ *Gr. Myth.* the goddesses of the seasons, justice, order, etc.

Hous·man (hous'mən), **A(lfred) E(dward)** 1859-1936; Eng. poet & classical scholar

Hous·ton (hyōōs'tən), **Samuel** 1793-1863; U.S. general & statesman: president of the Republic of Texas (1836-38; 1841-44): U.S. senator (1846-59)

How·ard (hou'ərd) ⟦ < the surname *Howard* ⟧ **1** a masculine name: dim. *Howie* **2 Catherine** c. 1520-42; 5th wife of HENRY VIII: beheaded **3 Henry** *see* SURREY, Earl of **4 Roy Wilson** 1883-1964; U.S. editor & newspaper publisher **5 Sidney Coe** (kō) 1891-1939; U.S. playwright

Howe (hou) **1 Elias** 1819-67; U.S. inventor of a sewing machine **2 Julia Ward** 1819-1910; U.S. social reformer & poet **3 Sir William** 5th Viscount Howe 1729-1814; commander in chief of Brit. forces in American Revolution (1775-78)

How·ells (hou'əlz), **William Dean** 1837-1920; U.S. novelist, critic, & editor

Hr·dlič·ka (hur'dlich kə), **A·leš** (ä'lesh) 1869-1943; U.S. anthropologist, born in Bohemia

Huás·car (wäs'kär) c. 1495-1533; Inca king of Peru, deposed by his half brother Atahualpa

Hu·bel (hyōō'bəl, yōō'-), **David Hun·ter** (hun'tər) 1926- ; U.S. neurophysiologist

Hu·bert (hyōō'bərt) ⟦ Fr < OHG *Huguberht*, lit., bright (in) spirit < *hugu*, mind, spirit + *beraht*, bright ⟧ a masculine name: equiv. It. *Uberto*

Hud·son (hud'sən) **1 Henry** died 1611; Eng. explorer, esp. of the waters about NE North America **2 W(illiam) H(enry)** 1841-1922; Eng. naturalist & writer

Hug·gins (hug'inz), **Sir William** 1824-1910; Eng. astronomer

Hugh (hyōō) a masculine name: var. *Hugo*

Hugh Capet *see* CAPET, Hugh

Hughes (hyōōz) **1 Charles Evans** 1862-1948; U.S. statesman & jurist: chief justice (1930-41) **2 Howard (Robard)** 1905-75; U.S. businessman **3 (James) Lang·ston** (laŋ'stən) 1902-67; U.S. poet & writer **4 Ted** (born *Edward James Hughes*) 1930- ; Eng. poet: poet laureate (1984-)

Hu·go (hyōō'gō; *for 2, also,* Fr ü gō') **1** a masculine name: see HUGH **2 Vic·tor Ma·rie** (vēk tôr' má rē') 1802-85; Fr. poet, novelist, & playwright

Hui·zing·a (hī'ziŋ ə), **Jo·han** (yō hän') 1872-1945; Du.

historian

Hull (hul), **Cor·dell** (kôr′del) 1871-1955; U.S. statesman: secretary of state (1933-44)

Hum·boldt (hoom′bôlt; *E* hum′bôlt), **Baron (Friedrich Heinrich) Al·ex·an·der von** (ä′lek sän′dər fôn) 1769-1859; Ger. scientist, explorer, & writer

Hume (hyōōm), **David** 1711-76; Scot. philosopher & historian

Hum·per·dinck (hoom′pər diŋk′; *E* hum′-), **Eng·el·bert** (eŋ′gəl bert′; *E*, -burt′) 1854-1921; Ger. composer

Hum·phrey (hum′frē) ‖ OE *Hunfrith* < Gmc **hun*, strength + OE *frith*, peace ‖ a masculine name: equiv. Ger. *Humfried*, It. *Onfredo*: also sp. **Hum′phry**

Hump·ty Dump·ty (hump′tē dump′tē) a short, squat character in an old nursery rhyme, a personification of an egg, who fell from a wall and broke into pieces

Hun·ting·ton (hun′tiŋ tən) **1 Col·lis Porter** (käl′is) 1821-1900; U.S. railroad builder **2 Samuel** 1731-96; Am. statesman: signer of the Declaration of Independence

Hu·nya·di (hoo′nyä dē), **Já·nos** (jä′nôsh) 1387-1456; Hung. general & national hero: also sp. **Hu′nya·dy**

Hus (hoos), **Jan** (yän) *Czech name of* John Huss

Hu Shih (hoo′ shë′, shē′) 1891-1962; Chin. diplomat, philosopher, & writer

Huss (hus), **John** *c.* 1369-1415; Bohemian religious reformer and martyr, burned as a heretic

Hus·sein I (hoo sān′) 1935- ; king of Jordan (1952-)

Hus·serl (hoos′ərl), **Edmund** 1859-1938; Ger. philosopher

Hus·ton (hyoo′stən, yoo′-), **John** 1906-87; U.S. film director

Hutch·ins (huch′inz), **Robert May·nard** (mā′nərd) 1899-1977; U.S. educator

Hutch·in·son (huch′in sən) **1 Anne** (born *Anne Marbury*) *c.* 1591-1643; Am. religious leader, born in England: a founder of Rhode Island **2 Thomas** 1711-80; colonial governor of Mass. (1771-74)

Hux·ley (huks′lē) **1 Al·dous (Leonard)** (ôl′dəs) 1894-1963; Eng. novelist & essayist, in the U.S. after *c.* 1935 **2 Andrew Fielding** 1917- ; Brit. biophysicist: halfbrother of Aldous & Julian **3 Sir Julian (Sorrell)** 1887-1975; Eng. biologist & writer: brother of Aldous **4 Thomas Henry** 1825-95; Eng. biologist & writer: grandfather of Aldous, Julian, & Andrew

Huy·gens, Huy·ghens (hī′gənz; *Du* hoi′gəns), **Christian** 1629-95; Du. physicist, mathematician, & astronomer

Hy·a·cin·thus (hī′ə sin′thəs) ⟦ L < Gr *Hyakinthos* < *hyakinthos*, wild hyacinth, bluebell, blue larkspur ⟧ *Gr. Myth.* a youth loved and accidentally slain by Apollo, who causes to grow from his blood a flower bearing the letters AI AI (a Greek cry of sorrow)

Hyde (hīd) **1 Douglas** 1860-1949; Ir. statesman & writer: president of Eire (1938-45) **2 Edward** *see* CLARENDON, 1st Earl of

Hy·ge·ia (hī jē′ə) ⟦ L *Hygea* < Gr *Hygeia, Hygieia* < *hygiēs*, healthy, sound < IE *su-gwiyēs*, living well < base *su-*, well + base *gwei-*, to live ⟧ *Gr. Myth.* the goddess of health

Hy·men (hī′mən) ⟦ L < Gr *Hymēn* < *hymēn*, membrane < IE *syumen-*, ligature < base *siw-* ⟧ *Gr. Myth.* the god of marriage

Hy·pe·ri·on (hī pir′ē ən) ⟦ L < Gr *Hyperiōn* ⟧ **1** *Gr. Myth.* a Titan, son of Uranus and Gaea, and father of the sun god Helios **2** *Gr. Myth.* Helios himself

Hyp·nos (hip′näs′) ⟦ Gr *Hypnos* < *hypnos*, sleep < IE *supnos* < base *swep-*, to sleep ⟧ *Gr. Myth.* the god of sleep, identified with the Roman Somnus: also **Hyp·nus** (hip′nəs)

I

I·a·go (ē ä′gō) *see* OTHELLO

I·an (ē′ən) a masculine name: see JOHN

Ibáñez *see* BLASCO IBÁÑEZ, Vicente

Iberville *see* D'IBERVILLE, Sieur

ibn-Rushd (ib′ən rōōsht′) *Ar.* name of AVERROËS

Ib·sen (ib′sən), **Hen·rik** (hen′rik) 1828-1906; Norw. playwright & poet

Ic·a·rus (ik′ə rəs; *also* ī′kə-) ⟦ L < Gr *Ikaros* ⟧ *Gr. Myth.* the son of Daedalus; escaping from Crete by flying with wings made by Daedalus, Icarus flies so high that the sun's heat melts the wax by which his wings are fastened, and he falls to his death in the sea

Ich·a·bod (ik′ə bäd′) ⟦ Heb *Ī-khābhōdh*, lit., according to pop. etym., inglorious: orig. meaning uncert. ⟧ a masculine name

Ic·ti·nus (ik tī′nəs) 5th cent. B.C.; Gr. architect who

designed the Parthenon

I·da (ī′də) ⟦ML < OHG: akin ? to ON *Ithunn*, goddess of youth⟧ a feminine name

I·dom·e·neus (ī däm′i nō̄s′, -nyō̄s′) *Gr. Legend* a king of Crete and leader of his subjects against Troy in the Trojan War

I·dun (ē′dō̄n′) *Norse Myth.* the goddess of spring, keeper of the golden apples of youth, and wife of Bragi: also **I·du·na** (ē′dō̄ nä′)

Ig·na·tius (ig nā′shəs) **1** ⟦L⟧ a masculine name **2** Saint (*c.* A.D. 50-*c.* 110); Christian martyr & bishop of Antioch: his day is Oct. 17

Ignatius (of) Loyola, Saint (born *Iñigo López de Recalde*) 1491-1556; Sp. priest: founder of the Society of Jesus (Jesuit order): his day is July 31

I·graine (ē grān′) ⟦akin ? to OFr *Iguerne* < ? Celt⟧ *Arthurian Legend* the mother of King Arthur

Ikh·na·ton (ik nät′n) died *c.* 1362 B.C.; king of Egypt (as *Amenhotep IV, c.* 1376-*c.* 1362) & religious reformer

Im·man·u·el (i man′yōō el′, -əl) ⟦Heb *'immānūēl* < *'im*, with + *ānū*, us + *ēl*, God, hence, lit., God with us⟧ **1** a masculine name: var. *Emmanuel, Manuel* **2** a name given by Isaiah to the Messiah of his prophecy (Isa. 7:14), often applied to Jesus (Matt. 1:23)

Im·o·gen (im′ə jen′) ⟦first recorded in Shakespeare's *Cymbeline* (First Folio): ? misprint for Holinshed's *Innogen*⟧ a feminine name: also **Im′o·gene** (-jēn′)

In·dra (in′drə) ⟦Sans⟧ the chief god of the early Hindu religion, associated with rain and thunderbolts

Indy, Vincent d' *see* D'INDY, (Paul Marie Théodore) Vincent

I·nez (ī′niz, ī′nez′, ī nez′) ⟦Sp *Iñez*⟧ a feminine name: see AGNES

Infinite (Being), the God

Inge (iŋ) **1 William** 1913-73; U.S. playwright **2 William Ralph** 1860-1954; Eng. theologian

In·ger·soll (iŋ′gər sôl′, -səl), **Robert Green** 1833-99; U.S. lawyer & lecturer: exponent of agnosticism

In·gres (an′gr′), **Jean Au·guste Do·mi·nique** (zhän ô güst′ dô mē nēk′) 1780-1867; Fr. painter

Ing·rid (iŋ′grid) ⟦< Scand; ult < ON *Ingvi*, name of a Gmc god + *rida*, ride⟧ a feminine name

In·ness (in′is), **George** 1825-94; U.S. painter

In·no·cent (in′ə sənt) **1** a masculine name, adopted

chiefly by several popes **2** Saint **Innocent I** (died A.D. 417); pope (401-417): his day is July 28 **3 Innocent II** (born *Gregorio Papareschi*) died 1143; pope (1130-43) **4 Innocent III** (born *Lotario de' Conti de' Segni*) c. 1161-1216; pope (1198-1216) **5 Innocent IV** (born *Sinibaldo de' Fieschi*) died 1254; pope (1243-54) **6 Innocent XI** (born *Benedetto Odeschalchi*) 1611-89; pope (1676-89)

I·nö·nü (ē nö nü′), **Is·met** (is met′) 1884-1973; Turk. statesman: president of Turkey (1938-50): prime minister (1923-24; 1925-37; 1961-65)

Invisible, the God

I·o (ī′ō′) ⟦ L < Gr *Iō* ⟧ *Gr. Myth.* a maiden loved by Zeus and changed into a heifer by jealous Hera or, in some tales, by Zeus to protect her: she is watched by Argus and is driven to Egypt, where she regains human form

Io·nes·co (yə nes′kō, ē′ə-), **Eugene** 1912- ; Fr. playwright, born in Romania

Iph·i·ge·ni·a (if′ə jə nī′ə) ⟦ L < Gr *Iphigeneia* ⟧ *Gr. Myth.* a daughter of Agamemnon, offered by him as a sacrifice to Artemis and, in some versions, saved by the goddess, who makes her a priestess

Ip·po·li·tov-I·va·nov (ē′pô lü′tôf ē vä′nôf), **Mi·kha·il Mi·khai·lo·vich** (mi khä ēl′ mi khī′lô vich) 1859-1935; Russ. composer

I·ra (ī′rə) ⟦ Heb 'irā, lit., watchful ⟧ a masculine name

I·rene (ī rēn′; *for 2* ī rē′nē) ⟦ < Fr or L: Fr *Irène* < L *Irene* < Gr *Eirēnē*, lit., peace ⟧ **1** a feminine name **2** *Gr. Myth.* the goddess of peace, daughter of Zeus and Themis: identified with the Roman Pax

I·ris (ī′ris) ⟦ L < Gr *Iris* < *iris* (the flower) < IE *wir- < base *wei-, to turn, bend ⟧ **1** a feminine name **2** *Gr. Myth.* the goddess of the rainbow: in the *Iliad*, she is the messenger of the gods

Ir·ma (ur′mə) ⟦ Ger, orig. contr. of *Irmenberta, Irmintrud, Irmgard,* etc. < OHG *Irmin,* cognomen of the Gmc war god Tiu ⟧ a feminine name

I·ron·sides (ī′ərn sīdz′) *name for* Oliver CROMWELL

Ir·ving (ur′viŋ) ⟦ north Brit surname, prob. orig. a place name ⟧ **1** a masculine name **2 Washington** 1783-1859; U.S. writer

Ir·win (ur′win) a masculine name: see ERWIN

I·saac (ī′zək) ⟦ LL(Ec) *Isaacus* < Gr(Ec) *Isaak* < Heb *yitshāq,* lit., laughter: see Gen. 17:17 ⟧ **1** a masculine name: dim. *Ike* **2** *Bible* one of the patriarchs, son of Abraham and Sarah, and father of Jacob and Esau: Gen. 21:3

Is·a·bel (iz'ə bel') 〚Sp, prob. an alteration of *Elizabeth* 〛 a feminine name: dim. *Bel*; var. *Isabelle, Isabella*

Is·a·bel·la (iz'ə bel'ə) 〚It〛 **1** a feminine name: dim. *Bella*: see ISABEL **2 Isabella I** 1451-1504; wife of Ferdinand V & queen of Castile (1474-1504): gave help to Columbus in his expedition: called **Isabella of Cas·tile** (kas tēl') **3 Isabella II** 1830-1904; queen of Spain (1833-68): deposed

Is·a·belle (iz'ə bel') 〚Fr〛 a feminine name: dim. *Belle*: see ISABEL

Is·a·dor·a (iz'ə dôr'ə) 〚var. of Gr *Isidōra*: see ISIDORE 〛 a feminine name: see ISIDORE

I·sa·iah (ī zā'ə; *chiefly Brit*, -zī-) 〚LL(Ec) *Isaias* < Gr(Ec) *Ēsaias* < Heb *yēsha 'yah*, lit., God is salvation 〛 **1** a masculine name **2** *Bible* a Hebrew prophet of the 8th cent. B.C.

Is·car·i·ot (is ker'ē ət) 〚LL(Ec) *Iscariota* < Gr(Ec) *Iskariōtēs* < ? Heb *ish-qĕrīyōth*, man of Kerioth (town in Palestine) 〛 *see* JUDAS (sense 1)

I·seult (i sōōlt') 〚Fr〛 ISOLDE

Ish·er·wood (ish'ər wood), **Christopher (William Brad-shaw)** 1904-86; U.S. writer, born in England

Ish·ma·el (ish'mā əl) 〚LL(Ec) *Ismaël* < Heb *yishmā'ē'l*, lit., God hears 〛 the son of Abraham and Hagar: he and his mother were outcasts: Gen. 21:9-21

Ish·tar (ish'tär') 〚Assyr-Bab < Akkadian, var. of *Ashdar*: see ASHTORETH 〛 *Bab. & Assyr. Myth.* the goddess of love, fertility, and war

Is·i·dore, Is·i·dor (iz'ə dôr') 〚 < Ger *Isdor* or Fr *Isidore*, both < L *Isidorus* < Gr *Isidōros* < *Isis* + *dōron*, gift; hence, lit., gift of Isis 〛 a masculine name: dim. *Izzy*; var. *Isadore, Isador*; fem. *Isadora*

Isidore of Se·ville (sə vil'), **Saint** (L. *Isidorus Hispalensis*) c. A.D. 560-636; Sp. bishop & scholar: his day is April 4

I·sis (ī'sis) 〚L < Gr〛 *Egypt. Myth.* the goddess of fertility, sister and wife of Osiris, usually represented with a cow's horns surrounding a solar (or lunar) disk

I·soc·ra·tes (ī säk'rə tēz') 436-338 B.C.; Athenian orator & rhetorician

I·sol·de (i sōl'də; *also* i sōld'; *Ger* ē zôl'də) 〚Ger < OFr

Isolt, Iseut < OHG *Isold*, prob. < *is*, ice + *waltan*, to rule, wield ‖ *Medieval Legend* **1** the Irish princess betrothed to King Mark of Cornwall and loved by Tristram **2** the daughter of the king of Brittany, married to Tristram Also **I·solt** (i sōlt′) See TRISTRAM

Is·ra·el (iz′rē əl, -rā-; *also* iz′rəl) ‖ OFr < LL(Ec) < Gr *Israēl* < Heb *yisrael*, lit., contender with God < *sara*, to wrestle + *el*, God ‖ **1** a masculine name: dim. *Izzy* **2** *Bible* Jacob: so named after wrestling with the angel: Gen. 32:28

Is·sa·char (is′ə kär′) Jacob's ninth son, whose mother was Leah: Gen. 30:18

I·thunn, I·thun (ē′thōōn) IDUN

I·van (ī′vən; *Russ* i vän′) ‖ Russ < Gr *Iōannēs*: see JOHN ‖ **1** a masculine name **2 Ivan III** 1440-1505; grand duke of Muscovy (1462-1505): called *the Great* **3 Ivan IV** 1530-84; grand duke of Muscovy (1533-84) & 1st czar of Russia (1547-84): called *the Terrible*

Ives (īvz), **Charles Edward** 1874-1954; U.S. composer

I·vy (ī′vē) ‖ < ModE *ivy* (the plant) < ME *ivi* < OE *ifig, ifegn*: orig. sense prob. "climber" ‖ a feminine name

Ix·i·on (iks′ī än′, -ən) ‖ L < Gr *Ixiōn* ‖ *Gr. Myth.* a Thessalian king who is bound to a revolving wheel in Tartarus because he sought the love of Hera

J

Jack (jak) ‖ ME *Jacke, Jake* < OFr *Jaque, Jaques* < LL(Ec) *Jacobus*, JACOB ‖ *nickname for* JOHN

Jack Frost frost or cold weather personified

Jack·son (jak′sən) **1 Andrew** (called *Old Hickory*) 1767-1845; U.S. general: 7th president of the U.S. (1829-37) **2 Robert H**(oughwout) 1892-1954; U.S. jurist: associate justice, Supreme Court (1941-54) **3 Thomas Jonathan** (called *Stonewall Jackson*) 1824-63: Confederate general in the Civil War

Jack the Ripper name given to the unidentified murderer of at least six London prostitutes in 1888

Ja·cob (jā′kəb) ‖ LL(Ec) *Jacobus* < Gr *Iakōbos* < Heb *Ja'aqob*, lit., seizing by the heel of (cf. Gen. 25:26) ‖ **1** a masculine name: dim. *Jake, Jack*; var. *James*; equiv. Fr. *Jacques*, It. *Giácomo* **2** *Bible* a son of Isaac, twin brother of Esau, and the father of the founders of the twelve tribes of Israel: also called

Israel: Gen. 25:24-34

Jac·que·line (jak'wə lin, jak'ə-) ⟦Fr, fem. of *Jacques:* see JACK⟧ a feminine name: dim. *Jacky, Jackie*

Ja·el (jā'əl) ⟦Heb *yāel*, lit., mountain goat⟧ *Bible* the woman who killed Sisera by hammering a tent peg through his head while he slept: Judg. 4:17-22

Jah·veh, Jah·ve (yä've) ⟦see YAHWEH⟧ JEHOVAH: also **Jah·weh** or **Jah·we** (yä'we, -wä)

Ja·kob·son (jā'kəb sən), **Ro·man** (**Osipovič**) (rō'mən) 1896-1982; U.S. linguist, born in Russia

James (jāmz) ⟦ME < OFr < LL(Ec) *Jacomus*, later form of *Jacobus:* see JACOB⟧ **1** a masculine name: dim. *Jamie, Jim, Jimmy;* fem. *Jamie:* see JACOB **2** *Bible a)* one of the twelve Apostles, Zebedee's son and brother of John: his day is July 25 (also **Saint James the Greater**) *b)* one of the twelve Apostles, Alphaeus' son: his day is May 3 (also **Saint James the Less**) *c)* a brother of Jesus: Gal. 1:19 **3 James I** 1566-1625; king of England (1603-25) & (as **James VI**) king of Scotland (1567-1625): son of Mary, Queen of Scots **4 James II** 1633-1701; king of England & (as **James VII**) king of Scotland (1685-88): deposed: son of Charles I **5 Henry** 1811-82; U.S. writer on religion & philosophy: father of Henry & William **6 Henry** 1843-1916; U.S. novelist, in England: son of Henry and brother of William **7 Jesse** (**Woodson**) 1847-82; U.S. outlaw **8 William** 1842-1910; U.S. psychologist & philosopher: exponent of pragmatism: son of Henry

James Edward *see* STUART, James Francis Edward

Jam·shid, Jam·shyd (jam shēd') ⟦Pers⟧ *Pers. Myth.* the king of the peris: because he boasts that he is immortal, he has to live as a human being on earth

Ja·ná·ček (yä'nə chek'), **Le·oš** (le'ôsh) 1854-1928; Czech composer

Jane (jān) ⟦Fr *Jeanne* < ML *Joanna:* see JOANNA⟧ a feminine name: dim. *Janet, Jenny*

Jane Doe *see* DOE

Jan·et (jan'it) a feminine name: dim. *Jan:* see JANE

Ja·net (zhȧ ne'), **Pierre** (**Marie Félix**) 1859-1947; Fr. psychologist

Jan·ice (jan'is) ⟦< JANE, JANET⟧ a feminine name: dim. *Jan*

Jan·sen (yän'sən; *E* jan'sən), **Cor·ne·lis** (kôr nä'lis) (L. name *Jansenius*) 1585-1638; Du. Rom. Catholic theologian

Ja·nus (jā′nəs) 〚L, lit., gate, arched passageway < IE base *yă-*, var. of *ei-*, to go 〛 *Rom. Myth.* the god who is guardian of portals and patron of beginnings and endings: he is shown as having two faces, one in front, the other at the back of his head

Ja·pheth (jā′feth′) 〚LL(Ec) < Gr(Ec) < Heb *yepheth,* lit., enlargement: cf. Gen. 9:27 〛 *Bible* the youngest of Noah's three sons: Gen. 5:32

Ja·ques (jā′kwēz) 〚OFr: see JACK〛 a cynically philosophical nobleman in Shakespeare's *As You Like It*

Jaques–Dal·croze (zhäk dàl krōz′), **É·mile** (ā mēl′) 1865-1950; Swiss composer: originated eurythmics

Jar·ed (jar′id) 〚LL(Ec) < Gr(Ec) < Heb *yeredh,* lit., descent: cf. Gen. 5:15 〛 a masculine name

Jar·ry (zhà rē′), **Alfred** 1873-1907; Fr. playwright

Jar·vis (jär′vis) 〚older *Gervas* < Norm var. of Fr *Gervais* < LL *Gervasius,* name of an early Christian saint and martyr 〛 a masculine name: var. *Jervis*

Ja·son (jā′sən) 〚L *Iāson* < Gr, lit., healer 〛 **1** a masculine name, and **2** *Gr. Myth.* a prince who leads the Argonauts, and, with Medea's help, gets the Golden Fleece

Jas·per (jas′pər) 〚OFr *Jaspar* < ? 〛 a masculine name: equiv. Fr. *Gaspard,* Ger. *Kasper,* Sp. *Gaspar*

Jas·pers (yäs′pərz), **Karl** 1883-1969; Ger. philosopher

Jau·rès (zhô res′), **Jean Lé·on** (zhän lā ōn′) 1859-1914; Fr. Socialist leader & journalist: assassinated

Jay (jā), **John** 1745-1829; Am. statesman & jurist: 1st chief justice of the U.S. (1789-95)

Jean (zhän; *for 2,* jēn) **1** *Fr. var. of* JOHN **2** a feminine name: dim. *Jeanie:* see JOANNA

Jeanne (jēn) a feminine name: dim. *Jeannette:* see JOANNA

Jeanne d'Arc (zhàn dàrk) *Fr. name of* JOAN OF ARC

Jean·nette (jə net′) a feminine name: dim. *Nettie, Netty:* see JEANNE

Jeans (jēnz), **Sir James (Hopwood)** 1877-1946; Eng. mathematician, physicist, astronomer, & writer

Jef·fers (jef′ərz), **(John) Robinson** 1887-1962; U.S. poet

Jef·fer·son (jef′ər sən), **Thomas** 1743-1826; Am. statesman: 3d president of the U.S. (1801-09): drew up the Declaration of Independence

Jeff·rey (jef′rē) a masculine name: dim. *Jeff:* see GEOFFREY

Je·hosh·a·phat (ji häsh′ə fat′, -häs′-) ‖ Heb *yehōshā-phāt*, lit., God has judged ‖ *Bible* a king of Judah in the 9th cent. B.C.: 2 Chron. 17-21

Je·ho·vah (ji hō′və) ‖ modern transliteration of the Tetragrammaton YHWH; the vowels appear through arbitrary transference of the vowel points of *Adōnāi*, my Lord: see YAHWEH ‖ God; (the) Lord

Je·hu (jē′hoo′, -hyoo′) ‖ Heb ‖ *Bible* a king of Israel in the 9th cent. B.C., described as a furious charioteer: 2 Kings 9

Je·kyll (jē′kəl; *popularly* jek′əl), **Dr.** a kind, good doctor in Robert Louis Stevenson's story *The Strange Case of Dr. Jekyll and Mr. Hyde*, who discovers drugs that enable him to transform himself into a vicious, brutal creature named Mr. Hyde and back again

Je·kyll (jē′kəl; *also* jek′əl), **Gertrude** 1843-1932; Eng. landscape architect

Jel·li·coe (jel′i kō′), **John Rush·worth** (rush′wurth′) 1st Earl Jellicoe 1859-1935; Eng. admiral

Je·mi·ma (jə mī′mə) ‖ Heb *yemīmāh*, lit., a dove ‖ a feminine name

Jen·ghiz Khan (jeŋ′gis kän′) *var. of* GENGHIS KHAN

Jen·ner (jen′ər) **1 Edward** 1749-1823; Eng. physician: introduced vaccination **2 Sir William** 1815-98; Eng. physician

Jen·ni·fer (jen′i fər) ‖ altered < GUINEVERE ‖ a feminine name: dim. *Jenni, Jennie, Jenny*

Jen·ny (jen′ē) a feminine name: see JANE, JENNIFER

Jeph·thah (jef′thə) ‖ Heb *Yiphtáh*, lit., God opens ‖ *Bible* a judge who sacrificed his daughter in fulfillment of a vow: Judg. 11:30-40

Jer·e·mi·ah (jer′ə mī′ə) ‖ LL(Ec) *Jeremias* < Gr(Ec) *Hieremias* < Heb *yirmeyāh*, lit., the Lord loosens (i.e., from the womb) ‖ **1** a masculine name: dim. *Jerry*; var. *Jeremy* **2** *Bible* a Hebrew prophet of the 7th and 6th cent. B.C.

Jer·e·my (jer′ə mē) a masculine name: see JEREMIAH

Jer·o·bo·am (jer′ə bō′əm) ‖ Heb *yārobh‘ām*, lit., prob., the people increases ‖ *Bible* the first king of Israel: 1 Kings 11:26-14:20

Je·rome (jə rōm′, jer′əm) ‖ Fr *Jérôme* < L *Hieronymus* < Gr *Hierōnymos* < *hieros*, holy (< IE base **eis-*, to move violently, excite) + *onyma*, name ‖ **1** a masculine name: dim. *Jerry* **2** Saint (born *Eusebius Hieron-*

ymus Sophronius) *c.* A.D. 340-420; monk & church scholar, born in Pannonia: author of the Vulgate: his day is Sept. 30

Jer·ry (jer'ē) a masculine name: see GERALD, GERARD, JEREMIAH, JEROME

Jes·per·sen (yes'pər sən, jes'-), (Jens) **Otto (Harry)** 1860-1943; Dan. linguist, noted for English studies

Jes·sa·mine (jes'ə min) ⟦ < MFr *jessemin,* jasmine ⟧ a feminine name

Jes·se (jes'ē) ⟦Heb *ytshai* ⟧ **1** a masculine name: dim. *Jess* **2** *Bible* the father of David: 1 Sam. 16

Jes·si·ca (jes'i kə) a feminine name

Jes·sie (jes'ē) a feminine name: var. of JESSICA

Je·su (jē'zoō, -soō; jā'-, yā'-) *archaic var. of* JESUS

Je·sus (jē'zəz, -zəs) ⟦LL(Ec) *Iesus* < Gr(Ec) *Iēsous* < Heb *yēshū'a,* contr. of *yehōshū'a* (JOSHUA), help of Jehovah < *yāh,* Jehovah + *hōshīa,* to help ⟧ **1** a masculine name **2** *c.* 8-4 B.C.-*c.* A.D. 29; founder of the Christian religion: see also CHRIST: also called **Jesus Christ** or **Jesus of Naz·a·reth** (naz'ə rəth) **3** the author of *Ecclesiasticus,* a book of the Apocrypha

Jev·ons (jev'ənz), **William Stanley** 1835-82; Eng. economist & logician

Jew·ett (joō'it), **Sarah Orne** (ôrn) 1849-1909; U.S. writer

Jez·e·bel (jez'ə bel', -bəl) ⟦Heb *'Izebhel* ⟧ *Bible* the wicked woman who married Ahab, king of Israel: 1 Kings 21:5-23; 2 Kings 9:30-37

Jill (jil) ⟦var. of *Gill,* contr. of *Gillian* < L *Juliana,* fem. of *Julianus* < *Julius,* name of a Roman gens ⟧ a feminine name

Jim (jim) *nickname for* JAMES

Ji·mé·nez (hē me'neth), **Juan Ra·món** (hwän rä mōn') 1881-1958; Sp. poet, in the Americas after 1937

Jim·my (jim'ē) *nickname for* JAMES: also sp. **Jim'mie**

Jin·nah (ji'nä', jin'ə), **Mohammed Ali** 1876-1948; Indian statesman: 1st governor general of Pakistan (1947-1948)

Jo·ab (jō'ab') ⟦LL(Ec) < Gr(Ec) *Iōab* < Heb *yō'ābh,* lit., Yahweh is (his) father ⟧ *Bible* the commander of David's army: 2 Sam. 10:7

Joan (jōn) a feminine name: see JOANNA

Jo·an·na (jō an'ə) ⟦ML, fem. of *Joannes:* see JOHN ⟧ a feminine name: var. *Joan, Jane, Jean, Joanne;* equiv. L. & Ger. *Johanna,* Fr. *Jeanne,* It. *Giovanna,* Sp.

Juana

Jo·anne (jō an′) a feminine name: see JOANNA

Joan of Arc (ärk) (Fr. name *Jeanne d'Arc*) 1412-31; Fr. heroine: defeated the English at Orléans (1429): burned at the stake for witchcraft: called the *Maid of Orléans*: also **Saint Joan of Arc**

Job (jōb) ⟦LL(Ec) < Gr(Ec) *Iōb* < Heb *'Iyyōbh*⟧ *Bible* a man who endured much suffering but did not lose his faith in God

Jo·cas·ta (jō kas′tə) ⟦L < Gr *Iokastē*⟧ *Gr. Myth.* the queen who unwittingly marries her own son, Oedipus, and kills herself when she finds out

Joc·e·lyn, Joc·e·lin (jäs′ə lin, jäs′lin) ⟦OFr *Joscelin* < OHG *Gauzelen*, dim. < *Gauta*, a Goth⟧ a feminine name

Jo·di, Jo·dy (jō′dē) a feminine and masculine name

Joe (jō) *nickname for* JOSEPH

Joe Blow [Slang] **1** *personification of* an average, ordinary man **2** a name used to refer to a man whose name is not known or whose typicalness is being emphasized

Joe College [Colloq.] *personification of* the typical male college student in the United States

Jo·el (jō′əl, -el′) ⟦LL(Ec) < Gr(Ec) *Iōēl* < Heb *yō'ēl*, lit., the Lord is God⟧ **1** a masculine name **2** *Bible* a Hebrew prophet, probably of the 5th cent. B.C.

Jof·fre (zhôf′r′), **Jo·seph Jacques Cé·saire** (zhō zef′ zhäk sā zer′) 1852-1931; Fr. general: commander in chief of Fr. forces in World War I

Jo·han·na (jō han′ə) a feminine name: see JOANNA

John (jän) ⟦ME *Jon* < OFr *Johan, Jehan, Jan* < ML *Johannes* < LL(Ec) *Joannes* < Gr(Ec) *Iōannes* < Heb *yōhānān*, contr. < *yehōhānān*, lit., Yahweh is gracious⟧ **1** a masculine name: dim. *Jack, Johnnie, Johnny;* equiv. Fr. *Jean,* Ger. *Johanne, Johannes, Hans,* Ir. *Sean, Shane, Shawn,* It. *Giovanni,* Pol. *Jan,* Russ. *Ivan,* Scot. *Ian, Jock,* Sp. *Juan,* Welsh *Evan;* fem. *Jane, Jean, Jeanne, Joan, Joanna, Joanne, Johanna* **2** *Bible a)* one of the twelve Apostles and one of the four Evangelists, to whom is ascribed the fourth Gospel, the three Letters of John, and the Book of Revelation: his day is Dec 27 (also **Saint John the Divine**) *b)* JOHN THE BAPTIST **3** (called *John Lackland*) *c.* 1167-1216; king of England (1199-1216):

forced by his barons to sign the Magna Carta: son of
Henry II_ **4 Saint John of the Cross** (born *Juan de
Yepes y Álvarez*) 1542-91; Sp. monk & mystic **5 John
III** (born *John Sobieski*) 1624-96; king of Poland
(1674-96) **6 John XXIII** (born *Angelo Giuseppe Ron-
calli*) 1881-1963; pope (1958-63) **7 Augustus (Edwin)**
1879-1961; Eng. painter

John Bar·ley·corn (bär'lē kôrn') *personification of* corn
liquor, malt liquor, etc.

John Bull ‖ title character in John Arbuthnot's *History
of John Bull* (1712) ‖ *personification of* England or an
Englishman

John Doe *see* DOE

John Henry *American Folklore* the hero, usually
depicted as black, of an American ballad, who died
after a contest pitting his strength with a sledge hammer against that of a steam drill

John·ny, John·nie (jän'ē) ‖ cf. JACK ‖ *nickname for* JOHN

Johnny Reb (reb) ‖ JOHNNY + *reb*(*el*) ‖ *personification of*
a Confederate soldier

John of Gaunt (gônt) Duke of Lancaster 1340-99;
founder of the house of Lancaster: son of Edward III

John Paul I (born *Albino Luciani*) 1912-78; pope (1978)

John Paul II (born *Karol Wojtyla*) 1920- ; pope (1978-)

John Q. Public *personification of* an ordinary or average
citizen, esp. of the U.S.

Johns (jänz), **Jasper** 1930- ; U.S. painter, sculptor, &
printmaker

John·son (jän'sən) **1 Andrew** 1808-75; 17th president of
the U.S. (1865-69) **2 James Wel·don** (wel'dən) 1871-
1938; U.S. writer & diplomat **3 Lyn·don Baines** (lin'
dən bānz') 1908-73; 36th president of the U.S. (1963-
69) **4 Philip Cour·tel·you** (kôr tel'yoo') 1906- ; U.S.
architect **5 Samuel** 1709-84; Eng. lexicographer,
writer, & critic: known as *Dr. Johnson*

Johns·ton (jänz'tən) **1 Albert Sidney** 1803-62; Confederate general **2 Joseph Eggleston** 1807-91; Confederate general

John the Baptist *Bible* the forerunner and baptizer of
Jesus: he was killed by Herod: Matt. 3

Join·ville (zhwan vēl'), **Jean de** (zhän də) *c.* 1224-1317;
Fr. chronicler

Jo·li·et, Jol·li·et (jō'lē et', jō'lē et'; *Fr* zhô lye'), **Louis**
1645-1700; Fr.-Cdn. explorer of the Mississippi

Jo·liot–Cu·rie (zhô lyō kü rē′) **1 (Jean) Fré·dé·ric** (frä dä rēk′) (born *Jean Frédéric Joliot*) 1900-58; Fr. nuclear physicist **2 I·rène** (ē ren′) (born *Irène Curie*) 1897-1956; Fr. nuclear physicist: wife of Frédéric & daughter of Pierre & Marie Curie

Jo·nah (jō′nə) ⟦LL(Ec) *Jonas* < Gr(Ec) *Iōnas* < Heb *jōnāh*, lit., a dove ⟧ **1** a masculine name: var. *Jonas* **2** *Bible* a Hebrew prophet: thrown overboard in a storm sent because he had disobeyed God, he was swallowed by a big fish, but three days later was cast up on the shore unharmed

Jon·a·than (jän′ə thən) ⟦Heb *yōnāthān*, contr. < *yehōnāthān*, lit., Yahweh has given ⟧ **1** a masculine name: dim. *Jon* **2** *Bible* Saul's oldest son, a close friend of David: 1 Sam. 18-20 **3** BROTHER JONATHAN

Jones (jōnz) **1 Howard Mum·ford** (mum′fərd) 1892-1980; U.S. educator & critic **2 In·i·go** (in′i gō′) 1573-1652; Eng. architect & stage designer **3 John Paul** (born *John Paul*) 1747-92; Am. naval officer in the Revolutionary War, born in Scotland **4 (Walter) David** 1895-1974; Eng. writer & artist

Jon·son (jän′sən), **Ben** *c.* 1572-1637; Eng. dramatist & poet

Jop·lin (jäp′lin), **Scott** 1868-1917; U.S. ragtime pianist & composer

Jor·daens (yôr′däns′), **Ja·cob** (yä′kôp) 1593-1678; Fl. painter

Jor·dan (jôrd′'n), **David Starr** (stär) 1851-1931; U.S. educator & naturalist

Jo·seph (jō′zəf, -səf) ⟦LL(Ec) < Gr(Ec) *Iōsēph* < Heb *yōsēph*, lit., may he add: see Gen. 30:24⟧ **1** a masculine name: dim. *Joe, Joey*; equiv. L. *Josephus*, It. *Guiseppe*, Sp. *José*; fem. *Josepha, Josephine* **2** *Bible a)* Jacob's eleventh son, whose mother was Rachel: Joseph was sold into slavery in Egypt by his jealous brothers but became a high official there: Gen. 30:22-24; 37; 45 *b)* the husband of Mary, mother of Jesus: Matt. 1:18-25: his day is March 19 (also called *Saint Joseph*) **3** *c.* 1840-1904; Nez Percé Indian chief

Jo·se·phine (jō′zə fēn, -sə-) ⟦Fr *Joséphine* < *Joseph*: see prec. ⟧ **1** a feminine name: dim. *Jo, Josie*; var. *Josepha* **2** 1763-1814; wife of Napoleon (1796-1809) & empress of France (1804-09): wife (1779-94) of Vicomte *Alexandre de Beauharnais* (1760-94) Fr.

army officer

Joseph of Ar·i·ma·the·a (ar'ə mə thē'ə) *Bible* a wealthy disciple who provided a tomb for Jesus' body: Matt. 27:57-60

Jo·se·phus (jō sē'fəs), **(Flavius)** A.D. 37-*c.* 95; Jewish historian

Josh·u·a (jäsh'yōō ə, jäsh'ōō ə) ⟦Heb *yehōshū'a,* lit., help of Jehovah: see JESUS⟧ **1** a masculine name: dim. *Josh* **2** *Bible* Moses' successor, who led the Israelites into the Promised Land

Jo·si·ah (jō sī'ə, -zī'ə) ⟦Heb *yōshīyāh,* lit., the Lord supports⟧ *Bible* a king of Judah in the 7th cent. B.C.: 2 Kings 22, 23

Jos·quin des Prez (or **Des·prez**) (zhôs kan' dā prā') *c.* 1440-1521; Fr. composer

Joule (jōōl), **James Prescott** 1818-89; Eng. physicist

Jove (jōv) ⟦< L *Jovis* (used as gen. of *Juppiter,* JUPITER) < OL *Jovis* (gen. *Jovis*) < IE **diwes,* gen. of **dyēus* < base **dei-,* to gleam, shine⟧ JUPITER

Jow·ett (jou'it, jō'-), **Benjamin** 1817-93; Eng. classical scholar & translator of Plato and others

Joyce (jois) ⟦< older *Jocosa* < L *jocosa,* fem. of *jocosus,* jocose⟧ **1** a feminine and masculine name **2 James (Augustine Aloysius)** 1882-1941; Ir. novelist

Juan (hwän, wän) a masculine name: fem. **Jua·ni·ta** (hwä nēt'ə, wä-)

Juá·rez (hwä'res', -rez'), **Be·ni·to Pa·blo** (be nē'tô pä'blô) 1806-72; Mex. statesman: president of Mexico (1861-65; 1867-72)

Ju·bal (jōō'bəl) ⟦Heb *yūbhāl*⟧ *Bible* one of Cain's descendants, a musician or inventor of musical instruments: Gen. 4:19-21

Ju·dah (jōō'də) ⟦Heb *yehūdhāh,* lit., praised⟧ **1** a masculine name: dim. *Jude;* fem. *Judith* **2** *Bible* Jacob's fourth son, whose mother was Leah: Gen. 29:35

Ju·das (jōō'dəs) ⟦ME < LL(Ec) < Gr(Ec) *Ioudas* < Heb *yehūdhāh,* prec.⟧ *Bible* **1** Judas Iscariot, the disciple who betrayed Jesus: Matt. 26:14, 48 **2** Jude, the Apostle **3** a brother of Jesus and James: Mark 6:3; Matt. 13:55

Ju·das (jōō'dəs), **Saint** *see* JUDE

Judas Maccabaeus *see* MACCABAEUS, Judas

Jude (jōōd) **1** a masculine name: see JUDAH **2** *Bible a)* one of the twelve Apostles: his day is Oct. 28 (also called *Judas, Saint Jude*) *b*) its author, perhaps the Judas called Jesus' brother See JUDAS

Ju·dith (jo͞od′ith) ⟦LL(Ec) < Gr(Ec) *Ioudith* < Heb *yehūdhīth,* fem. of *yehūdhāh,* JUDAH⟧ **1** a feminine name: dim. *Judy* **2** *Apocrypha* a Jewish woman who saved her people by killing Holofernes

Ju·dy (jo͞od′ē) **1** a feminine name: see JUDITH **2** Punch's wife in a puppet show

Jug·ger·naut (jug′ər nôt′) ⟦altered < Hindi *Jagannāth* < Sans *Jagannātha,* lord of the world < *jagat,* world + *nātha,* lord⟧ an incarnation of the Hindu god Vishnu, whose idol, it was formerly supposed, so excited his worshipers when it was hauled along on a large car during religious rites that they threw themselves under the wheels and were crushed

Ju·gur·tha (jo͞o gʉr′thə) died 104 B.C.; king of Numidia (*c.* 112-104 B.C.)

Jules (jo͞olz) a masculine name: see JULIUS

Jul·ia (jo͞ol′yə, jo͞o′lē ə) ⟦L, fem. of *Julius*: see JULIUS⟧ a feminine name: dim. *Juliet*; equiv. Fr. & Ger. *Julie*, It. *Giulia*

Jul·ian (jo͞ol′yən, jo͞o′lē ən) ⟦L *Julianus* < *Julius:* see JULIUS⟧ **1** a masculine name: dim. *Jule*; equiv. Fr. *Julien*, It. *Giuliano*; fem. *Juliana* **2** (L. name *Flavius Claudius Julianus*) A.D. 331-363; Rom. general: emperor of Rome (A.D. 361-363): called *Julian the Apostate*

Ju·li·an·a (jo͞o′lē an′ə; *for 2, Du* yü′lē ä′nə) ⟦L, fem. of prec.⟧ **1** a feminine name: equiv. Fr. *Julienne*, It. *Giuliana* **2** (born *Juliana Louise Emma Marie Wilhelmina*) 1909- ; queen of the Netherlands (1948-80): daughter of Wilhelmina

Jul·ie (jo͞o′lē) a feminine name: see JULIA

Ju·li·et (jo͞o′lē et′, -it; jo͞o′lē et′; jo͞ol′yit) ⟦Fr *Juliette*, dim. < L *Julia*⟧ **1** a feminine name: see JULIA **2** the heroine of Shakespeare's tragedy *Romeo and Juliet*: see ROMEO

Jul·ius (jo͞ol′yəs, jo͞o′lē əs) ⟦L, name of a Roman gens⟧ **1** a masculine name: dim. *Jule, Julie*; equiv. Fr. *Jules*, It. *Giulio*, Sp. *Julio*; fem. *Julia* **2 Julius II** (born *Giuliano della Rovere*) 1443-1513; pope (1503-13)

Julius Caesar *see* CAESAR, (Gaius) Julius

June (jo͞on) ⟦OFr < L *Junius* < *mensis Junius,* the month of *Juno*⟧ a feminine name

Jung (yoon), **Carl Gus·tav** (goos′täf′) 1875-1961; Swiss
psychologist & psychiatrist

Ju·no (jōō′nō) ⟦L⟧ *Rom. Myth.* the sister and wife of
Jupiter, queen of the gods, and goddess of marriage:
identified with the Greek Hera

Ju·pi·ter (jōō′pit ər) ⟦L *Juppiter,* orig. a voc. < bases of
Jovis, JOVE & *pater,* father⟧ *Rom. Myth.* the chief
deity, god of thunder and the skies: identified with the
Greek Zeus

Jupiter Plu·vi·us (plōō′vē əs) ⟦L, lit., Jupiter who brings
rain: *pluvius,* rainy < *pluere,* to rain, ult. < IE *pleu-,
to flow, pour < base *pel-,* to pour, fill⟧ Jupiter
regarded as the giver of rain

Jus·tin (jus′tin) ⟦L *Justinus* < *justus,* lawful, rightful,
proper < *jus,* right, law < IE *yewos,* fixed rule⟧ **1** a
masculine name: var. *Justus;* fem. *Justina* **2** Saint (*c.*
A.D. 100-*c.* 165); Christian apologist & martyr, born in
Samaria: his day is June 1: called *Justin Martyr*

Jus·ti·na (jus tē′nə, -tĭ′-) ⟦L, fem. of *Justinus:* see prec.⟧
a feminine name: dim. *Tina;* var. *Justine*

Jus·tin·i·an I (jus tin′ē ən) (L. name *Flavius Ancius Jus-
tinianus*) A.D. 483-565; Byzantine emperor (527-565):
known for the codification of Roman law: called *the
Great*

Ju·ve·nal (jōō′və nəl) (L. name *Decimus Junius
Juvenalis*) *c.* A.D. 60-*c.* 140; Rom. satirical poet

K

Kaf·ka (käf′kə), **Franz** (fränts) 1883-1924; Austrian-
Czech writer

Ka·ga·wa (kä′gä wä′), **To·yo·hi·ko** (tō′yō hē′kō) 1888-
1960; Jpn. social reformer & writer

Kai·ser (kī′zər), **Henry J(ohn)** 1882-1967; U.S. industrialist

Kalb, Johann *see* DE KALB, Johann

Ka·li (kä′lē) a Hindu goddess viewed both as destroying
life and as giving it

Ka·li·da·sa (kä′lē dä′sä) fl. 5th cent. A.D.; Hindu poet &
dramatist

Ka·ma (kä′mə) ⟦Sans *kāma,* desire, love, god of love <
IE *kang-* < base *ka-,* to desire⟧ *Hindu Myth.* the god
of love

Ka·me·ha·me·ha I (kä mä′hä mä′hä) *c.* 1758-1819; 1st

king of the Hawaiian Islands (1810-19): called *the Great*

Kan·din·sky (kan din′skē), **Was·si·li** (or **Va·si·li**) (vas′ə lē′) 1866-1944; Russ. painter in Germany & France

Kant (känt, kant), **Immanuel** 1724-1804; Ger. philosopher

Ka·pi·tza (kä′pi tsä′), **Pë·tr L**(**eonidovich**) (pyô′tər) 1894-1984; Soviet nuclear physicist

Ka·ra·jan (kär′ə yän′), **Herbert von** 1908-89; Austrian conductor

Kar·en (kar′ən) a feminine name: see CATHERINE

Kar·rer (kär′ər), **Paul** 1889-1971; Swiss chemist

Kast·ler (kàst ler′), **Al·fred** (àl fred′) 1902-84; Fr. physicist

Kate (kāt) a feminine name: dim. *Katie*: see CATHERINE

Kath·er·ine, **Kath·a·rine** (kath′ə rin, -ər in; kath′rin) a feminine name: dim. *Kate, Kathy, Kay, Kit, Kitty*: see CATHERINE: also **Kath·ryn** (kath′rin)

Kath·leen (kath′lēn, kath lēn′) ‖ Ir ‖ a feminine name: see CATHERINE

Kath·y (kath′ē) a feminine name: see CATHERINE, KATHERINE

Kauf·man (kôf′mən), **George S**(**imon**) 1889-1961; U.S. playwright

Ka·wa·ba·ta (kä′wä bä′tä), **Ya·su·na·ri** (yä′sōō nä′rē) 1899-1972; Jpn. writer

Kay (kā) **1** a feminine name: see KATHERINE **2** a masculine name **3** Sir *Arthurian Legend* a knight of the Round Table, the boastful and rude seneschal and foster brother of King Arthur

Ka·zan·tza·kis (kä′zän dzä′kēs′), **Ni·kos** (nē′kôs) 1885-1957; Gr. novelist

Kean (kēn), **Edmund** 1787-1833; Eng. actor

Kea·ton (kēt′n), **Bus·ter** (bus′tər) (born *Joseph Francis Keaton*) 1895-1966; U.S. comic film actor

Keats (kēts), **John** 1795-1821; Eng. poet

Ke·ble (kē′bəl), **John** 1792-1866; Eng. Anglican clergyman & poet: a founder of the Oxford movement

Keith (kēth) ‖ Scot < Gael base meaning "the wind" ‖ a masculine name

Kel·ler (kel′ər), **Helen Adams** 1880-1968; U.S. writer & lecturer: blind & deaf from infancy, she was taught to speak & read

Kel·ly (kel′ē) a feminine name

Kel·vin (kel′vin) ‖ < Eng surname ‖ **1** a masculine name **2** 1st Baron (*William Thomson*) 1824-1907; Brit. physicist & mathematician

Ke·mal A·ta·türk (ke mäl′ ät ä tʉrk′) 1881-1938; Turk. general: 1st president of Turkey (1923-38): also called *Mustafa Kemal* or *Kemal Pasha*

Kem·pis (kem′pis), **Thomas à** (born *Thomas Hamerken* or *Hammerlein*) *c.* 1380-1471; Ger. monk & scholar

Ken·drew (ken′drōō′), **Sir John Cow·der·y** (kou′dər ē) 1917- ; Brit. biochemist

Ken·nan (ken′ən), **George F(rost)** 1904- ; U.S. diplomat & historian

Ken·ne·dy (ken′ə dē) **1 John Fitzgerald** 1917-63; 35th president of the U.S. (1961-63): assassinated **2 Joseph Patrick** 1888-1969; U.S. businessman & diplomat: father of John & Robert **3 Robert Francis** 1925-68; U.S. lawyer & political leader: assassinated

Ken·neth (ken′əth) ‖ Scot < Gael *Caioneach*, lit., handsome ‖ a masculine name: dim. *Ken, Kenny*

Kent (kent) **1 James** 1763-1847; U.S. jurist **2 Rock·well** (räk′wel′) 1882-1971; U.S. artist

Kep·ler (kep′lər), **Jo·han·nes** (yô hän′əs) 1571-1630; Ger. astronomer & mathematician

Ke·ren·sky (kə ren′skē′; *Russ* kye′ryen skē), **A·lek·san·dr Fe·o·do·ro·vich** (ä′lyek sän′dər fyô′dô rô′vich) 1881-1970; Russ. revolutionary leader: prime minister of Russia (July-Nov., 1917), overthrown by the Bolshevik Revolution: in the U.S. after 1940

Kern (kʉrn), **Jerome (David)** 1885-1945; U.S. composer

Ker·ou·ac (ker′ōō ak′), **Jack** (born *Jean Louis Kerouac*) 1922-69; U.S. writer

Ket·ter·ing (ket′ər iŋ), **Charles Franklin** 1876-1958; U.S. electrical engineer & inventor

Kev·in (kev′in) ‖ Ir *Caomghin* < OIr *Coemgen*, lit., comely birth ‖ a masculine name

Key (kē), **Francis Scott** 1779-1843; U.S. lawyer: wrote "The Star-Spangled Banner"

Keynes (kānz), **John Maynard** 1st Baron Keynes 1883-1946; Eng. economist & writer

Kha·cha·tu·ri·an (kach′ə tōōr′ē ən, kä′chə-), **A·ram** (är′əm) 1903-78; Soviet composer

Kha·da·fy (kə dä′fē) *see* QADDAFI, Muammar al-

Khayyám, Omar *see* OMAR KHAYYÁM

Kho·mei·ni (kō mān′ē, kə-), Ayatollah **Ru·hol·la** (Mussaui) (roo hō′lə) 1900-89; fundamentalist religious leader of Iran (1979-89)

Kho·ra·na (kə rän′ə), **Har Go·bind** (här gō′bind′) 1922- ; U.S. biochemist, born in India

Khru·shchev (kroo′shôf′), **Ni·ki·ta Ser·gey·e·vich** (ni kē′tä syer gā′ye vich) 1894-1971; premier of the U.S.S.R. (1958-64)

Khu·fu (koo′foo′) fl. *c.* 2650 B.C.; king of Egypt, of the IVth dynasty: builder of the largest of the Great Pyramids

Kidd (kid), **Captain (William)** *c.* 1645-1701; Brit. privateer & pirate, born in Scotland: hanged

Kier·ke·gaard (kir′kə gärd′, -gôr′), **Sø·ren (Aabye)** (sö′rən) 1813-55; Dan. philosopher & theologian

Kil·mer (kil′mər), **(Alfred) Joyce** 1886-1918; U.S. poet

Kim·ber·ly (kim′bər lē) a feminine name: dim. *Kim, Kimmy*

King (kiŋ) **1 Martin Luther, Jr.** 1929-68; U.S. clergyman & leader in the black civil rights movement: assassinated **2 (William Lyon) Mackenzie** 1874-1950; Cdn. statesman: prime minister (1921-26; 1926-30; 1935-48)

King Lear (lir) the title character of a play by Shakespeare: Lear's division of his kingdom between his older daughters, Goneril and Regan, and disinheritance of his youngest, Cordelia, lead to civil strife and his own insanity and death

Kin·sey (kin′zē), **Alfred Charles** 1894-1956; U.S. zoologist: studied human sexual behavior in the U.S.

Kip·ling (kip′liŋ), **(Joseph) Rud·yard** (rud′yərd) 1865-1936; Eng. writer, born in India

Kirch·hoff (kir′H′hôf′), **Gus·tav Ro·bert** (goos′täf′ rō′bert′) 1824-87; Ger. physicist

Kirch·ner (kirk′nər, kir′H′nər), **Ernst Lud·wig** 1880-1938: Ger. painter & sculptor

Kis·sin·ger (kis′ən jər), **Henry Alfred** 1923- ; U.S. secretary of state (1973-77), born in Germany

Kit (kit) **1** a masculine name: see CHRISTOPHER **2** a feminine name: see CATHERINE, KATHERINE

Kitch·e·ner (kich′ə nər), **Horatio Herbert** 1st Earl Kitchener of Khartoum 1850-1916; Brit. military officer & statesman, born in Ireland

Kit·tredge (kit′rij), **George Ly·man** (lī′mən) 1860-1941; U.S. Shakespearean scholar & educator

Kit·ty (kit′ē) a feminine name: see CATHERINE, KATHER-

INE

Klee (klā), **Paul** 1879-1940; Swiss abstract painter

Klein (klīn), **Melanie** 1882-1960; Brit. psychoanalyst, born in Austria

Kleist (klīst), (**Bernd**) **Hein·rich Wil·helm von** (hīn'riH vil'helm' fōn) 1777-1811; Ger. playwright

Klem·per·er (klem'pər ər), **Otto** 1885-1973; Ger. conductor

Klimt (klimt), **Gus·tav** (gōos'täf') 1862-1918; Austrian painter

Kline (klīn), **Franz** 1910-62; U.S. painter

Knox (näks), **John** c. 1514-72; Scot. Protestant clergyman & religious reformer

Knut (k'nōot) *see* CANUTE

Koch (kōk; *Ger* kôkh), **Robert** 1843-1910; Ger. bacteriologist & physician

Ko·dály (kō di'), **Zol·tán** (zôl'tän') 1882-1967; Hung. composer

Koest·ler (kest'lər), **Arthur** 1905-83; Brit. writer & philosopher, born in Hungary

Ko·hel·eth (kō hel'eth) the author of Ecclesiastes, traditionally identified with Solomon

Kohl (kōl), **Hel·mut** (hel'mət; *Ger* hel'mōōt) 1930- ; chancellor of Germany (1990-); chancellor of West Germany (1982-90)

Ko·kosch·ka (kō kôsh'kə), **Os·kar** (äs'kər) 1886-1980; Brit. painter, born in Austria

Koll·witz (kôl'vits'), **Kä·the** (kā'tə) (born *Käthe Schmidt*) 1867-1945; Ger. painter, etcher, & lithographer

Kooning, Willem de *see* DE KOONING, Willem

Koop·mans (kōōp'mənz), **Tjal·ling Charles** (chä'liŋ) 1910-85; U.S. economist, born in the Netherlands

Korn·berg (kôrn'bʉrg'), **Arthur** 1918- ; U.S. biochemist

Kor·zyb·ski (kôr zip'skē), **Alfred** (**Habdank**) 1879-1950; U.S. semanticist, born in Poland

Kos·ci·us·ko (käs'ē us'kō; *Pol* kôsh chōōsh'kô), **Thaddeus** (born *Tadeusz Andrzej Bonawentura Kościuszko*) 1746-1817; Pol. patriot & general: served in the Am. army in the American Revolution

Kos·suth (käs'ōōth', kä sōōth'; *Hung* kô'shoot), **Louis** (Hung. name *Lajos Kossuth*) 1802-94; Hung. patriot & statesman

Ko·sy·gin (kə sē'gin), **A·lek·sei Ni·ko·la·e·vich** (ä'lyik sā'

nĕ′kô lä′yi vich′) 1904-80; Russ. statesman: premier of
the U.S.S.R. (1964-80)

Kous·se·vitz·ky (kōō′sə vit′skē), **Serge** (sɐrj, serzh)
(born *Sergey Aleksandrovich Kusevitsky*) 1874-1951;
U.S. orchestral conductor, born in Russia

Krafft–E·bing (kraft′ä′biŋ, kräft′-), Baron **Richard von**
1840-1902; Ger. neurologist

Kreis·ler (krīs′lər), **Fritz** (frits) 1875-1962; U.S. violinist
& composer, born in Austria

Kriem·hild (krēm′hilt′) ⟦ Ger < MHG *Kriemhilt* < Gmc
*grim-, a mask + **hild-*, battle ⟧ in the *Nibelungenlied*,
the wife of Siegfried and sister of Gunther: see also
GUDRUN

Kriss Krin·gle (kris′ kriŋ′gəl) ⟦ Ger *Christkindl* < *Christ*,
Christ + *kindl*, dim. of *kind*, child ⟧ SANTA CLAUS

Kris·ten (kris′tən) a feminine name: also **Kris′tin**

Krogh (krôg), **(Schack) August Steen·berg** (stēn′bərg)
1874-1949; Dan. physiologist

Kro·pot·kin (krô pôt′kin; *E* krə pät′kin), Prince **Pëtr A·**
lek·se·ye·vich (pyôt′r′ ä′lyik sā′yi vich′) 1842-1921;
Russ. anarchist & writer

Kru·ger (krōō′gər), **Paul** (born *Stephanus Johannes*
Paulus Kruger) 1825-1904; South African statesman:
president of the South African Republic (1883-1900)

Krupp (krup; *Ger* krѹop) family of Ger. steel & muni-
tions manufacturers in the 19th & 20th cent.

Ku·blai Khan (kōō′blī kän′, -blə-) *c.* 1216-94; Mongol
emperor of China (*c.* 1260-94): founder of the Mongol
dynasty: grandson of Genghis Khan: also **Ku·bla Khan**
(kōō′blə)

Kuhn (kѹon) **1 Richard** 1900-67; Austrian chemist **2**
Thomas S(amuel) 1922- ; U.S. historian & philosopher
of science

Kun (kѹon), **Bé·la** (bā′lä) 1886-*c.* 1937; Hung. Communist leader

Küng (kѹoŋ, kün), **Hans** 1928- ; Swiss theologian

K'ung Fu-tzu (kѹoŋ′ fōō′dzu′) *Chin. name of* CONFUCIUS

Ku·ro·sa·wa (kōō′rō sä′wä′), **A·ki·ra** (ä kē′rä′) 1910- ;
Jpn. motion-picture director

Ku·tu·zov (kə tōō′zôf′, -zôv′), **Mi·kha·il I·la·ri·o·no·vich**
(mē′khä ēl′ ē′lä rē ô nô′vich′) 1745-1813; Russ. field
marshal: defeated Napoleon at Smolensk (1812)

Kuyp (koip), **Aelbert** *alt. sp. of* Aelbert CUYP

Kuz·nets (kuz′nets′), **Simon** 1901-85; U.S. economist, born in Russia

Kyd (kid), **Thomas** 1558-94; Eng. dramatist

Kyle (kīl) a masculine and feminine name

L

La·ban (lā′bən) ⟦Heb *lavan*, lit., white⟧ *Bible* the father of Rachel and Leah: Gen. 29:16

La Bru·yère (lä′ brōō yer′; *Fr* là brü yer′), **Jean de** 1645-96; Fr. essayist & moralist

La·chaise (là shez′), **Gas·ton** (gàs tōn′) 1882-1935; U.S. sculptor, born in France

Lach·e·sis (lak′i sis) ⟦L < Gr *lachesis*, lit., lot < *lanchanein*, to obtain by lot or fate, happen⟧ *Gr. & Rom. Myth.* that one of the three Fates who determines the length of the thread of life

Lady the Virgin Mary: usually with *Our*

Lady of the Lake *Arthurian Legend* Vivian, mistress of Merlin; she lives in a castle surrounded by a lake

La·er·tes (lā ʉr′tēz′) ⟦L < Gr *Laertēs*⟧ **1** *Gr. Myth.* the father of Odysseus **2** in Shakespeare's *Hamlet*, the brother of Ophelia

La Farge (lə färzh′, färj′), **John** 1835-1910; U.S. artist

La·fa·yette (lä′fē et′, -fä-; laf′ē-; *Fr* là fà yet′), **Marquis de** (born *Marie Joseph Paul Yves Roch Gilbert du Motier*) 1757-1834; Fr. general & statesman: served (1777-81) in the Continental army in the American Revolution

La Fa·yette (lä′fē et′, -fä-; laf′ē-; *Fr* là fà yet′), **Comtesse de** (born *Marie Madeleine Pioche de La Vergne*) 1634-93; Fr. novelist

La·fitte (là fēt′), **Jean** *c.* 1780-*c.* 1826; Fr. pirate in the Gulf of Mexico: also sp. **Laf·fite′**

La Fol·lette (lə fäl′it), **Robert Marion** 1855-1925; U.S. legislator, reformer, & Progressive Party leader

La Fon·taine (lä′ fän tān′; *Fr* là fōn ten′), **Jean de** 1621-95; Fr. poet & writer of fables

La·ger·kvist (lä′gər kvist′; *Swed* lä′gər kvist′), **Pär (Fabian)** (par) 1891-1974; Swed. poet, novelist, & playwright

La·ger·löf (lä′gər lʉf′), **Sel·ma (Ottiliana Lovisa)** (sel′mä) 1858-1940; Swed. novelist

La·grange (là gränzh′), **Comte Jo·seph Louis de** (zhô zef lwe′ də) 1736-1813; Fr. mathematician & astronomer

La Guar·di·a (lə gwär'dē ə), **Fi·o·rel·lo H(enry)** (fē'ə rel' ō) 1882-1947; U.S. political leader: mayor of New York (1934-45)

Laing (laŋ), **R(onald) D(avid)** 1927-89; Brit. psychiatrist

La·ius (lā'yəs) ‖ L < Gr *Laios* ‖ *Gr. Myth.* a king of Thebes and the father of OEDIPUS

Lake (lāk), **Simon** 1866-1945; U.S. engineer & naval architect

Lake poets the English poets Wordsworth, Coleridge, and Southey, who lived in the Lake District

La·lo (lá lō'), **É·douard (Victor Antoine)** (ā dwär') 1823-92; Fr. composer

La·marck (lə märk'; *Fr* là màrk'), **Chevalier de** (born *Jean Baptiste Pierre Antoine de Monet*) 1744-1829; Fr. naturalist

La·mar·tine (lam'ər tēn'; *Fr* là màr tēn'), **Al·phonse Ma·rie Louis de (Prat de)** (àl fōns mà rē lwē'də) 1790-1869; Fr. poet

Lamb (lam) **1 Charles** (pen name *Elia*) 1775-1834; Eng. essayist & critic **2 Mary (Ann)** 1764-1847; Eng. writer: sister of Charles & coauthor with him of *Tales from Shakespeare* **3 Willis Eugene** 1913- ; U.S. physicist

Lamb, the Jesus

Lamb of God Jesus: so called by analogy with the paschal lamb: John 1:29, 36

Lan·ce·lot (làn'sə lət, -lät') ‖ Fr, double dim. < *Lance* < OHG *Lanzo*, lit., landed < *lant*, land ‖ *Arthurian Legend* the most celebrated of the Knights of the Round Table and the lover of Guinevere

Land (land), **Edwin Herbert** 1909-91; U.S. physicist, inventor, & industrialist

Lan·dau (län'dou'), **Lev (Davidovich)** (lyef) 1908-68; Soviet theoretical physicist

Lan·dor (lan'dər, -dôr'), **Walter Sav·age** (sav'ij) 1775-1864; Eng. writer & poet

Lan·dow·ska (län dôf'skä), **Wan·da** (vän'dä) 1879-1959; U.S. harpsichordist, born in Poland

Land·seer (land'sir), **Sir Edwin Henry** 1802-73; Eng. painter, esp. of animal pictures

Land·stei·ner (land'stī'nər; *Ger* länt'shtī'nər), **Karl** 1868-1943; U.S. pathologist & immunologist, born in Austria

Lang (laŋ) **1 Andrew** 1844-1912; Scot. writer **2 Fritz** 1890-1976; U.S. film director, born in Austria

Lang·er (laŋ'ər), **Susanne K(atherina)** (born *Susanne Katherina Knauth*) 1895-1985; U.S. philosopher

Lang·land (laŋ'lənd), **William** c. 1330-c. 1400; Eng. poet: also **Lang·ley** (laŋ'lē)

Lang·ley (laŋ'lē), **Samuel Pier·pont** (pir'pänt') 1834-1906; U.S. astronomer, physicist, & pioneer in airplane construction

Lang·muir (laŋ'myoor'), **Irving** 1881-1957; U.S. chemist

Lang·try (laŋ'trē), **Lillie** (born *Emily Charlotte Le Breton*) 1852-1929; Eng. actress

La·nier (lə nir'), **Sidney** 1842-81; U.S. poet

La·oc·o·ön (lā äk'ō än') ⟦L < Gr *Laokoōn*⟧ *Gr. Myth.* a priest of Troy who, with his two sons, is destroyed by two huge sea serpents after he warns the Trojans against the wooden horse

La·om·e·don (lā äm'ə dän') ⟦L < Gr *Laomedōn*⟧ *Gr. Myth.* father of Priam and founder of Troy

Lao·tzu (lou'dzu') 6th cent. B.C.; Chin. philosopher: reputed founder of Taoism: also sp. **Lao'–tze'** or **Lao'–tsze'**

La·place (là plàs'), **Marquis Pierre Si·mon de** (sē mōn' də) 1749-1827; Fr. mathematician & astronomer

Lard·ner (lärd'nər), **Ring(gold Wilmer)** 1885-1933; U.S. sports reporter & humorist

Lar·kin (lär'kin), **Philip (Arthur)** 1922-85; Brit. poet

La Roche·fou·cauld (là rôsh foo kō'), **Duc Fran·çois de** (frän swà'də) 1613-80; Fr. moralist & writer of maxims

La·rousse (lə roos', la-; *Fr* là roos'), **Pierre A·tha·nase** (à tà näz') 1817-75; Fr. lexicographer & grammarian

Lar·ry (lar'ē) a masculine name: see LAURENCE

La Salle (lə sal'; *Fr* là sàl'), **Sieur Ro·bert Ca·ve·lier de** (rô ber' kà və lyā' də) 1643-87; Fr. explorer in North America

Las Ca·sas (läs kä'säs'), **Bar·to·lo·mé de** (bär'tô lô mā' de) 1474-1566; Sp. missionary & historian in the Americas

Las·ki (las'kē), **Harold J(oseph)** 1893-1950; Eng. political scientist & socialist leader

Las·salle (lə sal'; *Ger* lä säl'), **Ferdinand** 1825-64; Ger. socialist & writer

Lat·i·mer (lat'ə mər), **Hugh** c. 1485-1555; Eng. Protestant bishop & religious reformer: burned at the stake

La Tour (là toor'), **Georges de** (zhôrzh də) 1593-1652;

Fr. painter

La·trobe (lə trōb′), **Benjamin Henry** 1764-1820; U.S. architect, born in England

Lat·ti·more (lat′ə môr′), **Rich·mond (Alexander)** (rich′mənd) 1906-84; U.S. scholar, translator, & poet

Laud (lôd), **William** 1573-1645; Eng. prelate: archbishop of Canterbury (1633-45): executed

Lau·ra (lôr′ə) ⟦prob. short for *Laurencia*, fem. of LAU-RENCE⟧ a feminine name: var. *Loretta, Lori, Lorinda*

Lau·rel (lôr′əl), **Stan(ley)** (born *Arthur Stanley Jefferson*) 1890-1965; U.S. motion-picture comedian, born in England

Lau·rence (lôr′əns) ⟦L *Laurentius*, prob. < *Laurentum*, town in Latium < ? *laurus*, laurel⟧ a masculine name: dim. *Larry*; var. *Lawrence*; equiv. Fr. *Laurent*, Ger. *Lorenz*, It. & Sp. *Lorenzo*; fem. *Laura*

Lau·ri·er (lô′rē ā′, lô′rē ā′), **Sir Wilfrid** 1841-1919; Cdn. statesman: prime minister (1896-1911)

La·val (là vál′; *E* lə val′), **Pierre** 1883-1945; Fr. politician: premier of France (1931-32; 1935-36): executed for treason

La·vin·i·a (lə vin′ē ə, -vin′yə) ⟦L⟧ a feminine name: var. *Lavina*

La·voi·sier (là vwà zyā′; *E* lə vwä′zē ā′), **An·toine Lau·rent** (än twàn lô rän′) 1743-94; Fr. chemist: guillotined

Law·rence (lôr′əns, lär′-) **1** a masculine name: see LAU-RENCE **2** **D(avid) H(erbert)** 1885-1930; Eng. novelist & poet **3** **Ernest O(rlando)** 1901-58; U.S. physicist **4** **Gertrude** (born *Gertrud Alexandra Dagmar Lawrence Klasen*) 1898-1952; Eng. actress **5** **Sir Thomas** 1769-1830; Eng. portrait painter **6** **T(homas) E(dward)** (changed name, 1927, to *Thomas Edward Shaw*) 1888-1935; Brit. adventurer & writer: called **Lawrence of Arabia**

Lax·ness (läks′nes), **Hall·dór (Kiljan)** (häl′dôr) (born *Halldór Gudjonsson*) 1902- ; Icelandic novelist

Lay·a·mon (lā′ə mən, lī′-) fl. *c.* 1200; Eng. poet and chronicler

Laz·a·rus (laz′ə rəs) ⟦LL(Ec) < Gr(Ec) *Lazaros* < Heb *el′azar*, lit., God has helped⟧ *Bible* **1** the brother of Mary and Martha, raised from the dead by Jesus: John 11 **2** the diseased beggar in Jesus' parable of the rich man and the beggar: Luke 16:19-31

Laz·a·rus (laz'ə rəs), **Emma** 1849-87; U.S. poet

Lea·cock (lē'käk'), **Stephen** (**Butler**) 1869-1944; Cdn. humorist & economist, born in England

Le·ah (lē'ə) ⟦Heb *Lē'āh*, gazelle⟧ **1** a feminine name **2** *Bible* the elder of the sisters who were wives of Jacob: Gen. 29:13-30

Lea·key (lē'kē), **L(ouis) S(eymour) B(azett)** 1903-72; Brit. anthropologist, born in Kenya

Le·an·der (lē an'dər) ⟦L < Gr *Leiandros* < ? *leōn*, lion + *anēr* (gen. *andros*), man, male: see ANDREW⟧ **1** a masculine name **2** *Gr. Legend* the lover of HERO

Lear (lir) **1** *see* KING LEAR **2** **Edward** 1812-88; Eng. humorist, illustrator, & painter

Lea·vis (lē'vis), **F(rank) R(aymond)** 1895-1978; Eng. literary critic

Le·brun (lə brën'), **Charles** (shȧrl) 1619-90; Fr. historical painter: also **Le Brun**

Leck·y (lek'ē), **William Edward Hart·pole** (härt'pōl') 1838-1903; Brit. historian, born in Ireland

Le·conte de Lisle (lə kōnt də lēl'), **Charles Ma·rie** (**René**) (shȧrl mȧ rē') 1818-94; Fr. poet

Le Cor·bu·sier (lə kôr bü zyā') (pseud. of *Charles-Édouard Jeanneret-Gris*) 1887-1965; Fr. architect, born in Switzerland

Le·da (lē'də) ⟦L < Gr *Lēda*⟧ *Gr. Myth.* a queen of Sparta and the wife of Tyndareus: she is the mother (variously by Tyndareus and by Zeus, who visited her in the form of a swan) of Clytemnestra, Helen of Troy, and Castor and Pollux

Led·bet·ter (led'bet'ər), **Hud·die** (hud'ē) (called *Leadbelly*) 1888-1949; U.S. blues singer

Led·er·berg (led'ər burg', lā'dər-), **Joshua** 1925- ; U.S. geneticist

Lee (lē) **1** ⟦var. of LEIGH; also short for LEROY⟧ a masculine and feminine name **2 Ann** 1736-84; Eng. mystic: founder of the Shakers in America (1776) **3 Charles** 1731-82; Am. general in the Revolutionary War, born in England **4 Henry** 1756-1818; Am. general in the Revolutionary War & statesman: called *Light-Horse Harry Lee* **5 Richard Henry** 1732-94; Am. Revolutionary statesman: signer of the Declaration of Independence: cousin of Henry **6 Robert E(dward)** 1807-70; commander in chief of the Confederate army in the Civil War: son of Henry **7 Tsung–Dao** (dzooŋ' dou') 1926- ; Chin. physicist in the U.S.

Leeu·wen·hoek (lā'vən hōōk'), **An·ton van** (än'tôn vän) 1632-1723; Du. naturalist & pioneer in microscopy

Le·gen·dre (lə zhän'dr'), **A·dri·en Ma·rie** (á drē an má rē') 1752-1833; Fr. mathematician

Lé·ger (lā zhā') **1 A·lex·is Saint–Lé·ger** (á lek sē san lā zhā') *see* ST. JOHN PERSE **2 Fer·nand** (fer nän') 1881-1955; Fr. painter

Legree, Simon *see* SIMON LEGREE

Le·hár (lā'här'), **Franz** (fränts) 1870-1948; Hung. composer of operettas

Leib·niz (līp'nits'), **Baron Gott·fried Wil·helm von** (gôt' frēt' vil'helm' fôn) 1646-1716; Ger. philosopher & mathematician: also sp. **Leib'nitz**

Leices·ter (les'tər), **Earl of** (*Robert Dudley*) c. 1532-88; Eng. courtier & general: favorite of Elizabeth I

Leif (lēf, lāf; lāv) ⟦ON *Leifr*, lit., descendant < base of *leifa*; akin to OE *læfan*, lit., to let remain⟧ a masculine name

Leif Ericson *see* ERICSON, Leif

Leigh (lē) ⟦< surname *Leigh* < ME *leye*, meadow⟧ a masculine and feminine name; var. *Lee*

Le·ly (lē'lē, lā'-), **Sir Peter** (born *Peter van der Faes*) 1618-80; Du. portrait painter in England

Lem·u·el (lem'yōō əl) ⟦Heb *lemū'ēl*, lit., belonging to God⟧ a masculine name: dim. *Lem*

Le·na (lē'nə, lā'-) a feminine name: var. *Lina*: see HELENA, MAGDALENE

L'En·fant (län fän'), **Pierre Charles** (pyer shárl') 1754-1825; Fr. engineer & architect who served in the Am. Revolutionary army & drew up plans for Washington, D.C.

Len·in (len'in; *Russ* lye'nyin), **V(ladimir) I(lyich)** (orig., surname *Ulyanov*; also called *Nikolai Lenin*) 1870-1924; Russ. leader of the Communist revolution of 1917: premier of the U.S.S.R. (1917-24)

Le·nore (lə nôr') a feminine name: see LEONORA

Le·o (lē'ō) ⟦L < *leo* (gen. *leonis*, lion < Gr *leōn* (gen. *leontos*)⟧ **1** a masculine name: var. *Leon*; fem. *Leona* **2** Saint Leo I (c. A.D. 400-461); pope (440-461): his day is November 10: called *the Great* **3** Saint Leo III (died A.D. 816); pope (795-816): his day is June 12 **4** Leo XIII (born *Gioacchino Pecci*) 1810-1903: pope (1878-1903)

Le·on (lē'än') a masculine name: see LEO

Le·o·na (lē ō'nə) a feminine name: see LEO

Leon·ard (len'ərd) ⟦Fr *Léonard* < OFr *Leonard* < OHG
Lewenhart, lit., strong as a lion < *lewo*, lion (< L *leo*:
see LEO) + *hart*, bold, hard⟧ a masculine name: dim.
Len, Lenny

Leonardo da Vinci *see* DA VINCI, Leonardo

Le·on·ca·val·lo (le ôn'kä väl'lô), **Rug·gie·ro** (r̅oo̅d je'rô)
1858-1919; It. operatic composer

Le·on·i·das (lē än'ə dəs) died 480 B.C.; king of Sparta (*c.*
491-480): defeated & killed by the Persians at Ther-
mopylae

Le·o·no·ra (lē'ə nôr'ə) a feminine name: dim. *Nora*; var.
Lenora, Lenore, Leonore: see ELEANOR

Le·o·nore (lē'ə nôr') a feminine name: var. of LEONORA

Le·ont·ief (lē änt'yef), **Was·si·ly** (vas'ə lē) 1906- ; U.S.
economist, born in Russia

Le·o·par·di (le'ô pär'dē), **Conte Gia·co·mo** (jä'kô mô)
1798-1837; It. poet

Le·o·pold (lē'ə pōld') ⟦Ger < OHG *Liutbalt* < *liut*, people (orig., prob., free man, akin to OE *leod*, man, king)
+ *balt*, strong, bold⟧ **1** a masculine name **2 Leopold I**
1640-1705; emperor of the Holy Roman Empire (1658-
1705) **3 Leopold I** 1790-1865; king of Belgium (1831-
65) **4 Leopold II** 1747-92; emperor of the Holy Roman
Empire (1790-92): son of Maria Theresa **5 Leopold II**
1835-1909; king of Belgium (1865-1909): son of Leopold I **6 Leopold III** 1901-83; king of Belgium (1934-
51): abdicated: son of Albert I

Lep·i·dus (lep'ə dəs), (**Marcus Aemilius**) died 13 B.C.;
Rom. triumvir (43-36 B.C.), with Antony & Octavian

Ler·mon·tov (ler'män tôf'), **Mi·kha·il Yur·ie·vich** (mē
khä ēl' y̅oo̅r'yə vich') 1814-41; Russ. poet & novelist

Le·roy (lə roi', lē'roi') ⟦ < Fr *le roi*, the king⟧ a masculine
name: also **LeRoy**

Le·sage (lə säzh'), **A·lain Re·né** (à lan rə nā') 1668-
1747; Fr. novelist & dramatist: also **Le Sage**

Les·lie (lez'lē, les'-) ⟦ < surname, orig. place name said to
be < *less lee* (*lea*), i.e., smaller meadow, dell⟧ a masculine and feminine name: dim. *Les*

Les·seps (les'əps; *Fr* le seps'), **Vicomte Fer·di·nand Ma·
rie de** (fer dē nän må rē' də) 1805-94; Fr. engineer &
diplomat: promoter & planner of the Suez Canal

Les·sing (les'iŋ) **1 Doris** (**May**) 1919- ; Brit. writer **2
Gott·hold E·phra·im** (gôt'hôlt' ā'frä im') 1729-81; Ger.

dramatist & critic

Les·ter (les'tər) 〚orig. surname < *Leicester*, city in central England〛 a masculine name: dim. *Les*

Le·ti·tia (li tish'ə) 〚< L *laetitia*, gladness < *laetus*, gay, glad〛 a feminine name: dim. *Letty*

Le·vi (lē'vī') 〚Heb, *lēwī*, lit., joining〛 **1** a masculine name: dim. *Lev* **2** *Bible* the third son of Jacob and Leah: Gen. 29:34

Lé·vi–Strauss (lā'vē strous'), **Claude** 1908- ; Fr. social anthropologist, born in Belgium

Lew·is (lōō'is) **1** a masculine name: dim. *Lew, Lewie*: see LOUIS **2** C(ecil) **Day** *see* DAY-LEWIS, C(ecil) **3** C(live) S(taples) 1898-1963; Brit. writer, born in Ireland **4** John L(lewellyn) 1880-1969; U.S. labor leader **5** Jerry Lee 1935- ; country music & rock singer and pianist **6** Mer·i·weth·er (mer'ē we*th*'ər) 1774-1809; Am. explorer: co-leader of the Lewis & Clark expedition (1804-06) to the Northwest **7** Sinclair 1885-1951; U.S. novelist **8** (Percy) Wynd·ham (win'dəm) 1884-1957; Brit. author & painter, born in the U.S.

Leyden, Lucas van *see* LUCAS VAN LEYDEN

Lib·by (lib'ē), W(illard) F(rank) 1908-80; U.S. chemist

Lich·ten·stein (lik'tən stīn', -stēn'), **Roy** 1923- ; U.S. painter

Lie (lē) **1** Jonas 1880-1940; U.S. painter, born in Norway **2** Jonas (Lauritz Edemil) 1833-1908; Norw. novelist: uncle of the painter **3** Tryg·ve (Halvdan) (trig'və) 1896-1968; Norw. statesman: 1st secretary-general of the United Nations (1946-53)

Lie·big (lē'biH), Baron Jus·tus von (yōōs'tōōs fôn) 1803-73; Ger. chemist

Lieb·knecht (lēp'kneHt'), **Karl** (kärl) 1871-1919; Ger. socialist leader

Lil·ith (lil'ith) 〚Heb *līlīth* < Assyr-Bab *lilītu*, lit., of the night〛 **1** in ancient Semitic folklore, a female demon or vampire that lives in desolate places **2** in medieval Jewish folklore, *a)* the first wife of Adam, before the creation of Eve *b)* a night witch who menaces infants

Li·li·u·o·ka·la·ni (li lē'ōō ō'kä lä'nē), **Lydia Ka·me·ke·ha** (kä'mä kā'hä) 1838-1917; queen of the Hawaiian Islands (1891-93)

Lil·li·an (lil'ē ən) 〚earlier *Lilion*, prob. < L *lilium*, lily〛 a feminine name: dim. *Lil, Lily, Lilly*: also **Lil'i·an**

Lil·y (lil'ē) 〚dim. of *Lilian* or < *lily*〛 a feminine name

Lin·coln (liŋ'kən), **Abraham** 1809-65; 16th president of the U.S. (1861-65): assassinated

Lind (lind), **Jenny** (born *Johanna Maria Lind;* Mme. *Otto Goldschmidt*) 1820-87; Swed. soprano: called the *Swedish Nightingale*

Lin·da (lin'də) a feminine name: see BELINDA

Lind·bergh (lind'bʉrg'), **Charles Augustus** 1902-74; U.S. aviator: made first nonstop solo flight from New York to Paris (1927)

Lind·say (lind'zē) **1** a feminine name: also **Lind'sey 2** (Nicholas) **Va·chel** (vā'chəl) 1879-1931; U.S. poet

Lin·nae·us (li nē'əs), **Car·o·lus** (kar'ə ləs) (Latinized form of *Karl von Linné*) 1707-78; Swed. botanist: considered the founder of the binomial nomenclature that is the basis of modern taxonomy

Li·o·nel (lī'ə nəl, -nel') ⟦Fr, dim. of *lion*, lion⟧ a masculine name

Lip·chitz (lip'shits'), **Jacques** (zhäk) (born *Chaim Jacob Lipchitz*) 1891-1973; U.S. sculptor, born in Lithuania

Li Peng (lē'peŋ') 1928- ; prime minister of China (1988-)

Lip·mann (lip'mən), **Fritz Albert** 1899-1986; U.S. biochemist, born in Germany

Li Po (lē'bō', -pō) A.D. 701-762; Chin. poet

Lip·pi (lip'ē; *It* lēp'pē) **1** Fi·lip·pi·no (fē'lēp pē'nō) *c.* 1457-1504; Florentine painter **2** Fra Fi·lip·po (fē lēp' pō) *c.* 1406-69; Florentine painter: father of Filippino: also called Fra Lip·po Lippi (lip'ō)

Lipp·mann (lip'mən), **Walter** 1889-1974; U.S. journalist

Lips·comb (lips'kəm), **William Nunn, Jr.** (nun) 1919- ; U.S. chemist

Li·sa (lē'sə, -zə) a feminine name: see ELIZABETH

Lisle *see* LECONTE DE LISLE & ROUGET DE LISLE

Lis·ter (lis'tər), **Joseph** 1st Baron Lister of Lyme Regis 1827-1912; Eng. surgeon: introduced antiseptic surgery

Liszt (list), **Franz** (fränts) 1811-86; Hung. composer & pianist

Li Tai Po (lē' tī' bō') Li Po

Little Corporal *name for* Napoleon BONAPARTE

Little John *Eng. Legend* a member of Robin Hood's band

Liv·ing·ston (liv'iŋ stən), **Robert R.** 1746-1813; Am. statesman; helped draft the Declaration of Independence

Liv·ing·stone (liv′iŋ stən), **David** 1813-73; Scot. missionary & explorer in Africa

Liv·y (liv′ē) (L. name *Titus Livius*) 59 B.C.-A.D. 17; Rom. historian

Llew·el·lyn (lōō el′in, lə wel′in; -ən) 〖Welsh *Llewelyn*, lit., prob., lionlike 〗 a masculine name: also **Llew·el′yn**

Lloyd (loid) 〖Welsh *Llwyd*, lit., gray 〗 a masculine name

Lloyd George, David 1st Earl Lloyd-George of Dwyfor 1863-1945; Brit. statesman: prime minister (1916-22)

Lo·ba·chev·ski (lô′bə chef′skē), **Ni·kò·lai I·va·no·vich** (nē kô lī′ ē vä′nô vich) 1793-1856; Russ. mathematician

Loch·in·var (läk′in vär′) the hero of a ballad in Sir Walter Scott's *Marmion*, who boldly rides off with his sweetheart just as she is about to be married to another

Locke (läk) **1 David Ross** *see* NASBY, Petroleum V. **2 John** 1632-1704; Eng. empirical philosopher

Lodge (läj), **Henry Cabot** 1850-1924; U.S. senator (1893-1924)

Loeb (lōb), **Jacques** (zhäk) 1859-1924; U.S. physiologist & biologist, born in Germany

Loe·wy (lō′ē), **Raymond (Fernand)** 1893-1986; U.S. industrial designer, born in France

Lof·ting (lôf′tiŋ), **Hugh (John)** 1886-1947; U.S. writer & illustrator, esp. of children's books, born in England

Lo·hen·grin (lō′ən grin′) *Gmc. Legend* a knight of the Holy Grail, son of Parsifal

Lo·is (lō′is) 〖LL(Ec) < Gr(Ec) *Lōis*: see 2 Tim. 1:5 〗 a feminine name

Lo·ki (lō′kē) 〖ON, lit., destroyer < IE base **leug-*, to break > Sans *rugná-*, broken 〗 *Norse Myth.* the god who constantly creates discord and mischief

Lo·max (lō′maks′), **Alan** 1915- ; U.S. scholar of folk music

Lom·bro·so (lôm brô′sô), **Ce·sa·re** (che′zä re) 1836-1909; It. physician & criminologist

Lon·don (lun′dən), **Jack** (born *John Griffith London*) 1876-1916; U.S. novelist & short-story writer

Long (lôŋ), **Hu·ey Pierce** (hyōō′ē) 1893-1935; U.S. political leader: assassinated

Long·fel·low (lôŋ′fel′ō), **Henry Wads·worth** (wädz′wurth′) 1807-82; U.S. poet

Lon·gi·nus (län jī'nəs), **Dionysius Cassius** *c.* A.D. 213-273; Gr. Platonic philosopher & rhetorician

Long·street (lôŋ'strēt'), **James** 1821-1904; Confederate general in the Civil War

Lope de Vega *see* VEGA, Lope de

Lorca, Federico García *see* GARCÍA LORCA, Federico

Lord 1 God: with *the* except in direct address 2 Jesus Christ: often with *Our*

Lord of hosts Jehovah; God

Lor·e·lei (lôr'ə lī') ⟦ Ger, altered by C. Brentano (1778-1842), Ger poet, after *Lurlei*, name of the rock (prob. lit., "ambush cliff") < MHG *luren*, to watch + *lei*, a cliff, rock ⟧ *Gmc. Folklore* a siren whose singing on a rock in the Rhine lures sailors to shipwreck on the reefs: orig. a character in literature

Lo·rentz (lō'rents), **Hen·drik An·toon** (hen'drik än'tōn) 1853-1928; Du. physicist

Lo·renz (lō'rents), **Kon·rad** (**Zacharias**) (kôn'rät) 1903-89; Austrian ethologist

Lo·ren·zo (lô ren'zō, lə-) a masculine name: see LAURENCE

Lo·ret·ta (lô ret'ə, lə-) ⟦ dim. of LAURA ⟧ a feminine name: see LAURA

Lo·ri (lôr'ē) a feminine name: see LAURA

Lo·rin·da (lô rin'də, lə-) a feminine name: see LAURA

Lor·na (lôr'nə) ⟦ apparently coined by R. D. Blackmore (1825-1900), Eng novelist < title of the Marquis of *Lorne* (1845-1914) ⟧ a feminine name

Lorrain, Claude *see* CLAUDE LORRAIN

Lor·raine (lô rān'; *Fr* lô ren') ⟦ Fr ⟧ a feminine name

Lot (lät) ⟦ Heb *Lōṭ* ⟧ *Bible* Abraham's nephew, who, warned by two angels, fled from the doomed city of Sodom: his wife looked back to see the destruction and was turned into a pillar of salt: Gen. 19:1-26

Lo·ti (lô tē'), **Pierre** (pseud. of *Louis Marie Julien Viaud*) 1850-1923; Fr. novelist

Lot·ta (lät'ə) a feminine name: see CHARLOTTE

Lot·tie, Lot·ty (lät'ē) a feminine name: see CHARLOTTE

Lou·is (lōō'ē; *for 1, usually* lōō'is; *Fr* lwē) ⟦ Fr < OFr *Loeis*; prob. via ML *Ludovicus* < OHG *Hludowig* < Gmc base **hluda-*, famous + **wiga-*, war, hence, lit., famous in war; in the form *Lewis*, sometimes an adaptation of Welsh *Llewelyn* ⟧ 1 a masculine name: dim. *Lou, Louie*; var. *Lewis*; equiv. L. *Ludovicus*, Ger. *Lud-*

wig, It. *Luigi,* Sp. *Luis,* Welsh *Llewellyn, Llewelyn;*
fem. *Louise* **2 Louis I** A.D.778-840; king of France &
emperor of the Holy Roman Empire (814-840): son &
successor of Charlemagne **3 Louis II de Bourbon** *see*
CONDÉ, Prince de **4 Louis IX** 1214-70; king of France
(1226-70): canonized as **Saint Louis,** his day is Aug. 25
5 Louis XI 1423-83; king of France (1461-83): son of
Charles VII **6 Louis XII** 1462-1515; king of France
(1498-1515) **7 Louis XIII** 1601-43; king of France
(1610-43): son of Henry IV **8 Louis XIV** 1638-1715;
king of France (1643-1715): his reign encompassed a
period of flourishing Fr. culture: son of Louis XIII **9
Louis XV** 1710-74; king of France (1715-74): great-
grandson of Louis XIV **10 Louis XVI** 1754-93; king of
France (1774-92): reign marked by the French Revolution: guillotined: grandson of Louis XV **11 Louis XVII**
1785-95; titular king of France (1793-95): son of Louis
XVI **12 Louis XVIII** 1755-1824; king of France (1814-
15; 1815-24): brother of Louis XVI

Lou·is (lōō'is), **Joe** (born *Joseph Louis Barrow*) 1914-81;
U.S. boxer: world heavyweight champion (1937-49)

Lou·i·sa (lōō ē'zə) ⟦It⟧ a feminine name: see LOUISE

Lou·ise (lōō ēz') ⟦Fr, fem. of LOUIS⟧ a feminine name:
dim. *Lou, Lulu;* var. *Eloise;* equiv. It. *Louisa*

Louis Napoleon (born *Charles Louis Napoléon Bona-
parte*) 1808-73; president of France (1848-52) & as
Napoleon III, emperor (1852-71): deposed: nephew of
Napoleon I

Louis Phi·lippe (fi lēp') 1773-1850; king of France
(1830-48): abdicated in Revolution of 1848

L'Ouverture *see* TOUSSAINT L'OUVERTURE

Louÿs (lwē), **Pierre** (born *Pierre Louis*) 1870-1925; Fr.
novelist & poet

Love 1 Cupid, or Eros, as the god of love **2** [Rare]
Venus

Love·lace (luv'lās'), **Richard** 1618-57; Eng. poet

Lov·ell (luv'əl), **Sir (Alfred Charles) Bernard** 1913- ;
Eng. astronomer

Low (lō) **1 Sir David** 1891-1963; Brit. political cartoonist, born in New Zealand **2 Juliette** (born *Juliette Gordon*) 1860-1927; U.S. founder of the Girl Scouts

Low·ell (lō'əl) **1 Abbott Lawrence** 1856-1943; U.S. educator **2 Amy** 1874-1925; U.S. poet & critic: sister of
Abbott **3 James Russell** 1819-91; U.S. poet, essayist, &

editor **4 Percival** 1855-1916; U.S. astronomer: brother of Abbott & Amy **5 Robert (Traill Spence, Jr.)** 1917-77; U.S. poet

Lowes (lōz), **John Livingston** 1867-1945; U.S. scholar, critic, & educator

Low·ry (lou′rē), **(Clarence) Malcolm** 1909-57; Brit. writer

Loy·o·la (loi ō′lə) *see* IGNATIUS (OF) LOYOLA, Saint

Lu·can (lōō′kən) (L. name *Marcus Annaeus Lucanus*) A.D. 39-65; Rom. poet, born in Spain

Lu·cas van Ley·den (lōō′käs′ vän lid′′n) (born *Lucas Jacobsz*) 1494-1533; Du. painter & etcher

Luce (lōōs), **Henry Robinson** 1898-1967; U.S. editor & publisher

Lu·ci·a (lōō chē′ə, -ä′, -sē′ə; lōō′sē ə, -shē ə, -shə) ⟦It < L: see LUCIUS, LUCY⟧ a feminine name: see LUCIUS, LUCY

Lu·cian (lōō′shən) ⟦L *Lucianus*, lit., of Lucius⟧ fl. 2d cent. A.D.; Gr. satirist, born in Syria

Lu·ci·fer (lōō′sə fər) ⟦ME < OE < L, morning star (in ML, Satan), lit., light-bringing < *lux* (gen. *lucis*), light + *ferre*, to bear⟧ *Theol.* SATAN; specif., in Christian theology, Satan as leader of the fallen angels: he was an angel of light until he revolted against God and, with the others, was cast into hell

Lu·cille (lōō sēl′) a feminine name: see LUCY

Lu·ci·na (lōō sī′nə) *Rom. Myth.* the goddess of childbirth: variously identified with Juno and Diana

Lu·cin·da (lōō sin′də) a feminine name: see LUCY

Lu·cius (lōō′shəs) ⟦L < *lux*, light⟧ a masculine name: fem. *Lucia*

Lu·cre·ti·a (lōō krē′shə, -shē ə) ⟦L⟧ a feminine name: equiv. Fr. *Lucrece*, It. *Lucrezia*

Lu·cre·ti·us (lōō krē′shəs, -shē əs) (born *Titus Lucretius Carus*) c. 96-c. 55 B.C.; Rom. poet & Epicurean philosopher

Lu·cul·lus (lōō kul′əs), **(Lucius Lucinius)** c. 110-c. 57 B.C.; Rom. general & consul: proverbial for his wealth & luxurious banquets

Lu·cy (lōō′sē) ⟦prob. via Fr *Lucie* < L *Lucia* fem. of *Lucius*: see LUCIUS⟧ **1** a feminine name: var. *Lucille, Lucile, Lucinda*; equiv. It. & Sp. *Lucia* **2** Saint (died c. A.D. 303); It. martyr: her day is Dec. 13

Lu·kács (lōō′käch′), **Györ·gy (Szegedi von)** (dyěr′dyə) 1885-1971; Hung. philosopher & literary critic

Luke (look) ⟦LL(Ec) *Lucas* < Gr(Ec) *Loukas*, prob. contr. of *Loukanos*⟧ **1** a masculine name **2** *Bible* one of the four Evangelists, a physician and companion of the Apostle Paul and the reputed author of the third Gospel and the Acts of the Apostles: his day is Oct. 18: also **Saint Luke**

Lul·ly (lü lē′), **Jean Bap·tiste** (zhän bȧ tēst′) (born *Giovanni Battista Lulli*) 1632-87; Fr. composer, chiefly of operas, born in Italy

Lu·lu (lōo′lōo) a feminine name: see LOUISE

Lu·na (lōo′nə) ⟦ME < L, the moon⟧ **1** *Rom. Myth.* the goddess of the moon: identified with the Greek Selene **2** the moon personified

Lunt (lunt), **Alfred** 1893-1977; U.S. actor

Lu·ther (lōo′thər), **Martin** ⟦Ger < OHG *Chlothar, Hludher* < Gmc base **hluda-*, famous + OHG *hari*, army, host: hence, lit., famous fighter⟧ 1483-1546; Ger. theologian & translator of the Bible: leader of the Protestant Reformation in Germany

Lu·tu·li (lə tōo′lē), **Albert** (**John Mvumbi**) 1898-1967; South African political leader, born in Zimbabwe: also **Lu·thu′li** (-thōo′-)

Lut·yens (luch′ənz), **Sir Edwin** (**Landseer**) 1869-1944; Eng. architect

Lux·em·burg (luk′səm burg′; *Ger* look′səm boork′), **Rosa** *c.* 1870-1919; Ger. socialist leader, born in Poland

Ly·cur·gus (lī kur′gəs) real or legendary Spartan lawgiver of about the 9th cent. B.C.

Lyd·gate (lid′gāt, -git), **John** *c.* 1370-*c.* 1450; Eng. poet

Lyd·i·a (lid′ē ə) ⟦LL(Ec) < Gr(Ec), orig. fem. of Gr *Lydios*, Lydian: see Acts 16:14⟧ a feminine name

Ly·ell (lī′əl), **Sir Charles** 1797-1875; Brit. geologist

Lyle (līl) ⟦ < Brit place name & surname⟧ a masculine and feminine name

Lyl·y (lil′ē), **John** *c.* 1554-1606; Eng. author & dramatist

Lynn (lin) ⟦prob. < Brit place name *Lynn* < Celt, as in Welsh *llyn*, a lake⟧ **1** a masculine name **2** a feminine name: var. *Lynne*

Ly·on (lī′ən), **Mary** 1797-1849; U.S. educator

Ly·san·der (lī san′dər) died 395 B.C.; Spartan naval and military commander

Ly·sim·a·chus (lī sim′ə kəs) *c.* 355-281 B.C.; Macedonian general: ruler of Thrace (323-281)

Ly·sip·pus (lī sip′əs) *c.* 360-*c.* 316 B.C.; Gr. sculptor

Lytton *see* BULWER-LYTTON, Edward George Earle Lytton

M

Mab (mab) *see* QUEEN MAB

Ma·bel (māʹbəl) ‖ < *Amabel* < L *amabilis*, lovable < *amare*, to love ‖ a feminine name

Mac·Ar·thur (mak ärʹthər, mək-), **Douglas** 1880-1964; U.S. general: commander in chief of Allied forces in the SW Pacific, World War II

Ma·cau·lay (mə kôʹlē) **1** Dame **Rose** 1881-1958; Eng. novelist **2 Thomas Bab·ing·ton** (babʹiŋ tən) 1st Baron Macaulay of Rothley 1800-59; Eng. historian, essayist, & statesman

Mac·beth (mək bethʹ, mak-) the title character of a play by Shakespeare: Macbeth, goaded by his ruthlessly ambitious wife, murders the king to gain the crown for himself

Mac·ca·bae·us (makʹə bēʹəs), **Judas** *see* MACCABEES

Mac·ca·bees (makʹə bēzʹ) ‖ LL(Ec) *Machabaei*, pl. of *Machabaeus*, surname of Judas < Gr(Ec) *Makkabaios* < ? Aram *maqqābā*, hammer: hence, lit., the hammerer ‖ family of Jewish patriots who, under Judas Maccabaeus, headed a successful revolt against the Syrians (175-164 B.C.) & ruled Palestine until 37 B.C.

Mac·Diar·mid (mək durʹmid), **Hugh** (pseud. of *Christopher Murray Grieve Scott*) 1892-1978; Scot. poet

Mac·don·ald (mək dänʹəld), **Sir John Alexander** 1815-91; Cdn. statesman, born in Scotland

Mac·Don·ald (mək dänʹəld), **(James) Ram·say** (ramʹzē) 1866-1937; Brit. statesman & Labour Party leader: prime minister (1924; 1929-35)

Mac·Dow·ell (mək douʹəl), **Edward Alexander** 1861-1908; U.S. composer

Mach·i·a·vel·li (makʹē ə velʹē), **Nic·co·lò (di Bernardo)** (nēʹkô lôʹ) 1469-1527; Florentine statesman & writer

Mac·ken·zie (mə kenʹzē) **1 Sir Alexander** *c.* 1763-1820; Cdn. explorer, born in Scotland **2 William Ly·on** (līʹən) 1795-1861; Cdn. journalist & insurgent leader, born in Scotland

Mac·Leish (mək lēshʹ), **Archibald** 1892-1982; U.S. poet

Mac·leod (mə kloudʹ), **John James Rick·ard** (rikʹərd) 1876-1935; Scot. physiologist: co-discoverer of insulin

Mac·Ma·hon (mȧk mȧ ōn′), **Comte Ma·rie Ed·mé Pa·trice Mau·rice de** (mȧ rē′ ed mä′ pȧ trēs′ mô rēs′ də) Duc de Magenta 1808-93; marshall of France: president of France (1873-79)

Mac·mil·lan (mak mil′ən, mək-), **(Maurice) Harold** 1894-1986; Eng. statesman: prime minister (1957-63)

Mac·Mil·lan (mak mil′ən, mək-), **Donald Bax·ter** (baks′ tər) 1874-1970; U.S. arctic explorer

Mac·Neice (mək nēs′), **Louis** 1907-63; Brit. poet, born in Ireland

Mac·pher·son (mək fur′sən), **James** 1736-96; Scot. poet: see OSSIAN

Mad·e·line (mad′′l in, -in′) a feminine name: see MAGDALENE

Ma·de·ro (mə der′ō; *Sp* mä *th*ā′rô), **Fran·cis·co In·da·le·cio** (frän sēs′kô ēn′dä le′syô) 1873-1913; Mex. revolutionist & statesman: president of Mexico (1911-13)

Madge (maj) a feminine name: see MARGARET

Mad·i·son (mad′ə sən) **1 Dol·ley** (däl′ē) (or, incorrectly, **Dolly**) (born *Dorothea Payne*) 1768-1849; wife of James **2 James** 1751-1836; 4th president of the U.S. (1809-17)

Ma·don·na (mə dän′ə) Mary, mother of Jesus

Mae (mā) a feminine name: see MARY

Mae·ce·nas (mĭ sē′nəs, mi-), **(Gaius Cilnius)** *c.* 70-8 B.C.; Rom. statesman & patron of Horace & Virgil

Mae·ter·linck (māt′ər liŋk′, met′-), **Count Maurice** 1862-1949; Belgian playwright, essayist, & poet

Mag·da·lene (mag′də lən, -lin, -lēn′; *also, for 2,* mag′ də lē′nə) ⟦LL(Ec) < Gr(Ec) *Magdalēnē*, lit., of Magdala, after *Magdala*, town on the Sea of Galilee⟧ **1** a feminine name: dim. *Lena*; var. *Madeline, Madelyn* **2** Mary Magdalene: Luke 8:2 (identified with the repentant woman in Luke 7:37) Also **Mag′da·len** (-lən)

Ma·gel·lan (mə jel′ən), **Ferdinand** *c.* 1480-1521; Port. navigator in the service of Spain: discovered the Strait of Magellan & the Philippine Islands

Mag·gie (mag′ē) a feminine name: see MARGARET

Ma·gi (mā′jī′) the wise men from the East (in later tradition, three in number) who came bearing gifts to the infant Jesus: Matt. 2:1-13

Ma·gritte (mȧ grēt′), **Re·né (François Ghislain)** (rə nā′) 1898-1967; Belgian painter

Mah·ler (mä′lər), **Gus·tav** (goos′täf′) 1860-1911; Austrian composer & conductor

Ma·hom·et (mə häm′it) *var. of* MOHAMMED

Ma·hound (mə hound′, -hōōnd′) 〚ME *Mahun* < OFr *Mahon*, contr. < *Mahomet*〛 **1** *archaic var. of* MOHAMMED **2** the Devil

Ma·ia (mā′ə, mī′-) **1** 〚Gr., lit., mother < *ma*, baby talk for *mētēr*, mother〛 *Gr. Myth.* one of the Pleiades, mother of Hermes by Zeus **2** 〚L, fem. of *Maius*, a deity (lit., ? he who brings increase, or the great one) < *Magnus* < *magnus*, great, big: later confused with Gr *Maia*〛 *Rom. Myth.* an earth goddess, sometimes identified with the Greek Maia: the month of May was named in her honor

Maid, the *name for* JOAN OF ARC

Maid Marian *Eng. Legend* Robin Hood's sweetheart

Maid of Or·lé·ans (ôr lā än′; E ôr′lē ənz) *name for* JOAN OF ARC

Mai·ler (mā′lər), **Norman** 1923- ; U.S. writer

Mail·lol (mà yôl′), **A·ris·tide** (à rēs tēd′) 1861-1944; Fr. sculptor

Mai·mon·i·des (mī män′ə dēz′) (born *Moses ben Maimon*) 1135-1204; Sp. rabbi, physician, & philosopher, in Egypt

Mainte·non (mant nōn′), **Marquise de** (born *Françoise d' Aubigné*) 1635-1719; 2d wife of Louis XIV

Mait·land (māt′lənd), **Frederic William** 1850-1906; Eng. legal historian & jurist

Ma·jor (mā′jər), **John** 1943- ; Brit. politician: prime minister (1990-)

Maker God

Mal·a·chi (mal′ə kī′) 〚Heb *mal'ākhī*, lit., my messenger〛 *Bible* a Hebrew prophet of the 5th cent. B.C.

Mal·a·mud (mal′ə məd, -mud′), **Bernard** 1914-86; U.S. writer

Mal·a·prop (mal′ə präp′), **Mrs.** 〚< ModE *malapropos* < Fr *mal à propos*, inappropriate〛 a character in Richard Sheridan's play *The Rivals* (1775), who makes ludicrous blunders in her use of words

Mal·colm (mal′kəm) 〚Celt *Maolcolm*, lit., servant of (St.) Columba〛 a masculine name

Malcolm X (eks) (born *Malcolm Little*) 1925-65; U.S. civil rights leader

Male·branche (màl bränsh′, mà lə-), **Ni·co·las (de)** (nē kô lä′) 1638-1715; Fr. philosopher

Ma·li·now·ski (mä'li nôf'skē), **Bro·ni·slaw (Kaspar)** (brô nē'släf) 1884-1942; U.S. anthropologist, born in Poland

Mal·lar·mé (må lår mā'), **Sté·phane** (stā fån') 1842-98; Fr. symbolist poet

Malmes·bur·y (mämz'bər ē, -brē), **William of** *see* WIL-LIAM OF MALMESBURY

Ma·lone (mə lōn'), **Edmund** (or **Edmond**) 1741-1812; Ir. literary critic & editor of Shakespeare's works

Mal·o·ry (mal'ə rē), **Sir Thomas** died *c.* 1471; Eng. writer: author of *Morte Darthur*, the first prose account in Eng. of the Arthurian legend

Mal·pi·ghi (mäl pē'gē), **Mar·cel·lo** (mär chel'lô) 1628-94; It. physiologist & pioneer in microscopic anatomy

Mal·raux (mål rō'), **An·dré** (än drä') 1901-76; Fr. writer & art historian

Mal·thus (mal'thəs), **Thomas Robert** 1766-1834; Eng. economist

Ma·nas·seh (mə nas'ə) ⟦Heb *mĕnaşşeh*, lit., causing to forget⟧ **1** *Bible* the elder son of Joseph: Gen. 41:52 **2** a king of Judah in the 7th cent. B.C. 2 Kings 21:1-18

Man·de·la (man del'ə), **Nelson (Rolihlahla)** 1918- ; South Afr. leader in the anti-apartheid movement

Man·de·ville (man'də vil'), **Sir John** 14th cent.; putative English author of a romanticized book of travels

Man·dy (man'dē) a feminine name: see AMANDA, MIRANDA

Ma·nes (mā'nēz') *var. of* MANI

Ma·net (må nā'), **É·douard** (ā dwår') 1832-83; Fr. impressionist painter

Ma·ni (mä'nē) *c.* A.D. 216-*c.* 276; Persian prophet

Man·i·chae·us, Man·i·che·us (man'i kē'əs) *var. of* MANI

Mann (män; *for* 2 man) **1** (**Luis**) **Hein·rich** (hin'riH) 1871-1950; Ger. writer: brother of Thomas **2 Horace** 1796-1859; U.S. educator **3 Thomas** (*Ger* tō'mäs) 1875-1955; Ger. novelist, in U.S. 1938-52

Man of Gal·i·lee (gal'ə lē') *name for* JESUS

Man of Sorrows a person alluded to by Isaiah (Isa. 53:3) and interpreted as being the Messiah: regarded by Christians as a name for Jesus

Mans·field (mans'fēld'), **Katherine** (born *Kathleen Mansfield Beauchamp*) 1888-1923; Brit. short-story writer, born in New Zealand

Man·sur (man soor') *c.* A.D. 712-775; Arab caliph (754-

775): founder of Baghdad: also **al'–Man·sur'** (al'-)

Man·te·gna (män te'nyä), **An·dre·a** (än dre'ä) 1431-1506; It. painter & engraver

Man·u·el (man'yōō əl) a masculine name: dim. *Manny*: see EMMANUEL

Ma·nu·ti·us (mə nōō'shē əs, -nyōō'-), **Al·dus** (ôl'dəs) (It. name *Aldo Manucci* or *Manuzio*) 1450-1515; It. printer

Man·zo·ni (män zō'nē; *It* män dzô'-), **A·les·san·dro** (**Francesco Tommaso Antonio**) (ä'les sän'drô) 1785-1873; It. poet & novelist

Mao Tse-tung (mou' dzu'dōōŋ') 1893-1976; Chinese communist leader: chairman of the People's Republic of China (1949-59) & of its Communist Party (1949-76): Pinyin *Mao Zedong*

Map (map), **Walter** c. 1140-c. 1209; Welsh poet & satirist: also, L. name, **Mapes** (māps, mä'pēz')

Ma·rat (må rå'), **Jean Paul** (zhän pôl) 1743-93; Fr. Revolutionary leader, born in Switzerland: assassinated by Charlotte Corday

Marc Antony *see* ANTONY, Mark

Mar·ceau (går sō'), **Marcel** 1923- ; Fr. mime

Mar·cel (mär sel') 1 a masculine name: see MARCELLUS 2 **Ga·bri·el** (gå brē el') 1889-1973; Fr. philosopher

Mar·cel·la (mär sel'ə) 〚L〛 a feminine name: see MARCELLUS

Mar·cel·lus (mär sel'əs) 〚L, dim. of *Marcus*〛 1 a masculine name: var. *Marcel*; fem. *Marcella* 2 (**Marcus Claudius**) c. 268-208 B.C.; Rom. statesman & general

Mar·cia (mär'shə) 〚L, fem. of *Marcius*, name of a Roman gens < *Marcus*, MARCUS〛 a feminine name: var. *Marsha*

Mar·ci·a·no (mär'sē ä'nō), **Rocky** (born *Rocco Francis Marchegiano*) 1923-69; U.S. boxer: world heavyweight champion (1952-56)

Mar·co·ni (mär kō'nē; *It* mär kô'nē), **Marchese Gu·gliel·mo** (gōō lyel'mô) 1874-1937; It. physicist: developed wireless telegraphy

Marco Polo *see* POLO, Marco

Mar·cus (mär'kəs) 〚L < *Mars*, MARS〛 a masculine name: var. *Mark*; fem. *Marcia*

Marcus Aurelius *see* AURELIUS, Marcus

Mar·duk (mär'dook') 〚Bab〛 *Bab. Myth.* the chief deity, orig. a local sun god

Mar·ga·ret (mär′gə rit, -grit) 〚ME < OFr *Margarete* < L *margarita*, a pearl < Gr *margarītēs* < *margaron*, a pearl, ult. < or akin to Sans *mañjaram*, a pearl, orig., bud〛 a feminine name: dim. *Greta, Madge, Maggie, Marge, Meg, Peg, Peggy;* var. *Margery, Margo, Margot, Marjorie;* equiv. Fr. *Marguerite,* Ger. *Margarete, Gretchen,* Ir. *Megan,* It. *Margherita,* Sp. *Margarita*

Margaret of An·jou (an′jōō′; *Fr* än zhōō′) 1430-82; queen of Henry VI of England (1445-61; 1470-71)

Margaret of Na·varre (nə vär′) 1492-1549; queen of Navarre (1544-49): writer & patroness of literature: also **Margaret of An·gou·lême** (än gōō lem′)

Margaret of Va·lois (và lwà′) 1553-1615; queen of Henry IV of France (1589-99): called *Queen Margot*

Mar·ger·y (mär′jər ē) 〚ME *Margerie* < OFr < L *margarita:* see MARGARET〛 a feminine name: dim. *Marge:* see MARGARET

Mar·got (mär′gō′, -gət) 〚Fr〛 a feminine name: see MARGARET: also **Mar′go′** (-gō′)

Mar·gue·rite (mär′gə rēt′) 〚see MARGARET〛 a feminine name

Ma·ri·a (mə rē′ə, -rī′-) a feminine name: see MARY

Mar·i·an (mer′ē ən, mar′-) 〚var. of MARION, but sp. as if < MARY + ANNE〛 a feminine name: var. *Marianne, Marianna*

Mar·i·anne (mer′ē an′, mar′-) 1 a feminine name: see MARIAN 2 *personification of* the French Republic: a woman in French Revolutionary costume

Maria Theresa 1717-80; archduchess of Austria: wife of Francis I (1708-65), emperor of the Holy Roman Empire: dowager empress (1765-80): queen of Bohemia & Hungary (1740-80): mother of Marie Antoinette

Ma·rie (mə rē′, ma-) a feminine name: see MARY

Marie An·toi·nette (mə rē′ an′twə net′; *Fr* mà rē än twà net′) 1755-93; wife of Louis XVI: queen of France (1774-92): daughter of Maria Theresa: guillotined

Marie de Médicis *see* MEDICI, Maria de'

Marie Louise 1791-1847; 2d wife of Napoleon I & empress of France (1810-15)

Mar·i·et·ta (mer′ē et′ə, mar′-) a feminine name: see MARY

Mar·i·lyn (mar′ə lin) a feminine name: see MARY

Ma·ri·net·ti (mar′ə net′ē, mär′-), (Emilio) Fi·lip·po Tom-

ma·so (fē lēp'pồ tôm mä'zồ) 1876-1944; It. poet

Mar·i·on (mer'ē ən, mar'-) ⟦Fr, orig. dim. of *Marie*, MARY⟧ 1 a masculine name 2 a feminine name: see MARY 3 Francis *c.* 1732-95; Am. general in the Revolutionary War: called the *Swamp Fox*

Ma·ri·tain (mȧ rē tan'), Jacques (zhäk) 1882-1973; Fr. philosopher

Mar·i·us (mer'ē əs), Gaius *c.* 157-86 B.C.; Rom. general & statesman

Ma·ri·vaux (mȧ rē võ'), Pierre Car·let de Cham·blain de (*Fr* pyer kȧr let shän bland' də) 1688-1763; Fr. playwright & novelist

Mar·jo·rie, Mar·jo·ry (mär'jə rē) a feminine name: see MARGARET

Mark (märk) 1 a masculine name: var. *Marc*: see MARCUS 2 *Bible* one of the four Evangelists, to whom is ascribed the second Gospel: his day is April 25: also **Saint Mark**

Mark Antony *see* ANTONY, Mark

Mark·ham (mär'kəm), (Charles) Edwin 1852-1940; U.S. poet

Marl·bor·ough (märl'bur'ō, -ə; *Brit* môl'bər ə), 1st Duke of (*John Churchill*) 1650-1722; Eng. general & statesman

Mar·lene (mär'lēn) a feminine name

Mar·lowe (mär'lō), Christopher 1564-93; Eng. dramatist & poet

Mar·quand (mär'kwänd', -kwənd), J(ohn) P(hillips) 1893-1960; U.S. novelist

Mar·quette (mär ket'), Jacques (zhäk) 1637-75; Fr. Jesuit missionary & explorer in North America: called *Père Marquette*

Mar·quis (mär'kwis), Don(ald Robert Perry) 1878-1937; U.S. humorist & journalist

Mars (märz) ⟦L⟧ 1 *Rom. Myth.* the god of war; identified with the Greek Ares 2 *personification of* war

Marsh (märsh), Reginald 1898-1954; U.S. painter

Mar·sha (mär'shə) a feminine name

Mar·shal (mär'shəl) ⟦< ModE *marshal* < *marescal* < OFr *mareschal* < Frank *marhskalk* or OHG *marahscalh*, lit., horse servant < *marah*, horse + *scalh*, servant < IE base *skel-*, to spring⟧ a masculine name: also **Mar'shall**

Mar·shall (mär'shəl) 1 George C(atlett) 1880-1959; U.S.

general & statesman: U.S. Army chief of staff (1939-45): secretary of state (1947-49) **2 John** 1755-1835; U.S. jurist: chief justice of the U.S. (1801-35) **3 Thurgood** (thur'good) 1908-93; U.S. jurist: associate justice, Supreme Court (1967-91)

Mar·ston (mär'stən), **John** 1576-1634; Eng. dramatist & satirist

Mar·tel (mär tel'), **Charles** *c.* A.D. 688-741; ruler of Austrasia (714-741) & of all the Franks (719-741): checked the Moorish invasion of Europe with a decisive victory near Tours (732): grandfather of Charlemagne

Mar·tha (mär'thə) ⟦LL(Ec) < Gr(Ec) < Aram *Mārthā*, lit., lady, fem. of *mār*, lord⟧ **1** a feminine name: equiv. Fr. *Marthe*, It. & Sp. *Marta* **2** *Bible* sister of Lazarus and Mary, chided by Jesus for being overly concerned with housework while he talked with Mary: Luke 10:40

Mar·tí (mär tē'), **Jo·sé (Julian)** (hô se') 1853-95; Cuban poet, essayist, & revolutionary patriot

Mar·tial (mär'shəl) (*Marcus Valerius Martialis*) *c.* A.D. 40-*c.* 104; Rom. epigrammatist & poet, born in Spain

Mar·tin (märt'n) ⟦Fr < L *Martinus* < Mars (gen. *Martis*), Mars: hence, lit., warlike⟧ **1** a masculine name **2** Saint (*c.* A.D. 316-*c.* 397) bishop of Tours: his day is Martinmas: also called **St. Martin of Tours** (toor; *Fr* tŏŏr) **3 Ar·cher John Porter** (är'chər) 1910- ; Eng. biochemist **4 Homer Dodge** (däj) 1836-97; U.S. painter

Mar·ti·neau (märt'n ō'), **Harriet** 1802-76; Eng. writer & economist

Mar·vell (mär'vəl), **Andrew** 1621-78; Eng. poet

Mar·vin (mär'vin) ⟦prob. ult. < Gmc **mari*, sea + **winiz*, friend⟧ a masculine name: var. *Mervin*

Marx (märks), **Karl (Heinrich)** 1818-83; Ger. social philosopher & economist, in London after 1850: founder of modern socialism

Mar·y (mer'ē, mar'ē; *also* mā'rē) ⟦ME *Marie* < OE < LL(Ec) *Maria* < Gr *Maria, Mariam* < Heb *Miryām* or Aram *Maryām*, lit., rebellion⟧ **1** a feminine name: dim. *Mamie, Molly, Polly*; masc. & fem. *Marie, Marion*; var. *Mae, Maria, Marietta, Marilyn, May, Miriam*; equiv. Ir. *Maureen, Moira*, Fr. *Marie, Marion*, Ger., It., & Sp. *Maria*, Pol. *Marya* **2** *Bible a)* mother of Jesus: Matt. 1:18-25: often referred to as the (*Blessed*) *Virgin Mary, Saint Mary b)* sister of Mar-

tha and Lazarus: Luke 10:38-42 *c*) MARY MAGDALENE
(see MAGDALENE, sense 2) **3 Mary I** (*Mary Tudor*)
1516-58; queen of England (1553-58): daughter of
Henry VIII & Catherine of Aragon: wife of Philip II of
Spain **4 Mary II** 1662-94; queen of England, Scotland,
and Ireland (1689-94), ruling jointly with her husband,
William III: daughter of James II

Mary, Queen of Scots (*Mary Stuart*) 1542-87; queen of
Scotland (1542-67): beheaded

Mary Magdalene MAGDALENE (sense 2)

Ma·sac·cio (mä sät′chô) (born *Tommaso Guidi*) 1401-
28; Florentine painter

Ma·sa·ryk (mä′sä rik; *E* mas′ə rik) **1 Jan** (yän) 1886-
1948; Czech statesman: son of Tomáš **2 To·máš Gar·
rigue** (tô′mäsh gà rēg′) 1850-1937; Czech statesman:
1st president of Czechoslovakia (1918-35)

Mas·ca·gni (mäs kän′yē), **Pie·tro** (pye′trô) 1863-1945;
It. composer

Mase·field (mās′fēld′), **John** 1878-1967; Eng. writer: poet
laureate (1930-1967)

Mas·i·nis·sa (mas′ə nis′ə) *c.* 238-148 B.C.; Numidian king
who fought as a Roman ally against Hannibal

Mas·sa·soit (mas′ə soit′) died 1661; chief of the Wampanoag Indians: signed a treaty with the Pilgrims of Plymouth in 1621

Mas·sé·na (mà sā nà′), **An·dré** (än drā′) Duc de Rivoli,
Prince d'Essling 1758-1817; Fr. marshal under Napoleon

Mas·se·net (mas′ə nā′; *Fr* màs ne′), **Jules** (Émile Frédéric) (zhül) 1842-1912; Fr. composer

Mas·sine (mà sēn′), **Lé·o·nide** (lā ô nēd′) 1896-1979;
U.S. ballet dancer & choreographer, born in Russia

Mas·sin·ger (mas′in jər), **Philip** 1583-1640; Eng. dramatist

Mas·si·nis·sa (mas′ə nis′ə) *alt. sp. of* MASINISSA

Master Jesus Christ: with *our, the,* etc.

Mas·ters (mas′tərz), **Edgar Lee** 1869-1950; U.S. poet

Math·er (math′ər, math-) **1 Cot·ton** (kät′′n) 1663-1728;
Am. clergyman & writer **2 In·crease** (in′krēs′) 1639-
1723; Am. clergyman & writer: father of Cotton

Math·ews (math′yōoz′), **Mit·ford M(cLeod)** (mit′fərd)
1891-1985; U.S. lexicographer & educator

Ma·til·da, Ma·thil·da (mə til′də) ‖ ML *Matilda,
Mathildis* < OHG *Mahthilda* < *maht*, might, power +

hiltia, battle; hence, lit., powerful (in) battle ‖ a feminine name: dim. *Mattie, Matty, Maud, Tilda, Tilly*

Ma·tisse (må tēs'), **Hen·ri** (än rē') 1869-1954; Fr. painter

Mat·thew (math'yōō') ‖ME *Matheu* < OFr < LL(Ec) *Matthaeus* < Gr(Ec) *Matthaios, Matthias*, contr. < *Mattathias* < Heb *mattithyāh*, lit., gift of God‖ 1 a masculine name: dim. *Mat*(*t*); var. *Matthias*; equiv. Fr. *Mathieu*, Ger. & Swed. *Matthaus*, It. *Matteo*, Sp. *Mateo* 2 *Bible* one of the four Evangelists, a customs collector to whom is ascribed the first Gospel: his day is Sept. 21: also **Saint Matthew**

Mat·thi·as (mə thī'əs) ‖Gr: see MATTHEW‖ *Bible* one of the Apostles, chosen by lot to replace Judas Iscariot: Acts 1:26: his day is May 14: also **Saint Matthias**

Maud, Maude (môd) a feminine name: see MATILDA

Maugham (môm), (**William**) **Som·er·set** (sum'ər set') 1874-1965; Eng. novelist & playwright

Mau·pas·sant (mō pä sän'; *E* mō'pə sänt'), (**Henri René Albert**) **Guy de** (gē də) 1850-93; Fr. writer of novels & short stories

Mau·reen (mô rēn') ‖Ir *Mairin*, dim. of *Maire*, MARY‖ a feminine name

Mau·ri·ac (mô'rē ak'; *Fr* mô ryak'), **Fran·çois** (frän swä') 1885-1970; Fr. novelist & essayist

Mau·rice (mô rēs'; môr'is, mär'-) ‖Fr < LL *Mauritius* < *Maurus*, a Moor‖ a masculine name: var. *Morris*; equiv. Ger. *Moritz*, It. *Maurizio*, Sp. *Mauricio*

Maurice of Nas·sau (nä'sou') Prince of Orange 1567-1625; Du. statesman & military leader

Mau·rois (mô rwä'), **An·dré** (än drā') (born *Émile Salomon Wilhelm Herzog*) 1885-1967; Fr. writer

Mau·ry (môr'ē), **Matthew Fon·taine** (fän tān') 1806-73; U.S. naval officer & oceanographer

Max (maks) a masculine name: fem. *Maxine*: see MAXI-MILIAN

Max·im (mak'sim) 1 **Hiram Percy** 1869-1936; U.S. inventor: son of Sir Hiram 2 **Sir Hiram Stevens** 1840-1916; Brit. engineer & inventor of weapons & explosives, born in the U.S. 3 **Hudson** 1853-1927; U.S. chemist & inventor of explosives: brother of Sir Hiram

Max·i·mil·ian (mak'sə mil'yən) ‖blend of the L names *Maximus* & *Aemilianus*‖ 1 a masculine name: dim. *Max* 2 (born *Ferdinand Maximilian Joseph*) 1832-67;

archduke of Austria: emperor of Mexico (1864-67); executed **3 Maximilian I** 1459-1519; emperor of the Holy Roman Empire (1493-1519) **4 Maximilian II** 1527-76; emperor of the Holy Roman Empire (1564-76)

Max·ine (maks ēn′) ⟦fem. of MAX⟧ a feminine name: see MAX

Max·well (maks′wel′, -wəl), **James Clerk** (klärk) 1831-79; Scot. physicist

May (mā) ⟦contr. of MARY, MARGARET, often assoc. with the name of the month⟧ a feminine name

Ma·ya (mä′yä′) ⟦Sans *māyā*⟧ *Hinduism* the goddess Devi, or Shakti, consort of Siva

Ma·ya·kov·ski (mä′yä kôf′skē), **Vla·di·mir** (Vladimirovich) (vlä dē′mir′) 1893-1930; Russ. poet

May·nard (mā′nərd, -närd′) ⟦ME < Anglo-Fr *Mainard* < OHG *Maganhard* < *magan*, power, strength (< IE base **māgh-*, to be able) + *hart*, strong, hard⟧ a masculine name

May·o (mā′ō) **1 Charles Horace** 1865-1939: U.S. surgeon **2 William James** 1861-1939; U.S. surgeon; brother of Charles Horace

Mays (māz), **Wil·lie** (Howard, Jr.) (wil′ē) 1931- ; U.S. baseball player

Ma·za·rin (ma za ran′; *E* ma′zə rin′), **Jules** (zhül) Cardinal (born *Giulio Mazarini*) 1602-61; Fr. statesman & prelate, born in Italy

Maz·zi·ni (mät tsē′nē, mäd dzē′nē), **Giu·sep·pe** (jōō zep′pe) 1805-72; It. patriot & revolutionist

Mc·Clel·lan (mə klel′ən), **George Brin·ton** (brint′′n) 1826-85; Union general in the Civil War

Mc·Cor·mack (mə kôr′mək), **John** 1884-1945; U.S. tenor, born in Ireland

Mc·Cor·mick (mə kôr′mik), **Cyrus Hall** 1809-84; U.S. inventor of the reaping machine

Mc·Cul·lers (mə kul′ərz), **Carson** (born *Carson Smith*) 1917-67; U.S. writer

Mc·Guf·fey (mə guf′ē), **William Holmes** 1800-73; U.S. educator: editor of a series of school readers

Mc·Kin·ley (mə kin′lē), **William** 1843-1901; 25th president of the U.S. (1897-1901): assassinated

Mc·Lu·han (mə klōō′ən), (Herbert) **Marshall** 1911-80; Cdn. writer & educator

Mc·Mil·lan (mək mil′ən), **Edwin Mat·ti·son** (mat′ə sən)

1907-91; U.S. chemist

Mead (mēd), **Margaret** 1901-78; U.S. anthropologist

Meade (mēd) **1 George Gordon** 1815-72; Union general in the Civil War **2 James Edward** 1907- ; Eng. economist

Mea·ny (mē'nē), **George** 1894-1980; U.S. labor leader: president of the AFL-CIO (1955-79)

Med·a·war (med'ə wər), **Peter Brian** 1915-87; Eng. immunologist

Me·de·a (mē dē'ə, mə-) ⟦L < Gr *Mēdeia*⟧ *Gr. Myth.* a sorceress who helps Jason get the Golden Fleece and, later, when deserted by him, kills their children

Me·di·ci (med'ə chē'; *It* me'dē chē') **1** family of rich, powerful bankers, merchants, & rulers of Florence & Tuscany in the 14th, 15th, & 16th cent., also noted as patrons of art & literature **2 Catherine de'** 1519-89; queen of Henry II of France (1547-59): Fr. name **Cathe·rine de Mé·di·cis** (kȧ trēn' də mä dē sēs') **3 Cos·i·mo de'** (kô'zē mô' de) 1389-1464; head of the Florentine Republic: called *the Elder* **4 Cosimo I de'** 1519-74; grand duke of Tuscany (1569-74): called *the Great* **5 Giu·lio de'** (jo͞o'lyô de) *see* CLEMENT VII **6 Lo·ren·zo de'** (lô ren'tsô de) 1449-92; ruler of Florence (1469-92): called *the Magnificent* **7 Maria de'** 1573-1642; queen of Henry IV of France (1600-10): queen regent (1610-17): Fr. name **Ma·rie de Mé·di·cis** (mȧ rē' də mä dē sēs')

Me·du·sa (mə do͞o'sə, -dyo͞o'-; -zə) ⟦ME *Meduse* < L *Medusa* < Gr *Medousa*, lit., ruler < *medein*, to govern < IE base **med-*, to measure, consider, wise counselor, doctor⟧ *Gr. Myth.* one of the three Gorgons, slain by Perseus

Meer (mer, mir), **Jan van der** *see* VERMEER, Jan

Me·gae·ra (mə jir'ə) ⟦L < Gr *Megaira*, lit., the exalted one (a euphemism) < **megaros*, great < *megas* < IE base **meĝ(h)-*, large⟧ *Gr. & Rom. Myth.* one of the three Furies

Meg·an (meg'ən, mē'gən) ⟦Ir⟧ a feminine name: see MARGARET

Mehe·met A·li (me met' ä lē') 1769-1849; viceroy of Egypt (1805-48)

Mei·ji (mā'jē') ⟦Jpn, lit., enlightened peace⟧ reign name of the emperor Mutsuhito of Japan

Me·ir (me ir'), **Gol·da** (gōl'də) (born *Goldie Mabovitch*, later *Goldie Myerson*) 1898-1978; Israeli statesman, born in Russia: prime minister of Israel (1969-74)

Meis·so·nier (me sô nyā'), **Jean Lou·is Er·nest** (zhän lwē er nest') 1815-91; Fr. painter

Meit·ner (mīt'nər), **Li·se** (lē'zə) 1878-1968; Austrian nuclear physicist, in the U.S. & Sweden

Me·lanch·thon (mə laŋk'thən), **Philipp** (born *Philipp Schwarzerd*) 1497-1560; Ger. Protestant reformer

Mel·a·nie (mel'ə nē) a feminine name

Mel·ba (mel'bə), **Dame Nellie** (*Helen Porter Mitchell Armstrong*) 1861-1931; Austral. soprano

Mel·bourne (mel'bərn), **2d Viscount** (*William Lamb*) 1779-1848; Eng. statesman: prime minister (1834; 1835-41)

Mel·chi·or (mel'kē ôr'), **Lau·ritz** (**Lebrecht Hommel**) (lou'rits) 1890-1973; U.S. tenor, born in Denmark

Mel·chiz·e·dek (mel kiz'ə dek', -kē'zə-) ⟦Heb *malkī-tsedheq*, lit., king of righteousness⟧ *Bible* the priest and king of Salem who blessed Abraham: Gen. 14:18

Mel·e·a·ger (mel'ē ā'jər) ⟦L < Gr *Meleagros*⟧ *Gr. Myth.* the son of the queen of Calydon and slayer of the Calydonian boar: he is sometimes also listed as one of the Argonauts

Me·lin·da (mə lin'də) a feminine name: var. *Malinda*

Me·lis·sa (mə lis'ə) ⟦Gr, lit., a bee < *meli*, honey < IE base **melit-*⟧ a feminine name

Mel·lon (mel'ən), **Andrew William** 1855-1937; U.S. financier: secretary of the treasury (1921-32)

Mel·pom·e·ne (mel päm'ə nē') ⟦L < Gr *Melpomenē* < *melpein*, to sing⟧ *Gr. Myth.* the Muse of tragedy

Mel·ville (mel'vil) ⟦after the surname (orig. place name)⟧ **1** a masculine name: var. *Melvil* **2 Herman** 1819-91; U.S. novelist

Mel·vin (mel'vin) ⟦< ? *mæl*, *mæthel*, council + *wine*, friend, protector⟧ a masculine name

Mem·ling (mem'liŋ), **Hans** c. 1430-94; Fl. painter, prob. born in Germany: also **Mem'linc** (-liŋk)

Mem·non (mem'nän') ⟦L < Gr *Memnōn*⟧ *Gr. Myth.* an Ethiopian king killed by Achilles in the Trojan War and made immortal by Zeus

Me·nan·der (mə nan'dər) c. 342-c. 291 B.C.; Athenian comic dramatist

Men·ci·us (men'shē əs, -shəs) (L. name of *Meng-tzu*) c. 372-c. 289 B.C.; Chin. Confucian philosopher

Menck·en (meŋ'kən), **H(enry) L(ouis)** 1880-1956; U.S. writer, editor, & critic

Men·del (men'dəl), **Gre·gor Jo·hann** (grā'gôr yō'hän') 1822-84; Austrian monk & botanist: founder of genetics

Men·de·le·ev (men'də lā'əf), **Dmi·tri I·va·no·vich** (də mē'trē ē vä'nồ vich') 1834-1907; Russ. chemist

Men·dels·sohn (men'dəl sōn', -zōn'; -sən) **1 Fe·lix** (fā' liks) (full name *Jakob Ludwig Felix Mendelssohn-Bartholdy*) 1809-47; Ger. composer: grandson of Moses **2 Moses** 1729-86; Ger. Jewish philosopher

Men·e·la·us (men'ə lā'əs) ⟦L < Gr *Menelaos*⟧ *Gr. Myth.* a king of Sparta: son of Atreus and husband of Helen of Troy

Men·e·lik II (men'ə lik) 1844-1913; emperor of Ethiopia (1889-1913)

Me·nén·dez de A·vi·lés (mə nen'dez' dā ä'vē läs'), **Pe·dro** (pe'drō) 1519-74; Sp. naval officer & explorer: founded St. Augustine, Fla., in 1565

Me·nes (mē'nēz') *c.* 3100 B.C.; traditionally, 1st king of the 1st dynasty of ancient Egypt

Meng·tzu (muŋ'dzu') *see* MENCIUS

Men·ning·er (men'iŋ ər), **Karl Augustus** 1893-1990; U.S. psychiatrist

Me·not·ti (mə nät'ē), **Gian Car·lo** (jän kär'lō) 1911- ; It. operatic composer, in the U.S.

Men·tor (men'tər, -tôr) ⟦L < Gr *Mentōr*, lit., adviser⟧ *Gr. Myth.* the loyal friend and advisor of Odysseus, and teacher of his son, Telemachus

Men·u·hin (men'yōō in), **Ye·hu·di** (yə hōō'dē) 1916- ; U.S. violinist

Men·zies (men'zēz'), **Sir Robert Gordon** 1894-1978; Austral. statesman: prime minister (1939-41; 1949-66)

Meph·i·stoph·e·les (mef'ə stäf'ə lēz') ⟦Ger, earlier *Miphostophiles* < ? Heb *mēphîtz*, destroyer + *tōphél*, liar⟧ a devil in medieval legend and later literary and operatic works, to whom Faust, or Faustus, sells his soul for knowledge and power: also **Me·phis·to** (mə fis'tō)

Mer·ca·tor (mər kāt'ər), **Ge·rar·dus** (jə rär'dəs) ⟦L calque of (*Gerhard*) *Kremer*, lit., dealer, merchant⟧ 1512-94; Fl. geographer & cartographer

Merchant of Ven·ice (ven'is), **the** Antonio, the merchant in Shakespeare's play *The Merchant of Venice*, who borrows money from SHYLOCK

Mer·cu·ry (mur′kyoo rē) ⟦L *Mercurius*, Mercury, of Etr orig.⟧ *Rom. Myth.* the messenger of the gods, god of commerce, manual skill, eloquence, cleverness, travel, and thievery: identified with the Greek Hermes

Mer·e·dith (mer′ə dith) ⟦Welsh, prob. < *mor*, sea + base of *differaf*, I protect; lit., sea protector⟧ **1** a masculine and feminine name **2 George** 1828-1909; Eng. novelist & poet **3 Owen** (pseud. of *Edward Robert Bulwer-Lytton*, 1st Earl of Lytton) 1831-91; Eng. poet & diplomat

Mer·gen·thal·er (mur′gən thäl′ər, -thôl′-), **Ott·mar** (ät′mär′) 1854-99; U.S. inventor of the Linotype, born in Germany

Mé·ri·mée (mā rē mā′), **Pros·per** (prôs per′) 1803-70; Fr. novelist, essayist, & historian

Mer·leau-Pon·ty (mer lō pōn tē′), **Maurice** 1908-61; Fr. philosopher

Mer·lin (mur′lin) ⟦ML *Merlinus* < Welsh *Myrrdin* < Brythonic **Mori-dünon* < **mori*, sea + Proto-Celt **dunom*, hill, fortified hill, fort, hence, lit., sea-hill or sea-fortress⟧ *Arthurian Legend* a magician and seer, helper of King Arthur

Mer·ton (murt′′n), **Thomas** 1915-68; U.S. religious, writer, & mystic

Mer·vin (mur′vin) ⟦prob. var. of MARVIN⟧ a masculine name: var. *Mervyn, Merwin, Merwyn*: see MARVIN

Me·shach (mē′shak′) ⟦Heb *mēshakh*⟧ *Bible* one of the three captives who came out of the fiery furnace miraculously unharmed: Dan. 3

Mes·sa·li·na (mes′ə li′nə), **Va·le·ri·a** (və lir′ē ə) *c.* A.D. 22-48; Rom. empress: 3d wife of Claudius I: notorious for her dissolute life: executed

Mes·siaen (mā syan′), **O·li·vi·er** (Eugène Prosper Charles) (ō lē vyā′) 1908-92; Fr. composer

Mes·si·ah (mə si′ə) ⟦used by the Geneva translators (1560) for LL(Ec) *Messias* & ME *Messie*, both (ME via OFr < LL) < Gr(Ec) *Messias* < Aram *měshīḥā*, Heb *māshīaḥ*, lit., anointed⟧ *Christianity* Jesus, regarded as the realization of the prophecy that the Messiah would come, and hence called *the Christ*: also **Mes·si·as** (-əs)

Metch·ni·koff (mech′ni kôf′), **É·lie** (ā lē′) (Russ. *Ilya Ilyich Mechnikov*) 1845-1916; Russ. biologist & bacteriologist, in France

Me·thu·se·lah (mə thoo'zə lə, -thyoo'-) ⟦Heb *methūshelah*, lit., ? man of the dart, or ? man of She-lah (a Babylonian deity)⟧ *Bible* one of the patriarchs, who lived 969 years: Gen. 5:27

Met·ter·nich (met'ər nik), Prince (**Klemens Wenzel Nepomuk Lothar**) **von** 1773-1859; Austrian statesman & diplomat

Mey·er·beer (mi'ər bir', -ber'), **Gia·co·mo** (jä'kə mō') (born *Jakob Liebmann Beer*) 1791-1864; Ger. operatic composer

Mi·cah (mi'kə) ⟦Heb *mĪkhā(yah)*, lit., who is like (God)?⟧ *Bible* a Hebrew prophet of the 8th cent. B.C.

Mi·chael (mi'kəl) ⟦LL(Ec) < Gr (LXX & N.T.) *Michaēl* < Heb *mĪkhā'ēl*, lit., who is like God?⟧ **1** a masculine name: dim. *Mike, Mickey*; equiv. Fr. *Michel*, It. *Michele*, Sp. *Miguel*; fem. *Michelle, Michele* **2** *Bible* one of the archangels

Mi·chel·an·ge·lo (mi'kəl an'jə lō', mik'əl-) (full name *Michelangelo Buonarroti*) 1475-1564; It. sculptor, painter, architect, & poet

Miche·let (mēsh le'), **Jules** (zhül) 1798-1874; Fr. historian

Mi·chelle, Mi·chele (mi shel', mē-) a feminine name: see MICHAEL

Mi·chel·son (mi'kəl sən), **Albert Abraham** 1852-1931; U.S. physicist, born in Germany

Mic·kie·wicz (mits kye'vich), **A·dam** (ä'däm) 1798-1855; Pol. poet

Mi·das (mi'dəs) *Gr. Myth.* a king of Phrygia granted the power of turning everything that he touches into gold

Mid·dle·ton (mid'l tən), **Thomas** 1580-1627; Eng. dramatist

Mies van der Ro·he (mēz' van dər rō'ə), **Ludwig** 1886-1969; U.S. architect, born in Germany

Mil·dred (mil'drid) ⟦OE *Myldthryth* < *milde*, mild + *thryth*, power, strength⟧ a feminine name: dim. *Mil, Millie, Milly*

Miles (mīlz) ⟦OFr *Miles, Milon* < OHG *Milo*, lit., mild, peaceful⟧ a masculine name

Mil·haud (mē yō'), **Da·rius** (dà ryüs') 1892-1974; Fr. composer

Mil·i·cent (mil'ə sənt) a feminine name: see MILLICENT

Mill (mil) **1 James** 1773-1836; Scot. philosopher, historian, & economist **2 John Stuart** 1806-73; Eng. philosopher & economist: son of James

Mil·lais (mi lā′), **Sir John Everett** 1829-96; Eng. painter

Mil·lay (mi lā′), **Edna St. Vincent** 1892-1950; U.S. poet

Mil·ler (mil′ər) **1 Arthur** 1915- ; U.S. playwright **2 Henry** 1891-1980; U.S. writer **3 Joa·quin** (wä kēn′) (pseud. of *Cincinnatus Heine Miller*) c. 1837-1913; U.S. poet **4 Joe** 1684-1738; Eng. stage comedian: *Joe Miller's Jest-book* (1739), a book of jokes attributed to him, was published after his death

Mil·let (mi lā′; *Fr* mē ye′, -le′), **Jean Fran·çois** (zhän frän swä′) 1814-75; Fr. painter

Mil·li·cent (mil′i sənt) ⟦OFr *Melisent* < OHG *Amalaswind* < *amal*, work + *swind-*, strong, akin to Goth *swinths*⟧ a feminine name

Mil·li·kan (mil′i kən), **Robert Andrews** 1868-1953; U.S. physicist

Milne (miln), **A(lan) A(lexander)** 1882-1956; Eng. playwright, novelist, & writer of children's books

Mi·lo (mī′lō) a famous Greek athlete, c. 520 B.C.

Mil·stein (mil′stīn′), **Nathan** 1904-92; U.S. violinist, born in Russia

Mil·ti·a·des (mil tī′ə dēz′) died c. 489 B.C.; Athenian general: defeated the Persians at Marathon in 490

Mil·ton (milt′'n) ⟦after surname or place name *Milton* < OE *Middel-tun* (lit., Middletown) & OE *Mylen-tun* (lit., Mill town)⟧ **1** a masculine name: dim. *Milt, Miltie* **2 John** 1608-74; Eng. poet

Mi·mir (mē′mir′) ⟦ON *Mimir*, redupl. of Gmc *mer-* < IE base *(s)mer-*, to remember⟧ *Norse Myth.* a giant guarding the spring of wisdom at the root of the tree Ygdrasil

Mind *Christian Science* God: in full **Divine Mind**

Mi·ner·va (mə nur′və) ⟦L, prob. < Etr⟧ **1** a feminine name: dim. *Minnie* **2** *Rom. Myth.* the goddess of wisdom, technical skill, and invention: identified with the Greek Athena

Min·gus (miŋ′gəs), **Char·lie** (chär′lē) (born *Charles Mingus*) 1922-79; U.S. jazz musician & composer

Min·ne·wit (min′ə wit), **Peter** *alt. sp.* of Peter Minuit

Mi·nos (mī′näs′) ⟦Gr *Minōs*⟧ *Gr. Myth.* a king of Crete, son of Zeus by Europa: after he dies he becomes one of the three judges of the dead in the lower world: see also Minotaur

Min·o·taur (min'ə tôr') ⟦ME *Minotaure* < L *Mino-taurus* < Gr *Minōtauros* < *Minōs*, Minos + *tauros*, a bull⟧ *Gr. Myth.* a monster with the body of a man and the head of a bull (in some versions, with the body of a bull and the head of a man), confined by Minos in a labyrinth built by Daedalus, and annually fed seven youths and seven maidens from Athens, until killed by Theseus: see also PASIPHAË

Min·u·it (min'yōō it), Peter *c.* 1580-1638; 1st Du. director of New Netherland (1626-31)

Mi·ra·beau (mir'ə bō'; *Fr* mē rà bō'), Comte (**Honoré Gabriel Riqueti**) de 1749-91; Fr. revolutionist, orator, & statesman

Mi·ran·da (mə ran'də) ⟦L, fem. of *mirandus,* strange, wonderful < *mirari,* to wonder at < *mirus,* wonderful < IE base **(s)mei-,* to smile⟧ a feminine name: dim. *Mandy*

Mir·i·am (mir'ē əm) ⟦Heb *miryām*⟧ **1** a feminine name: see MARY **2** *Bible* the sister of Moses and Aaron: Ex. 15:20

Mi·ró (mē rō'), **Jo·an** (zhōō än', hwän) 1893-1983; Sp. painter

Mi·shi·ma (mish'i mä'), **Yu·ki·o** (yōō'kē ō') 1925-70; Jpn. writer

Mis·tral (mēs träl') **1 Fré·dé·ric** (frā dā rēk') 1830-1914; Fr. Provençal poet **2 Ga·bri·e·la** (gä'brē ā'lä) (born *Lucila Godoy Alcayaga*) 1889-1957; Chilean poet

Mitch·ell (mich'əl) **1 Maria** 1818-89; U.S. astronomer **2 Peter Dennis** 1920-92; Eng. chemist **3 William** (called *Billy*) 1879-1936; U.S. army officer & aviation pioneer

Mith·ras (mith'rəs, -ras') ⟦L < Gr *Mithras* < OPers *Mithra*⟧ the ancient Persian god of light and truth, opponent of darkness and evil: also **Mith'ra** (-rə)

Mith·ri·da·tes VI (mith'rə dāt'ēz) *c.* 132-63 B.C.; king of Pontus (120-63): called *the Great*

Mi·tro·pou·los (mə trä'pə ləs, -trô'pōō lôs'), **Di·mi·tri** (də mē'trē) 1896-1960; U.S. conductor, born in Greece

Mit·ter·rand (mē te rän'; *E* mēt'ər änd', mit'-), **Fran·çois** (**Maurice**) (frän swä') 1916- ; Fr. statesman: president of France (1981-)

Mne·mos·y·ne (nē mäs'i nē', -mäz'-) ⟦L < Gr *mnē-mosynē,* memory < *mnasthai,* to remember < IE base **men-,* to think⟧ *Gr. Myth.* the goddess of memory, and mother (by Zeus) of the Muses

Mo·ab (mō′ab′) ⟦LL(Ec) < Gr(Ec) < Heb *mō′ābh*⟧ *Bible* a son of Lot: Gen. 19:37

Mo·di·glia·ni (mō′dēl yä′nē), **A·me·de·o** (ä′mä dā′ō) 1884-1920; It. painter, in France

Mo·dred (mō′dred′) *Arthurian Legend* treacherous nephew of King Arthur: they kill each other in battle

Mohammed (mō ham′id) ⟦Ar *Muḥammad,* lit., praise-worthy⟧ **1** c. A.D. 570-632; Arab prophet: founder of Islam **2 Mohammed II** 1430-81; sultan of Turkey (1451-81): captured Constantinople (1453)

Mohammed Ali *var. of* MEHEMET ALI

Mohammed Re·za Pah·la·vi (rē zä′ pä′lə vē) 1919-80; shah of Iran (1941-79); deposed

Mo·lech (mō′lek′) ⟦LL(Ec) *Moloch* < Gr(Ec) (in LXX) < Heb *mōlōkh, mōlekh*⟧ an ancient Phoenician and Ammonite god, to whom children were sacrificed by burning

Mo·lière (mōl yer′, mō′lē er′; *Fr* mô lyer′) (born *Jean Baptiste Poquelin*) 1622-73; Fr. dramatist

Mol·ly (mäl′ē) *nickname for* MARY

Mol·nár (mōl′när′, môl′-), **Fe·renc** (fe′rents) 1878-1952; Hung. playwright & novelist, later in the U.S.

Mo·loch (mō′läk′) MOLECH

Mo·lo·tov (mäl′ə tôf′, mō′-; -tôv′), **V(yacheslav) M(ikhailovich)** (born *Vyacheslav Mikhailovich Skriabin*) 1890-1986; Russ. statesman: foreign minister of the U.S.S.R. (1939-49; 1953-56)

Molt·ke (môlt′kə) **1** Count **Hel·muth (Johannes Ludwig) von** (hel′mōōt fôn) 1848-1916; Ger. general **2** Count **Helmuth (Karl Bernhard) von** 1800-91; Ger. field marshal: uncle of Helmuth

Momm·sen (mäm′zən, -sən), **The·o·dor** (tā′ə dôr′) 1817-1903; Ger. historian

Mo·mus (mō′məs) ⟦L < Gr *Mōmos,* lit., blame, ridicule⟧ *Gr. Myth.* the god of mockery and censure

Mo·na (mō′nə) ⟦Ir *Muadhnait,* dim. of *muadh,* noble⟧ a feminine name

Monck, George *alt. sp. of* George MONK

Mon·dri·an (män′drē än′), **Piet** (pēt) (born *Pieter Cornelis Mondriaan*) 1872-1944; Du. painter, in France & the U.S.

Mo·net (mō nā′, mə-; *Fr* mô ne′), **Claude** 1840-1926; Fr. impressionist painter

Mon·i·ca (män′i kə) ⟦LL < ?⟧ a feminine name

Monk (muŋk) **1 George** 1st Duke of Albemarle 1608-70; Eng. general & politician **2 The·lo·ni·ous** (Sphere) (thə lō′nē əs) 1920-82; U.S. jazz pianist & composer

Mon·mouth (män′məth), **Duke of** (*James Scott*) 1649-85; illegitimate son of Charles II & pretender to the Eng. throne: led an insurrection against James II: executed

Mo·nod (mô nō′), **Jacques Lu·ci·en** (zhäk lü syan′) 1910-76; Fr. biochemist

Mon·roe (mən rō′) **1 James** 1758-1831; 5th president of the U.S. (1817-25) **2 Marilyn** (born *Norma Jean Mortenson*, later changed to *Norma Jean Baker*) 1926-62; U.S. film actress

Mon·ta·gu (män′tə gyo͞o′), **Lady Mary Wort·ley** (wurt′ lē) (born *Mary Pierrepont*) 1689-1762; Eng. writer

Mon·ta·gue (män′tə gyo͞o′) the family name of Romeo in Shakespeare's *Romeo and Juliet*

Mon·taigne (män tän′; *Fr* mōn ten′y′), **Mi·chel Ey·quem de** (mē shel e kem′ də) 1533-92; Fr. essayist

Mon·ta·le (mōn tä′lā), **Eu·ge·nio** (ä′o͞o jä′nyô) 1896-1981; It. poet

Mont·calm (mänt′käm′; *Fr* mōn kälm′), **Lou·is Jo·seph de** (lwē zhō zef′ də) (full name *Louis Joseph de Montcalm-Gozon*, Marquis *de Saint Véran*) 1712-59; Fr. general defeated & killed by Brit. forces under Wolfe at Quebec

Mon·tes·quieu (mōn tes kyö′; *E* män′təs kyo͞o′), (Baron **de la Brède et de**) (born *Charles Louis de Secondat*) 1689-1755; Fr. jurist & political philosopher

Mon·tes·so·ri (mänt′ə sôr′ē; *It* mōn′tes sô′rē), **Maria** 1870-1952; It. educator

Mon·teux (mōn tö′), **Pierre** 1875-1964; U.S. orchestra conductor, born in France

Mon·te·ver·di (mänt′ə ver′dē; *It* mōn′te ver′dē), **Clau·dio** (**Giovanni Antonio**) (klou′dyô) 1567-1643 It. composer

Mon·te·zu·ma II (mänt′ə zo͞o′mə) *c.* 1480-1520; Aztec emperor of Mexico (1502-20)

Mont·fort (mänt′fərt) **1 Simon de** *c.* 1160-1218; Fr. soldier: led crusade against Albigenses **2 Simon de** Earl of Leicester, *c.* 1208-65; Eng. statesman & soldier: son of Simon (Fr. soldier)

Mont·gom·er·y (munt gum′ər ē), **Bernard Law** (lô) 1st Viscount Montgomery of Alamein 1887-1976; Brit.

field marshal in World War II

Mon·ther·lant (môn ter län'), **Hen·ri** (Millon) **de** (än rē' də) 1896-1972; Fr. novelist & playwright

Mood·y (mōōd'ē) **1 Dwight Ly·man** (lī'mən) 1837-99; U.S. evangelist **2 William Vaughn** 1869-1910; U.S. poet & playwright

Moore (moor) **1 George** (**Augustus**) 1852-1933; Ir. novelist, playwright, & critic **2 G(eorge) E(dward)** 1873-1958; Eng. philosopher **3 Henry** 1898-1986; Eng. sculptor **4 Marianne** (**Craig**) 1887-1972; U.S. poet **5 Thomas** 1779-1852; Ir. poet

Mo·ra·vi·a (mō rä'vē ə; *It* mô rä'vyä), **Al·ber·to** (äl ber' tô) (born *Alberto Pincherle*) 1907-90; It. writer

Mor·de·cai (môr'də kī') ⟦Heb *mordēkhai*⟧ **1** a masculine name: dim. *Mordy* **2** *Bible* the cousin of Esther (in the Book of Esther), who saved the Jews from the destruction planned by Haman

Mor·dred (môr'dred') MODRED

More (môr) **1 Hannah** 1745-1833; Eng. writer, esp. of religious tracts **2 Sir Thomas** 1478-1535; Eng. statesman & writer: executed: canonized in 1935: also called **Saint Thomas More**

Mor·gan (môr'gən) ⟦Welsh, lit., sea dweller (< *mor*, sea, ult. < IE base **mori*), akin to Ir *Muirgen*⟧ **1** a masculine name **2 Daniel** 1736-1802; Am. Revolutionary general **3 Sir Henry** *c.* 1635-88; Welsh buccaneer in the Spanish Main **4 John Hunt** 1825-64; Confederate general in the Civil War **5 J(ohn) P(ierpont)** 1837-1913; U.S. financier **6 John Pier·pont** (pir'pänt') 1867-1943; U.S. financier: son of J. P. Morgan **7 Lewis Henry** 1818-81; U.S. anthropologist **8 Thomas Hunt** 1866-1945; U.S. geneticist

Mor·gan le Fay (môr'gən lə fā') ⟦OFr *Morgain la fée*, lit., Morgan the fairy < Celt, as in OIr *Morrigain*, queen of the incubi, sorceress < **mor-* (< IE base **mer-*, to rub, seize) + OIr *rigain*, queen < IE base **reg-*, to rule⟧ *Arthurian Legend* the evil fairy half sister of King Arthur; in other legends, variously a water spirit, lake fairy, etc.

Mor·gen·thau (môr'gən thô'), **Henry, Jr.** 1891-1967; U.S. public official: secretary of the treasury (1934-45)

Mor·i·son (môr'ə sən), **Samuel Eliot** 1887-1976; U.S. historian

Mo·ri·sot (mô rē zō'), **Berthe** (bert) 1841-95; Fr.

impressionist painter

Mor·nay (môr nā′), **Phi·lippe de** (fē lēp′ də) Seigneur du
Plessis-Marly 1549-1623; Fr. diplomat & Huguenot
leader: also *Duplessis-Mornay*

Mor·phe·us (môr′fē əs, -fyōōs-) [[ME < L < Gr *Mor-
pheus*, prob. < *morphē*, form: hence, orig., one who
shapes (dreams)]] *Gr. Myth.* the god of dreams, son of
Hypnos

Mor·ris (môr′is, mär′-) [[var. of MAURICE]] **1** a masculine name: dim. *Morrie, Morry* **2 Gou·ver·neur** (guv′ər
nir′) 1752-1816; Am. statesman & diplomat **3 Robert**
1734-1806; Am. financier & patriot **4 William** 1834-
96; Eng. poet, artist, craftsman, & socialist

Mor·ri·son (môr′ə sən), **To·ni** (tō′nē) 1931- ; U.S. writer

Mors (môrz, môrs) [[L < *mors*, death, akin to *mori*, to
die < IE base **mer*-, to die, be worn out]] *Rom. Myth.*
death personified as a god: identified with the Greek
Thanatos

Morse (môrs), **Samuel F(inley) B(reese)** 1791-1872; U.S.
artist & inventor of the telegraph

Mor·ti·mer (môrt′ə mər) [[< Norm surname < place
name]] a masculine name: dim. *Mort, Morty*

Mor·ton (môrt′'n) [[orig. surname & place name < OE
Mor-tun < *mor*, a swamp, moor + *tun*, town]] **1** a
masculine name: dim. *Mort, Morty* **2 Ferdinand
Joseph** (called *Jelly Roll*) 1890-1941; U.S. jazz pianist
& composer **3 William Thomas Green** 1819-68; U.S.
dentist: introduced the use of ether for anesthesia
(1846)

Mo·ses (mō′zəz, -zəs) [[LL(Ec) < Gr(Ec) *Mōsēs* < Heb
mōsheh, prob. < Egypt *mes, mesu*, child, son]] **1** a
masculine name: dim. *Mo, Mose* **2** *Bible* the leader
who brought the Israelites out of slavery in Egypt and
led them to the Promised Land, received the Ten
Commandments from God, and gave laws to the people

Moses, Anna Mary Robertson 1860-1961; U.S. primitive
painter: called *Grandma Moses*

Möss·bau·er (mös′bou′ər), **Ru·dolf Lud·wig** (rōō′dôlf′
lōōt′viH′) 1929- ; Ger. physicist

Mother Goose 1 the imaginary narrator of a collection
of tales (*c.* 1697) by Charles Perrault **2** the imaginary
creator of a collection of nursery rhymes first published in London perhaps as early as 1765

Mother Hub·bard (hub'ərd) a character in an old nursery rhyme

Mother Nature *personification of* the power, force, principle, etc. that seems to regulate the physical universe

Mother of God *name for* VIRGIN MARY

Moth·er·well (mu*th*'ər wel'), **Robert** 1915-91; U.S. painter

Mot·ley (mät'lē), **John Lo·throp** (lō'thrəp) 1814-77; U.S. historian & diplomat

Mott (mät), **Lucretia** (born *Lucretia Coffin*) 1793-1880; U.S. abolitionist & women's rights advocate

Mount·bat·ten (mount bat'ʼn) **Louis (Francis Albert Victor Nicholas)** ⟦ orig. transl. of Ger *Battenberg* ⟧ 1st Earl Mountbatten of Burma 1900-79; Brit. admiral

Moussorgsky, Modest *alt. sp. of* Modest Petrovich MUSSORGSKY

Mo·zart (mō'tsärt'), **Wolf·gang A·ma·de·us** (vôlf'gäŋk' ä' mä dā'oos) 1756-91; Austrian composer

Mu·bar·ak (mōō bär'ək), **(Muhammad) Hos·ni** (häs'nē) 1929- ; Egyptian statesman: pres. of Egypt (1981-)

Mu·ham·mad (moo ham'əd) *var. of* MOHAMMED

Muir (myoor), **John** 1838-1914; U.S. naturalist, explorer, & writer, born in Scotland

Mul·ler (mul'ər), **H(ermann) J(oseph)** 1890-1967; U.S. biologist & geneticist

Mül·ler (mul'ər, myōōl'-; mül'-), **(Friedrich) Max** (maks; mäks) 1823-1900; Eng. philologist, mythologist, & Orientalist, born in Germany

Mul·li·ken (mul'i kən), **Robert San·der·son** (san'dər sən) 1896-1986; U.S. physicist & chemist

Mul·ro·ney (mul rō'nē), **(Martin) Brian** 1939- ; prime minister of Canada (1984-93)

Mum·ford (mum'fərd), **Lewis** 1895-1990; U.S. social philosopher & architectural critic

Munch (mooŋk), **Ed·vard** (ed'värt') 1863-1944; Norw. painter

Mun·chau·sen (mun'chou'zən, moon'-; -chô'-), **Baron** (*Karl Friedrich Hieronymus von Münchhausen*) 1720-97; Ger. soldier & adventurer known for his exaggerated tales of his exploits, esp. as collected by Rudolf Erich Raspe (1737-94), Ger. writer in England

Mun·ro (mən rō'), **H(ector) H(ugh)** *see* SAKI

Mu·ra·sa·ki Shi·ki·bu (mōō'rä sä'kē shē'kē bōō'), **Lady** *c.* A.D. 978-*c.* 1031; Jpn. novelist & poet

Mu·rat (mü *rà′*), **Jo·a·chim** (zhô à shan′) 1767-1815; Fr. marshal under Napoleon: king of Naples (1808-15)

Mur·doch (mʉr′däk′), (**Jean**) **Iris** 1919- ; Eng. writer, born in Ireland

Mu·ri·el (myoor′ē əl) ⟦prob. < Celt, as in Ir *Muirgheal* < *muir*, the sea + *geal*, bright⟧ a feminine name

Mu·ril·lo (moo rē′lyō; *E* myoo ril′ō, mə-), **Bar·to·lo·mé Es·te·ban** (bär′tô lô mä′ es tä′bän′) 1617-82; Sp. painter

Mur·ray (mʉr′ē, mu′rē) ⟦after the surname *Murray* < ? Celt, as in Welsh *mor*, the sea⟧ **1** a masculine name **2** (**George**) **Gilbert** (**Aimé**) 1866-1957; classical scholar & statesman, born in Australia **3** **Sir James Augustus Henry** 1837-1915; lexicographer, born in Scotland **4** **Lind·ley** (lind′lē) 1745-1826; Am. grammarian, in England

Mur·row (mʉr′ō), **Edward R**(**oscoe**) 1908-65; U.S. radio & TV journalist

Muse (myōoz) *n.* ⟦OFr < L *musa* < Gr *mousa*, a Muse, music, eloquence < ? IE base **mendh-*, to pay attention to, be lively > ON *munda*, to strive⟧ *Gr. Myth.* any of the Muses

Mus·es (myōoz′iz) *Gr. Myth.* the nine goddesses who preside over literature and the arts and sciences: Calliope, Clio, Euterpe, Melpomene, Terpsichore, Erato, Polyhymnia (or Polymnia), Urania, and Thalia

Mus·set (mü se′), (**Louis Charles**) **Al·fred de** (àl fred′ də) 1810-57; Fr. poet & writer

Mus·so·li·ni (mōōs′sô lē′nē; *E* moos′ə lē′nē, mus′-), **Be·ni·to** (be nē′tô) 1883-1945; It. dictator: Fascist prime minister of Italy (1922-43): executed: called *Il Duce*

Mus·sorg·sky (mə sôrk′skē, -sôrg′-), **Mo·dest Pe·tro·vich** (mō dest′ pi trō′vich) 1839-81; Russ. composer

Mus·ta·fa Ke·mal (moos′tä fä′ ke mäl′) *see* Kemal Atatürk

Mu·tsu·hi·to (moot′sə hēt′ō) 1852-1912; emperor of Japan (1867-1912): see also Meiji

Muy·bridge (mī′brij′), **Ead·weard** (ed′wərd) 1830-1904; Eng. photographer

My·ra (mī′rə) ⟦< ? Ir *Moira*, *Moyra*⟧ a feminine name

Myr·dal (mir′däl′, mʉr′-, mür′-), (**Karl**) **Gun·nar** (gun′är, -ər) 1898-1987; Swed. economist & sociologist

My·ron (mī′rən) ⟦prob. < Gr *Myrōn*⟧ **1** a masculine name **2** Gr. sculptor of the 5th cent. B.C.

Myr·tle (murt''l) ⟦ < ModE *myrtle* (the evergreen plant) < ME *mirtille* < OFr *myrtille* < ML *myrtillus*, dim. < L *myrtus* < Gr *myrtos* ⟧ a feminine name

N

Na·bo·kov (nä bô′kôf, nä′bə kôf′), **Vladimir** 1899-1977; U.S. writer & teacher, born in Russia

Na·both (nā′bäth) ⟦Heb *nābhōth*⟧ *Bible* a vineyard owner, killed at Jezebel's behest so that Ahab could seize the vineyard: 1 Kings 21

Na·der (nā′dər), **Ralph** 1934- ; U.S. lawyer & consumer advocate

Na·dine (nə dēn′, nā-) ⟦Fr < ? Russ *nadyezhda*, hope⟧ a feminine name

Na·hum (nā′əm, -həm) ⟦Heb *naḥūm*, lit., comfort⟧ *Bible* a Hebrew prophet of the 7th cent. B.C.

Na·mi·er (nā′mē ər), Sir **Lewis Bernstein** 1888-1960; Brit. historian, born in Russia

Nan·cy (nan′sē) ⟦prob. by faulty division of *mine Ancy*, dim. form of ME *Annis*, AGNES, confused with ANNE: see ANNA⟧ a feminine name: dim. *Nan*

Nan·nette, Na·nette (na net′) a feminine name: see ANNA

Nan·sen (nän′sən; nan′-), **Fridt·jof** (frit′yäf) 1861-1930; Norw. arctic explorer, naturalist, & statesman

Na·o·mi (nā ō′mē, na-; nā′ə mī′) ⟦Heb *nō'omī*, lit., my delight⟧ **1** a feminine name **2** *Bible* the mother-in-law of Ruth: Ruth 1

Naph·ta·li (naf′tə lī′) ⟦Heb < *naphtulim*; wrestlings: see Gen. 30:8⟧ *Bible* Jacob's sixth son, whose mother was Bilhah: Gen. 30:7-8

Na·pi·er (nā′pē ər, nə pir′), **John** 1550-1617; Scot. mathematician: inventor of logarithms

Na·po·le·on (nə pō′lē ən, -pōl′yən) **1** *see* BONAPARTE, Napoleon: in full **Napoleon I 2 Napoleon II** (born *François Charles Joseph Napoléon Bonaparte*), Duke of Reichstadt, 1811-32; titular emperor of France: son of Napoleon I & Marie Louise **3 Napoleon III** *see* LOUIS NAPOLEON

Nar·cis·sus (när sis′əs) ⟦L < Gr *Narkissos*⟧ *Gr. Myth.* a beautiful youth who, after Echo's death, is made to pine away for love of his own reflection in a spring and changes into the narcissus

Nas·by (naz'bē), **Pe·tro·le·um V.** (pə trō'lē əm) (pseud. of *David Ross Locke*) 1833-88; U.S. humorist

Nash (nash), **Ogden** 1902-71; U.S. writer of humorous verse

Nashe (nash), **Thomas** 1567-1601; Eng. satirist & pamphleteer: also sp. **Nash**

Nas·sau (nä'sou') princely family of the former German duchy, which, as the House of Orange, has ruled the Netherlands since 1815

Nas·ser (nas'ər), **Ga·mal Ab·del** (gä mäl' äb'dəl) 1918-70; Egypt. statesman: president of Egypt (1956-58): president of the United Arab Republic (1958-70)

Nast (nast), **Thomas** 1840-1902; U.S. political cartoonist & illustrator, born in Germany

Nat·a·lie (nat''l ē) ⟦Fr < LL *Natalia* < L *natalis* (*dies*), natal (day), name given to children born on Christmas Day⟧ a feminine name: equiv. Russ. *Natasha*

Na·than (nā'thən) ⟦Heb *nāthán*, lit., he has given⟧ **1** a masculine name: dim. *Nat, Nate* **2** *Bible* a prophet who rebuked David for the death of Uriah: 2 Sam. 12:1-14 **3 George Jean** 1882-1958; U.S. drama critic & editor

Na·than·a·el (nə than'yəl, -ē əl) ⟦LL(Ec) < Gr(Ec) *Nathanaēl* < Heb *něthan'ēl*, lit., God has given⟧ **1** a masculine name: dim. *Nat*: also sp. **Nathaniel 2** *Bible* one of the disciples of Jesus: John 1:45: see also BARTHOLOMEW

Na·tion (nā'shən), **Car·ry** (kar'ē) (born *Carry Amelia Moore*) 1846-1911; U.S. agitator for temperance

Nat·ta (nä'tä'), **Giu·lio** (jōōl'yō) 1903-79; It. chemist

Nau·sic·a·ä (nô sik'ā ə, -ē ə) in Homer's *Odyssey*, King Alcinoüs's daughter, who discovers, and secures safe passage for, the shipwrecked Odysseus

Naz·a·rene (naz'ə rēn', naz'ə rēn'), **the** Jesus

Neal (nēl) ⟦ME *Nel, Neel, Nele*, prob. < Ir *Niul* (Gael *Niall*) < *niadh*, a champion⟧ a masculine name

Neb·u·chad·nez·zar (neb'yə kəd nez'ər, neb'ə-) ⟦ult. < Akkadian *Nabū-kudur-uṣur*⟧ died 562 B.C.; king of Babylonia (*c.* 605-562), who conquered Jerusalem, destroyed the Temple, & deported many Jews into Babylonia (586 B.C.): 2 Kings 24; Dan. 1-4: also **Neb'u·chad·rez'zar** (-rez'ər)

Nec·ker (nā ker'; *E* nek'ər), **Jacques** (zhäk) 1732-1804; Fr. statesman & financier, born in Switzerland: father of Madame de Staël

Ned (ned) ⟦by faulty division of *mine Ed*⟧ a masculine name: see EDGAR, EDMUND, EDWARD

Né·el (nā el′), **Louis** (Eu·gè·ne Fé·lix) 1904- ; Fr. physicist

Nef·er·ti·ti (nef′ər tē′tē) 14th cent. B.C.; queen of Egypt & wife of Ikhnaton: also **Nef′re·te′te** (-rə-)

Ne·he·mi·ah (nē′hi mī′ə, nē′ə-) ⟦Heb *nehemyāh*, lit., comfort of *Jah* (God)⟧ *Bible* a Hebrew leader of *c.* 5th cent. B.C.

Neh·ru (nā′rōō), **Ja·wa·har·lal** (jə wä′hər läl′) 1889-1964; Indian nationalist leader in India's movement for independence: prime minister (1947-64)

Neil (nēl) a masculine name: see NEAL

Neil·son (nēl′sən), **William Allan** 1869-1946; U.S. educator & editor, born in Scotland

Nell (nel) a feminine name: see HELEN, ELEANOR

Nel·lie, Nel·ly (nel′ē) a feminine name: see HELEN, ELEANOR

Nel·son (nel′sən) ⟦< the surname *Nelson* < ME *Nel* (see NEAL) + *son*, son⟧ 1 a masculine name 2 **Hora·tio** Viscount Nelson 1758-1805; Eng. admiral

Nem·e·sis (nem′ə sis) ⟦L < Gr *nemein*, to distribute, deal out, govern < IE base **nem-*, to assign, take, arrange⟧ *Gr. Myth.* the goddess of retributive justice, or vengeance

Nep·tune (nep′tōōn′, -tyōōn′) ⟦ME < L *Neptunus*, prob. < IE **nebhtus* < base **nebh-*, moist⟧ 1 *Rom. Myth.* the god of the sea: identified with the Greek Poseidon 2 the sea personified

Ne·re·us (nir′ē əs, nir′yōōs′) ⟦L < Gr *Nereus*, prob. < IE **(s)nāu-* < base **(s)na-*, to flow⟧ *Gr. Myth.* a benevolent sea god, father of the fifty Nereids

Nernst (nernst), **Wal·ther Her·mann** (väl′ter her′män′) 1864-1941; Ger. physicist & chemist

Ne·ro (nir′ō) (*Nero Claudius Caesar Drusus Germanicus*, born *Lucius Domitius Ahenobarbus*) A.D. 37-68; emperor of Rome (54-68): notoriously cruel & depraved

Ne·ru·da (ne rōō′thä; *E* nə rōō′də), **Pa·blo** (pä′blô) (born *Ricardo Eliezer Neftalí Reyes Basoalto*) 1904-73; Chilean poet

Ner·vi (ner′vē), **Pier Lu·i·gi** (pir lōō ē′jē) 1891-1979; It. engineer & architect

Nes·tor (nes'tər, -tôr') ⟦L < Gr *Nestōr*, lit., the one who returns, akin to *neomai*, I return < IE base **nes-*, to unite, be concealed > Goth *nasjan*, to save, OE *nesan*, to survive⟧ **1** a masculine name **2** *Gr. Myth.* a wise old counselor on the side of the Greeks at Troy

Net·tie, Net·ty (net'ē) a feminine name: see ANTOINETTE, HENRIETTA, JEANNETTE

Nev·el·son (nev'əl sən), **Louise** 1900-88; U.S. sculptor, born in Russia

Nev·il, Nev·ille (nev'əl) ⟦< Norm surname *Nevil, Néville,* after *Neuville,* town in Normandy (lit., new city)⟧ a masculine name: also **Nev'ile** or **Nev'ill**

New·comb (nōō'kəm, nyōō'-), **Simon** 1835-1909; U.S. astronomer, born in Canada

New·man (nōō'mən, nyōō'-), **John Henry** Cardinal Newman, 1801-90; Eng. theologian & writer

New·ton (nōōt''n, nyōōt''n) ⟦after surname *Newton* < common Eng place name *Newton* < OE *neowa tun,* new town⟧ **1** a masculine name **2** Sir **Isaac** 1642-1727; Eng. mathematician & natural philosopher: formulated the laws of gravity & motion & the elements of differential calculus

Ney (nā), **Mi·chel** (mē shel') Duc d'Elchingen, Prince de La Moskova, 1769-1815; Fr. military leader under Napoleon I: executed

Nich·o·las (nik'ə ləs) ⟦ME < OFr *Nicolas* < L *Nicolaus* < Gr *Nikolaos* < *nikē,* victory + *laos,* the people⟧ **1** a masculine name; *Nick;* equiv. L. *Nicolaus,* Fr. & Sp. *Nicolas,* Ger. *Nikolaus,* It. *Niccolo,* Russ. *Nikolai* **2 Nicholas I** 1796-1855; czar of Russia (1825-55) **3** Saint (*c.* A.D. 800-867); pope (858-867): his day is Nov. 13: called *the Great* **4 Nicholas II** 1868-1918; last czar of Russia (1894-1917): forced to abdicate; executed **5** Saint (4th cent. A.D.); bishop of Myra: patron saint of Russia, of Greece, & of young people, sailors, etc.: his day is Dec. 6: cf. SANTA CLAUS

Nicholas of Cu·sa (kyōō'sə, -zə) 1401-64; Ger. cardinal, philosopher, & mathematician

Nick (nik) a masculine name: see NICHOLAS

Nic·o·las (nik'ə ləs) a masculine name: see NICHOLAS

Nic·ole (ni kōl'; *Fr* nē kōl') ⟦Fr fem. of *Nicolas:* see NICHOLAS⟧ a feminine name: dim. *Nicky, Nikki;* var. *Nicola*

Nie·buhr (nē'boor) **1 Bar·thold Ge·org** (bär'tôlt' gā'ôrk')

1776-1831; Ger. historian, born in Denmark **2 Rein·
hold** (rīn'hōld') 1892-1971; U.S. clergyman & Protestant theologian

Nie·mey·er (nē'mī'ər), **Oscar** (born *Oscar Niemeyer
Soares Filho*); 1907- ; Brazilian architect

Nie·möl·ler (nē'mö lər), **(Friedrich Gustav Emil) Mar·tin**
(mär'tēn) 1892-1984; Ger. Protestant leader

Nie·tzsche (nē'chə), **Frie·drich Wil·helm** (frē'driH' vil'
helm') 1844-1900; Ger. philosopher

Night·in·gale (nīt''n gāl'), **Florence** 1820-1910; Eng.
nurse in the Crimean War: regarded as the founder of
modern nursing

Ni·jin·sky (ni zhēn'ski; *E* nə jin'skē), **Vas·lav** (vás láf')
1890-1950; Russ. ballet dancer

Ni·ke (nī'kē) ⟦Gr *Nikē*, prob. < IE base **nēik-*, to attack
> OE *(ga)næstan*, to fight⟧ *Gr. Myth.* the winged god-
dess of victory

Nim·itz (nim'its), **Chester William** 1885-1966; U.S.
admiral in World War II

Nim·rod (nim'räd') ⟦Heb *nimrōdh*⟧ *Bible* the son of
Cush, referred to as a mighty hunter: Gen. 10:8-9

Nine, the the nine Muses

Ni·o·be (nī'ō bə') ⟦L < Gr *Niobē*⟧ *Gr. Myth.* a queen of
Thebes, daughter of Tantalus, who, weeping for her
slain children, is turned into a stone from which tears
continue to flow

Nix·on (nik'sən), **Richard M(ilhous)** 1913- ; 37th president of the U.S. (1969-74): resigned under threat of
impeachment

Njorth (nyôrth) ⟦ON *Njörthr*⟧ *Norse Myth.* one of the
Vanir, father of Frey and Freya: also **Njord** (nyôrd)

Nkru·mah (ən krōō'mə), **Kwa·me** (kwä'mē) 1909-72;
president of Ghana (1960-66)

No·ah (nō'ə) ⟦Heb *nōah*, lit., rest, comfort⟧ **1** a masculine name **2** *Bible* the patriarch commanded by God to
build the ark on which he, his family, and two of every
kind of creature survived the Flood: Gen. 5:28-10:32

No·bel (nō bel'), **Al·fred Bern·hard** (àl'fred ber'nàrd)
1833-96; Swed. industrialist, philanthropist, & inventor of dynamite: established the Nobel prizes

No·el (nō'əl) ⟦OFr *Nouel, Noel*, lit., natal: see NOEL: cf.
NATALIE⟧ a masculine and feminine name

No·gu·chi (nō gōō'chē) **1 Hi·de·yo** (hē'de yō') 1876-
1928; U.S. bacteriologist, born in Japan **2 I·sa·mu** (ē'

sä mōō′) 1904-88; U.S. sculptor

No·ra (nôr′ə) ⟦Ir, contr. of *Honora, Eleanor, Leonora*⟧ a feminine name: see ELEANOR, LEONORA

Nor·dau (nôr′dou′), **Max Simon** (born *Max Simon Südfeld*) 1849-1923; Ger. writer, physician, & Zionist leader, born in Hungary

Nor·den·skjöld (nōōr′dən shüld′), Baron **Nils A·dolf E·rik** (nils ä′dôlf ā′rik) 1832-1901; Swed. arctic explorer, born in Finland

Nor·ma (nôr′mə) ⟦< ? L *norma,* carpenter's square, rule⟧ a feminine name

Nor·man (nôr′mən) ⟦< OE *Northman,* OHG *Nordemann,* lit., Northman⟧ a masculine name: dim. *Norm*

Norn (nôrn) ⟦ON *norn* < IE base *(s)ner-, *(s)nur-,* to snarl, mutter⟧ *Norse Myth.* any of the three goddesses, representing the past, present, and future, who determine the destiny of gods and mortals

Nor·ris (nôr′is) **1 Frank** (born *Benjamin Franklin Norris, Jr.*) 1870-1902; U.S. novelist **2 George William** 1861-1944; U.S. senator (1913-43)

Nor·rish (nôr′ish), **Ronald George** (Wreyford) 1897-1978; Eng. chemist

North (nôrth), **Frederick** 2d Earl of Guilford 1732-92; Eng. statesman: prime minister of Great Britain (1770-82): called *Lord North*

North·cliffe (nôrth′klif′), Viscount (*Alfred Charles William Harmsworth*) 1865-1922; Eng. newspaper publisher, born in Ireland

Nos·tra·da·mus (näs′trə dā′məs, nô′strə dä′-) (born *Michel de Notredame*) 1503-66; Fr. astrologer

Nox (näks) ⟦L < *nox,* night < IE base *nekwt-*⟧ *Rom. name for* NYX

Noyes (noiz), **Alfred** 1880-1958; Eng. poet

Nu·re·yev (nōō rā′yef), **Rudolf** (Hametovich) 1938-93; ballet dancer, born in the Soviet Union

Nye (nī), **Edgar Wilson** (pseud. *Bill Nye*) 1850-96; U.S. humorist

Nyx (niks) ⟦Gr < *nyx,* night < IE base *nekwt-*⟧ *Gr. Myth.* the goddess of night

O

Oates (ōts), **Titus** 1649-1705; Eng. fabricator of the Popish Plot, a supposed Rom. Catholic plot (1678) to massacre Protestants, burn London, and kill the king

O·ba·di·ah (ō′bə dī′ə) ⟦ult. < Heb 'ōbhadhyāh, lit., servant of the Lord⟧ **1** a masculine name **2** *Bible* a Hebrew prophet

O·ber·on (ō′bər än′, -ən′) ⟦Fr < OFr *Auberon*⟧ *Eng. Folklore* the king of fairyland and husband of Titania

O'Ca·sey (ō kā′sē), **Sean** (shôn) 1880-1964; Ir. playwright

Occam, William of *see* OCKHAM, William of

O·ce·a·nus (ō sē′ə nəs) ⟦L < Gr *Ōkeanos*, the outer sea (in contrast to the Mediterranean)⟧ *Gr. Myth.* a Titan, father of the Oceanides and ruler of the sea before Poseidon

O·cho·a (ō chō′ə), **Se·ve·ro** (sə ver′ō) 1905- ; U.S. biochemist, born in Spain

Ochs (äks), **Adolph Simon** 1858-1935; U.S. newspaper publisher

Ock·ham (äk′əm), **William of** *c.* 1285-*c.* 1349; Eng. philosopher

O'Con·nell (ō kän′əl), **Daniel** 1775-1847; Ir. nationalist leader

O'Con·nor (ō kän′ər) **1 (Mary) Flan·ner·y** (flan′ər ē) 1925-64; U.S. writer **2 Frank** (born *Michael John O'Donovan*) 1903-66; Ir. author **3 Sandra Day** 1930- ; associate justice, U.S. Supreme Court (1981-) **4 Thomas Pow·er** (pou′ər) 1848-1929; Ir. journalist & nationalist leader: called *Tay Pay*

Oc·ta·vi·a (äk tā′vē ə) ⟦L, fem. of *Octavius*⟧ **1** a feminine name: see OCTAVIUS **2** died 11 B.C.; wife of Mark Antony

Oc·ta·vi·an (-ən) *see* AUGUSTUS (the emperor)

Oc·ta·vi·us (-əs) ⟦L < *octavus*, eighth⟧ a masculine name: fem. *Octavia*

O·dets (ō dets′), **Clifford** 1906-63; U.S. playwright

O·din (ō′din) ⟦Dan < ON *Othinn*, akin to OE *Woden*⟧ *Norse Myth.* the chief deity, god of art, culture, war, and the dead: identified with the Germanic Woden

O·do·a·cer (ō′dō ā′sər) *c.* A.D. 435-493; 1st barbarian ruler of Italy (476-493)

O·do·va·car (ō′dō vä′kər) *var. of* ODOACER

O·dys·se·us (ō dis′ē əs, ō dis′yōōs′) ⟦Gr⟧ the hero of the *Odyssey*, a king of Ithaca and one of the Greek leaders in the Trojan War: Latin name *Ulysses*

Oed·i·pus (ed′i pəs; *also* ē′di-) ⟦L < Gr *Oidipous* (<

oidein, to swell + *pous,* foot: lit., swollen foot) ⟧ *Gr. Myth.* the son of Laius and Jocasta, king and queen of Thebes, who, raised by the king of Corinth, later returns to Thebes and unwittingly kills his father and marries his mother

Oe·no·ne (ē nō′nē) ⟦ L < Gr *Oinōnē* ⟧ *Gr. Myth.* a nymph deserted by her husband, Paris, for Helen of Troy

O'Fao·láin (ō′fə lôn′), **Seán** (shôn) 1900-91; Ir. author

Of·fen·bach (ôf′ən bäk′; *Fr* ôf en bäk′), **Jacques** (zhȧk) (born *Jakob Eberscht*) 1819-80; Fr. composer of operettas, born in Germany

O'Fla·her·ty (ō fla′hər tē), **Li·am** (lē′əm) 1897-1984; Ir. writer

Og·den (äg′dən, ôg-), **C(harles) K(ay)** 1889-1957; Eng. educator & linguist: devised Basic English

O·gle·thorpe (ō′gəl thôrp′), **James Edward** 1696-1785; Eng. general: founder of the colony of Georgia (1733)

O'Har·a (ō har′ə), **John** 1905-70; U.S. author

O. Henry *see* HENRY, O.

O'Hig·gins (ō hig′ənz; *Sp* ô ē′gēns), **Ber·nar·do** (ber när′dō) 1778-1842; Chilean revolutionary leader: 1st president of Chile (1817-23)

Oi·strakh (oi′sträkh), **David (Fyodorovich)** 1908-74; Russ. violinist

O'Keeffe (ō kēf′), **Georgia** 1887-1986; U.S. painter

O'Kel·ly (ō kel′ē), **Sean T(homas)** (shôn) 1882-1966; Ir. nationalist leader: president of Ireland (1945-59)

O·laf (ō′ləf, -läf) ⟦ON *Olafr, Aleifr* < **anulaibar,* lit., descendant of the (original) ancestor < **anu* (< IE **an-,* ancestor > L *anus,* old woman) + *-laibar* (> Leifr, LEIF) ⟧ **1** a masculine name **2 Olaf I** (born *Olaf Tryggvasson*) c. 964-1000; king of Norway (995-1000): subject of many legends **3 Saint Olaf II** (born *Olaf Haraldsson*) c. 995-1030; king of Norway (1015-28): patron saint of Norway: his day is July 29 **4 Olaf V** 1903-91; king of Norway (1957-91): son of Haakon VII Also sp. **O'lav**

Old·cas·tle (ōld′kas′əl), **Sir John** Lord Cobham, *c.* 1378-1417; Eng. Lollard leader: executed as a heretic

Ol·den·burg (ōld′'n bʉrg′), **Claes** (klas) 1929- ; U.S. sculptor, born in Sweden

Old Harry the Devil; Satan

Old Hickory *name for* Andrew JACKSON

Old Man of the Sea in the *Arabian Nights,* an old man who clung to the back of Sinbad for many days and nights

Old Nick 〚 prob. contr. < NICHOLAS 〛 the Devil; Satan

Old Pretender *name for* James Francis Edward STUART

Ol·ga (äl′gə, ôl′-, ōl′-) 〚 Russ < ON *Helga,* holy < *heilagr,* akin to OE *heilag,* holy 〛 a feminine name

Ol·ive (äl′iv) 〚 ME *oliva* < L, an olive 〛 a feminine name: var. *Olivia*

Ol·i·ver (äl′ə vər) 〚 Fr *Olivier:* form assimilated to OFr *olivier,* olive tree < L *olivarius,* but prob. < MLowG *alfihar,* lit., elf-army < *alf,* elf + *hari,* a host, army 〛 **1** a masculine name **2** one of Charlemagne's twelve peers, a friend of Roland: see ROLAND

O·liv·i·a (ō liv′ē ə, ə-) a feminine name: see OLIVE

O·liv·i·er (ō liv′ē ā′), **Laurence (Kerr)** Baron Olivier of Brighton 1907-89; Brit. actor

Olm·sted (ōm′sted′, äm′-, -stəd), **Frederick Law** (lô) 1822-1903; U.S. landscape architect

O·lym·pi·a (ō lim′pē ə, ə-) 〚 L < Gr, fem. of *Olympios,* lit., of Olympus 〛 a feminine name

O·mar Khay·yám (ō′mär kī yäm′, ō′mər kī yam′) died 1123; Pers. poet & mathematician: author of *The Rubáiyát,* translated into English by Edward FitzGerald

Om·nip·o·tence (äm nip′ə təns) God

Om·nip·o·tent (-tənt), **the** God

Om·nis·cient (äm nish′ənt; *Brit & Cdn,* -nis′ē ənt), **the** God

Om·pha·le (äm′fə lē′) *Gr. Myth.* a queen of Lydia in whose service Hercules, dressed as a woman, does womanly tasks for three years to appease the gods

O'Neill (ō nēl′), **Eugene (Gladstone)** 1888-1953; U.S. playwright

On·sa·ger (ôn′säg′ər), **Lars** (lärz) 1903-76; U.S. chemist, born in Norway

O·phe·lia (ō fēl′yə) 〚 prob. < Gr *ōphelia,* a help, succor 〛 **1** a feminine name **2** in Shakespeare's *Hamlet,* Polonius's daughter, in love with Hamlet

Op·pen·heim·er (äp′ən hī′mər), **J(ulius) Robert** 1904-67; U.S. nuclear physicist

Ops (äps) 〚 L, lit., strength, riches < IE **ops,* a work < base **op-,* to work, riches 〛 *Rom. Myth.* the wife of Saturn and goddess of the harvest: identified with the

Greek Rhea

Or·ange (ôr′inj, är′-) name of the ruling family of the Netherlands: see NASSAU

Or·cus (ôr′kəs) *Rom. Myth.* Pluto, or Dis

O·res·tes (ō res′tēz′) ⟦L < Gr *Orestēs* < *oros*, mountain < IE base *er-, to set in motion, elevate⟧ *Gr. Myth.* son of Agamemnon and Clytemnestra, who, with the aid of his sister Electra, avenges the murder of his father by killing his mother and her lover Aegisthus

Orff (ôrf), **Carl** 1895-1982; Ger. composer

Or·i·gen (ôr′i jən, är′-; -jen′) (L. name *Origenes Adamantius*) *c.* A.D. 185-*c.* 254; Christian theologian & scholar, born in Alexandria

O·ri·on (ō rī′ən, ə-) ⟦ME < L < Gr *Ōriōn*⟧ *Gr. & Rom. Myth.* a hunter whom Diana loves but accidentally kills

Or·lan·do (ôr lan′dō; *also, for 2, It* ôr län′dō) ⟦It⟧ **1** a masculine name: see ROLAND **2 Vit·to·rio E·ma·nue·le** (vēt tô′ryô e′mä nwe′le) 1860-1952; It. statesman: premier of Italy (1917-19)

Or·lé·ans (ôr lā än′; *E* ôr′lē ənz) **1** a branch of the house of Bourbon, one of whose members (Louis Philippe) ruled France, 1830-48 **2 Louis Phi·lippe Jo·seph Duc d'** (lwē′ fē lēp′ zhô zef′) 1747-93; Fr. revolutionist: guillotined: father of Louis Philippe

Or·mazd (ôr′məzd, -mazd′) ⟦Pers < OPers *Auramazda* < Avestan *Ahuro-Mazdao*, wise lord < *ahura*, a god (see OSCAR) + *mazdah-*, name of the highest god < IE *mendh-*, to direct one's mind toward < base *men-*, to think + *dhē-*, to put⟧ Zoroastrianism the supreme deity and creator of the world, or the spirit of good: cf. AHRIMAN: also sp. **Or′muzd**

O·roz·co (ô rôs′kô), **Jo·sé Cle·men·te** (hô se′ kle men′ te) 1883-1949; Mex. painter

Or·phe·us (ôr′fē əs, -fyōōs′) ⟦L < Gr⟧ *Gr. Myth.* a poet-musician with magic musical powers who descends to the underworld and tries to lead his wife, Eurydice, back from the dead but fails because he breaks the injunction not to look back at her until they reach the upper world

Or·son (ôr′sən) ⟦< Fr *ourson*, dim. of *ours*, a bear < L *ursus*⟧ a masculine name

Or·te·ga y Gas·set (ôr te′gä ē gä set′), **Jo·sé** (hô se′) 1883-1955; Sp. essayist & philosopher

Or·ville (ôr'vil) 〚Fr; orig. place name〛 a masculine
name

Or·well (ôr'wel, -wəl), **George** (pseud. of *Eric Arthur
Blair*) 1903-50; Eng. writer

Os·born (äz'bərn), **Henry Fair·field** (fer'fēld') 1857-1935;
U.S. paleontologist & biologist

Os·borne (äz'bərn, -bôrn) **1 John** (**James**) 1929- ; Eng.
playwright **2 Thomas Mott** (mät) 1859-1926; U.S.
prison reformer

Os·car (äs'kər) 〚OE *Osgar* < *os,* a god, akin to ON *áss*
(< IE **ansu-,* a spirit, demon > Avestan *ahura*) + *gar,*
a spear〛 **1** a masculine name **2 Oscar II** 1829-1907;
king of Norway & Sweden (1872-1905), then of Sweden alone

Os·ce·o·la (äs'ē ō'lə) *c.* 1804-38; leader of the Seminole
Indians

O·si·ris (ō sī'ris) 〚L < Gr < Egypt *Us-àr*〛 *Egypt. Myth.*
the god of the lower world and judge of the dead,
brother and husband of Isis

Os·man (äz'mən, äs'-; *Turk* äs'män') 〚Turk *Othman* <
Ar *'Uthmān*〛 *c.* 1259-1326; Turkish leader & founder
of the Ottoman dynasty

Os·si·an (äsh'ən, äs'ē ən) 〚Gael *Oisīn,* dim. of *os,* a
fawn〛 *Gael. Folklore* a bard and hero of the 3d cent.:
James Macpherson published pieces of poetic prose
(1761-65) which he falsely claimed were his transla-
tions of Ossian's poetry from old Gaelic manuscripts

Os·si·etz·ky (ôs'ē et'skē), **Carl von** (kärl fôn) 1889-1938;
Ger. journalist & pacifist

Ost·wald (ôst'vält), **Wil·helm** (vil'helm) 1853-1932; Ger.
chemist, born in Latvia

Os·wald (äz'wəld, -wôld') 〚OE *Osweald* < *os,* a god +
weald, power, ult. < IE base *wal-,* to be strong〛 a
masculine name: dim. *Ozzie*

O·thel·lo (ō thel'ō) the title character of a play by
Shakespeare: Othello, a noble Moor, is made madly
jealous by the villainous Iago and kills his faithful and
loving wife, Desdemona

O·thin (ō'thin) ODIN

Oth·man (äth'mən; *Turk Ar* ooth män') OSMAN

O·tis (ōt'əs) **1** 〚orig. family name: popularized as given
name in honor of James Otis〛 a masculine name **2
James** 1725-83; Am. Revolutionary statesman

Ot·to (ät'ō) 〚OHG *Otho, Odo* < *auda,* rich〛 **1** a masculine name **2 Otto I** A.D. 912-973; king of Germany (936-973) & emperor of the Holy Roman Empire (962-973): called *the Great*

Our Lady Mary, the mother of Jesus; Virgin Mary

Ov·id (äv'id) (L. name *Publius Ovidius Naso*) 43 B.C.-c. A.D. 17; Rom. poet

Ow·en (ō'ən) ⟦Welsh < *Owein*, earlier *Ewein*, < Celt *Esuganyos*, akin to Gr *Eugenios*: see EUGENE⟧ **1** a masculine name **2 Robert** 1771-1858; Brit. industrialist & socialist **3 Wilfred** (wil'frid) 1893-1918; Eng. poet

P

Pa·de·rew·ski (pad'ə ref'skē; *Pol* pä'de *ref*'skē), **I·gnace Jan** (ē'nyás' yän') 1860-1941; Pol. pianist & composer: prime minister of Poland (1919)

Pa·ga·ni·ni (pag'ə nē'nē; *It* pä'gä nē'nē), **Nic·co·lò** (nēk'kō lô') 1782-1840; It. violinist & composer

Page (pāj), **Walter Hines** (hīnz) 1855-1918; U.S. journalist, editor, & diplomat

Pag·et (paj'it), **Sir James** 1814-99; Eng. surgeon & pathologist

Paine (pān) **1 Robert Treat** (trēt') 1731-1814; Am. jurist & statesman **2 Thomas** 1737-1809; Am. Revolutionary patriot, writer, & political theoretician, born in England

Pal·es·tri·na (pal'ə strē'nə; *It* pä'les trē'nä), **Gio·van·ni Pier·lu·i·gi da** (jō vän'nē pyer loo ē'jē dä) *c.* 1525-94; It. composer

Pa·ley (pā'lē), **William** 1743-1805; Eng. theologian & philosopher

Pal·grave (pal'grāv'), **Francis Turner** 1824-97; Eng. anthologist

Pal·la·dio (päl lä'dyō), **An·dre·a** (än dre'ä) (born *Andrea di Pietro*) 1508-80; It. architect

Pal·las (pal'əs) ⟦L < Gr⟧ *Gr. Myth.* ATHENA: also **Pallas Athena**

Palm·er (päm'ər), **Samuel** 1805-81; Eng. landscape painter & etcher

Palm·er·ston (päm'ər stən), **3d Viscount** (*Henry John Temple*) 1784-1865; Brit. statesman: prime minister (1855-58; 1859-65)

Pam·e·la (pam'ə lə) ⟦apparently coined by SIDNEY for a

character in his *Arcadia* (1590)] a feminine name

Pan (pan) ⟦L < Gr⟧ *Gr. Myth.* a god of fields, forests, wild animals, flocks, and shepherds, represented as having the legs (and, sometimes, horns and ears) of a goat: identified with the Roman Faunus

Pan·da·rus (pan′də rəs) ⟦L < Gr *Pandaros*⟧ a leader of the Lycians in the Trojan War: in medieval romances and in Boccaccio, Chaucer, and Shakespeare, he acts as the go-between for Troilus and Cressida

Pan·do·ra (pan dôr′ə) ⟦L < Gr *Pandōra* < *pan*, all (< IE base **keu-*, a swelling, arch) + *dōron*, a gift (< IE base **do-*, to give) ⟧ *Gr. Myth.* the first mortal woman: out of curiosity she opens a box, letting out all human ills into the world (or, in a later version, letting all human blessings escape and be lost, leaving only hope)

Pank·hurst (paŋk′hurst′), **Em·me·line** (em′ə lin′, -lēn′) (born *Emmeline Goulden*) 1858-1928; Eng. suffragist

Pan·ta·gru·el (pan′tə grōō el′, -grōō′əl; pan tag′rōō el′; *Fr* pän tȧ grü el′) ⟦< ? name of a minor devil referred to in writings of the late 15th c.⟧ the boisterous, giant son of Gargantua in Rabelais′ *Gargantua and Pantagruel*: he is a jovial drunkard characterized by rough, extravagant humor

Pan·ta·loon (pan′tə lōōn′) ⟦Fr *Pantalon* < It *Pantalone*, name of a character in Italian comedy, from the Venetian patron saint *Pantalone* or *Pantaleone* (< Gr *pantos*, gen. of *pan*: see PANDORA + *leōn*, lion): also, the garment worn by this character⟧ **1** a stock character in commedia dell′arte, usually a slender, foolish old man wearing tight trousers extending to the feet **2** a similar figure in modern pantomime, the butt of the clown′s jokes

Pan·urge (pan′urj′; *Fr* pȧ nürzh′) ⟦Fr < Gr *panourgos*, knavish, ready for anything < *pan* (see PANDORA) + *-ourgos*, worker < *ergon*, work⟧ the mirthful, roguish, cowardly companion of Pantagruel in Rabelais′ *Gargantua and Pantagruel*

Panza, Sancho *see* SANCHO PANZA

Pa·o·lo (pä′ô lô) *see* FRANCESCA DA RIMINI

Par·a·cel·sus (par′ə sel′səs), **Phi·lip·pus Au·re·o·lus** (fi lip′əs ô rē′ə ləs) (born *Theophrastus Bombastus von Hohenheim*) 1493-1541; Swiss physician & alchemist

Par·cae (pär′sē) ⟦L, pl. of *Parca*, one of the Fates, orig., a birth-goddess < *parere*, to give birth < IE base **per-*, to give birth to ‖ FATES

Pa·ré (pà rā′), **Am·broise** (än brwäz′) *c.* 1517-90; Fr. surgeon

Pa·re·to (pä re′tô), **Vil·fre·do** (vēl fre′dô) 1848-1923; It. economist & sociologist in Switzerland

Par·is (par′is) ‖ L < Gr ‖ *Gr. Legend* a son of Priam, king of Troy: his kidnapping of Helen, wife of Menelaus, causes the Trojan War

Park (pärk), **Mun·go** (muŋ′gō) 1771-1806; Scot. explorer in Africa

Par·ker (pär′kər) **1 Char·lie** (chär′lē) (born *Charles Christopher Parker, Jr.*) 1920-55; U.S. jazz musician **2 Dorothy** (born *Dorothy Rothschild*) 1893-1967; U.S. writer **3** Sir **Gilbert** (born *Horatio Gilbert George Parker*) 1862-1932; Cdn. novelist in England **4 Theo·dore** 1810-60; U.S. clergyman, social reformer, & abolitionist

Park·man (pärk′mən), **Francis** 1823-93; U.S. historian

Par·men·i·des (pär men′ə dēz′) 5th cent. B.C.; Gr. Eleatic philosopher

Par·nell (pär nel′, pärn′əl), **Charles Stewart** 1846-91; Ir. nationalist leader

Parr (pär), **Catherine** 1512-48; 6th & last wife of Henry VIII of England

Par·ring·ton (par′iŋ tən), **Vernon Louis** 1871-1929; U.S. literary historian

Par·rish (par′ish), **Max·field** (maks′fēld) 1870-1966; U.S. illustrator & painter

Par·ry (par′ē), Sir **William Edward** 1790-1855; Eng. naval officer & arctic explorer

Par·sons (pär′sənz), **Tal·cott** (tôl′kät, täl′-; -kət) 1902-79; U.S. sociologist

Par·then·o·pe (pär then′ə pē′) ‖ L < Gr *Parthenopē* ‖ *Gr. Myth.* the siren who throws herself into the sea after her songs fail to lure Odysseus into a shipwreck

Par·tridge (pär′trij), **Eric** (**Honeywood**) 1894-1979; Brit. lexicographer, born in New Zealand

Pas·cal (pas kal′; *Fr* pàs kàl′), **Blaise** (blez) 1623-62; Fr. mathematician, physicist, & philosopher

paschal lamb [*often* **P- L-**] *Christianity name for* Jesus Christ

Pa·siph·a·ë (pə sif′ā ē′) ‖ L < Gr *Pasiphaē* ‖ *Gr. Myth.* the wife of Minos and mother of the Minotaur by a white bull belonging to Minos

Pas·sy (pá sē′) **1** Fré·dé·ric (frā dā rēk′) 1822-1912; Fr. economist **2 Paul É·douard** (pôl ā dwár′) 1859-1940; Fr. phonetician: principal originator of the International Phonetic Alphabet: son of Frédéric

Pas·ter·nak (pas′tər nak′), **Boris (Leonidovich)** 1890-1960; Russ. poet & novelist

Pas·teur (pas tʉr′; Fr pás tër′), **Louis** 1822-95; Fr. chemist & bacteriologist

Pa·ter (pā′tər), **Walter (Horatio)** 1839-94; Eng. essayist & critic

Pa·ton (pāt′′n), **Alan (Stewart)** 1903-88; South African novelist

Pa·tri·cia (pə trish′ə, -trē′shə) ⟦L, fem. of patricius, patrician < patres, senators, lit., fathers, pl. of pater, father < IE *pətér⟧ a feminine name: dim. Pat, Patty

Pat·rick (pa′trik) ⟦L patricius, a patrician⟧ **1** a masculine name: dim. Paddy, Pat, Rick; fem. Patricia **2** Saint (c. A.D. 385-c. 461); Brit. missionary in, and patron saint of, Ireland: his day is March 17

Pa·tro·clus (pə trō′kləs, pa′trō-) ⟦L < Gr Patroklos⟧ Gr. Myth. a Greek warrior and friend of Achilles, slain by Hector in the Trojan War

Pat·ti (pät′tē; E pat′ē), **A·de·li·na** (ä′de lē′nä) (born Adela Juana Maria Patti) 1843-1919; It. operatic soprano, born in Spain

Pat·ton (pat′′n), **George S(mith)** 1885-1945; U.S. general

Paul (pôl) ⟦L Paulus (or Gr Paulos), Rom. surname, prob. < paulus, small: akin to paucus, few⟧ **1** a masculine name: equiv. L. Paulus, It. Paulo, Sp. Pablo: fem. Paula, Pauline **2** (original name Saul) died c. A.D. 67: a Jew of Tarsus who became the Apostle of Christianity to the Gentiles: author of several Letters in the New Testament: his day is June 29: also **Saint Paul 3 Paul I** 1754-1801: czar of Russia (1796-1801): son of Catherine II & Peter III **4 Paul III** (born Alessandro Farnese) 1468-1549; pope (1534-49) **5 Paul VI** (born Giovanni Battista Montini) 1897-1978; pope (1963-78)

Paul·a (pôl′ə) ⟦L, fem. of prec.⟧ a feminine name: see PAUL

Paul Bun·yan (bun′yən) American Folklore a giant lumberjack who, with the help of his blue ox, Babe, performed various superhuman feats

Pau·li (pou′lē), **Wolf·gang** (woolf′gaŋ′; Ger vôlf′gäŋk′) 1900-58; U.S. physicist, born in Austria

Paul·ine (pô lēn') 〚L *Paulina*, fem. of *Paulinus* < L *Paulus*, PAUL〛 a feminine name

Paul·ing (pôl'iŋ), **Li·nus (Carl)** (lī'nes) 1901- ; U.S. chemist

Pau·sa·ni·as (pô sā'nē əs) 2d cent. A.D.; Gr. historian & geographer, probably born in Lydia

Pa·va·rot·ti (pä'və rôt'ē; *It* pä'vä rôt'tē), **Lu·cia·no** (lōō chä'nô) 1935- ; It. operatic tenor

Pav·lov (pav'lôv'; *Russ* pà'vlôf'), **I·van Pe·tro·vich** (i vàn' pye trô'vich) 1849-1936; Russ. physiologist

Pav·lo·va (päv lō'və, pav-; *Russ* pàv'lô və'), **An·na (Matveyevna)** (än'ä) 1881-1931; Russ. ballet dancer

Pax (päks; *also* paks) the Roman goddess of peace, identified with the Greek Irene

Paz (päs; *E also* päz), **Oc·ta·vio** (ôk tä'vyô) 1914- ; Mex. poet

Pea·bod·y (pē'bäd'ē, -bəd ē), **George** 1795-1869; U.S. merchant & philanthropist, in England

Pea·cock (pē'käk'), **Thomas Love** (luv) 1785-1866; Eng. novelist & poet

Peale (pēl) **1 Charles Will·son** (wil'sən) 1741-1827; Am. portrait painter **2 James** 1749-1831; Am. painter: brother of Charles **3 Rem·brandt** (rem'brant') 1778-1860: Am. painter: son of Charles

Pearl (purl) 〚< ModE *pearl* (the gem) < ME *perle* < MFr < VL *perla, perula*, altered < L *perna*, a sea mussel〛 a feminine name

Pear·son (pir'sən), **Lester Bowles** (bōlz) 1897-1972; Cdn. statesman: prime minister (1963-68)

Pear·y (pir'ē), **Robert Edwin** 1856-1920; U.S. arctic explorer: the leader of an expedition generally regarded as being the first to reach the North Pole (1909)

Pe·cos Bill (pā'kōs') *American Folklore* a frontier cowboy, who performed such superhuman feats as digging the Rio Grande

Peel (pēl), **Sir Robert** 1788-1850; Brit. statesman: prime minister (1834-35; 1841-46)

Peeping Tom *Eng. Legend* a Coventry tailor who was struck blind after peeping at Lady Godiva

Peg·gy (peg'ē) a feminine name: see MARGARET

Pei (pā), **I(eoh) M(ing)** 1917- ; U.S. architect, born in China

Peirce (purs), **Charles San·ders** (san'dərz) 1839-1914;

U.S. philosopher & mathematician

Pe·la·gi·us (pə lā′jē əs) *c.* A.D. 360-*c.* 420 Brit. monk & theologian

Pe·le·us (pē′lē əs, pēl′yōōs′) *Gr. Myth.* a king of the Myrmidons, father of Achilles

Pe·li·as (pē′lē əs, pel′ē-) ⟦ L < Gr ⟧ *Gr. Myth.* a king of Thessaly and the uncle and guardian of Jason, whom he sends in search of the Golden Fleece

Pe·lop·i·das (pi läp′i dəs) died 364 B.C.; Theban general

Pe·lops (pē′läps′) ⟦ L < Gr, prob. < *pellos*, dark + *ops*, face ⟧ *Gr. Myth.* the son of Tantalus: he is killed and served to the gods as food by his father, but later is restored to life by them

Pen·de·rec·ki (pen′də ret′skē), **Krzysz·tof** (kris′tôf′, krə zish′tôf′) 1933- ; Pol. composer

Pe·nel·o·pe (pə nel′ə pē) ⟦ L < Gr *Pēnelopē* ⟧ **1** a feminine name: dim. *Penny* **2** Odysseus's wife, who waits faithfully for his return from the Trojan War

Penn (pen), **William** 1644-1718; Eng. Quaker leader: founder of Pennsylvania

Pen·nell (pen′əl), **Joseph** 1857-1926; U.S. etcher, book illustrator, & writer

Pen·zi·as (pent′sē əs), **Ar·no Allan** (är′nō) 1933- ; U.S. physicist, born in Germany

Pep·in the Short (pep′in) *c.* A.D. 714-768; king of the Franks (751-768): father of Charlemagne

Pepys (pēps), **Samuel** 1633-1703; Eng. government official, known for his diary

Per·ci·val (pur′si vəl) ⟦ OFr *Perceval*, prob. < *perce val*, pierce valley: apparently coined by CHRÉTIEN DE TROYES (12th c.) ⟧ **1** a masculine name; dim. *Percy*: also **Per′ce·val 2** PERCIVALE

Per·ci·vale (pur′si vəl) ⟦ see prec. ⟧ *Arthurian Legend* a knight who is allowed to see the Holy Grail

Per·cy (pur′sē) ⟦ dim. of *Percival;* also after Fr *Perci*, village in Normandy ⟧ **1** a masculine name: see PERCIVAL **2** Sir **Henry** 1364-1403; Eng. soldier & rebel against Henry IV: called *Hotspur* **3 Thomas** 1729-1811; Eng. bishop & collector of early English & Scottish ballads

Per·el·man (per′əl mən; purl′mən), **S(idney) J(oseph)** 1904-79; U.S. humorist

Pé·rez de Cué·llar (pā′räs dā kwä′yär), **Ja·vier** (hä vyer′) 1920- ; Peruvian diplomat: secretary-general of the United Nations (1982-91)

Per·go·le·si (per'gō lā'zē, -sē), **Gio·van·ni Bat·tis·ta** (jô vän'nē bät tēs'tä) 1710-36; It. composer

Per·i·cles (per'i klēz') c. 495-429 B.C.; Athenian statesman & general

Per·kins (pʉr'kinz), **Frances** 1882-1965; U.S. social worker: secretary of labor (1933-45)

Per·rault (pe rō'), **Charles** (shȧrl) 1628-1703; Fr. writer & compiler of fairy tales

Per·rin (pe ran'), **Jean Bap·tiste** (zhän bȧ tēst') 1870-1942; Fr. physicist

Per·ry (per'ē) ⟦? orig., a dim. of *Pers* < Fr *Piers* < L *Petrus*, PETER⟧ **1** a masculine name **2 Matthew Cal·braith** (kal'breth') 1794-1858; U.S. naval officer: negotiated U.S.-Japanese trade treaty (1854) **3 Oliver Haz·ard** (haz'ərd) 1785-1819; U.S. naval officer: defeated the Brit. fleet on Lake Erie (1813): brother of Matthew **4 Ralph Barton** 1876-1957; U.S. philosopher & educator

Perse, St. John *see* ST. JOHN PERSE

Per·seph·o·ne (pər sef'ə nē) ⟦L < Gr *Persephonē*⟧ *Gr. Myth.* the daughter of Zeus and Demeter, abducted by Hades (Pluto) to be his wife in the lower world: identified with the Roman Proserpina

Per·se·us (pʉr'sē əs, -syōōs') ⟦L < Gr⟧ *Gr. Myth.* the son of Zeus and Danae, and slayer of Medusa: he marries Andromeda after rescuing her from a sea monster

Per·shing (pʉr'shiŋ), **John Joseph** 1860-1948; U.S. general: commander in chief of American Expeditionary Forces, World War I

Per·u·gi·no (per'ōō jē'nō), **Il** (ēl) (born *Pietro di Cristoforo Vannucci*) c. 1446-1523; It. painter

Pe·rutz (pə rōōts'), **Max Ferdinand** 1914- ; Brit. molecular biologist, born in Austria

Pes·ta·loz·zi (pes'tə lät'sē), **Jo·hann Hein·rich** (yô'hän' hin'riH) 1746-1827; Swiss educational reformer

Pé·tain (pā tan'), **Hen·ri Phi·lippe** (än rē fē lēp') 1856-1951; Fr. general: premier of Fr. government at Vichy (1940-44): convicted of treason (1945)

Pe·ter (pēt'ər) ⟦ME < LL(Ec) *Petrus* < Gr *Petros* (< *petros*, stone, *petra*, rock) used as transl. of Aram *kēphā*, rock⟧ **1** a masculine name: dim. *Pete*: equiv. L. *Petrus*, Fr. *Pierre*, It. *Pietro*, Sp. *Pedro*, Russ. *Pëtr* **2** *Bible* (original name *Simon*) died c. A.D. 64: one of the twelve Apostles, a fisherman, to whom the Letters of Peter are ascribed: considered the first pope: his day is June 29: also *Simon Peter* or *Saint Peter* **3 Peter I** 1672-1725; czar of Russia (1682-1725): called *Peter the Great* **4 Peter II** 1923-70; king of Yugoslavia (1934-45): son of Alexander I **5 Peter III** 1728-62; czar of Russia (1762): assassinated, & succeeded by his wife, Catherine II

Peter Pan the title character of J. M. Barrie's play (1904), a young boy who runs away to "Never-Never Land" and never grows up

Pe·ti·pa (pə tē pä′), **Ma·rius** (mä′ ryüs′) 1818-1910; Fr. dancer & choreographer in Russia

Pe·tö·fi (pet′ə fē; *Hung* pe′tö fē), **Sán·dor** (shän′dôr′) 1823-49; Hung. poet & patriot

Pe·trarch (pē′trärk′) (It. name *Francesco Petrarca*) 1304-74; It. lyric poet & scholar

Pe·trie (pē′trē), Sir (**William Matthew**) **Flin·ders** (flin′dərz) 1853-1942; Eng. archaeologist & Egyptologist

Pe·tro·ni·us (pi trō′nē əs), (**Gaius**) died A.D. 66; Rom. satirist: often called *Petronius Arbiter*

Pevs·ner (*for 1* pefs′nər & *Fr* pevz ner′; *for 2* pevz′nər) **1 An·toine** (än twän′) 1886-1962; Fr. sculptor & painter, born in Russia: brother of Naum Gabo **2** Sir **Ni·ko·laus** (**Barnhard Leon**) (nik′ə ləs) 1902-85; Brit. art historian, born in Germany

Phae·dra (fē′drə, fē′-) 〖L < Gr *Phaidra*〗 *Gr. Myth.* daughter of Minos and wife of Theseus: she kills herself after her stepson, Hippolytus, rejects her advances: see HIPPOLYTUS

Phae·drus (fē′drəs) 1st cent. A.D.; Rom. writer of fables and reputed translator of some of Aesop's fables

Pha·ë·thon (fā′ə thän′) 〖L *Phaethon* < Gr *Phaethōn*, lit., shining (< *phaethein*, to shine) < *phaos*, light < IE base *bhā-, to shine〗 *Class. Myth.* son of Helios, the sun god: he unsuccessfully tries to drive his father's sun chariot and almost sets the world on fire, but Zeus strikes him down with a thunderbolt

Phe·be (fē′bē) a feminine name: see PHOEBE

Phei·dip·pi·des (fī dip′i dēz′) 〖prob. altered (by HERODOTUS) after *Philippides*〗 5th cent. B.C.; Athenian courier who ran to Sparta to seek aid against the Persians before the battle of Marathon

Phid·i·as (fid′ē əs) 5th cent. B.C.; Gr. sculptor

Phi·dip·pi·des (fĭ dip'ĭ dēz') *alt. sp. of* PHEIDIPPIDES

Phi·le·mon (fĭ lē'mən, fī-) ⟦ L < Gr *Philēmōn*, lit., affectionate < *philein*, to love ⟧ *Gr. Myth.* the husband of BAUCIS

Phil·ip (fil'ip) ⟦ L *Philippus* < Gr *Philippos*, lit., fond of horses < *philos*, loving + *hippos*, horse ⟧ **1** a masculine name: dim. *Phil*; var. *Phillip*; equiv. L. *Philippus*, Fr. *Philippe*, Ger. *Philipp*, It. *Filippo*, Sp. *Felipe*; fem. *Philippa* **2** one of the twelve Apostles: his day is May 1: also **Saint Philip 3** (Ind. name *Metacomet*) died 1676; chief of the Wampanoag Indians (1662-76): led a war against New England colonists: son of Massasoit: called *King Philip* **4** *Prince* 1921- ; Duke of Edinburgh, born in Greece: husband of Elizabeth II of England **5** *Saint* (1st cent. A.D.); a deacon of the early Christian church: his day is June 6 **6** *Philip II* 382-336 B.C.; king of Macedonia (359-336): father of Alexander the Great **7** *Philip II* 1165-1223; king of France (1180-1223): also called **Philip Augustus 8** *Philip II* 1527-98; king of Spain (1556-98) & (as **Philip I**) of Portugal (1580-98): sent Armada against England (1588) **9** *Philip IV* 1268-1314; king of France (1285-1314): moved the papacy to Avignon (1309): called *the Fair* **10** *Philip V* 1683-1746; 1st Bourbon king of Spain (1700-46)

Phi·lip·pa (fĭ lip'ə) ⟦ fem. of prec. ⟧ a feminine name: see PHILIP

Philip the Good 1396-1467; duke of Burgundy (1419-67)

Phil·lip (fil'ip) a masculine name: see PHILIP

Phil·lips (fil'ips), **Wen·dell** (wen'dəl) 1811-84; U.S. abolitionist, reformer, & orator

Phil·lis (fil'is) a feminine name: see PHYLLIS

Phil·oc·te·tes (fil'äk tē'tēz') *Gr. Legend* the Greek warrior who kills Paris in the Trojan War with a poisoned arrow given him by Hercules

Phi·lo (**Ju·dae·us**) (fī'lō jōō dē'əs) *c.* 20 B.C.-*c.* A.D. 50 Hellenistic Jewish philosopher of Alexandria

Phil·o·me·la (fil'ō mē'lə) ⟦ L < Gr < *philein*, to love + *melos*, song ⟧ *Gr. Myth.* a princess of Athens raped by Tereus, husband of her sister Procne: the gods change Philomela into a nightingale, Procne into a swallow, and Tereus into a hawk

Phin·e·as (fin'ē əs) ⟦ LL *Phinees* < Gr < Heb *pīnĕḥās*, prob. < Egypt *pe-neḥase*] a masculine name

Pho·ci·on (fō'sē än') *c.* 402-*c.* 317 B.C.; Athenian statesman & general

Phoe·be (fē'bē) 〚L < Gr *Phoibē,* fem. of *Phoibos:* see fol. 〛 1 a feminine name 2 *Gr. Myth.* Artemis as goddess of the moon: identified with the Roman Diana 3 [Old Poet.] the moon personified

Phoe·bus (fē'bəs) 〚ME *Phebus* < L *Phoebus* < Gr *Phoibos,* bright one < *phoibos,* bright 〛 1 *Gr. Myth.* Apollo as god of the sun 2 [Old Poet.] the sun personified

Phyfe (fīf), **Duncan** (born *Duncan Fife*) 1768-1854; U.S. cabinetmaker & furniture designer, born in Scotland

Phyl·lis (fil'is) 〚L < Gr, lit., leaf, ult. < IE base *bhel-,* to swell, sprout 〛 a feminine name: dim. *Phyl*

Pia·get (pyä zhä'; *Fr* pyá zhe'), **Jean** (zhän) 1896-1980; Swiss psychologist & philosopher

Pi·cas·so (pi kä'sō, -kas'ō), **Pa·blo** (pä'blō) 1881-1973; Sp. painter & sculptor in France

Pic·card (pi kärd'; *Fr* pē kár') 1 **Au·guste** (ô güst') 1884-1962; Swiss physicist in Belgium: known for balloon ascents into the stratosphere & descents in a bathyscaph 2 **Jean Fé·lix** (zhän fā lēks') 1884-1963; U.S. chemist & aeronautical engineer, born in Switzerland: also known for balloon ascents: twin brother of Auguste

Pick·er·ing (pik'ər iŋ) 1 **Edward Charles** 1846-1919; U.S. astronomer & physicist 2 **William Henry** 1858-1938; U.S. astronomer: brother of Edward

Pick·ett (pik'it), **George Edward** 1825-75; Confederate general

Pick·wick (pik'wik), **Mr. (Samuel)** the naive, benevolent president of the Pickwick Club in Charles Dickens' *Pickwick Papers* (1836)

Pi·co del·la Mi·ran·do·la (pē'kō del'ə mə ran'dō lə; *It* pē'kô del'lä mē *r*än'dô lä'), **Count Gio·van·ni** (jô vän' nē) 1463-94; It. humanist

Pied Piper (of Ham·e·lin) (ham'ə lin) *Gmc. Legend* a musician who rid Hamelin of its rats by leading them with his piping to the river, where they drowned: in revenge for not being paid, he piped the village children to a mountain, where they disappeared

Pierce (pirs), **Franklin** 1804-69; 14th president of the U.S. (1853-57)

Pi·erre (pē er′; *Fr* pyer) 〚Fr: see PETER〛 a masculine name: see PETER

Pi·er·rot (pē′ər ō′; *Fr* pye rō′) 〚Fr, dim. of *Pierre*, PETER〛 a stock comic character in old French pantomime, having a whitened face and wearing loose white pantaloons and a jacket with large buttons

Pike (pīk), **Zeb·u·lon Montgomery** (zeb′yoo lən) 1779-1813; U.S. general & explorer

Pi·late (pī′lət), **Pon·tius** (pun′chəs, -shəs; päŋ′-; *also* pän′ tē əs) 1st cent. A.D.; Rom. procurator of Judea, Samaria, & Idumaea (*c.* 26-*c.* 36) who condemned Jesus to be crucified

Pinck·ney (piŋk′nē), **Charles Cotes·worth** (kōts′wərth) 1746-1825; Am. statesman & diplomat

Pin·dar (pin′dər, -där′) *c.* 522-*c.* 438 B.C.; Gr. lyric poet

Pi·ne·ro (pi nir′ō), **Sir Arthur Wing** (wiŋ) 1855-1934; Eng. playwright

Pink·er·ton (piŋk′ər tən), **Allan** 1819-84; U.S. private detective, born in Scotland

Pin·ter (pin′tər), **Harold** 1930- ; Eng. playwright

Pin·zón (pēn thōn′) **1 Mar·tín A·lon·so** (mär tēn′ ä lôn′ sō) *c.* 1440-93; Sp. navigator with Columbus; commanded the *Pinta* **2 Vi·cen·te Yá·ñez** (vē then′te yä′ nyeth) *c.* 1460-*c.* 1524 Sp. navigator with Columbus; commanded the *Niña*: brother of Martín

Pi·ran·del·lo (pir′ən del′ō; *It* pē′rän del′lô), **Lu·i·gi** (loo ē′jē) 1867-1936; It. playwright & novelist

Pi·ra·ne·si (pir′ə nä′zē; *It* pē′rä ne′zē), **Giam·bat·ti·sta** (jäm′bät tē′stä) 1720-78; It. architect & engraver

Pi·sa·no (pē sä′nō, -zä′-), **Ni·co·la** (nē kô′lä) *c.* 1220-*c.* 1284; It. sculptor & architect

Pis·ca·tor (pis kä′tôr), **Erwin** 1893-1966; Ger. theatrical director & producer

Pi·sis·tra·tus (pi sis′trə təs, pī-) died 527 B.C.; tyrant of Athens (variously from 560 to 527)

Pis·sar·ro (pi sär′ō; *Fr* pē sà rō′), **Ca·mille** (kà mē′y′) 1830-1903; Fr. painter, born in the Virgin Islands

Pis·ton (pis′tən), **Walter** 1894-1976; U.S. composer

Pit·man (pit′mən), **Sir Isaac** 1813-97; Eng. inventor of a system of shorthand

Pitt (pit) **1 William** 1st Earl of Chatham 1708-78; Eng. statesman: prime minister (1766-68): called *the Great Commoner* **2 William** 1759-1806; Eng. statesman: prime minister (1783-1801; 1804-06): son of William

Pi·us (pī'əs) **1** a masculine name, adopted chiefly by several popes **2 Pius II** (born *Enea Silvio de Piccolomini*) 1405-64; pope (1458-64) **3 Pius VII** (born *Luigi Barnaba Chiaramonti*) 1742-1823; pope (1800-23) **4 Pius IX** (born *Giovanni Maria Mastai-Ferretti*) 1792-1878; pope (1846-78) **5** Saint **Pius X** (born *Giuseppe Sarto*) 1835-1914; pope (1903-14): his day is Aug. 21 **6 Pius XI** (born *Achille Ratti*) 1857-1939; pope (1922-39) **7 Pius XII** (born *Eugenio Pacelli*) 1876-1958; pope (1939-58)

Pi·zar·ro (pi zär'ō; *Sp* pē thär'rô), **Fran·cis·co** (frän thēs'kô) *c.* 1474-1541; Sp. conqueror of Peru

Planck (pläŋk), **Max (Karl Ernst Ludwig)** (mäks) 1858-1947; Ger. physicist

Plan·tag·e·net (plan taj'ə nit) name of the ruling family of England (1154-1399)

Plath (plath), **Sylvia** 1932-63; U.S. poet

Pla·to (plāt'ō) ⟦Gr *Platōn*⟧ *c.* 427-*c.* 347 B.C.; Gr. philosopher

Plau·tus (plôt'əs), **(Titus Maccius)** *c.* 254-184 B.C.; Rom. writer of comic dramas

Plé·iade (plā yàd') ⟦Fr < L *Pleiades* < Gr: see fol.⟧ a group of seven French poets of the 16th cent. who favored the use of classical forms

Ple·ia·des (plē'ə dēz', plī'-; -yə-) *Gr. Myth.* the seven daughters of Atlas and Pleione, placed by Zeus among the stars

Plin·y (plin'ē) **1** (L. name *Gaius Plinius Secundus*) A.D. 23-79; Rom. naturalist & writer: called *the Elder* **2** (L. name *Gaius Plinius Caecilius Secundus*) *c.* A.D. 62-*c.* 113; Rom. writer & statesman: nephew of Pliny the Elder: called *the Younger*

Plo·ti·nus (plō tī'nəs) A.D. 205-270; Rom. Neoplatonic philosopher, born in Egypt

Plu·tarch (plōō'tärk') *c.* A.D. 46-*c.* 120; Gr. biographer & historian

Plu·to (plōōt'ō) ⟦L < Gr *Ploutōn* < *ploutos*, wealth akin to *plein*, to float, swim < IE base **pel-*, to fill⟧ *Gr. & Rom. Myth.* the god ruling over the lower world: also called *Hades* by the Greeks and *Dis* or *Orcus* by the Romans

Plu·tus (plōōt'əs) ⟦L < Gr *Ploutos* < *ploutos*, wealth: see prec.⟧ *Gr. Myth.* the blind god of wealth

Po·ca·hon·tas (pō'kə hänt'əs) *c.* 1595-1617; North

American Indian princess: reputed to have saved Captain John Smith from execution

Poe (pō), **Edgar Allan** 1809-49; U.S. poet, short-story writer, & critic

Poin·ca·ré (pwȧn kȧ rā′) **1 Jules Hen·ri** (zhül än rē′) 1854-1912; Fr. mathematician **2 Ray·mond** (rā mōn′) 1860-1934; Fr. statesman: prime minister (1912-13; 1922-24; 1926-29): president (1913-20): cousin of Jules

Pole (pōl), **Reginald** 1500-58; Eng. cardinal: last Rom. Catholic archbishop of Canterbury (1556-58)

Po·li·tian (pō lish′ən) (born *Angelo Ambrogini*) 1454-94; It. humanist & poet

Polk (pōk), **James Knox** 1795-1849; 11th president of the U.S. (1845-49)

Pol·lock (päl′ək) **1 Sir Frederick** 3d Baronet 1845-1937; Eng. jurist & writer on law **2 Jackson** 1912-56; U.S. abstract painter

Pol·lux (päl′əks) 〚L, earlier *Polluces* < Gr *Polydeukēs*〛 *Gr. & Rom. Myth.* the immortal twin of Castor: see DIOSCURI

Pol·ly (päl′ē) feminine name: see MARY

Po·lo (pō′lō), **Mar·co** (mär′kō) 1254-1324; Venetian traveler in E Asia

Po·lo·ni·us (pə lō′nē əs) in Shakespeare's *Hamlet*, a verbose, sententious old courtier, father of Ophelia and Laertes

Po·lyb·i·us (pō lib′ē əs) *c.* 200-*c.* 118 B.C.; Gr. historian

Pol·y·carp (päl′i kärp′), **Saint** (2d cent. A.D.); Gr. bishop of Smyrna: Christian martyr: his day is Feb. 23

Pol·y·cli·tus, **Pol·y·clei·tus** (päl′i klīt′əs) 5th cent. B.C.; Gr. sculptor: also **Pol·y·cle′tus** (-klēt′-)

Pol·yg·no·tus (päl′ig nōt′əs) 5th cent. B.C.; Gr. painter

Pol·y·hym·ni·a (päl′i him′nē ə) 〚L < Gr *Polymnia* < *poly-* < *polys*, much, many < IE **pelu*, large amount < base **pel-*, to pour, fill + *hymnos*, hymn〛 *Gr. Myth.* the Muse of sacred poetry: also **Po·lym′ni·a** (pō lim′-)

Pol·y·ni·ces (päl′i nī′sēz′) 〚Gr *Polyneikēs*, lit., great wrangler < *polys*, much (see prec.) + *neikos*, quarrel, akin to *Nikē*: see NIKE〛 *Gr. Legend* a son of Oedipus and Jocasta

Pol·y·phe·mus (päl′i fē′məs) in Homer's *Odyssey*, a Cyclops who confines Odysseus and his companions in a cave until Odysseus blinds him so that they can escape

Po·mo·na (pō mō′nə) ⟦L < *pomum*, fruit⟧ *Rom. Myth.* the goddess of fruits and fruit trees

Pom·pa·dour (päm′pə dôr′, -dŏŏr′; *Fr* pōn på dŏŏr′), Marquise **de** (born *Jeanne Antoinette Poisson*) 1721-64; mistress of Louis XV

Pom·pey (päm′pē, -pā′) (L. name *Gnaeus Pompeius Magnus*) 106-48 B.C.; Rom. general & triumvir

Pon·ce de Le·ón (pän′sā dā′ lā ōn′, -sē-; päns′də lē′ən; *Sp* pôn′the *the* leôn′) *c.* 1460-1521; Sp. explorer: discovered Florida while seeking the Fountain of Youth

Pon·chi·el·li (pän′kē el′ē, pôn′-; *It* pôn kyel′lē), **A·mil·ca·re** (ä mēl′kä rä′) 1834-86; It. operatic composer

Pon·ti·ac (pänt′ē ak′) *c.* 1720-69; Ottawa Indian chief

Pontius Pilate *see* PILATE, Pontius

Pope (pōp) **1 Alexander** 1688-1744; Eng. poet **2 John** 1822-92; Union general in the Civil War

Pop·per (päp′ər), Sir **Karl Rai·mund** (rī′moont′) 1902- ; Brit. philosopher, born in Austria

Por·se·na (pôr′si nə), **Lars** (lärz) 6th cent. B.C.; Etruscan king who, according to legend, attacked Rome in an unsuccessful attempt to restore Tarquin to the throne: also **Por·sen·na** (pôr sen′ə)

Por·ter (pôrt′ər) **1 Cole** (kōl) *c.* 1893-1964; U.S. composer of popular songs **2 David** 1780-1843; U.S. naval officer & diplomat **3 David Dix·on** (dik′sən) 1813-91; Union admiral in the Civil War: son of David **4** Sir **George** 1920- ; Brit. chemist **5 Katherine Anne** 1890-1980; U.S. short-story writer, essayist, & novelist **6 Rodney Robert** 1917-85; Brit. biochemist **7 William Sydney** *see* HENRY, O.

Por·tia (pôr′shə) ⟦L *Porcia*, fem. of *Porcius*, name of a Roman gens, prob. < *porcus*, a pig⟧ **1** a feminine name **2** the heroine of Shakespeare's *Merchant of Venice*

Po·sei·don (pō sī′dən) ⟦L < Gr *Poseidōn*⟧ *Gr. Myth.* god of the sea and of horses: identified with the Roman Neptune

Post (pōst), **Emily** (born *Emily Price*) 1873-1960; U.S. writer on etiquette

Po·tem·kin (pō tem′kin, pə-; *Russ* pu tyôm′kin), **Gri·go·ri A·le·ksan·dro·vich** (grē gô′rē ä′lyek sän′drô vich′) 1739-91; Russ. field marshal & statesman: favorite of Catherine the Great

Pot·ter (pät′ər), **Be·a·trix** (bē′ə triks′) 1866-1943; Eng.

writer & illustrator of children's books

Pou·lenc (pōō la*n*k′), **Fran·cis** (frä*n* sēs′) 1899-1963; Fr. composer

Pound (pound) **1 Ezra (Loomis)** 1885-1972; U.S. poet, in Italy (1924-45; 1958-72) **2 Roscoe** 1870-1964; U.S. educator & legal scholar

Pous·sin (pōō sa*n*′), **Ni·co·las** (nē kô lä′) 1594-1665; Fr. painter

Pow·ell (pou′əl; *for 1* pō′əl) **1 Anthony (Dymoke)** 1905- ; Eng. novelist **2 Cecil Frank** 1903-69; Brit. physicist **3 Lewis Franklin, Jr.** 1907- ; associate justice, U.S. Supreme Court (1972-) **4 John Wesley** 1834-1902; U.S. explorer & geologist

Pow·ys (pō′is) **1 John Cow·per** (kōō′pər) 1872-1963; Eng. novelist & critic **2 T(heodore) F(rancis)** 1875-1953; novelist: brother of John

Prax·it·e·les (praks it′ə lēz′) 〚L < Gr *Praxitelēs*〛 4th cent. B.C.; Athenian sculptor

Pre·log (pre′lōg′), **Vladimir** 1906- ; Swiss chemist, born in Yugoslavia

Pres·cott (pres′kət), **William Hick·ling** (hik′li*n*) 1796-1859; U.S. historian

Pres·ley (prez′lē), **El·vis (Aron)** (el′vis) 1935-77; U.S. rock-and-roll singer

Pres·ter John (pres′tər) a legendary medieval Christian king and priest said to have ruled either in the Far East or in Ethiopia

Pretender in English history, the son or the grandson of James II: see OLD PRETENDER, YOUNG PRETENDER

Pré·vost d'Ex·iles (prā vō deg zēl′), **An·toine Fran·çois** (ä*n* twàn frä*n* swà′) 1697-1763; Fr. novelist: called **Abbé Prévost**

Pri·am (prī′əm) 〚L *Priamus* < Gr *Priamos*〛 Gr. Legend the last king of Troy, who reigned during the Trojan War: he was the father of Hector and Paris

Pri·a·pus (prī ā′pəs) 〚L < Gr *Priapos*〛 Gr. & Rom. Myth. a god, son of Dionysus and Aphrodite, personifying the male procreative power

Price (pris), **(Mary) Le·on·tyne** (lē än′tēn′) 1927- ; U.S. operatic soprano

Pride (prīd), **Thomas** died 1658; Eng. army officer: in 1648 brought about the expulsion (Pride's Purge) of over 100 Royalist & Presbyterian Members of Parliament

Priest·ley (prēst′lē) **1** J(ohn) B(oynton) 1894-1984; Eng. novelist, playwright, & literary critic **2** Joseph 1733-1804; Eng. scientist & theologian, in the U.S. after 1794: discoverer of oxygen

Pri·go·gine (pri gô′gin; prē′gô zhēn′), **Il·ya** (il yä′) 1917- ; Belgian chemist, born in Russia

Prince of Darkness name for SATAN

Prince of Peace name for Jesus Christ

Pri·or (prī′ər), **Matthew** 1664-1721; Eng. poet

Pris·ci·an (prish′ən, -ē ən) (L. name *Priscianus Caesariensis*) fl. A.D. 500: Latin grammarian

Pris·cil·la (pri sil′ə) 〖L, dim. of *Prisca*, fem. of *Priscus*, a Roman surname < *priscus*, ancient, primitive, akin to OL *pri*, before 〗 a feminine name

Pro·clus (prō′kləs, prä′kləs) *c*. A.D. 410-485 Gr. Neoplatonic philosopher, born in Constantinople

Proc·ne (präk′nē) 〖L < Gr *Proknē*〗 Gr. Myth. sister of Philomela and wife of Tereus, transformed into a swallow by the gods: see PHILOMELA

Pro·co·pi·us (prō kō′pē əs) 6th cent. A.D.; Byzantine historian

Pro·crus·tes (prō krus′tēz′) 〖L < Gr *Prokroustēs* < *prokrouein*, to beat out, stretch out < *pro*-, before + *krouein*, to strike 〗 Gr. Myth. a giant of Attica who seizes travelers, ties them to a bedstead, and either stretches them or cuts off their legs to make them fit it

prodigal son Bible a wastrel son who was welcomed back warmly on his homecoming in repentance: Luke 15:11-32

Pro·ko·fi·ev (prō kôf′ē ef′, -kō′fē-), **Ser·gey (Sergeyvich)** (ser gā′) 1891-1953; Russ. composer

Pro·me·the·us (prō mē′thē əs) 〖L < Gr *Promētheus*, lit., forethought < *promēthes*, thinking before < *pro*-, before + *manthanein*, to learn < IE *mendh*-, to pay attention to, be alert 〗 Gr. Myth. a Titan who steals fire from heaven for the benefit of mankind: in punishment, Zeus chains him to a rock where a vulture (or eagle) comes each day to eat his liver, which grows back each night

Pro·per·ti·us (prō pur′shəs, -shē əs), **Sex·tus** (seks′təs) *c*. 50-*c*. 15 B.C.; Rom. poet

Prophet, the 1 among Muslims, Mohammed **2** among Mormons, Joseph Smith

Pro·ser·pi·na (prō sur′pi nə) 〖L〗 Rom. Myth. the

daughter of Ceres and wife of Pluto: identified with the Greek Persephone: also **Pro·ser·pi·ne** (präs'ər pīn', prō sur'pi nē')

Pros·per·o (präs'pər ō') the deposed, magic-working Duke of Milan in Shakespeare's *The Tempest*, exiled on an island with his daughter Miranda

Pro·tag·o·ras (prō tag'ə rəs) *c.* 481-*c.* 411 B.C.; Gr. philosopher: one of the principal Sophists

Pro·te·us (prō'tē əs) 〚ME *Protheus* < L *Proteus* < Gr *Prōteus*〛 *Gr. Myth.* a minor sea god and servant of Poseidon: he can change his form or appearance at will

Prou·dhon (proo dōn'), **Pierre Jo·seph** (pyer zhō zef') 1809-65; Fr. socialist & writer

Proust (proost), **Marcel** 1871-1922; Fr. novelist

Prov·i·dence (präv'ə dəns) God, as the guiding power of the universe

Pru·dence (prood''ns) 〚LL, fem. of *Prudentius* < L *prudentia*, prudence〛 a feminine name: dim. *Prue*

Psalm·ist (säm'ist), **the** King David, to whom all or certain of the Psalms are variously attributed

Psy·che (sī'kē) 〚L < Gr *psychē*, the soul, akin to *psychein*, to blow, cool < IE base **bhes-*, to blow〛 *Rom. Folklore* a maiden who, after undergoing many hardships due to Venus' jealousy of her beauty, is reunited with Cupid and made immortal by Jupiter

Ptah (p'tä, p'täkh) 〚Egypt *ptḥ*〛 *Egypt. Myth.* the chief god of Egyptian Memphis, creator of gods and mortals

Ptol·e·my (täl'ə mē) **1** (L. name *Claudius Ptolomaeus*) 2d cent. A.D.; Alexandrian astronomer, mathematician, & geographer **2 Ptolemy I** *c.* 367-283 B.C.; general of Alexander the Great: 1st king of the Ptolemaic dynasty (323-285): called *Ptolemy Soter* ("Savior") **3 Ptolemy II** 309-246 B.C.; king of Egypt (285-246): son of Ptolemy I: called *Ptolemy Philadelphus*

Puc·ci·ni (poo chē'nē), **Gia·co·mo** (jä'kō mō') 1858-1924; It. operatic composer

Pu·las·ki (poo läs'kē), **Cas·i·mir** (kaz'i mir') 1748-79; Pol. general in the American Revolutionary army

Pul·it·zer (pool'it sər, pyoo'lit-), **Joseph** 1847-1911; U.S. newspaper owner & philanthropist, born in Hungary

Punch (punch) 〚contr. after *Punchinello*, earlier *Polichinello*, a character in a Neapolitan puppet play < It *Pulcinella* < VL **pullicinus* < LL *pullicenus*, young chicken, dim. of L *pullus*, chicken, small animal

< IE base *pōu-, *pu-, small child, small animal ‖ the male character of the puppet show *Punch and Judy*, a hook-nosed, humpbacked figure

Pun·chi·nel·lo (pun'chə nel'ō) ‖ see prec. ‖ a prototype of Punch

Pu·pin (pyōō pēn'), **Michael Id·vor·sky** (id vôr'skē) 1858-1935; U.S. physicist & inventor, born in Hungary

Pur·cell (pur'səl), **Henry** *c.* 1659-95; Eng. composer

Push·kin (pōōsh'kin), **A·lek·san·dr Ser·ge·ye·vich** (ä'lyik sän'dr' syer gyä'yə vich) 1799-1837; Russ. poet

Put·nam (put'nəm), **Israel** 1718-90; Am. general in the Revolutionary War

Pu·vis de Cha·vannes (pü vēd' shȧ vȧn'), **Pierre** 1824-98; Fr. painter

Pyg·ma·li·on (pig māl'ē ən, -yən) ‖ L < Gr *Pygmaliōn* ‖ *Gr. Legend* a king of Cyprus and a sculptor: see GALA-TEA

Pyle (pīl), **Ernest Taylor** (called *Ernie*) 1900-45; U.S. journalist

Pym (pim), **John** *c.* 1583-1643; Eng. parliamentary leader

Pyr·a·mus and This·be (pir'ə məs ənd thiz'bē) Babylonian lovers in ancient mythology: Pyramus, mistakenly thinking Thisbe has been killed by a lioness, kills himself, and Thisbe, finding his body, kills herself

Pyr·rhus (pir'əs) **1** *Gr. Myth.* Achilles' son **2** *c.* 318-272 B.C.; king of Epirus (*c.* 305-272 B.C.)

Py·thag·o·ras (pi thag'ə rəs) 6th cent. B.C.; Gr. philosopher & mathematician, born on Samos

Q

Q *pseud. of* Sir Arthur Thomas QUILLER-COUCH

Qad·da·fi (kə dä'fē), **Mu·am·mar al–** (mōō'ə mär' al'-) 1942- ; Libyan political leader: prime minister (1969-): also **Qa·dha'fi**

Quarles (kwôrlz), **Francis** 1592-1644; Eng. poet

Queen Mab (mab) *Eng. Folklore* a fairy queen who controls people's dreams

Quen·tin (kwent''n) ‖ Fr < L *Quintinus* < *Quintus*, Roman praenomen < *quintus*, the fifth ‖ a masculine name: var. *Quintin*

Ques·nay (kā ne'), **Fran·çois** (frän swä') 1694-1774; Fr. economist & physician

Quet·zal·co·atl (ket säl'kō ät''l) a principal god of the

Aztecs, symbolized by a feathered serpent

Que·zon (kā'sän'), **Ma·nuel Luis** (män wel' lōō ēs') 1878-1944; Philippine statesman: 1st president of the Philippines (1935-44): in full **Manuel Lu·is Quezon y Mo·li·na** (ē mō lē'nə)

Quil·ler-Couch (kwil'ər kōōch'), Sir **Arthur Thomas** (pseud. *Q*) 1863-1944; Eng. writer

Quin·cy (kwin'zē), **Josiah** 1744-75; Am. Revolutionary patriot

Quintero, Joaquín Álvarez *see* ÁLVAREZ QUINTERO, Joaquín

Quin·til·ian (kwin til'yən) (L. name *Marcus Fabius Quintilianus*) *c.* A.D. 35-*c.* 96; Rom. rhetorician, born in Spain

Quin·tin (kwint'ʼn) a masculine name: dim. *Quint*: see QUENTIN

Qui·ri·nus (kwi rī'nəs) ⟦L⟧ *Rom. Myth.* an early god of war: later identified with Romulus

Quixote, Don *see* DON QUIXOTE

R

Ra (rä) ⟦Egypt *rˁ*, sun, day⟧ *Egypt. Myth.* the sun god and principal deity: usually depicted as having the head of a hawk and wearing the solar disk as a crown

Ra·be·lais (rab'ə lā'; *Fr* rȧ ble'), **Fran·çois** (frän swȧ') *c.* 1494-1553; Fr. satirist & humorist

Ra·bi (rä'bē), **I(sidor) I(saac)** 1898-1988; U.S. physicist, born in Austria

Ra·chel (*for 1 & 2*, rā'chəl; *for 3, Fr* rȧ shel') ⟦LL(Ec) < Gr(Ec) *Rhachēl* < Heb *rachel*, lit., ewe⟧ **1** a feminine name: dim. *Rae* **2** *Bible* the younger of the two wives of Jacob, and mother of Joseph and Benjamin: Gen. 29-35 **3** (born *Élisa Félix*) *c.* 1820-58; Fr. actress, born in Switzerland

Rach·ma·ni·noff (rak man'i nôf'), **Ser·gei V(assilievich)** (ser gā') 1873-1943; Russ. composer, conductor, & pianist: also sp. **Rach·man'i·nov'** (-nôf')

Ra·cine (ra sēn'; *Fr* rȧ sēn'), **Jean Bap·tiste** (zhän bȧ tēst') 1639-99; Fr. poet & dramatist

Rae (rā) a feminine name: see RACHEL

Rae·burn (rā'bərn), Sir **Henry** 1756-1823: Scot. painter

Rail-Splitter, the *name for* Abraham LINCOLN

Ra·leigh (rô'lē, rä'lē), Sir **Walter** *c.* 1552-1618; Eng.

statesman, explorer, & poet: beheaded: also sp. **Ra'legh**

Ralph (ralf; *Brit usually* rāf) 〚ON *Rathulfr* (akin to OE *Rædwulf*) < *rath,* counsel + *ulfr,* wolf〛 a masculine name: equiv. Fr. *Raoul*

Ra·ma (rä'mə) 〚Sans *Rāma*〛 any of three of the incarnations of the Hindu god Vishnu, esp. the seventh: see RAMACHANDRA

Ra·ma·chan·dra (rä'mə chun'drə) 〚Sans *Rāmacandra*〛 Rama, the seventh incarnation of the Hindu god Vishnu: the hero of the Ramayana

Ra·meau (ra mō'), **Jean Phi·lippe** (zhän fē lēp') 1683-1764; Fr. composer & organist

Ram·e·ses (ram'ə sēz) *var. of* RAMSES

Ra·mo·na (rə mō'nə) 〚Sp〛 a feminine name: see RAYMOND

Ram·say (ram'zē) **1** Allan 1686-1758; Scot. poet & bookseller **2** George *see* DALHOUSIE, Earl of **3** Sir William 1852-1916; Brit. chemist, born in Scotland

Ram·ses (ram'sēz', -zēz') **1** name of 11 Egyptian kings who ruled from *c.* 1315 to *c.* 1090 B.C. **2** Ramses I died *c.* 1314; founder of the dynasty **3** Ramses II died 1225; king (1292-25): often identified as the pharaoh of Exodus **4** Ramses III died 1167; king (*c.* 1198-67)

Ran·dal, Ran·dall (ran'dəl) 〚< OE *Randwulf* (or ON *Ranthulfr*) < *rand,* shield + *wulf,* wolf〛 a masculine name

Ran·dolph (ran'dôlf') 〚ML *Randulfus* < OE *Randwulf:* see prec.〛 **1** a masculine name **2** John 1773-1833; U.S. statesman & orator

Ran·ke (räŋ'kə), **Le·o·pold von** (lā'ō pôlt' fôn) 1795-1886; Ger. historian

Ran·som (ran'səm), **John Crowe** (krō) 1888-1974; U.S. poet & critic

Raph·a·el (rā'fē əl, -fä-; -el'; *also,* & *for* 3 *usually,* rä'fä el', rä'fä el'; -fī-, -fä-) 〚LL(Ec) < Gr(Ec) *Rhaphaēl* < Heb *refael,* lit., God hath healed〛 **1** a masculine name **2** an archangel mentioned in the Apocrypha **3** (born *Raffaello Santi* or *Sanzio*) 1483-1520; It. painter & architect

Rask (räsk), **Ras·mus Chris·tian** (räs'mŏŏs krēs'tyän) 1787-1832; Dan. philologist

Ras·mus·sen (räs'mŏŏ sən), **Knud** (**Johan Victor**) (kə nŏŏ*th*') 1879-1933; Dan. arctic explorer

Ras·pu·tin (ras pyŏŏt'in), **Gri·go·ri Ye·fi·mo·vich** (gri gô'ri ye fē'mə vich) (orig. surname *Vilkin*) c. 1871-1916; Russ. religious mystic & faith healer

Ra·the·nau (rä'tə nou'), **Wal·ther** (väl'tər) 1867-1922; Ger. industrialist & statesman: assassinated

Rau·schen·berg (rou'shən bərg'), **Robert** 1925- ; U.S. artist

Ra·vel (rà vel'), **Mau·rice** (**Joseph**) (mô rēs') 1875-1937; Fr. composer

Ray (rā) a masculine name: see RAYMOND

Ray, Man (man) 1890-1976; U.S. painter & photographer

Ray·leigh (rā'lē), 3d Baron (*John William Strutt*) 1842-1919; Eng. physicist

Ray·mond (rā'mənd) ⟦NormFr *Raimund* < Frank *Raginmund*, lit., wise protection < Gmc **ragina-*, counsel (as in Goth *ragin*, judgment) + **mund-*, hand, protection (as in OHG *munt*)⟧ a masculine name: dim. *Ray*; fem. *Ramona*

Read (rēd), **Sir Herbert** (**Edward**) 1893-1968; Eng. poet & critic

Reade (rēd), **Charles** 1814-84; Eng. novelist

Rea·gan (rā'gən), **Ronald** (**Wilson**) 1911- ; 40th president of the U.S. (1981-89)

Reaper, the the GRIM REAPER

Re·bec·ca (ri bek'ə) ⟦LL(Ec) < Gr(Ec) *Rhebekka* < Heb *rivka*, lit., noose, connection⟧ 1 a feminine name: dim. *Becky, Reba* 2 *Bible* the wife of Isaac and mother of Jacob and Esau: Gen 25:20: usually sp. **Re·bek'ah**

Ré·ca·mier (rā kà myā'), **Madame** (born *Jeanne Françoise Julie Adelaïde Bernard*) 1777-1849; Fr. social leader in intellectual & literary circles

Red Cloud 1822-1909; Dakota Indian chief

Re·don (rə dōn'), **O·di·lon** (ô dē lôn') 1840-1916; Fr. painter & lithographer

Reed (rēd) 1 **John** 1887-1920; U.S. journalist & radical 2 **Walter** 1851-1902; U.S. army surgeon & bacteriologist

Re·gan (rē'gən) in Shakespeare's *King Lear*, the younger of Lear's two cruel and disloyal daughters

Re·gi·na (ri jī'nə, -jē'-) ⟦L, a queen, fem. of *rex*, king < IE base **reg-*, straight, stretch out, put in order⟧ a feminine name: dim. *Gina*

Reg·i·nald (rej'i nəld) ⟦ML *Reginaldus* < OHG *Raganald, Raginold* < Gmc **ragina-*, **ragna-*, judgment, counsel + *waldan, to rule⟧ a masculine name:

dim. *Reggie*; var. *Reynold*; equiv. Fr. *Regnault*, *Renaud*, Ger. *Reinhold*, It. *Rinaldo*, Sp. *Reynaldos*

Reg·u·lus (reg′yōō ləs), (**Marcus Atilius**) died *c.* 250 B.C.; Rom. consul & general in the 1st Punic War

Rehn·quist (ren′kwist′), **William H(ubbs)** 1924- ; associate justice, U.S. Supreme Court (1972-86): chief justice of the U.S. (1986-)

Re·ho·bo·am (rē′hə bō′əm) ⟦Heb *rechavam*, lit., prob., enlarger of the people⟧ *Bible* the first king of Judah: 2 Chron. 9:31-12:16

Rein·hardt (rīn′härt) **1 Ad(olph)** 1913-67: U.S. painter **2 Djan·go** (jaŋ′gō) (born *Jean Baptiste*) 1910-53; Belgian jazz guitarist **3 Max** (born *Max Goldmann*) 1873-1943; Austrian theatrical director & producer in Germany and later in the U.S.

Re·marque (rə märk′), **E·rich Ma·ri·a** (er′ik mə rē′ə) (born *Erich Paul Remark*) 1898-1970; U.S. novelist, born in Germany

Rem·brandt (rem′bränt′, -brant′) (born *Rembrandt Harmensz van Rijn*) 1606-69; Du. painter & etcher

Rem·ing·ton (rem′iŋ tən), **Frederic** 1861-1909; U.S. painter, sculptor, & illustrator

Re·mus (rē′məs) ⟦L⟧ *Rom. Myth.* the twin brother of ROMULUS

Re·nan (rə nan′, -nän′; *Fr* rə nän′), (**Joseph**) **Er·nest** (er nest′) 1823-92; Fr. historian & essayist

Re·nee (rə nā′) a feminine name

Re·noir (rən wär′, ren′wär′; *Fr* rə nwär′) **1 Jean** 1894-1979; Fr. film director: son of Pierre Auguste **2 Pierre Au·guste** (pyer ô güst′) 1841-1919; Fr. painter

Re·spi·ghi (*re* spē′gē), **Ot·to·ri·no** (ôt′tô rē′nô) 1879-1936; It. composer

Reu·ben (rōō′bən) ⟦via LL(Ec) < Gr(Ec) < Heb *reuven*, lit., behold, a son < *reu*, imper. of *raa*, to see + *ben*, son⟧ **1** a masculine name: dim. *Rube*, *Ruby* **2** *Bible* the eldest son of Jacob and Leah: Gen. 29:32

Reu·ther (rōō′thər), **Walter** (**Philip**) 1907-70; U.S. labor leader

Re·vere (rə vir′), **Paul** 1735-1818; Am. silversmith & patriot: rode from Boston to Lexington (April 18, 1775) to warn the colonists that British troops were coming

Rex (reks) ⟦L, a king: see REGINA⟧ a masculine name

Rey·nard (ren′ərd, rā′nərd, rā′närd′) ⟦OFr *Renard*,

Renart < OHG *Reginhart* < Gmc *ragina, counsel, judgment (< IE base **reĝ-*, to put in order) + *hard*, bold, brave ‖ the fox in the medieval beast epic *Reynard the Fox*; hence, a proper name for the fox in fable and folklore

Reyn·old (ren'əld) a masculine name: see REGINALD

Reyn·olds (ren'əldz), Sir **Joshua** 1723-92; Eng. portrait painter

Rhad·a·man·thus (rad'ə man'thəs) ‖ L < Gr *Rhadamanthos* ‖ *Gr. Myth.* a son of Zeus and Europa, rewarded for his exemplary justice by being made, after his death, a judge of the dead in the lower world: also **Rhad'a·man'thys** (-this)

Rhe·a (rē'ə) ‖ L < Gr ‖ *Gr. Myth.* daughter of Uranus and Gaea, wife of Cronus, and mother of Zeus, Poseidon, Hades, Demeter, Hera, and Hestia: identified with the Roman Ops and the Phrygian Cybele

Rhe·a Sil·vi·a (rē'ə sil'vē ə) *Rom. Myth.* a vestal virgin who breaks her vows and becomes by Mars the mother of Romulus and Remus

Rho·da (rō'də) ‖ L *Rhode* < Gr *Rhodē* < *rhodon*, rose < OPers *wṛda* > Ar *ward* ‖ a feminine name

Rhodes (rōdz), **Cecil John** 1853-1902; Brit. financier & colonial administrator in South Africa

Ri·be·ra (ri ber'ə; *Sp* rē ber'rä), **Jo·sé** (hô se') c. 1588-c. 1652; Sp. painter in Naples: called *Lo Spagnoletto*

Ri·car·do (ri kär'dō), **David** 1772-1823; Eng. economist

Rice (rīs), **Elmer** (born *Elmer Reizenstein*) 1892-1967; U.S. playwright

Rich·ard (rich'ərd) ‖ ME *Rycharde* < OFr *Richard* < OHG *Richart* < Gmc **rik-*, king (akin to L *rex*: see REGINA) + *harthuz, strong ‖ **1** a masculine name: dim. *Dick, Rich, Rick*; equiv. It. *Riccardo*, Sp. *Ricardo* **2 Richard I** 1157-99; king of England (1189-99): son of Henry II: called **Richard Coeur de Li·on** (kʉrd' lē ōn', kʉr' də lē'ən) **3 Richard II** 1367-1400; king of England (1377-99): last Plantagenet king: deposed: son of Edward, the Black Prince **4 Richard III** 1452-85; king of England (1483-85): last king of the house of York

Richard Roe (rō) ‖ see DOE ‖ a name used in law courts, legal papers, etc. to refer to a person whose actual name is unknown, esp. to the second person of two when both names are unknown (the first person being referred to as *John Doe*)

Rich·ards (rich′ərdz) **1** I(vor) A(rmstrong) 1893-1979; Eng. literary critic in the U.S. **2 Theodore William** 1868-1928; U.S. chemist

Rich·ard·son (rich′ərd sən) **1 Henry Handel** (pseud. of *Ethel Florence Lindesay Richardson Robertson*) 1870-1946; Austral. novelist **2 Henry Hobson** 1838-86; U.S. architect **3 Sir Owen (Willans)** 1879-1959; Eng. physicist **4 Sir Ralph (David)** 1902-83; Brit. actor **5 Samuel** 1689-1761; Eng. novelist

Ri·che·lieu (rish′lōō′, -ə lōō′; *Fr* rē shə lyö′), **Duc de** (born *Armand Jean du Plessis*) 1585-1642; Fr. cardinal & statesman: chief minister of Louis XIII (1624-42)

Rich·ter (rik′tər), **Burton** 1931- ; U.S. physicist

Rick·en·back·er (rik′ən bak′ər), **Edward Vernon** 1890-1973; U.S. aviator & aviation executive

Ride (rīd), **Sally K(risten)** 1951- ; U.S. astronaut: 1st U.S. woman in space (1983)

Rid·ley (rid′lē), **Nicholas** c. 1500-55; Eng. bishop & Protestant reformer: burned at the stake for heresy

Ri·en·zi (rē en′zē), **Co·la di** (kô′lä dē) c. 1313-54; Rom. patriot & political reformer

Riis (rēs), **Jacob August** 1849-1914; U.S. journalist & social reformer, born in Denmark

Ri·ley (rī′lē), **James Whit·comb** (hwit′kəm) 1849-1916; U.S. poet

Ril·ke (ril′kə), **Rai·ner Ma·ri·a** (rī′nər mä rē′ä) 1875-1926; Austrian lyric poet, born in Prague

Rim·baud (ram bō′; *Fr* ran bō′), **(Jean Nicolas) Ar·thur** (àr tür′) 1854-91; Fr. poet

Rim·sky-Kor·sa·kov (rim′skē kôr′sə kôf′), **Ni·ko·lai An·dre·ye·vich** (nē kô li′ än dryā′ye vich) 1844-1908; Russ. composer: also sp. **Rim′ski–Kor′sa·koff′**

Rine·hart (rīn′härt′), **Mary Roberts** 1876-1958; U.S. mystery-story writer & playwright

Rip van Win·kle (rip′ van wiŋ′kəl) the title character of a story (1819) by Washington Irving: Rip awakens after a twenty-year sleep to find everything changed

Ri·ta (rēt′ə) ⟦ It ⟧ a feminine name

Ri·ve·ra (rē ve′rä; *E* ri ver′ə), **Die·go** (dye′gô) 1886-1957; Mex. painter

Riv·ers (riv′ərz), **Larry** (born *Yitzroch Loiza Grossberg*) 1923- ; U.S. painter

Ri·zal (rē säl′), **Jo·sé** (hô se′) 1861-96; Philippine patriot, novelist, & poet: shot for alleged conspiracy against Spain

Riz·zio (rit′sē ō′), **David** *c.* 1533-66; It. musician: secretary to & favorite of Mary, Queen of Scots: murdered

Robbia, Luca Della *see* DELLA ROBBIA, Luca

Rob·bins (rä′bənz), **Jerome** 1918-   ; U.S. dancer & choreographer

Rob·ert (räb′ərt) ⟦OFr < OHG *Hruodperht* < *hruod-*, fame, praise < IE base **kar-*, to praise, boast + *perht*, bright ⟧ 1 a masculine name: dim. *Bob, Rob, Robby, Robbie, Robin*; var. *Rupert*; fem. *Roberta, Robin* 2 **Robert I** died 1035; duke of Normandy (*c.* 1028-35): father of William the Conqueror 3 **Robert I** *see* BRUCE, Robert (the)

Ro·ber·ta (rə bur′tə, rō-) ⟦fem. of prec.⟧ a feminine name: see ROBERT

Robe·son (rōb′sən), **Paul** 1898-1976; U.S. singer & actor

Ro·bes·pierre (rōbz′pyer′, -pir′; *Fr* rô bes pyer′), **Max·i·mi·lien** (**François Marie Isidore de**) (måk sē mē lya*n*′) 1758-94; Fr. revolutionist & Jacobin leader: guillotined

Rob·in (rä′bən) a feminine and masculine name: see ROBERT

Robin Good·fel·low (good′fel′ō) *Eng. Folklore* a mischievous sprite or fairy: identified with Puck

Robin Hood (hood) *Eng. Legend* a 12th-cent. outlaw who lived with his followers in Sherwood Forest and robbed the rich to help the poor

Rob·in·son (rä′bən sən) 1 **Edwin Ar·ling·ton** (är′liŋ tən) 1869-1935; U.S. poet 2 **Jack Roosevelt** (called *Jackie*) 1919-72; U.S. baseball player 3 **Sir Robert** 1886-1975; Brit. chemist

Robinson Cru·soe (krōō′sō′) the title hero of Daniel Defoe's novel (1719), a sailor who, shipwrecked on a tropical island, survives by various ingenious contrivances until rescued years later

Ro·cham·beau (rō′sham bō′; *Fr* rô shän bō′), **Comte de** (*Jean Baptiste Donatien de Vimeur*) 1725-1807; Fr. general: commanded Fr. forces against the British in the Am. Revolutionary War

Rock·e·fel·ler (räk′ə fel′ər) 1 **John D**(avison) 1839-1937; U.S. industrialist & philanthropist 2 **John D**(avison)**, Jr.** 1874-1960; U.S. industrialist & philanthropist: son of John Davison 3 **Nelson A**(ldrich) 1908-79; vice president of the U.S. (1974-77): son of John Davison, Jr.

Rock·ne (räk′nē), **Knute** (**Kenneth**) (nōōt) 1888-1931; U.S. football coach, born in Norway

Rock·well (räk′wel′), **Norman** 1894-1978; U.S. illustrator

Rod·er·ick (räd′ər ik) 〚ML *Rodericus* < OHG *Hrodrich* < *hruod-*, fame (see ROBERT) + Gmc **rik-*, a king (akin to L *rex:* see REGINA)〛 a masculine name: dim. *Rod*; equiv. Sp. *Roderigo*

Rod·gers (rä′jərz), **Richard** 1902-79; U.S. composer

Ro·din (rô dan′), (**François**) **Au·guste** (**René**) (ô güst′) 1840-1917; Fr. sculptor

Rod·ney (räd′nē) 〚< surname *Rodney*, after *Rodney Stoke*, England〛 a masculine name: dim. *Rod*

Roe·bling (rō′bliŋ), **John A**(**ugustus**) 1806-69; U.S. civil engineer & bridge designer, born in Germany

Roent·gen (rent′gən; *Ger* rënt′gən), **Wil·helm Kon·rad** (vil′helm′ kôn′rät′) 1845-1923; Ger. physicist: discoverer of X-rays

Roeth·ke (ret′kə), **Theodore** 1908-63; U.S. poet

Rog·er (rä′jər) 〚OFr < OHG *Ruodiger, Hrodger* (akin to OE *Hrothgar*) < *hruod-, ruod-*, fame (see ROBERT) + **ger*, spear〛 a masculine name

Rog·ers (rä′jərz) **1 Bruce** 1870-1957; U.S. typographer & book designer **2 Robert** 1731-95: Am. frontier soldier **3 Will** (born *William Penn Adair Rogers*) 1879-1935; U.S. humorist & actor

Ro·get (rō′zhā′), **Peter Mark** 1779-1869; Eng. writer & physician: compiler of a thesaurus

Ro·land (rō′lənd, räl′ənd) 〚Fr < OHG *Hruodland* < *hruod-*, fame (see ROBERT) + *land,* land〛 **1** a masculine name: equiv. It. *Orlando* **2** a legendary hero famous for his strength, courage, and chivalrous spirit who appears in the *Chanson de Roland* and other stories of the Charlemagne cycle

Rol·land (rô län′), **Ro·main** (rô man′) 1866-1944; Fr. writer

Rol·lo (räl′ō) *c.* A.D. 860-*c.* 931 Norse conqueror of Normandy: 1st duke of Normandy (911-927)

Ro·mains (rô man′), **Jules** (zhül) (born *Louis Farigoule*) 1885-1972; Fr. novelist, poet, & playwright

Ro·ma·nov (rō′mə nôf′, rō mä′nôf′) **1** name of the ruling family of Russia from 1613 to 1917 **2 Mi·kha·il Feo·do·ro·vich** (mē khä ēl′ fyô′dô rô vich) 1598-1645; 1st Romanov czar & founder of the dynasty Also sp.

Ro′ma·noff′

Rom·berg (räm′bʉrg′), **Sigmund** 1887-1951: U.S. composer, born in Hungary

Ro·me·o (rō′mē ō′) 〚It < *Romolo* < L *Romulus*〛 the hero of Shakespeare's tragedy *Romeo and Juliet* (c. 1595), son of Montague and lover of Juliet, daughter of Capulet: at the death of the lovers their feuding families become reconciled

Rom·mel (räm′əl), **Erwin (Johannes Eugen)** 1891-1944; Ger. field marshal in World War II

Rom·ney (rum′nē, räm′-), **George** 1734-1802; Eng. painter

Rom·u·lus (räm′yoo ləs) 〚L〛 *Rom. Myth.* a son of Mars and founder and first king of Rome, deified as Quirinus: he and his twin brother Remus, left as infants to die in the Tiber, are suckled by a she-wolf

Ron·ald (rän′əld) 〚Scot < ON *Rögnvaldr,* akin to OHG *Raganald:* see REGINALD〛 a masculine name: dim. *Ron*

Ron·sard (rōn sȧr′), **Pierre de** 1524-85; Fr. poet

Rönt·gen (rent′gən; *Ger* rënt′gən), **Wilhelm Konrad** *alt. sp. of* Wilhelm Konrad ROENTGEN

Roo·se·velt (rō′zə vəlt, -velt′; rōō′zə-) **1** a masculine name **2 (Anna) Eleanor** 1884-1962; U.S. writer & delegate at UN: wife of Franklin **3 Franklin Del·a·no** (del′ə nō′) 1882-1945; 32d president of the U.S. (1933-45) **4 Theodore** 1858-1919; 26th president of the U.S. (1901-09)

Root (rōōt), **Elihu** 1845-1937; U.S. statesman: secretary of state (1905-09)

Ros·a·lie (rō′zə lē′, räz′ə-) 〚Fr, prob. < L *rosalia,* annual ceremony of hanging garlands of roses on tombs < *rosa,* rose〛 a feminine name

Ros·a·lind (räz′ə lind) 〚Sp *Rosalinda,* as if from *rosa linda,* pretty rose, but prob. ult. < OHG *Roslindis* < Gmc *hros,* horse + *lindi,* lithe〛 a feminine name

Ros·a·mond, Ros·a·mund (räz′ə mənd, rō′zə-) 〚ME *Rosamunda* < OFr *Rosamonde* or Sp *Rosamunda* < ML *Rosamunda,* as if < L *rosa munda,* clean rose, but ult. < OHG *Hrosmund* < Gmc *hros,* horse + **mund-,* hand, protection〛 a feminine name: dim. *Roz*

Ros·coe (räs′kō) 〚< ?〛 a masculine name

Rose (rōz) 〚< ModE *rose* (the flower) < ME < OE < L *rosa* < Gr *rhodou* < OPers *wṛda*〛 a feminine name: dim. *Rosie;* var. *Rosita;* equiv. It. & Sp. *Rosa*

Rose·crans (rōz'kranz'), **William Starke** (stärk) 1819-98: Union general in the Civil War

Rose·mar·y (rōz'mer'ē) ⟦ < ModE *rosemary* (the herb), altered (after *rose* (the flower) & MARY) < earlier *ros-marine* < L *ros marinus* (also *ros maris*), lit., dew of the sea < *ros*, dew + *marinus*, marine ⟧ a feminine name: var. **Rose·ma·rie** (rōz'mə rē')

Ro·si·ta (rō zēt'ə) a feminine name: see ROSE

Ross (rôs) **1 Betsy** (Mrs. *Elizabeth Griscom Ross*) 1752-1836; Am. woman reputed to have made the first Am. flag **2 Harold W**(allace) 1892-1951; U.S. magazine editor **3 Sir James Clark** 1800-62; Brit. polar explorer **4 Sir John** 1777-1856; Brit. arctic explorer, born in Scotland: uncle of Sir James **5 Sir Ronald** 1857-1932; Eng. pathologist, born in India

Ros·set·ti (rə zet'ē, -set'ē) **1 Christina** (**Georgina**) 1830-94; Eng. poet **2 Dante Gabriel** 1828-82; Eng. Pre-Raphaelite painter & poet: brother of Christina

Ros·si·ni (rō sē'nē), **Gio·ac·chi·no** (**Antonio**) (jô'äk kē'nō) 1792-1868; It. composer

Ros·tand (rôs tän'), **Ed·mond** (ed mōn') 1868-1918; Fr. dramatist & poet

Ro·stov·tzeff (rə stôf'tsef), **M**(ichael) **I**(vanovich) 1870-1952; U.S. historian, born in Russia

Roth·ko (räth'kō'), **Mark** (born *Marcus Rothkovich*) 1903-70; U.S. painter, born in Russia

Roth·schild (rôths'chīld', rôth'-; *Ger* rōt'shilt') **1** name of a family of European bankers **2 Mey·er An·selm** (mī'ər än'zelm) 1743-1812; Ger. founder of the banking house of Rothschild: also **Meyer Am·schel** (äm'shəl) **3 Nathan Meyer** 1777-1836; Eng. banker, born in Germany: son of Meyer Anselm

Rou·ault (rōō ō'), **Georges** (zhôrzh) 1871-1958; Fr. painter

Rou·get de Lisle (or **L'Isle**) (rōō zhed lēl'), **Claude Jo·seph** (klōd zhō zef') 1760-1836; Fr. army officer & composer: wrote the *Marseillaise*

Rous (rous), **Francis Pey·ton** (pāt''n) 1879-1970; U.S. pathologist

Rous·seau (rōō sō') **1 Hen·ri** (än rē') 1844-1910; Fr. primitive painter: called *Le Douanier* (The Customs Officer) **2 Jean Jacques** (zhän zhäk') 1712-78; Fr. political philosopher & writer, born in Switzerland **3** (**Pierre Étienne**) **Thé·o·dore** (tā ô dôr') 1812-67; Fr.

landscape painter

Ro·we·na (rō ē'nə, rō wē'-) ⟦< ? OE *Hrothwina* < *hroth,* fame, akin to OHG *hruod-* (see ROBERT) + *wina,* a friend, fem. of *wine:* see EDWIN⟧ a feminine name

Row·land (rō'lənd) a masculine name: see ROLAND

Row·land·son (rō'lənd sən), **Thomas** 1756-1827; Eng. caricaturist & painter

Rox·anne (räks an') a feminine name: dim. *Roxie;* var. *Roxanna*

Roy (roi) ⟦as if < OFr *roy* (Fr *roi*), a king, but prob. < Gael *rhu,* red⟧ a masculine name

Royce (rois), **Josiah** 1855-1916; U.S. philosopher

Ru·bens (rōō'bənz), **Peter Paul** 1577-1640; Fl. painter

Ru·bin·stein (rōō'bin stīn') **1 An·ton** (**Grigorevich**) (än' tôn) 1829-94; Russ. pianist & composer **2 Ar·tur** (är' toor') 1887-1982; U.S. pianist, born in Poland

Ru·by (rōō'bē) ⟦< ModE *ruby* (the gem) < ME < OFr *rubi,* ult. < L *rubeus,* reddish, ult. < IE **rudhso-:* see RUSSELL⟧ a feminine name

Ru·dolf I (rōō'dôlf) 1218-91; Ger. king & emperor of the Holy Roman Empire (1273-91): founder of the Hapsburg dynasty: also called **Rudolf I of Hapsburg**

Ru·dolph (rōō'dôlf', -dälf') ⟦Ger *Rudolf* < OHG *Rudolf, Hrodulf* < *hruod-,* fame (see ROBERT) + *wolf,* wolf⟧ a masculine name: dim. *Rudy;* var. *Rodolph, Rolf, Rollo;* equiv. Fr. *Rodolphe,* Ger. *Rudolf,* It. & Sp. *Rodolfo*

Ru·fus (rōō'fəs) ⟦L, red-haired, red⟧ a masculine name

Ruis·dael (rois'däl', ris'-; *Du* rēs'däl'), **Ja·cob van** (yä'kôp vän') *c.* 1628-82; Du. landscape painter

Rum·ford (rum'fərd), **Count** *see* THOMPSON, Benjamin

Rum·pel·stilts·kin (rum'pəl stilt'skin') *Gmc. Folklore* a dwarf who saves the life of a king's bride by spinning flax into gold in exchange for her first child: he agrees to free her from the bargain if she can guess his name, which she does

Run·yon (run'yən), (**Alfred**) **Da·mon** (dā'mən) 1884-1946; U.S. journalist & short story writer

Ru·pert (rōō'pərt) ⟦Ger *Ruprecht, Rupprecht:* see ROBERT⟧ a masculine name

Ru·rik (rōō'rik) died A.D. 879; Scand. chief regarded as the founder of the 1st Russian dynasty (*c.* 862-1598)

Rush (rush), **Benjamin** 1745-1813; Am. physician: signer of the Declaration of Independence

Rus·kin (rus′kin), **John** 1819-1900; Eng. writer, art critic, & social reformer

Rus·sell (rus′əl) ⟦< surname *Russell,* orig. dim. of Fr *roux,* reddish < OFr *rous* < L *russus,* reddish < IE **rudhso-* < base **reudh-,* red⟧ 1 a masculine name: dim. *Russ:* also **Rus′sel** 2 **Bertrand (Arthur William)** 3d Earl Russell, 1872-1970; philosopher, mathematician, & writer, born in Wales 3 **George William** (pseud. *Æ* or *A.E.*) 1867-1935; Ir. poet & essayist 4 **Lord John** 1st Earl Russell of Kingston Russell, 1792-1878; Eng. statesman: prime minister (1846-52; 1865-66): grandfather of Bertrand 5 **Lillian** (born *Helen Louise Leonard*) 1861-1922; U.S. singer & actress

Rus·tin (rus′tin), **Bay·ard** (bī′ərd) 1910-87; U.S. civil rights leader

Ruth (rо̄о̄th) ⟦LL(Ec) < Heb *rut,* prob. contr. < *re'ut,* companion⟧ 1 a feminine name 2 *Bible* a Moabite widow deeply devoted to her mother-in-law, Naomi, for whom she left her own people to later become the wife of Boaz of Bethlehem 3 **George Herman** (called *Babe*) 1895-1948; U.S. baseball player

Ruth·er·ford (ru*th*′ər fərd), **Joseph Franklin** 1869-1942; U.S. leader of Jehovah's Witnesses

Rut·ledge (rut′lij) 1 **Ann** *c.* 1813-35; alleged fiancée of young Abraham Lincoln 2 **Edward** 1749-1800; Am. statesman: signer of the Declaration of Independence 3 **John** 1739-1800; Am. statesman: brother of Edward

Ruys·dael (rois′däl′, rīs′-; *Du* rēs′däl′), **Jacob van** *alt. sp.* of Jacob van RUISDAEL

Ruy·ter (roi′tər, rī′-), **Mi·chiel A·dri·aans·zoon de** (mē khēl′ ä′drē än′sən də) 1607-76; Du. admiral

Ru·žič·ka (rо̄о̄′zhĕch kä′), **Le·o·pold** (lä′ô̂ pôlt′) 1887-1976: Swiss chemist, born in Yugoslavia

Ry·an (rī′ən) a masculine name

Ry·der (rīd′ər), **Albert Pink·ham** (piŋk′əm) 1847-1917; U.S. painter

Ryle (rīl) 1 **Gilbert** 1900-76; Brit. philosopher 2 **Sir Martin** 1918-84; Brit. astronomer

S

Saa·di (sä′dē) *alt. sp.* of SADI

Saa·ri·nen (sär′i nen′, -nən) 1 **Ee·ro** (ā′rō) 1910-61; U.S. architect, born in Finland 2 **(Gottlieb) E·liel** (ēl′yel)

1873-1950; Finn. architect, in the U.S. after 1923: father of Eero

Sa·ba·tier (så bå tyā'), **Paul** (pôl) 1854-1941; Fr. chemist

Sa·bin (sā'bin), **Albert B(ruce)** 1906-93; U.S. physician & bacteriologist, born in Russia: developed an oral vaccine to prevent poliomyelitis

Sac·co (sak'ō; *It* säk'kô), **Ni·co·la** (nē kô'lä) 1891-1927; It. anarchist in the U.S.: together with Bartolomeo VANZETTI, charged with murder & payroll theft in 1920: their conviction & execution aroused international protest, being regarded by many as the result of political bias

Sachs (saks; *Ger* zäks), **Hans** 1494-1576; Ger. Meistersinger, a cobbler by trade

Sack·ville (sak'vil'), **Thomas** 1st Earl of Dorset & Baron Buckhurst 1536-1608; Eng. statesman & poet

Sa·dat (sä dät'), **An·war** (el–) (än'wär', än wär') 1918-81; president of Egypt (1970-81): assassinated

Sade (sad, säd; *Fr* såd), **Marquis de** (full name Comte *Donatien Alphonse François de Sade*) 1740-1814; Fr. soldier & novelist, whose writings describe sexual aberrations

Sa·di (sä'dē) (born *Muslih-ud-Din*) c. 1184-c. 1291; Pers. poet

Sa·die (sä'dē) a feminine name: see SARAH

Sa·gan (sā'gən), **Carl (Edward)** 1934- ; U.S. astronomer & writer

Sage (sāj), **Russell** 1816-1906; U.S. financier

Sainte–Beuve (sant böv'), **Charles Au·gus·tin** (shårl ô güs tan') 1804-69; Fr. literary critic & writer

Saint–Ex·u·pé·ry (san teg zü pā rē'), **An·toine de** (än twän' də) 1900-44; Fr. aviator & writer

Saint–Gau·dens (sänt gôd'′nz), **Augustus** 1848-1907; U.S. sculptor, born in Ireland

Saint–Just (san zhüst'), **Louis An·toine Lé·on de** (lwē än twän' lā ôn' də) 1767-94; Fr. revolutionist

Saint–Saëns (san säns'), **(Charles) Ca·mille** (kå mē'y') 1835-1921; Fr. composer

Saints·bur·y (sānts'ber'ē, -bər ē), **George (Edward Bateman)** 1845-1933; Eng. literary critic

Saint–Si·mon (san sē môn') **1** Comte de (*Claude Henri de Rouvroy*) 1760-1825; Fr. social philosopher **2** Duc de (*Louis de Rouvroy*) 1675-1755; Fr. courtier & writer

Sa·kha·rov (sä'kə rôf, -räf'; sak'ə-), **An·drei (Dmi-**

trievich) (än'drä) 1921-89; Russ. nuclear physicist: political dissident & human rights activist

Sa·ki (sä'kē) (pseud. of *Hector Hugh Munro*) 1870-1916; Brit. short-story writer & novelist, born in Burma

Sal·a·din (sal'ə din) (born *Salah-ad-Din Yusuf ibn-Ayyub*) 1137-93; sultan of Egypt & Syria (1174-93)

Sa·la·zar (sä'lə zär'), **An·to·nio de O·li·vei·ra** (än tô' nyoo dē ô'lē vā'rə) 1889-1970; prime minister & dictator of Portugal (1932-68)

Sal·in·ger (sal'in jər), **J(erome) D(avid)** 1919- ; U.S. novelist & short-story writer

Salis·bur·y (sôlz'ber'e, -bə rē; salz'-), 3d Marquess of (*Robert Arthur Talbot Gascoyne-Cecil*) 1830-1903; Eng. statesman

Salk (sôlk), **Jo·nas E(dward)** (jō'nəs) 1914- ; U.S. physician & bacteriologist: developed a vaccine to prevent poliomyelitis

Sal·lust (sal'əst) (L. name *Gaius Sallustius Crispus*) 86-*c.* 35 B.C.; Rom. historian

Sal·ly (sal'ē) a feminine name: see SARAH

Sa·lo·me (sə lō'mē, sal'ə mā') ‖ LL(Ec) < Gr(Ec) *Salōmē* < Heb *shalom*, lit., peace ‖ *traditional name of* the daughter of Herodias: her dancing pleased Herod so much that he granted her request for the head of John the Baptist: see Matt. 14:8

Sal·o·mon (sal'ə mən), **Haym** (hīm) 1740-85; Am. financier & patriot, born in Poland: helped finance the Am. Revolutionary War

Sa·man·tha (sə man'thə) a feminine name

Sam·son (sam'sən) ‖ LL(Ec) < Gr(Ec) *Sampsōn* < Heb *shimshon* < ? *shemesh*, sun: interpretation of name uncert. ‖ **1** a masculine name: var. **Samp'son 2** *Bible* an Israelite judge noted for his great strength: betrayed to the Philistines by Delilah: Judges 13-16

Sam·u·el (sam'yoo əl, -yool) ‖ LL(Ec) < Gr(Ec) *Samouēl* < Heb *shemuel*, lit., name of God ‖ **1** a masculine name: dim. *Sam, Sammy* **2** *Bible* a Hebrew judge and prophet

Sam·u·el·son (sam'yoo əl sən, -yool-), **Paul (Anthony)** 1915- ; U.S. economist & educator

San·cho Pan·za (san'chō pan'zə; *Sp* sän'chô pän'thä) the simple, credulous squire to Cervantes' Don Quixote: his practical, peasant common sense contrasts with the visionary idealism of his master

Sand (sand; *Fr* sänd, sän), **George** (pseud. of *Amandine Aurore Lucie Dupin*, Baronne *Dudevant*) 1804-76; Fr. novelist

Sand·burg (sand′bʉrg′), **Carl** 1878-1967; U.S. poet, writer, & ballad collector

San·dra (san′drə, sän′-) a feminine name: see ALEXANDRA

Sang·er (saŋ′ər) **1 Frederick** 1918- ; Brit. biochemist **2 Margaret** (born *Margaret Higgins*) 1883-1966; U.S. nurse: leader in birth-control education

San Mar·tín (sän′ mär tēn′), **Jo·sé de** (hô se′ de) 1778-1850; South American revolutionary leader, born in Argentina

San·ta (san′tə) *short for* SANTA CLAUS

San·ta An·na (san′tä ä′nä), **An·to·nio Ló·pez de** (än tô′nyô lô′pes de) *c.* 1795-1876: Mex. revolutionist & general: president (1833-35; 1841-44; 1846-47; 1853-55)

San·ta Claus, San·ta Klaus (san′tə klôz′) 〚 < Du dial. *Sinterklaas, Sante Klaas* < *Sant Nikolaas*, Saint NICHOLAS 〛 *Folklore* a fat, white-bearded, jolly old man in a red suit, who lives at the North Pole, makes toys for children, and distributes gifts at Christmastime: also called *Saint Nicholas, Saint Nick*

San·ta·ya·na (san′tē an′ə, -ä′nə; *Sp* sän′tä yä′nä), **George** (born *Jorge Augustín Nicolás de Santayana*) 1863-1952; U.S. philosopher & writer, born in Spain

Sa·pir (sə pir′), **Edward** 1884-1939; U.S. linguist & anthropologist, born in Pomerania

Sap·phi·ra (sə fī′rə) 〚LL(Ec) *Saphira* < Gr(Ec) *Sappheirē* < Aram word meaning "beautiful" 〛 *Bible* the wife of Ananias, struck dead with her husband for lying: Acts 5:1-10

Sap·pho (saf′ō) fl. early 6th cent. B.C.; Gr. lyric poet of Lesbos

Sar·a (ser′ə, sar′-) a feminine name: see SARAH

Sar·ah (ser′ə, sar′-) 〚Heb *sara*, lit., princess, fem. of *sar*, prince 〛 **1** a feminine name: dim. *Sadie, Sal, Sally;* var. *Sara* **2** *Bible* the wife of Abraham and mother of Isaac: see Gen. 17:15

Sa·rai (ser′ī′) *Bible* Sarah: so called before God's covenant with Abraham: Gen. 17:15

Sar·dou (sȧr dōō′), **Vic·to·rien** (vēk tô ryan′) 1831-1908; Fr. dramatist

Sar·gent (sär′jənt), **John Singer** 1856-1925; U.S. painter in Europe

Sar·gon (sär'gän') 1 fl. c. 2300 B.C.; founder of the Akkadian kingdom 2 Sargon II died 705 B.C.; king of Assyria (722-705)

Sa·roy·an (sə roi'ən), **William** 1908-81; U.S. writer

Sar·pe·don (sär pēd''n, -pē'dän') ⟦L < Gr *Sarpēdōn*⟧ *Gr. Myth.* a son of Zeus and Europa, who becomes king of Lycia and is allowed to live three generations: in some versions, he is killed by Patroclus in the Trojan War

Sar·to (sär'tô), **An·dre·a del** (än dre'ä del) (born *Andrea d'Agnolo di Francesco*) 1486-1531; Florentine painter

Sar·tre (sàr'tr'; *E* sär'trə), **Jean–Paul** (zhän pôl) 1905-80; Fr. philosopher, playwright, & novelist

Sas·soon (sa sōōn'), **Siegfried (Lorraine)** 1886-1967; Eng. writer & poet

Sa·tan (sāt''n) ⟦ME < OE < LL(Ec) < Gr(Ec) < Heb *satan*, adversary, prob. < *śṭn*, to be adverse, plot against⟧ 1 *Judaism* any of various celestial beings functioning as accuser or critic of man 2 *Christian Theol.* the great enemy of man and of goodness; the Devil: usually identified with Lucifer, the chief of the fallen angels

Sa·tie (sà tē'), **E·rik (Alfred Leslie)** (e *r*ēk') 1866-1925; Fr. composer

Sat·urn (sat'ərn) ⟦ME *Saturne* < OE < L *Saturnus* < Etr⟧ *Rom. Myth.* the god of agriculture: identified with the Greek Cronus

Saul (sôl) ⟦< LL(Ec) *Saul* (for 2, *Saulus*) < Gr(Ec) *Saoul* (for 2, *Saulos*) < Heb *shaul*, lit., asked (i.e., of God) < *shaal*, to ask⟧ 1 *Bible* the first king of Israel: 1 Sam. 9 2 *orig. name of* the Apostle PAUL

Saus·sure (sō sür'), **Fer·di·nand de** (fer dē nän' də) 1857-1913; Swiss linguist

Sav·ior, Sav·iour (sāv'yər) 1 God 2 Jesus Christ

Sa·vo·na·ro·la (sä·vô nä rô'lä; *E* sav'ə nə rō'lə), **Gi·ro·la·mo** (jē rô'lä mô') 1452-98; It. monk: religious & political reformer: burned at the stake for heresy

Sax·o Gram·mat·i·cus (sak'sō grə mat'i kəs) c. 1150-c. 1220; Dan. historian

Sca·li·a (skə lē'ə), **An·to·nin** (an'tə nin) 1936- ; U.S. jurist: associate justice, U.S. Supreme Court (1986-)

Scan·der·beg (skan'dər beg') (born *George Castriota*) c. 1403-68; Alb. leader & national hero

Scar·a·mouch (skar'ə moͦosh', -moͦoch') 〚Fr *Scara-mouche* < It *Scaramuccia*, lit., a skirmish〛 a stock character in old Italian comedy, depicted as a braggart and poltroon

Scar·lat·ti (skär lät'tē) **1** A·les·san·dro (ä'les sän'drô) 1660-1725; It. composer **2 (Giuseppe)** Do·me·ni·co (dô me'nē kô') 1685-1757; It. composer: son of Alessandro

Scar·ron (skȧ rōn'), **Paul** (pôl) 1610-60; Fr. poet & dramatist

Sche·he·ra·za·de (shə her'ə zä'də, -zäd') 〚Ger < Pers *Shīrazād*〛 in *The Arabian Nights*, the Sultan's bride, who saves her life by maintaining the Sultan's interest in the suspenseful tales she tells

Schel·ling (shel'iŋ), **Fried·rich Wil·helm Jo·seph von** (frē'driH vil'helm yō'zef fôn) 1775-1854; Ger. philoso-pher

Schia·pa·rel·li (skyä'pä rel'lē), **Gio·van·ni Vir·gi·nio** (jô vän'nē vir jē'nyô) 1835-1910; It. astronomer

Schie·le (shē'lə), **E·gon** (e'gôn) 1890-1918; Austrian painter

Schil·ler (shil'ər), **(Jo·hann Chris·toph) Fried·rich von** (frē'driH fôn) 1759-1805; Ger. dramatist & poet

Schle·gel (shlā'gəl) **1** Au·gust Wil·helm von (ou'goost vil'helm fôn) 1767-1845; Ger. poet, critic & translator **2 (Karl Wilhelm) Fried·rich von** (frē'driH fôn) 1772-1829; Ger. critic & philosopher: brother of August

Schlei·er·ma·cher (shli'ər mä'khər), **Frie·drich Ernst Da·ni·el** (frē'driH ernst dä'nē el) 1768-1834; Ger. theologian & philosopher

Schle·sing·er (shlā'ziŋ ər, shles'in jər) **1 Arthur M(eier)** 1888-1965; U.S. historian **2 Arthur M(eier), Jr.** 1917- ; U.S. historian: son of Arthur

Schlie·mann (shlē'män), **Hein·rich** (hīn'riH) 1822-90; Ger. archaeologist

Schna·bel (shnä'bəl), **Ar·tur** (är'toor) 1882-1951; U.S. pianist & composer, born in Austria

Schnitz·ler (shnits'lər), **Ar·thur** (är'toor) 1862-1931; Austrian playwright & novelist

Schön·berg (shän'bərg, shōn'-; *Ger* shön'berk'), **Arnold** 1874-1951; U.S. composer, born in Austria

School·craft (skoͦol'kraft'), **Henry Rowe** (rō) 1793-1864; U.S. ethnologist

Scho·pen·hau·er (shō'pən hou'ər), **Arthur** 1788-1860; Ger. pessimist philosopher

Schrö·ding·er (shrö′diŋ ər), **Er·win** (er′vēn) 1887-1961; Austrian physicist

Schu·bert (shōō′bərt; *Ger* shōō′bert), **Franz (Peter)** (fränts) 1797-1828; Austrian composer

Schu·man (shōō′mən), **William (Howard)** 1910-92; U.S. composer

Schu·mann (shōō′män), **Robert (Alexander)** 1810-56; Ger. composer

Schum·pe·ter (shoom′pā tər), **Joseph A(lois)** 1883-1950; U.S. economist, born in Austria

Schurz (shoorts), **Carl** 1829-1906; U.S. statesman, journalist, & Union general, born in Germany

Schütz (shüts), **Hein·rich** (hin′riH) 1585-1672; Ger. composer

Schuy·ler (skī′lər), **Philip John** 1733-1804; Am. Revolutionary general & statesman

Schweit·zer (shvīt′sər; *E* shwīt′sər), **Al·bert** (äl′bert) 1875-1965; Alsatian medical missionary, theologian, & musician in Africa

Scip·i·o (sip′ē ō) 1 (*Publius Cornelius Scipio Africanus*) *c.* 237-*c.* 183 B.C.; Rom. general: defeated Hannibal (202) in the 2d Punic War: called *Major* or *the Elder* 2 (*Publius Cornelius Scipio Aemilianus Africanus Numantinus*) *c.* 185-*c.* 129 B.C.; Rom. general & statesman: destroyed Carthage (146): grandson (through adoption) of Scipio the Elder: called *Minor* or *the Younger*

Scott (skät) 1 a masculine name: dim. *Scotty* 2 **Dred** (dred) *c.* 1795 -1858; U.S. black slave: his claim to be free as a result of living in free territory was denied in a controversial Supreme Court decision (1857) 3 **Robert Fal·con** (fôl′kən) 1868-1912; Eng. naval officer & antarctic explorer 4 Sir **Walter** 1771-1832; Scot. poet & novelist 5 **Win·field** (win′fēld′) 1786-1866; U.S. general

Scotus *see* DUNS SCOTUS, John

Scratch ⟦altered (infl. by *scratch*) < ME *skratte* < ON *skratti*, monster, sorcerer, akin to OHG *scraz*, goblin < IE base **(s)ker-*, to shrink⟧ [*sometimes* s-] the Devil: usually **Old Scratch**

Scria·bin (skryä′bēn; *E* skrē ä′bin), **A·lek·san·dr (Niko·layevich)** (ä′lyik sän′dr′) 1872-1915; Russ. composer & pianist

Scribe (skrēb), **Au·gus·tin Eu·gène** (ô güs tan′ ö zhen′)

1791-1861; Fr. dramatist & librettist

Scripps (skrips), **Edward Wyl·lis** (wil′is) 1854-1926; U.S. newspaper publisher

Scrooge (skrōōj) *n.* ⟦after Ebenezer *Scrooge*, character in Charles Dickens' *A Christmas Carol* (1843)⟧ [*also* s-] a hard, miserly misanthrope

Sea·borg (sē′bôrg), **Glenn T**(heodore) 1912- ; U.S. nuclear chemist

Sean (shôn, shän) a masculine name

Se·bas·tian (sə bas′chən) ⟦L *Sebastianus* < Gr *Sebastianos*, lit., a man of *Sebastia*, ancient name of Sivas, or a man of *Sebaste*, name of Samaria after the time of Herod the Great⟧ **1** a masculine name **2** Saint (died *c.* A.D. 288); Christian martyr of Rome: his day is Jan. 20

Se·fer·is (sə fer′əs), **George** (pseud. of *Georgios Stylianou Sepheriades*) 1900-71; Gr. poet, critic, & diplomat

Se·go·via (se gô′vyä; *E* sə gō′vē ə), **An·drés** (än dres′) *c.* 1893-1987; Sp. guitarist & composer

Selassie *see* HAILE SELASSIE

Se·le·ne (si lē′nē) ⟦Gr *Selēnē* < *selēnē*, the moon < *selas*, light, gleam < ? IE base **swel-*, to burn, smolder⟧ *Gr. Myth.* the goddess of the moon: later identified with Artemis

Se·leu·cus I (sə lōō′kəs) died 280 B.C.; Macedonian general & founder of the Seleucid dynasty: called *Seleucus Nicator*

Sel·ma (sel′mə) ⟦< ? Gr *selma*, a ship⟧ a feminine name

Selz·nick (selz′nik), **David O**(liver) 1902-65; U.S. film producer

Sem·e·le (sem′ə lē′) ⟦L < Gr *Semelē*⟧ *Gr. Myth.* the daughter of Cadmus, and mother of Dionysus: seeing Zeus in all his glory, she is consumed in his lightning

Se·me·nov (sim yô′nəf; *Russ* syi myô′nəf), **Ni·ko·lai** (**Nikolaevich**) (nik′ə li′; *Russ* nyi ku li′) 1896-1986; Russ. chemist

Se·mir·a·mis (si mir′ə mis) *Bab. Legend* a queen of Assyria noted for her beauty, wisdom, and sexual exploits: reputed founder of Babylon: based on a historical queen of the 9th cent. B.C.

Sen·dak (sen′dak), **Maurice Bernard** 1928- ; U.S. writer & illustrator

Sen·e·ca (sen′i kə), (**Lucius Annaeus**) *c.* 4 B.C.-A.D. 65; Rom. philosopher, dramatist, & statesman

Sen·ghor (sän gôr′), **Lé·o·pold Sé·dar** (lā ô pôld′ sä dår′) 1906- ; Senegalese statesman: president of Senegal (1960-80)

Sen·nach·er·ib (sə nak′ər ib) died 681 B.C.; king of Assyria (705-681): son of Sargon II

Sen·nett (sen′it), **Mack** (mak) (born *Michael Sinnott*) 1884-1960; U.S. film producer & director, esp. of slapstick comedies, born in Canada

Se·quoy·ah (si kwoi′ə) *c.* 1760-1843; Cherokee scholar and leader: created Cherokee syllabary: also sp. **Se·quoy′a**

Se·ra·pis (sə rā′pis) ⟦ L < Gr *osorāpis* < Egypt *wsyr-hp*, Osiris-Apis ⟧ *Egypt. Myth.* a god of the lower world, whose cult spread to Greece and Rome

Ser·kin (sur′kin), **Rudolf** 1903-91; U.S. pianist, born in Bohemia

serpent [*often* S-] Satan, in the form he assumed to tempt Eve: Gen. 3:1-5

Ser·ra (ser′ä), **Ju·ni·pe·ro** (hoō nē′pe rô′) (born *Miguel José Serra*) 1713-84; Sp. missionary in W North America

Ser·ve·tus (sər vēt′əs), **Michael** (Sp. name *Miguel Serveto*) 1511-53; Sp. theologian: burned at the stake for heresy

Ser·vice (sur′vis), **Robert** (**William**) 1874-1958; Cdn. writer, born in England

Ses·sions (sesh′ənz), **Roger** (**Huntington**) 1896-1985; U.S. composer

Set (set) ⟦ Gr *Sēth* < Egypt *sth, śtsh* ⟧ *Egypt. Myth.* a god of evil, represented as having an animal's head with square-tipped ears

Seth¹ (seth) ⟦ LL(Ec) < Gr(Ec) *Sēth* < Heb *shet*, lit., appointed < *shat*, to put ⟧ **1** a masculine name **2** *Bible* the third son of Adam: Gen. 4:25

Seth² (sät) *var. of* SET

Se·ton (sēt′'n) **1** Saint **Elizabeth Ann** (born *Elizabeth Ann Bayley*) (1774-1821); Am. Rom. Catholic leader: 1st native-born Am. saint: her day is Jan. 4 **2 Ernest Thompson** (born *Ernest Seton Thompson*) 1860-1946; U.S. naturalist, writer, & illustrator, born in England

Seu·rat (sö rá′), **Georges** (**Pierre**) (zhôrzh) 1859-91; Fr. painter: noted for his use of pointillism

Seuss (soōs), **Dr.** *pseud. of* Theodor Seuss GEISEL

Seversky, Alexander *see* DE SEVERSKY, Alexander

P(rocofieff)

Se·ver·us (sə vir′əs), (**Lucius Septimius**) A.D. 146-211; Rom. emperor (193-211)

Sé·vi·gné (sā vē nyā′), Marquise **de** (born *Marie de Rabutin-Chantal*) 1626-96; Fr. writer

Sew·all (sōō′əl), **Samuel** 1652-1730; Am. jurist, born in England: presided over witchcraft trials at Salem

Sew·ard (sōō′ərd), **William Henry** 1801-72; U.S. statesman: secretary of state (1861-69)

Sey·mour (sē′môr) ⟦orig. Eng family name, prob. < OE *sæ*, sea + *mor*, hill⟧ **1** a masculine name **2 Jane** *c.* 1509-37; 3d wife of Henry VIII: mother of Edward VI

Sfor·za (sfôr′tsä) **1** Count **Car·lo** (kär′lô) 1873-1952; It. statesman & anti-Fascist leader **2 Fran·ces·co** (frän ches′kô) 1401-66; It. condottiere & duke of Milan **3 Lu·do·vi·co** (lōō′dô vē′kô) 1451-1508; duke of Milan & patron of da Vinci: son of Francesco: also **Lo′do·vi′co** (lô′-)

Sha·drach (sha′drak′, shā′-) ⟦Heb *shadrach*: prob. a made-up name intended to sound Babylonian: see Dan. 1:7⟧ *Bible* one of the three captives who came out of the fiery furnace miraculously unharmed: Dan. 3:12-27

Shaftes·bur·y (shafts′ber′ē, shäfts′-; -bər ē), 1st Earl of (*Anthony Ashley Cooper*) 1621-83; Eng. statesman: lord chancellor (1672-73)

Shah Ja·han (shä′ jə hän′) 1592-1666; Mogul emperor of India (1628-58): builder of the Taj Mahal

Shahn (shän), **Ben(jamin)** 1898-1969; U.S. painter, born in Lithuania

Shake·speare (shāk′spir), **William** 1564-1616; Eng. poet & dramatist: also sp. **Shake′spear, Shake′spere,** or **Shak′spere**

Sha·mash (shä′mäsh′) ⟦< Akkadian *shamshu*, sun⟧ *Bab. & Assyr. Myth.* the sun god, responsible for summer warmth and the success of crops, and a symbol for justice

Shane (shān) a masculine name

Shan·non (shan′ən) **1** a masculine and feminine name **2 Claude El·wood** (el′wood) 1916- ; U.S. mathematician

Shap·ley (shap′lē), **Har·low** (här′lô) 1885-1972; U.S. astronomer

Shar·on (sher′ən) ⟦< ?⟧ a feminine name

Shaw (shô) **1 George Bernard** 1856-1950; Brit. dramatist & critic, born in Ireland **2 Henry Wheeler** *see* BILLINGS, Josh **3 Thomas Edward** *see* LAWRENCE, T(homas) E(dward)

Shawn (shôn) **1** a masculine name **2 Ted** (born *Edwin Myers Shawn*) 1891-1972; U.S. dancer & choreographer: husband of Ruth St. Denis

Shays (shāz), **Daniel** *c.* 1747-1825; Am. Revolutionary soldier: leader of an insurrection (Shays' Rebellion) in W Mass. (1786-87), protesting high land taxes

She·ba (shē'bə), **Queen of** *Bible* the queen who visited King Solomon to investigate his reputed wisdom: 1 Kings 10:1-13

Shei·la (shē'lə) ⟦Ir⟧ a feminine name: see CECILIA

Shel·ley (shel'ē) **1** a feminine name **2 Mary Woll·stone·craft** (wool'stən kraft') 1797-1851; Eng. novelist: daughter of Mary Wollstonecraft & William Godwin: second wife of Percy **3 Percy Bysshe** (bish) 1792-1822; Eng. poet

Shem (shem) ⟦Heb *shem*⟧ *Bible* the eldest of Noah's three sons: Gen. 5:32

Shep·ard (shep'ərd) **1 Alan** (**Bartlett**) 1923- ; U.S. astronaut: 1st American in space (1961) **2 Sam** (born *Samuel Shepard Rogers*) 1943- ; U.S. playwright

Sher·i·dan (sher'i dən) **1 Philip Henry** 1831-88; Union general in the Civil War **2 Richard Brins·ley** (brinz'lē) 1751-1816; Brit. dramatist & politician, born in Ireland

Sher·lock Holmes (shʉr'läk' hōmz', -hōlmz') a fictitious British detective with great powers of deduction, the main character in many stories by A. Conan Doyle

Sher·man (shʉr'mən) **1 John** 1823-1900; U.S. statesman: brother of William **2 Roger** 1721-93; Am. statesman: signer of the Declaration of Independence **3 William Tecumseh** 1820-91; Union general in the Civil War

Sher·wood (shʉr'wood), **Robert Em·met** (em'it) 1896-1955; U.S. playwright

Shir·ley (shʉr'lē) ⟦orig. a surname < the place name *Shirley* (England) < OE *scire*, shire + *leah*, meadow, lea: hence lea where the shire moot was held⟧ a feminine name: dim. *Shirl*; var. *Sheryl*

Shi·va (shē'və) *var. of* SIVA

Shock·ley (shäk'lē), **William** (**Bradford**) 1910-89; U.S.

physicist, born in Great Britain

Sho·lo·khov (shô'lô khôf), **Mi·kha·il** (**Aleksandrovich**) (mē khä ēl') 1905-84; Russ. novelist

Sho·sta·ko·vich (shô'stä kô'vich; *E* shäs'tə kō'vich), **Dmi·tri** (d'mē'trē) 1906-75; Russ. composer

Shu·lam·ite (shoo'lə mīt') the name of the maiden in the Song of Solomon, 6:13

Shy·lock (shī'läk') the Jewish moneylender in Shakespeare's *Merchant of Venice*

Si·be·li·us (si bā'lē oos; *E* sə bāl'yəs), **Jean** (zhän) (born *Johan Julius Christian Sibelius*) 1865-1957; Finn. composer

Sib·yl (sib'əl) [[L *Sibylla* < *sibylla*, a woman consulted as a prophetess < Gr]] a feminine name

Sick·ert (sik'ərt), **Walter Richard** 1860-1942; Brit. painter & etcher

Sid·dhar·tha (sid där'tə) *see* BUDDHA

Sid·dons (sid'nz), **Sarah** (born *Sarah Kemble*) 1755-1831; Eng. actress

Sid·ney (sid'nē) [[< the surname *Sidney*, prob. reduced < *St. Denis*]] **1** a masculine and feminine name: dim. *Sid* **2** Sir **Philip** 1554-86; Eng. poet, soldier, & statesman

Sieg·fried (sig'frēd, sēg'-; *Ger* zēk'frēt') [[Ger < Gmc **segu-*, power, victory + **frith-*, peace, protection]] *Gmc. Legend* a hero who wins the treasure of the Nibelungs, kills a dragon, and helps Gunther win Brunhild for a wife

Sie·mens (sē'mənz; *Ger* zē'məns), Sir **William** (born *Karl Wilhelm von Siemens*) 1823-83; Brit. engineer & inventor, born in Germany

Sien·kie·wicz (shen kye'vich), **Hen·ryk** (hen'rik) 1846-1916; Pol. novelist

Sig·is·mund (sij'is mənd, sig'-; *Ger* zē'gis moont') 1368-1437; Holy Roman emperor (1411-37)

Sig·mund (sig'mənd) [[< Ger *Siegmund* & ON *Sigmundr* < Gmc **sig-*, victory + **mund-*, hand, protection]] a masculine name

Si·gurd (sig'ərd) the hero of the Volsunga Saga: identified with the Germanic Siegfried

Si·kor·sky (si kôr'skē), **I·gor** (**Ivanovich**) (ē'gôr) 1889-1972; U.S. aeronautical engineer, born in Russia

Si·las (sī'ləs) [[LL(Ec) < Gr(Ec) < Aram *sh'îlâ*, lit., asked for]] a masculine name: dim. *Si*

Si·le·nus (sī lē'nəs) ⟦L < Gr *Seilēnos*⟧ the foster father and tutor of Dionysus and leader of the satyrs, traditionally pictured as a fat, drunken, jovial old man with pointed ears

Si·lo·ne (sē lô'ne; *E* sə lō'nē), **Ig·na·zio** (ē nyä'tsyô) (born *Secondo Tranquilli*) 1900-78; It. writer

Sil·va·nus (sil vā'nəs) *Rom. Myth.* a minor deity of fields and woods

Sil·ves·ter (sil ves'tər) a masculine name: see SYLVESTER

Sil·vi·a (sil'vē ə) a feminine name: see SYLVIA

Si·me·non (sēm nōn'; *E* sē'mə nōn'), **Georges (Joseph Christian)** (zhôrzh) 1903-89; Fr. novelist, born in Belgium

Sim·e·on (sim'ē ən) ⟦LL(Ec) *Symeon* < Gr(Ec) *Symeōn* < Heb *shim'on*, lit., heard < *sham'a*, to hear⟧ **1** a masculine name **2** *Bible a*) the second son of Jacob and Leah: Gen. 29:33; Num. 1:22 *b*) a pious man who, on seeing the infant Jesus in the Temple, spoke the words later set to the canticle "Nunc Dimittis": Luke 2:25-32

Simeon Sty·li·tes (stī lit'ēz'), Saint (*c.* A.D. 390-c. 459); Syrian monk who lived & preached on the top of a pillar near Antioch for over 30 years: his day is Jan. 5

Si·mon (sī'mən) ⟦ME < LL(Ec) < Gr(Ec) *Simōn, Seimōn* < Heb *shim'on*, lit., heard: see SIMEON⟧ **1** a masculine name: dim. *Si* **2** *Bible a*) one of the twelve Apostles, called *Peter* or **Simon Peter** (see PETER) *b*) one of the twelve Apostles, called **Simon the Canaanite** (or **the Zealot**): Mark 3:18: his day is Oct. 28 (also **Saint Simon**) *c*) a brother or relative of Jesus: Mark 6:3

Simon, Herbert Alexander 1916- ; U.S. social scientist & economist

Si·mon·i·des (sī män'ə dēz') *c.* 556-c. 468 B.C.; Gr. lyric poet: also **Simonides of Ke·os** (kā'äs')

Simon Le·gree (lə grē') the villainous slave overseer in H. B. Stowe's *Uncle Tom's Cabin*

Simon Ma·gus (mā'gəs) a Samaritan magician whose offer of money to learn how to impart the Holy Ghost to others angered Peter: Acts 8:9-24

Simple Simon a foolish character in a nursery rhyme

Si·na·tra (si nä'trə), **Frank** (born *Francis Albert Sinatra*) 1915- ; U.S. popular singer & film actor

Sin·bad the Sailor (sin'bad') a merchant in *The Arabian*

Nights who makes seven adventurous voyages

Sin·clair (sin kler′), **Up·ton** (**Beall, Jr.**) (up′tən) 1878-1968; U.S. novelist & socialist

Sind·bad (sin′bad, sind′-) SINBAD THE SAILOR

Sing·er (siŋ′ər) **1** Isaac Ba·shev·is (bä shev′is) 1904-91; U.S. writer in Yiddish, born in Poland **2** Isaac Mer·ritt (mer′it) 1811-75; U.S. inventor: improved the sewing machine

Si·quei·ros (sē ke′rôs), (**José**) **Da·vid Al·fa·ro** (dä vēd′ äl fä′rô) 1896-1974; Mex. painter, esp. of murals

Sis·er·a (sis′ər ə) 〖Heb *sisera*; prob. of Hittite orig.〗 *Bible* a military leader of the Canaanites against the Israelites, murdered by Jael: Judg. 4:17-22

Sis·ley (sēs lā′; *E* sis′lē), **Al·fred** (äl fred′) 1839-99; Fr. painter

Sis·mon·di (sēs mō̃n dē′; *E* sis män′dē), **Jean Charles Lé·o·nard Si·monde de** (zhän shȧrl lä ô nȧr′ sē mō̃nd′ də) 1773-1842; Swiss historian & economist

Sis·y·phus (sis′ə fəs) 〖L < Gr *Sisyphos*〗 *Gr. Myth.* a greedy king of Corinth doomed forever in Hades to roll a heavy stone uphill, only to have it always roll down again

Sit·ter (sit′ər), **Wil·lem de** (vil′əm də) 1872-1934; Du. astronomer

Sitting Bull *c.* 1834-90; a principal chief of the Dakota Indians: fought in the Battle of the Little Bighorn

Sit·well (sit′wəl, -wel) **1** Dame **Edith** 1887-1964; Eng. poet & critic: sister of Osbert & Sacheverell **2** Sir **Os·bert** (äz′bərt) 1892-1969; Eng. poet & essayist **3** Sa·chev·er·ell (sə shev′ər əl) 1897-1988; Eng. poet & art critic

Si·va (sē′və, shē′-) 〖Hindi < Sans, auspicious〗 Hindu god of destruction and reproduction, a member of the supreme Hindu trinity: see BRAHMA, VISHNU

Skeat (skēt), **W**(**alter**) **W**(**illiam**) 1835-1912; Eng. philologist & lexicographer

Skel·ton (skelt′'n), **John** *c.* 1460-1529; Eng. poet

Sloan (slōn), **John** 1871-1951; U.S. painter & etcher

Sme·ta·na (sme′tä nȧ; *E* smet′'n ə), **Be·dřich** (bed′ər zhikh) 1824-84; Czech composer

Smith (smith) **1 Adam** 1723-90; Scot. economist **2 Alfred E**(**manuel**) 1873-1944; U.S. politician **3 Bes·sie** (bes′ē) *c.* 1898-1937; U.S. blues singer **4 David** (**Roland**) 1906-65; U.S. sculptor & painter **5** Captain

John c. 1580-1631; Eng. colonist in America: cf. POCA-
HONTAS **6 Joseph** 1805-44; U.S. founder of the Mormon Church **7 Sydney** 1771-1845; Eng. clergyman &
essayist **8 William** 1769-1839; Eng. geologist

Smok·ey (smō′kē) *trademark for* a cartoon figure of a
bear dressed as a forest ranger, used as the symbol of
the need for preventing forest fires

Smol·lett (smäl′it), **Tobias (George)** 1721-71; Brit. novelist, born in Scotland

Smuts (smuts), **Jan Chris·ti·aan** (yän′ kris′tē än) 1870-
1950; South African general: prime minister (1919-24;
1939-48)

Snor·ri Stur·lu·son (snô′rē stʉr′lə sən) c. 1179-1241; Ice.
historian & poet

Snow (snō), **C(harles) P(ercy)** Baron Snow of Leicester
1905-80; Eng. novelist & physicist

So·bies·ki (sō byes′kē), **John** *see* JOHN III

Soc·ra·tes (säk′rə tēz′) c. 470-399 B.C.; Athenian philosopher & teacher

Sod·dy (säd′ē), **Frederick** 1877-1956; Brit. chemist

Sol (säl) ⟦ME < L < **sawol, *saol* < IE base **sāwel-,
swen- > sun, Gr *hēlios*, Goth *sauil*, sun⟧ **1** *Rom.
Myth.* the sun god: identified with the Greek Helios **2**
the sun personified

Sol·o·mon (säl′ə mən) ⟦LL(Ec) *Solomon, Salomon* <
Gr(Ec) *Solomōn, Salōmōn* < Heb *shelomo*, lit., peace-
ful < *shalom*, peace⟧ **1** a masculine name: dim. *Sol* **2**
king of Israel: he built the first temple and was noted
for his wisdom: son & successor of DAVID: 2 Sam. 12:24

So·lon (sō′lən, -län′) c. 640-c. 559 B.C.; Athenian statesman & lawgiver: framed the democratic laws of Athens

Sol·y·man I (säl′i mən) *var. of* SULEIMAN (I)

Sol·zhe·ni·tsyn (sōl′zhə nēt′sin), **A·lek·san·dr
(Isayevich)** (al′ik san′dər) 1918- ; Russ. writer, esp. of
novels: exiled in 1974

Som·nus (säm′nəs) ⟦L, sleep < IE **swopnos* < base
*swep-, to sleep > Gr *hypnos*, sleep, Sans *svapiti*, (he)
sleeps, OE *swefan*, to sleep⟧ *Rom. Myth.* the god of
sleep: identified with the Greek Hypnos

Son, the *Christian Theol.* Jesus Christ, as the second
person of the Trinity

Son of God (or **Man**) *Christian Theol. name for* Jesus
Christ

So·phi·a (sō fē′ə, -fī′ə) ⟦< Gr *sophia*, skill, wisdom <

sophos, wise ‖ a feminine name: dim. *Sophie, Sophy*

Soph·o·cles (säf′ə klēz′) *c.* 496-406 B.C.; Gr. writer of tragic dramas

So·rel (sȏ rel′; *E* sə rel′), **Georges (Eugène)** (zhȏrzh) 1847-1922; Fr. social philosopher

Sou·sa (sōō′zə, -sə), **John Philip** 1854-1932; U.S. bandmaster & composer of marches

Sou·ter (sōōt′ər), **David** 1939- ; U.S. jurist: associate justice, Supreme Court (1990-)

Sou·they (sou′thē, suth′ē), **Robert** 1774-1843; Eng. poet & writer: poet laureate (1813-43)

Sou·tine (sōō tēn′), **Cha·im** (khī′im) 1894-1943; Fr. painter, born in Lithuania

Soy·er (soi′ər) **1 Moses** 1899-1974; U.S. painter, born in Russia **2 Raphael** 1899-1987; U.S. painter, born in Russia: twin brother of Moses

So·yin·ka (shô yiŋ′kə), **Wo·le** (wō′lā) (born *Akinwande Oluwole Soyinka*) 1934- ; Nigerian playwright

Spark (spärk), **Muriel (Sarah)** (born *Muriel Sarah Camberg*) 1918- ; Brit. writer

Spar·ta·cus (spärt′ə kəs) died 71 B.C.; Thracian slave & gladiator in Rome: leader of a slave revolt

Spen·cer (spen′sər) ‖ < the surname *Spencer* < ME *spenser,* butler, steward < OFr *despencier* < *despense,* larder, buttery < ML *dispensa* < L, fem. pp. of *dispendere,* to weigh out < *dis-,* out + *pendere,* to weigh < IE base **(s)pen(d)-,* to pull, stretch ‖ **1** a masculine name: var. *Spenser* **2 Herbert** 1820-1903; Eng. philosopher

Spen·der (spen′dər), **Stephen** 1909- ; Eng. poet & critic

Speng·ler (speŋ′lər; *Ger* shpeŋ′lər), **Oswald** 1880-1936; Ger. philosopher

Spen·ser (spen′sər) **1** a masculine name: see SPENCER **2 Edmund** *c.* 1552-99; Eng. poet

Sper·ry (sper′ē) **1 Elmer Ambrose** 1860-1930; U.S. inventor, electrical engineer, & manufacturer **2 Roger Wol·cott** (wool′kät) 1913- ; U.S. neurobiologist

Sphinx (sfiŋks) *Gr. Myth.* a sphinx at Thebes that strangles passersby who are unable to guess its riddle

Spi·no·za (spi nō′zə), **Ba·ruch** (bə rōōk′) (Eng. *Benedict*) 1632-77; Du. philosopher

Spock (späk), **Benjamin (McLane)** 1903- ; U.S. pediatrician, writer of books on child care, & social activist

Sta·cy (stā′sē) a feminine and masculine name: also **Sta′**

cey

Staël (stäl), Madame de Baronne de Staël-Holstein (born *Anne Louise Germaine Necker*) 1766-1817; Fr. writer & mistress of a popular salon

Stag·i·rite (staj′ə rīt′), the *name for* ARISTOTLE

Sta·lin (stä′lin), **Joseph** (born *Iosif Vissarionovich Dzhugashvili*) 1879-1953; Soviet premier (1941-53): general secretary of the Communist party of the U.S.S.R. (1922-53)

Stan·dish (stan′dish), **Miles** (or **Myles**) *c.* 1584-1656; Eng. colonist: military leader of Plymouth Colony

Stan·hope (stan′əp), **Philip Dor·mer** (dôr′mər) *see* CHESTERFIELD, 4th Earl of

Stan·i·slav·sky (stan′i släf′skē, stän′-), **Kon·stan·tin** (kän′stən tēn′) (born *Konstantin Sergeyevich Alekseyev*) 1863-1938; Russ. actor, director, & teacher of acting

Stan·ley (stan′lē) ⟦ < the surname *Stanley* < the place name *Stanley* < OE *stan leah,* stone lea ⟧ **1** a masculine name: dim. *Stan* **2** Sir **Henry Morton** (born *John Rowlands*) 1841-1904; Brit. journalist & explorer in Africa **3 Wen·dell Meredith** (wen′dəl) 1904-71; U.S. biochemist

Stan·ton (stant″n) **1 Edwin McMas·ters** (mək mas′tərz) 1814-69; U.S. statesman: secretary of war (1862-68) **2 Elizabeth Ca·dy** (kā′dē) 1815-1902; U.S. reformer & suffragist leader

Sta·ti·us (stā′shē əs, stā′shəs), **Pub·li·us Pa·pin·i·us** (pub′lē əs pə pin′ē əs) *c.* A.D. 45-*c.* 96; Rom. poet

St. Den·is (sānt′ den′is), **Ruth** (born *Ruth Dennis*) *c.* 1877-1968; U.S. dancer & choreographer: wife of Ted Shawn

Steele (stēl), Sir **Richard** 1672-1729; Brit. essayist & dramatist, born in Ireland

Steen (stān), **Jan** (yän) 1626-79; Du. painter

Ste·fans·son (stef′an sən), **Vil·hjal·mur** (vil′hyoul′mər) 1879-1962; U.S. arctic explorer, born in Canada

Stei·chen (stī′kən), **Edward** 1879-1973; U.S. photographer, born in Luxembourg

Stein (stīn), **Gertrude** 1874-1946; U.S. writer in France

Stein·beck (stīn′bek′), **John** (**Ernst**) 1902-68; U.S. novelist & short-story writer

Stein·metz (stīn′mets), **Charles Proteus** 1865-1923; U.S. electrical engineer & inventor, born in Germany

Stel·la (stel′ə) ⟦ < L *stella*, a star (dim. < *sterela) < IE base *ster-, a star ⟧ a feminine name: see ESTELLE

Sten·dhal (sten′däl; *Fr* stan dàl′) (pseud. of *Marie Henri Beyle*) 1783-1842; Fr. novelist and essayist

Sten·tor (sten′tôr′) ⟦ L < Gr *Stentōr*, akin to *stenein*, to rumble, roar < IE base **(s)ten*- > L *tonare*, to thunder ⟧ a Greek herald in the Trojan War, described in the *Iliad* as having the voice of fifty men

Steph·a·nie (stef′ə nē) ⟦ var. of *Stephana*, fem. of *Stephanus:* see fol. ⟧ a feminine name

Ste·phen (stē′vən) ⟦ L *Stephanus* < Gr *Stephanas* < *stephanos*, a crown < *stephein*, to encircle, crown ⟧ **1** a masculine name: dim. *Steve*; var. *Steven*; equiv. L. *Stephanus*, Fr. *Étienne*, Ger. *Stephan*, It. *Stefano*, Sp. *Esteban*, Russ. *Stepen*; fem. *Stephanie* **2** *Bible* one of the seven chosen to assist the Apostles (Acts 6 & 7); the 1st Christian martyr: his day is Dec. 26: called **Saint Stephen 3 Stephen** (sometimes *Stephen of Blois*) c. 1097-1154: king of England (1135-54): grandson of William the Conqueror **4 Stephen I** 975-1038; king of Hungary (1001-38): as **Saint Stephen**, his day is Aug. 16 **5** Sir **Leslie** 1832-1904; Eng. critic & philosopher: father of Virginia Woolf

Ste·phens (stē′vənz) **1 Alexander Hamilton** 1812-83; U.S. statesman: vice president of the Confederacy (1861-65) **2 James** 1882-1950; Ir. poet & novelist **3 John Lloyd** 1805-52; U.S. explorer & archaeologist

Ste·phen·son (stē′vən sən) **1 George** 1781-1848; Eng. engineer: developed the steam locomotive **2 Robert** 1803-59; Eng. engineer & bridge builder: son of George

Stern (sturn) **1 Isaac** 1920- ; U.S. violinist, born in Russia **2 Otto** 1888-1969; U.S. physicist, born in Germany

Sterne (sturn), **Laurence** 1713-68; Brit. novelist & clergyman, born in Ireland

Steu·ben (stoo′bən; *Ger* shtoi′bən), Baron **Frederick William Augustus von** 1730-94; Prus. military officer: served as Am. general in the American Revolution

Ste·ven (stē′vən) a masculine name: see STEPHEN

Ste·vens (stē′vənz) **1 John Paul** 1920- ; associate justice, U.S. Supreme Court (1975-) **2 Thaddeus** 1792-1868; U.S. statesman & abolitionist **3 Wallace** 1879-1955; U.S. poet

Ste·ven·son (stē′vən s′n), **Robert Louis** (**Balfour**) 1850-94; Scot. novelist, poet, & essayist

Stew·art (stōō'ərt, styōō'-) **1** a masculine name: see
STUART **2** James **(Maitland)** (called *Jimmy*) 1908- ;
U.S. film actor **3** Potter 1915-1985; U.S. jurist: associate justice, U.S. Supreme Court (1958-81)

Stieg·litz (stēg'lits), **Alfred** 1864-1946; U.S. photographer

Stim·son (stim'sən), **Henry L(ewis)** 1867-1950; U.S. statesman: secretary of state (1929-33): secretary of war (1911-13; 1940-45)

St. John, Henry *see* BOLINGBROKE, 1st Viscount

St. John Perse (purs) (pseud. of *Alexis Saint-Léger Léger*) 1887-1975; Fr. diplomat & poet

St. Lau·rent (san lô rän'), **Louis Stephen** 1882-1973; Cdn. statesman: prime minister (1948-57)

Stock·hau·sen (shtôk'hou'zən), **Karl·heinz** (kärl'hīnts) 1928- ; Ger. composer

Sto·kow·ski (stə kôf'skē, -kou'-), **Leopold (Boleslawowicz Stanislaw Antoni)** 1882-1977; U.S. orchestra conductor, born in England

Stone (stōn) **1** Edward **Du·rell** (də rel') 1902-78; U.S. architect **2** Harlan Fiske 1872-1946; U.S. jurist: chief justice of the U.S. (1941-46) **3** Lucy (Mrs. *Henry Brown Blackwell*) 1818-93; U.S. reformer & suffragist

Stop·pard (stäp'ərd), **Tom** 1937- ; Brit. playwright, born in Czechoslovakia

Sto·ry (stôr'ē), **Joseph** 1779-1845; U.S. jurist: associate justice, U.S. Supreme Court (1811-45)

Stowe (stō), **Harriet (Elizabeth) Beecher** 1811-96; U.S. novelist: sister of Henry Ward Beecher

Stra·bo (strā'bō) *c.* 63 B.C.-*c.* A.D. 21; Gr. geographer

Stra·chey (strā'chē), **(Giles) Lyt·ton** (lit''n) 1880-1932; Eng. biographer

Stra·di·va·ri (strä'dē vä'rē), **An·to·nio** (än tô'nyô) (L. name *Antonius Stradivarius*) 1644-1737; It. violin maker

Straf·ford (straf'ərd), **1st Earl of** (*Thomas Wentworth*) 1593-1641; Eng. statesman: advisor of Charles I: beheaded

Straus (strous; *Ger* shtrous), **Oscar** (or **Oskar**) 1870-1954; Fr. composer, born in Austria

Strauss (shtrous; *E* strous) **1** Jo·hann (yō'hän) 1825-99; Austrian composer, esp. of waltzes **2** Rich·ard (riH' ärt) 1864-1949; Ger. composer & conductor

Stra·vin·sky (strə vin'skē; *Russ* strä vēn'ski), **I·gor**

(Feodorovich) (ē'gôr) 1882-1971; U.S. composer & conductor, born in Russia

Strind·berg (strind'bŭrg, strin'-; *Swed* strin'bar'y'), (Johan) August 1849-1912; Swed. dramatist & novelist

Stu·art (stōō'ərt, styōō'-) ‖ < the family name *Stuart* < ? OE *stiweard*, steward ‖ 1 a masculine name 2 name of the ruling family of Scotland (1371-1603) & of England & Scotland (1603-1714) except during the Commonwealth (1649-60) 3 **Charles Edward** 1720-88; Eng. prince: grandson of James II: called *The Young Pretender, Bonnie Prince Charlie* 4 **Gilbert (Charles)** 1755-1828; U.S. portrait painter 5 **J(ames) E(well) B(rown)** (called *Jeb*) 1833-64; Confederate general 6 **James Francis Edward** 1688-1766; Eng. prince: son of James II: called *The Old Pretender*

Stubbs (stubz), **George** 1724-1806; Eng. painter

Stuy·ve·sant (stī'və sənt), **Peter** 1592-1672; last Du. governor of New Netherland (1646-64)

Sty·ron (stī'rən), **William** 1925- ; U.S. writer

Suck·ling (suk'liŋ), **Sir John** 1609-42; Eng. poet

Su·cre (sōō'kre), **An·to·nio Jo·sé de** (än tō'nyô hô se' de) 1795-1830; South American liberator: 1st president of Bolivia (1826-28)

Su·der·mann (zōō'dər män'; *E* sōō'dər mən), **Her·mann** (her'män') 1857-1928; Ger. playwright & novelist

Sue·to·ni·us (swi tō'nē əs) (*Gaius Suetonius Tranquillus*) *c.* A.D. 69-*c.* 140; Rom. biographer & historian

Su·har·to (sōō här'tō) 1921- ; president of Indonesia (1967-)

Su·kar·no (sōō kär'nō) *c.* 1902-70; Indonesian statesman: president of Indonesia (1945-67)

Su·lei·man (I) (sōō'lä män') *c.* 1494-1566; sultan of the Ottoman Empire (1520-66): called *the Magnificent*

Sul·la (sul'ə) (*Lucius Cornelius Sulla Felix*) 138-78 B.C.; Rom. general: dictator of Rome (82-79)

Sul·li·van (sul'ə vən) 1 **Sir Arthur Seymour** 1842-1900; Eng. composer: see GILBERT, Sir William Schwenck 2 **John L(awrence)** 1858-1918; U.S. prizefighter 3 **Louis Hen·ri** (hen'rē) 1856-1924; U.S. architect

Sul·ly (sul'ē; *also, for 1, Fr* sü lē') 1 **Duc de** (*Maximilien de Béthune*) 1560-1641; Fr. statesman 2 **Thomas** 1783-1872; U.S. painter, born in England

Sul·ly-Pru·dhomme (sü lē prü dôm'), **Re·né Fran·çois Ar·mand** (rə nā' frän swä' àr män') 1839-1907; Fr.

poet & critic

Sum·ner (sum'nər) **1 Charles** 1811-74; U.S. statesman & abolitionist **2 William Graham** 1840-1910; U.S. sociologist & economist

Sun·day (sun'dā, -dē), **William Ashley** (called *Billy*) 1862-1935; U.S. evangelist

Sung (soon) Chin. dynasty (960-1279 A.D.), noted for achievement in art & literature

sun god the sun personified and worshiped as a god

Sun Yat-sen (soon' yät'sen') 1866-1925; Chin. political & revolutionary leader

Supreme Being God

Sur·rey (sur'ē), **Earl of** (*Henry Howard*) c. 1517-47; Eng. poet & courtier: executed for treason

Su·san (soo'zən) ⟦Fr *Susanne* < LL(Ec) *Susanna* < Gr(Ec) *Sousanna* < Heb *shoshana*, lily⟧ a feminine name: dim. *Sue, Susie, Suzy*; var. *Susanna, Susannah*; equiv. Fr. *Susanne, Suzanne*

Su·san·na, Su·san·nah (soo zan'ə) a feminine name: see SUSAN

Suth·er·land (suth'ər lənd), **Dame Joan** 1926- ; Austral. operatic soprano

Su·vo·rov (soo vô'rôf), **Count A·lek·san·dr** (*Vasilievich*) (ä'lyik sän'dr') 1729-1800; Russ. field marshal

Sven·ga·li (sven gä'lē, sfen-) *n.* ⟦for the evil hypnotist, *Svengali*, in the novel *Trilby* (1894) by DU MAURIER⟧ a person who attempts to dominate another, usually with evil or selfish intentions

Swe·den·borg (swēd'n bôrg'; *Swed* sväd'n bôr'y'), **Emanuel** (born *Emanuel Swedberg*) 1688-1772; Swed. scientist, mystic, & religious philosopher

Sweet (swēt), **Henry** 1845-1912; Eng. linguist

Swift (swift), **Jonathan** 1667-1745; Eng. satirist, born in Ireland

Swin·burne (swin'bərn), **Algernon Charles** 1837-1909; Eng. poet & critic

Swith·in, Swith·un (swith'ən, swith'-), **Saint** (c. A.D. 800-c. 862); Eng. prelate: his day is July 15

Syb·il (sib'əl) a feminine name: see SIBYL

Syd·ney (sid'nē) a masculine name: see SIDNEY

Syl·ves·ter (sil ves'tər) ⟦L *Silvester* < *silvestris*, of a wood or forest < *silva*, wood⟧ a masculine name

Syl·vi·a (sil'vē ə) ⟦L *Silvia* < *silva*, forest⟧ a feminine name: dim. *Syl, Sylvie*

Sym·onds (sim'ənz, -əndz), **John Ad·ding·ton** (ad'iŋ tən) 1840-93; Eng. poet, writer, & scholar

Synge (siŋ) **1** (**Edmund**) **John Mil·ling·ton** (mil'iŋ tən) 1871-1909; Ir. dramatist **2 Richard Laurence Mil·lington** 1914- ; Brit. biochemist

Szell (sel, zel), **George** 1897-1970; U.S. orchestra conductor & pianist, born in Hungary

Szi·lard (zē'lärd, si'-; zi lärd'), **Leo** 1898-1964; U.S. nuclear physicist, born in Hungary

Szold (zōld), **Henrietta** 1860-1945; U.S. Zionist leader

T

Tab·i·tha (tab'i thə) ⟦LL(Ec) < Gr(Ec) *Tabeitha* < Aram *tavita,* lit., roe, gazelle⟧ a feminine name

Tac·i·tus (tas'i təs), (**Publius Cornelius**) *c.* A.D. 55-*c.* 120; Rom. historian

Taft (taft) **1 Lo·ra·do** (lə rä'dō) 1860-1936; U.S. sculptor **2 William Howard** 1857-1930; 27th president of the U.S. (1909-13): chief justice of the U.S. (1921-30)

Ta·gore (tə gôr'), **Sir Ra·bin·dra·nath** (rə bēn'drə nät') 1861-1941; Indian (Bengali) poet

Taine (ten; *E* tān), **Hip·po·lyte A·dolphe** (ē pô lēt à dôlf') 1828-93; Fr. literary critic & historian

Tal·ley·rand (tal'i rand'; *Fr* tàl rän', tà le-) (born *Charles Maurice de Talleyrand-Périgord*) Prince of Benevento 1754-1838; Fr. statesman & diplomat

Tal·lis (tal'is), **Thomas** *c.* 1510-85; Eng. composer

Ta·los (tā'läs') *Gr. Myth.* **1** an inventor killed because of jealousy by Daedalus, his uncle **2** a man of brass given by Zeus to Minos, King of Crete, as a watchman

Ta·ma·yo (tä mä'yô), **Ru·fi·no** (rōō fē'nô) 1899-1991; Mex. painter

Tam·er·lane (tam'ər lān') ⟦after *Timur lenk,* Timur the lame⟧ *c.* 1336-1405; Mongol warrior whose conquests extended from the Black Sea to the upper Ganges

Tamm (täm), **I·gor** (**Evgenyevich**) (ē'gôr') 1895-1971; Soviet physicist

Tam·my (tam'ē) a feminine name

Tan·cred (taŋ'krid) *c.* 1078-1112; Norman leader of the 1st Crusade

Ta·ney (tô'nē), **Roger B**(**rooke**) 1777-1864; U.S. jurist: chief justice of the U.S. (1836-64)

Tan·guy (tän gē'), **Yves** (ēv) 1900-55; U.S. painter, born in France

Tann·häu·ser (tän'hoi'zər; tan'-) 〚Ger〛 a German knight and minnesinger of the 13th cent., dealt with in legend as a knight who seeks absolution after giving himself up to revelry in Venusberg

Tan·ta·lus (tan'tə ləs) 〚L < Gr *Tantalos*〛 *Gr. Myth.* a king, son of Zeus, doomed in the lower world to stand in water that always recedes when he tries to drink it and under branches of fruit that always remain just out of reach

Tan·ya (tän'yə) a feminine name

Tar·bell (tär'bel', -bəl), **Ida M**(inerva) 1857-1944; U.S. journalist & author

Tar·king·ton (tär'kiŋ tən), **(Newton) Booth** 1869-1946; U.S. novelist

Tar·pe·ia (tär pē'ə) *Rom. Myth.* a girl who treacherously opens the Capitoline citadel to the invading Sabines, who then crush her to death with their shields

Tar·quin (tär'kwin) (*Lucius Tarquinius Superbus*) semi-legendary Etruscan king of Rome (*c.* 534-*c.* 510 B.C.)

Tar·ti·ni (tär tē'nē), **Giu·sep·pe** (joo zep'pe) 1692-1770; It. violinist, composer, & musical theoretician

Tar·tuffe (tär toof'; *Fr* tȧr tüf') 〚Fr < It *Tartufo*, lit., a truffle〛 the title hero, a religious hypocrite, of a satirical comedy (1664-69) by Molière

Tar·zan (tär'zən, -zan') *n.* 〚after *Tarzan*, jungle-raised hero of stories by Edgar Rice Burroughs〛 [*also* t-] any very strong, virile, and agile man: often used ironically or humorously

Tas·man (täs'män'; *E* taz'mən), **A·bel Jans·zoon** (ä'bəl yän'sōn) *c.* 1603-59; Du. navigator who discovered Tasmania & New Zealand

Tas·so (täs'sô; *E* tas'ō), **Tor·qua·to** (tôr kwä'tô) 1544-95; It. epic poet

Tate (tāt) **1 (John Orley) Allen** 1899-1979; U.S. poet & critic **2 Nahum** 1652-1715; Brit. poet & dramatist, born in Ireland: poet laureate (1692-1715)

Ta·tum (tāt'əm) **1 Art**(hur) 1910-56; U.S. jazz pianist **2 Edward L**(awrie) 1909-75; U.S. biochemist

Taw·ney (tô'nē), **R**(ichard) **H**(enry) 1880-1962; Brit. economic historian

Tay·lor (tā'lər) **1 (James) Bay·ard** (bī'ərd, bā'ärd') 1825-78; U.S. poet, journalist, & translator **2 Jeremy** 1613-67; Eng. bishop & theological writer **3 Zachary** 1784-

1850; U.S. general: 12th president of the U.S. (1849-50)

Tchai·kov·sky (chī kôf'skē), **Peter Il·ich** (il'yich) 1840-93; Russ. composer: also **Pëtr Il·yich Tschai·kow·sky** (pyô'tr' il yēch' chī kôf'skē)

Tche·kov (che'kôf'), **Anton** *alt. sp. of* Anton Pavlovich CHEKHOV: also **Tche'khov**

Teach (tēch), **Edward** *see* BLACKBEARD

Teas·dale (tēz'dāl'), **Sara** 1884-1933; U.S. poet

Te·cum·seh (ti kum'sə) *c.* 1768-1813; chief of the Shawnee Indians: attempted to unite the W Indian tribes

Ted (ted) *nickname for:* 1 EDWARD 2 THEODORE Also **Ted'dy** (-ē)

Teil·hard de Char·din (te yàr də shàr dan'), **Pierre** 1881-1955; Fr. paleontologist, geologist, & philosopher

Tek·a·kwith·a (tek'ə kwith'ə), **Catherine** (also called *Kateri*) 1656-1680; North American Indian religious; beatified: called *Lily of the Mohawks*: also sp. **Teg'a·kwith'a** (teg'ə-) or **Teg'a·koui'ta** (-kwēt'ə)

Te·lem·a·chus (tə lem'ə kəs) ⟦L < Gr *Tēlemachos*⟧ *Gr. Legend* the son of Odysseus and Penelope: he helps his father slay his mother's suitors

Te·le·mann (te'lə män'), **Ge·org Phi·lipp** (gā ôrk' fē'lip) 1681-1767; Ger. composer

Tell (tel), **William** *see* WILLIAM TELL

Tel·ler (tel'ər), **Edward** 1908- ; U.S. nuclear physicist, born in Hungary

Tel·lus (tel'əs) ⟦L < *tellus*, the earth < IE base **telo-*, flat surface⟧ *Rom. Myth.* the goddess of the earth: identified with the Greek Gaea

Tem·ple (tem'pəl), **Sir William** 1628-99; Brit. diplomat & writer

Tempter, the the Devil; Satan

Ten·iers (ten'yərz; *Fl* tə nirs') 1 **David** 1582-1649; Fl. painter: called *the Elder* 2 **David** 1610-90; Fl. painter: son of Teniers the Elder: called *the Younger*

Ten·niel (ten'yəl), **Sir John** 1820-1914; Eng. illustrator & caricaturist

Ten·ny·son (ten'i sən), **Alfred** 1st Baron Tennyson 1809-92; Eng. poet: poet laureate (1850-92): called *Alfred, Lord Tennyson*

Ter Borch (tur bôrkh'), **Ge·rard** (gā'rärt) 1617-81; Du. painter: also written **Ter·borch'**

Ter·ence (ter'əns) ⟦L *Terentius,* name of a Roman

gens ‖ **1** a masculine name: dim. *Terry* **2** (L. name *Publius Terentius Afer*) *c.* 195-*c.* 159 B.C.; Rom. writer of comedies

Te·re·sa (tə rē′sə, -zə; *Sp* te re′sä) **1** a feminine name: see THERESA **2 Mother** (born *Agnes Gonxha Bojaxhiu*) 1910- ; Rom. Catholic missionary in India, born in Yugoslavia **3 Saint** (1515-82); Sp. Carmelite nun: her day is Oct. 12: called **Teresa of A·vi·la** (ä′vē lä′; *E* av′i lə)

Te·resh·ko·va (te′resh kô′və), **Va·len·ti·na** (**Vladi·mirovna**) (vä′len tē′nə) 1937- ; Soviet cosmonaut: 1st woman in space (1963)

Te·re·us (tē′rē əs) ‖ L < Gr *Tēreus* ‖ Gr. Myth. a king of Thrace: see PHILOMELA

Ter·ma·gant (tur′mə gənt) ‖ ME *Tervagant* < OFr, name of an imaginary Muslim deity prob. introduced by the Crusaders ‖ an imaginary deity supposed by medieval Christians to be worshiped by Muslims and represented in morality plays as a boisterous, over-bearing figure

Ter·mi·nus (tur′mə nəs) *Rom. Myth.* the deity presiding over boundaries and landmarks

Terp·sich·o·re (tərp sik′ə rē′) ‖ Gr *Terpsichorē* < *terp-sichoros*, delighting in the dance < *terpein*, to delight in + *choros*, a dance ‖ Gr. Myth. the Muse of the dance

Ter·ry (ter′ē) **1** a masculine name: see TERENCE **2** a feminine name: var. *Terri*: see THERESA **3 Dame Ellen** (**Alice** or **Alicia**) 1848-1928; Eng. actress

Ter·tul·li·an (tər tul′ē ən, -tul′yen) (L. name *Quintus Septimius Florens Tertullianus*) *c.* A.D. 160-*c.* 230; Rom. church father, born in Carthage

Tes·la (tes′lə), **Ni·ko·la** (nik′ə lə) 1856-1943; U.S. inventor, born in Croatia

Te·thys (tē′this) ‖ L < Gr *Tēthys* ‖ Gr. Myth. a daughter of Uranus and wife of Oceanus, by whom she is the mother of the Oceanides

Tet·zel (tet′səl), **Jo·hann** (yō′hän′) *c.* 1465-1519; Ger. Dominican monk & inquisitor: opposed by Luther

Thack·er·ay (thak′ər ē), **William Make·peace** (māk′pēs′) 1811-63; Eng. novelist

Thad·de·us, Thad·e·us (thad′ē əs, tha dē′əs) ‖ ME < LL(Ec) *Thaddaeus* < Gr(Ec) *Thaddaios* ‖ a masculine name: dim. *Thad*

Tha·li·a (thā′lē ə, thāl′yə; *for 2, usually* thə lī′ə) ‖ L < Gr

Thaleia < *thallein*, to flourish, bloom < IE base **dhal-*, to blossom > Alb *dal*, (I) sprout] *Gr. Myth.* **1** the Muse of comedy and pastoral poetry **2** Bloom, one of the three Graces

Than·a·tos (than'ə täs') [Gr, lit., death < IE **dhwen-*, dark, clouded] *Gr. Myth.* death personified: identified with the Roman Mors

Thant (thänt, tänt; thant), **U** (o͞o) 1909-74; Burmese statesman & diplomat: secretary-general of the United Nations (1962-71)

Thatch·er (thach'ər), **Margaret** (**Hilda**) (born *Margaret Hilda Roberts*) 1925- ; Brit. politician: prime minister (1979-90)

Thay·er (thā'ər, ther), **Syl·va·nus** (sil vā'nəs) 1785-1872; U.S. army officer & educator: reorganized the U.S. Military Academy at West Point

Thel·ma (thel'mə) [< ?, but often a var. of SELMA] a feminine name

The·mis (thē'mis) *Gr. Myth.* a goddess of law and justice, daughter of Uranus and Gaea: represented as holding aloft a scale for weighing opposing claims

The·mis·to·cles (thə mis'tə klēz') *c.* 525-*c.* 460 B.C.; Athenian statesman & naval commander

The·oc·ri·tus (thē ä'kri təs) 3d cent. B.C.; Gr. poet

The·o·dor·a (thē'ə dôr'ə) [Gr *Theodōra:* see fol.] a feminine name: dim. *Dora*

The·o·dore (thē'ə dôr') [L *Theodorus* < Gr *Theodōros* < *theos*, god + *dōron*, gift] a masculine name: dim. *Ted, Teddy*; fem. *Theodora*: also **The'o·dor'**

The·od·o·ric (thē äd'ə rik) [LL *Theodoricus*, altered (after *Theodorus*, Theodore) < Goth **Thiudoreiks* < *thiuda*, folk, akin to OHG *thioda* < IE **teutā-*, crowd < base **teu-*, to swell + *reiks*, ruler, leader, ult. < IE base **reĝ-*, straight, stretch out, put in order] *c.* A.D. 454-526; king of the Ostrogoths (474-526)

The·o·do·si·us (thē'ə dō'shē əs, -shəs) [LL < Gr *Theodosios* < *theos*, god < IE base *dhēs-*, used in religious terms + *dosis*, gift < IE base **do-*, to give] **1** a masculine name: fem. *Theodosia* **2** (*Flavius Theodosius*) *c.* A.D. 346-395; Rom. general: emperor of Rome (379-395): called *the Great*

The·o·phras·tus (thē'ə fras'təs) [L < Gr *Theophrastos* < *theos*, god < IE base **dhēs-*, used in religious terms + *phrazein*, to speak, plan, observe, guard: hence, lit.,

? divinely protected ⟧ *c.* 372-*c.* 287 B.C.; Gr. philosopher & natural scientist

The·re·sa (tə rē'sə, -zə) ⟦ < Fr *Thérèse* or Port *Theresa* < L *Therasia* < ? ⟧ **1** a feminine name: dim. *Terry, Tess;* var. *Teresa* **2** *see* TERESA, Saint **3** *see* THÉ-RÈSE, Saint

Thé·rèse (tā'rez'; *E* tə rēs'), Saint (1873-97); Fr. Carmelite nun: her day is Oct. 3: called **Thérèse of Li·sieux** (lē zyö')

Ther·si·tes (thər sīt'ēz') ⟦ L < Gr *Thersitēs* < dial. (Lesbian) *thersos*, boldness, for *tharsos* < IE base **dhers-*, to dare, be bold ⟧ in the *Iliad*, an ugly, loud, abusive Greek soldier in the Trojan War

The·se·us (thē'sē əs) ⟦ L < Gr *Thēseus* ⟧ Gr. Legend the principal hero of Attica, son of Aegeus and king of Athens, famed esp. for his killing of the Minotaur

Thes·pis (thes'pis) 6th cent. B.C.; Gr. poet: traditionally the originator of Gr. tragedy

The·tis (thēt'is) ⟦ L < Gr *Thetis* ⟧ Gr. Myth. one of the Nereids and mother of Achilles

Thiers (tyer), **Louis A·dolphe** (lwē á dôlf') 1797-1877; Fr. statesman & historian

Thisbe *see* PYRAMUS AND THISBE

Thom·as (täm'əs) ⟦ ME < LL(Ec) < Gr(Ec) *Thōmas* < Heb *teom*, Aram *teoma*, lit., a twin ⟧ **1** a masculine name: dim. *Tom, Tommy;* fem. *Thomasina* **2** *Bible* (called *Didymus, the Twin*) one of the twelve Apostles, who doubted at first the resurrection of Jesus: John 20:24-29: his day is Dec. 21: also *Saint Thomas* **3 Clarence** 1948- ; associate justice, U.S. Supreme Court (1991-) **4 Dyl·an (Marlais)** (dil'ən) 1914-53; Welsh poet **5 George Henry** 1816-70; Union general in the Civil War **6 Norman (Mattoon)** 1884-1968; U.S. Socialist leader **7 (Philip) Edward** 1878-1917; Eng. poet **8 Seth** 1785-1859; U.S. clock manufacturer

Thomas à Becket *see* BECKET, Saint Thomas à

Thomas à Kempis *see* KEMPIS, Thomas à

Thomas Aquinas *see* AQUINAS, Saint Thomas

Thomp·son (tämp'sən, täm-) **1 Benjamin** Count Rumford 1753-1814; Brit. scientist & statesman, born in America **2 David** 1770-1857; Cdn. explorer, born in England **3 Francis** 1859-1907; Eng. poet

Thom·son (täm'sən, tämp'-) **1 Sir George Pag·et** (paj'it) 1892-1975; Eng. physicist **2 James** 1700-48; Scot.

poet **3 James** (pseud. *B.V.*; i.e., *Bysshe Vanolis*) 1834-
82; Scot. poet **4** Sir J(ohn) **Arthur** 1861-1933; Scot.
naturalist & writer **5** Sir **Joseph John** 1856-1940; Eng.
physicist: father of Sir George **6 Virgil** 1896-1989;
U.S. composer **7 William** *see* KELVIN, 1st Baron

Thor (thôr) ⟦ON *Thorr* < IE base **(s)ten*-, loud rustling,
deep noise⟧ *Norse Myth.* the god of thunder, war, and
strength, and the son of Odin, armed with a magic
hammer

Tho·reau (thôr′ō; thô rō′, thə-), **Henry David** (born
David Henry Thoreau) 1817-62; U.S. naturalist &
writer

Thorn·dike (thôrn′dīk′), **Edward Lee** 1874-1949; U.S.
psychologist, educator, & lexicographer

Thorpe (thôrp), **Jim** (born *James Francis Thorpe*) 1888-
1953; U.S. athlete

Thoth (thōth; tōt) ⟦L < Gr *Thōth* < Egypt *dhwty*⟧
Egypt. Myth. the god of wisdom, learning, and magic,
the scribe of the gods: represented as having a human
body and the head of either a dog or an ibis

Thu·cyd·i·des (thōō sid′i dēz′) *c.* 460-*c.* 400 B.C.;
Athenian historian

Thur·ber (thur′bər), **James (Grover)** 1894-1961; U.S.
writer, humorist, & cartoonist

Thy·es·tes (thī es′tēz′) ⟦L < Gr *Thyestēs*⟧ *Gr. Myth.* a
brother of Atreus and son of Pelops: see ATREUS

Ti·ber·i·us (tī bir′ē əs) (*Tiberius Claudius Nero Caesar*)
42 B.C.-A.D. 37; Rom. emperor (A.D. 14-37)

Tie·po·lo (tye′pô lô), **Gio·van·ni Bat·tis·ta** (jô vän′nē bät
tēs′tä) 1696-1770; Venetian painter

Tif·fa·ny (tif′ə nē) a feminine name

Tig·lath–pi·le·ser III (tig′lath′ pī lē′zər, -pi-) died *c.* 727
B.C.; king of Assyria (*c.* 745-*c.* 727)

Ti·ki (tē′kē) ⟦Polynesian: prob. < Maori⟧ *Polynesian
Myth.* the first man, or the god who creates him

Til·den (til′dən), **Samuel Jones** 1814-86; U.S. politician

Til·lich (til′ik), **Paul (Johannes)** 1886-1965; U.S. theologian, born in Germany

Til·ly (til′ē), Count of (*Johann Tserklaes*) 1559-1632; Fl.
general in the Thirty Years' War

Time FATHER TIME

Tim·o·thy (tim′ə thē) ⟦Fr *Timothée* < L *Timotheus* <
Gr *Timotheos* < *timē*, honor < IE base **kwei*-, to heed,
value + *theos*, god < IE base **dhēs*-, used in religious

terms ‖ a masculine name: dim. *Tim, Timmy*

Ti·mur (tē mŏŏr′) *var. of* TAMERLANE

Ti·na (tē′nə) a feminine name: see CHRISTINE, ERNES-
TINE, JUSTINA

Tin·ber·gen (tin′ber′kən) **1** Jan (yän) 1903- ; Du.
economist **2** Ni·ko·laas (nē′kŏ̂ läs′) 1907-88; Du.
ethologist: brother of Jan

Tin·dale, **Tin·dal** (tin′dəl), **William** *alt. sp. of* William
TYNDALE

Tin·to·ret·to (tin′tə ret′ō; *It* tēn′tô ret′tô), **Il** (ēl) (born
Jacopo Robusti) 1518-94; Venetian painter

Tip·pe·ca·noe (tip′i kə nŏŏ′) *name for* William Henry
HARRISON

Tip·pett (tip′it), Sir **Michael** (**Kemp**) 1905- ; Brit. composer

Ti·re·si·as (tī rē′sē əs) ‖ L < Gr *Teiresias* ‖ *Gr. Myth.* a
blind soothsayer of Thebes

Tir·so de Mo·li·na (tir′sō dä′ mō lē′nə) (pseud. of
Gabriel Téllez) c. 1584-1648; Sp. dramatist

Ti·siph·o·ne (ti sif′ə nē′) ‖ Gr *Tisiphonē*, lit., the
avenger of blood < *tisis*, vengeance + *phonos*,
bloodletting, murder < IE **gwhonos*, a beating < base
*gwhen-, to beat, strike ‖ *Gr. & Rom. Myth.* one of the
three Furies

Ti·tan (tīt′'n) ‖ ME < L < Gr (pl. *Titanes*) ‖ *old poet.
name for* HELIOS —*n. Gr. Myth.* any of a race of giant
deities who are overthrown by the Olympian gods

Ti·ta·ni·a (ti tā′nē ə, tī-) *Eng. Folklore* the queen of
fairyland and wife of Oberon

Ti·tho·nus (ti thō′nəs) ‖ L < Gr *Tithōnos* ‖ *Gr. Myth.*
the son of Laomedon and the lover of Eos: she obtains
immortality for him but not eternal youth, so that he
shrivels up and is turned into a grasshopper

Ti·tian (tish′ən) (It. name *Tiziano Vecellio*) c. 1490-1576;
Venetian painter

Ti·to (tē′tō), Marshal (born *Josip Broz*) 1892-1980;
Yugoslav Communist party leader: prime minister
(1945-53) & president (1953-80) of Yugoslavia

Ti·tus (tīt′əs) ‖ L ‖ **1** a masculine name **2** (*Titus Flavius
Sabinus Vespasianus*) A.D. 39-81; Rom. general &
emperor (79-81): son of Vespasian

Ti·u (tē′ŏŏ) ‖ OE *Tiw*, akin to OHG *Ziu* < IE **deiwos*,
god < IE base **dhēs-*, used in religious terms ‖ the god
of war and the sky: identified with the Norse Tyr

To·bi·as (tō bī′əs, tə-) 〚LL(Ec) < Gr(Ec) *Tōbias* < Heb *toviya*, lit., God is good < *tov*, good + *ya*, God〛 **1 a** masculine name: dim. *Toby*: var. *Tobiah* **2** TOBIT

To·bin (tō′bin), **James** 1918- ; U.S. economist

To·bit (tō′bit) *Apocrypha* a Hebrew captive in Nineveh

Tocque·ville (tōk′vil′; *Fr* tôk vēl′), **A·le·xis (Charles Henri Maurice Clérel) de** (á lek sē′ də) 1805-59; Fr. author & statesman

Todd (täd) **1** a masculine name **2** Baron **Alexander (Robertus)** 1907- ; Brit. organic chemist

To·jo (tō′jo), **Hi·de·ki** (hē′de kē′) 1884-1948; Jpn. general & statesman: prime minister (1941-44)

To·ku·ga·wa (tō′kōō gä′wä) Japanese noble family that held the shogunate and exercised control over Japan and its emperors (1603-1867)

Tol·kien (täl′kēn′), **J(ohn) R(onald) R(euel)** 1892-1973; Eng. novelist, scholar, & linguist

Tol·stoy or **Tol·stoi** (täl′stoi′, tōl′-; *Russ* tôl stoi′), Count **Leo Ni·ko·la·ye·vich** (nē′kô lä′ye vich′) 1828-1910; Russ. novelist & social theoretician: Russ. given name *Lev*

Tom·baugh (täm′bô′), **Clyde William** 1906- ; U.S. astronomer: discovered Pluto (1930)

Tom Thumb a tiny hero of many English folk tales

To·ny (tō′nē) a masculine name: see ANTHONY

Ton·ya (tän′yə, tō′-) a feminine name: dim. *Toni;* var. *Tonia*: see ANTONIA

Tor·que·ma·da (tôr′kə mäd′ə; *Sp* tôr′ke mä′*th*ä), **To·más de** (tô mäs′ *th*e) 1420-98; Sp. Dominican monk: first Grand Inquisitor of the Spanish Inquisition

Tor·ri·cel·li (tôr′ə chel′ē; *It* tôr′rē chel′lē), **E·van·ge·lis·ta** (e′vän je lēs′tä) 1608-47; It. physicist & mathematician: discovered principle of the barometer

Tos·ca·ni·ni (täs′kə nē′nē; *It* tôs′kä nē′nē), **Ar·tu·ro** (är toor′ō; *It* är tōō′rô) 1867-1957; It. orchestral conductor, esp. in the U.S.

Tou·louse–Lau·trec (tōō lōōz′lō trek′), **Hen·ri (Marie Raymond) de** (än rē′ də) 1864-1901; Fr. painter & lithographer

Tou·ré (tōō rā′), **Sé·kou** (sā kōō′) 1922-84; president of Guinea (1958-84)

Tous·saint L'Ou·ver·ture (tōō san lōō ver tür′) (born *Pierre François Dominique Toussaint*) c. 1743-1803; Haitian liberator & general

Toyn·bee (toin'bē), **Arnold J**(oseph) 1889-1975; Eng. historian

Tra·cy (trā'sē) a feminine name

Tra·jan (trā'jən) (L. name *Marcus Ulpius Trajanus*) c. A.D. 53-117; Rom. general & statesman, born in Spain: Rom. emperor (98-117)

Tre·vel·yan (tri vil'yən) **1** George Macaulay 1876-1962; Eng. historian **2** Sir George Otto 1838-1928; Eng. historian & politician: father of George Macaulay

Tril·ling (tril'iŋ), **Lionel** 1905-75; U.S. critic & author

Trismegistus *see* HERMES TRISMEGISTUS

Tris·tan (tris'tən) a masculine name: see TRISTRAM

Tris·tram (tris'trəm) ⟦OFr *Tristan, Tristan,* altered (infl. by L *tristis,* sad) < Celt *Drystan < drest,* tumult, din⟧ **1** a masculine name: dim. *Tris;* var. *Tristam, Tristan* **2** *Medieval Legend* a knight sent to Ireland by King Mark of Cornwall to bring back the princess Isolde to be the king's bride: Isolde and Tristram fall in love and tragically die together; in some versions, Tristram marries another Isolde, a princess of Brittany

Tri·ton (trīt'ʼn) ⟦L < Gr *Tritōn;* ? akin to OIr *triath,* sea⟧ *Gr. Myth.* a sea god, son of Poseidon and Amphitrite, represented as having the head and upper body of a man and the tail of a fish and as carrying a conch-shell trumpet

Tro·i·lus (troi'ləs, trō'ə ləs) ⟦ME < L < Gr *Trōilos*⟧ *Gr. Legend* a son of King Priam, killed by Achilles: in medieval romance and in works by Boccaccio, Chaucer, and Shakespeare, Troilus was the lover of Cressida

Trol·lope (träl'əp), **Anthony** 1815-82; Eng. novelist

Trot·sky (trät'skē), **Leon** (born *Lev Davidovich Bronstein*) 1879-1940; Russ. revolutionist: commissar of war (1918-24) under Lenin: exiled (1929)

Troyes, Chrétien de *see* CHRÉTIEN DE TROYES

Tru·deau (trōō dō', trōō'dō'), **Pierre Elliott** 1919- ; prime minister of Canada (1968-79; 1980-84)

Tru·dy (trōō'dē) a feminine name: see GERTRUDE

Truf·faut (trōō fō'; *Fr* trü fō'), **Fran·çois** (frän swä') 1932-84; Fr. film director

Tru·man (trōō'mən), **Harry S** 1884-1972; 33d president of the U.S. (1945-53)

Trum·bull (trum'bəl) **1 John** 1756-1843; U.S. painter **2**

Jonathan 1710-85; Am. Revolutionary patriot: father of John

Truth (trōōth), **So·journ·er** (sō'jʉrn'ər) (orig. a slave called *Isabella*) *c.* 1797-1883; U.S. abolitionist & women's-rights advocate

Tschaikowsky *see* TCHAIKOVSKY, Peter Ilich

Tsve·ta·ye·va (sfə tä'yə və), **Ma·ri·na** (**Ivanovna**) (mə rē'nə) 1892-1941; Russ. poet, essayist, & critic

Tu·bal–cain (tōō'bəl kān', tyōō'-) *Bible* a worker in brass and iron: Gen. 4:22

Tub·man (tub'mən) **1 Harriet** *c.* 1820-1913; U.S. abolitionist **2 William V**(acanarat) **S**(hadrach) 1895-1971; president of Liberia (1944-71)

Tu·dor (tōō'dər, tyōō'-) **1** ruling family of England (1485-1603), descended from **Owen Tudor** (died 1461), a Welsh nobleman who married the widow of Henry V **2 Antony** (born *William Cook*) 1908-87; Brit. dancer & choreographer in the U.S.

Tul·ly (tul'ē) *old Eng. name for* (Marcus Tullius) CICERO

Tu·renne (tōō ren'; *Fr* tü ren'), **Vicomte de** (də) (*Henri de La Tour d'Auvergne*) 1611-75; Fr. marshal

Tur·ge·nev (tōōr gän'əf, -yəf), **I·van Ser·ge·e·vich** (ē vän' syir gyä'yə vyich') 1818-83; Russ. novelist: also sp. **Tur·ge'nieff** or **Tur·ge'niev**

Tur·got (tür gō'), **Anne Ro·bert Jacques** (än rô ber zhäk') Baron de l'Aulne, 1727-81; Fr. economist & statesman

Tu·ring (toor'iŋ, tyoor'-), **Alan Math·i·son** (math'i sən) 1912-54; Brit. mathematician: pioneer in computer theory

Tur·ner (tʉr'nər) **1 Frederick Jackson** 1861-1932; U.S. historian **2 J**(oseph) **M**(allord) **W**(illiam) 1775-1851; Eng. painter **3 Nat** 1800-31; U.S. slave, who led an abortive revolt (1831)

Tur·pin (tʉr'pin), **Dick** 1706-39; Eng. highwayman: hanged

Tus·saud (tōō sō'; *popularly* tə sôd'), **Madame** (born *Marie Gresholtz*) 1760-1850; Swiss waxworks exhibitor in London

Tut·ankh·a·men (tōōt'äŋk ä'mən) fl. *c.* 1355 B.C.; Egypt. king of the 18th dynasty: tomb discovered in 1922: also sp. **Tut'ankh·a'mun** or **Tut'ankh·a'mon**: popularly called **King Tut** (tut)

Twain (twān), **Mark** *pseud. of* Samuel Langhorne CLEM-

ENS

Tweed (twēd), **William Mar·cy** (mär′sē) 1823-78; U.S. politician & corrupt Tammany leader: called *Boss Tweed*

Twee·dle·dum and Twee·dle·dee (twēd″l dum′ ′n twēd″l dē′) two almost identical brothers in *Through the Looking Glass*, by Lewis Carroll

Twelve, the the Twelve Apostles

Twelve Apostles the twelve disciples chosen by Jesus to go forth to teach the gospel

Ty·che (tī′kē) ⟦Gr *Tychē*, akin to *teuchein*, to prepare < IE base **dheugh-*, to press⟧ *Gr. Myth.* the goddess of chance: identified with the Roman Fortuna

Ty·de·us (tī′dē əs, tid′ē-) ⟦L < Gr⟧ *Gr. Legend* the father of Diomedes and one of the Seven against Thebes

Ty·ler (tī′lər) **1 John** 1790-1862; 10th president of the U.S. (1841-45) **2 Wat** (wät) died 1381; Eng. rebel: leader of the Peasants' Revolt: also **Walter Tyler**

Tyn·dale (tin′dəl), **William** *c.* 1494-1536; Eng. religious reformer & translator of the Bible: executed for heresy

Tyn·dar·e·us (tin der′ē əs) ⟦L < Gr *Tyndareos*⟧ *Gr. Myth.* a king of Sparta, husband of LEDA

Ty·phoid Mary (tī′foid′) *n.* ⟦orig. nickname for *Mary Mallon* (died 1938), typhoid-carrying cook in New York⟧ **1** a person who is a carrier of typhoid **2** a person who spreads any kind of disease, infection, or corruption

Tyr (tir, tür) ⟦ON: for IE base see TIU⟧ *Norse Myth.* the god of war and son of Odin, noted for his courage

U

Uc·cel·lo (ōō chel′lō, ōōt-), **Pa·o·lo** (pou′lō) (born *Paolo di Dono*) *c.* 1397-1475; It. painter

U·dall (yōōd″l), **Nicholas** 1505-56; Eng. schoolmaster, translator, & playwright

Uh·land (ōō′länt′), **Jo·hann Lud·wig** (yō′hän′ lōōt′viH′) 1787-1862; Ger. poet & literary historian

U·la·no·va (ōō lä′nə və), **Ga·li·na** (Sergeyevna) (gə lē′ nə) 1910- ; Soviet ballerina

Ul·bricht (ōōl′briHt′), **Wal·ter** (väl′tər) 1893-1973; chief of state of East Germany (1960-73)

Ul·fi·las (ul′fi ləs) ⟦LGr for Goth *Wulfila*, lit., little wolf

< *wulfs*, wolf + -*ila*, dim. suffix: cf. ATTILA] *c.* A.D. 311-
c. 383; bishop of the Goths: translated the Bible into
Gothic: also **Ul′fi·la** (-lə)

U·lys·ses (yoo lis′ēz′) [ML, for L *Ulixes* < ?] **1** a masculine name **2** *Latin name for* ODYSSEUS

U·na (ōō′nə, yōō′-) [Ir *Una, Oonagh;* also < L *una*, one]
a feminine name

U·na·mu·no (ōō′nä mōō′nō), **Mi·guel de** (mē gel′ *the*)
1864-1936; Sp. philosopher & writer

Uncle Sam [extended < abbrev. *U.S.*] [Colloq.] the
U.S. (government or people), personified as a tall,
spare man with chin whiskers, dressed in a red, white,
and blue costume of swallow-tailed coat, striped trousers, and tall hat with a band of stars

Uncle Tom *n.* [after the main character, an elderly
black slave, in Harriet Beecher Stowe's antislavery
novel, *Uncle Tom's Cabin* (1852)] a black whose
behavior toward whites is regarded as fawning or ser-
vile: a term of contempt

Und·set (oon′set′), **Sig·rid** (sig′rid) 1882-1949; Norw.
novelist

Un·ter·mey·er (un′tər mī′ər), **Louis** 1885-1977; U.S.
poet, anthologist, & critic

Up·dike (up′dīk′), **John (Hoyer)** 1932- ; U.S. novelist

U·ra·ni·a (yōō rā′nē ə) [L < Gr *Ourania*, lit., the heav-
enly one < *Ouranos*, fol.] *Gr. Myth.* the Muse of
astronomy

U·ra·nus (yoor′ə nəs, yōō rān′əs) [LL < Gr *Ouranos*,
lit., heaven] *Gr. Myth.* a god who is the personification of the heavens, the son and husband of Gaea
(Earth) and father of the Titans, Furies, and Cyclopes:
he is overthrown by his son Cronus (Saturn)

Ur·ban II (ur′bən) *c.* 1042-99; pope (1088-99)

U·rey (yoor′ē), **Harold Clay·ton** (klāt′'n) 1893-1981; U.S.
chemist

U·ri·ah (yōō rī′ə) [Heb *uriya*, lit., God is light < *or*,
light, brightness (akin to *ur*, fire) + *ya*, Jehovah] **1** a
masculine name **2** *Bible* a Hittite captain whose beautiful wife, Bathsheba, David lusted after: David
arranged for Uriah to die in battle and then married
Bathsheba: 2 Sam. 11

U·ri·el (yoor′ē əl) [Heb *uriel*, lit., light of God < *or*, light
(see prec.) + *el*, God] in angelology and literature, a
principal angel or archangel

Ur·quhart (ur'kərt, -kärt'), Sir **Thomas** 1611-60; Scot. writer & translator

Ur·su·la (ur'sə lə) ⟦ML, dim. of L *ursa*, she-bear⟧ **1** a feminine name **2** Saint (*c.* 4th cent.) a legendary Christian British princess said to have been killed along with 11,000 virgins, by the Huns at Cologne

U·shas (ōō'shäs') ⟦Sans *Uṣas*, dawn⟧ the Hindu, or Vedic, goddess of the dawn

Ussh·er (ush'ər), **James** 1581-1656; Ir. archbishop & theologian

U Thant *see* THANT, U

U·ther (yōō'thər) *Arthurian Legend* a king of Britain and the father of King Arthur

U·tril·lo (ōō tril'ō, yōō-; *Fr* ü trē yō'), **Maurice** 1883-1955; Fr. painter

Uve·dale (yōōv'dāl'), **Nicholas** *var.* of Nicholas UDALL

V

Val·de·mar (väl'də mär') *alt. sp. of* WALDEMAR I

Va·lens (vā'lənz), (**Flavius**) *c.* A.D. 328-378; emperor of the Eastern Roman Empire (364-378): brother of Valentinian I

Val·en·tine (val'ən tīn') ⟦ME < L *Valentinus* < *Valens*, a masculine name < *valens*, prp. of *valere*, to be strong < IE base **wal-*⟧ **1** a masculine name **2** Saint (3d cent. A.D.); Christian martyr of Rome: his day is Feb. 14

Val·en·tin·i·an (val'ən tin'ē ən) ⟦L *Valentinius*⟧ **1** masculine name adopted by three Roman emperors **2** **Valentinian I** *c.* A.D. 321-375; ruled, 364-375: brother of Valens **3** **Valentinian II** *c.* A.D. 371-392; ruled, 375-392: son of Valentinian I **4** **Valentinian III** *c.* A.D. 419-455; ruled, 425-455

Val·en·ti·no (val'ən tē'nō), **Rudolph** (born *Rodolfo Alfonzo Raffaelo Pierre Filibert Guglielmi di Valentina d'Antonguolla*) 1895-1926; U.S. motion-picture actor, born in Italy

Va·le·ri·an (və lir'ē ən) (L. name *Publius Licinius Valerianus*) *c.* A.D. 190-260; Rom. emperor (253-260)

Val·e·rie (val'ər ē) a feminine name: dim. *Val*; equiv. Fr. *Valérie*: also **Va·ler·i·a** (və lir'ē ə)

Va·lé·ry (vȧ lā rē'), **Paul** (**Ambroise**) (pôl) 1871-1945; Fr. poet & essayist

Vallejo 260

Val·le·jo (və lā'hō, -lä'ō), **Cé·sar** (sā'zär) 1892-1938; Peruvian poet

Va·lois (và lwá') ruling family of France (1328-1589)

Van·brugh (van brō͞o'; *Brit usually* van'brə), Sir John 1664-1726; Eng. dramatist & architect

Van Bu·ren (van byoor'ən), **Martin** 1782-1862; 8th president of the U.S. (1837-41)

Van·der·bilt (van'dər bilt), **Cornelius** 1794-1877; U.S. capitalist & railroad & steamship industrialist

van der Waals (vän dər vâlz'), **Jo·han·nes Di·de·rik** (yô hän'əs dē'də rik) 1837-1923; Du. physicist

Van Do·ren (van dôr'ən) **1 Carl** (**Clinton**) 1885-1950; U.S. editor & writer **2 Mark** (**Albert**) 1894-1972; U.S. poet & literary critic: brother of Carl

Van Dyck (van dīk'), Sir **Anthony** 1599-1641; Fl. painter, in England after 1632: also sp. **Van·dyke'**

Vane (vān), Sir **Henry** (or **Harry**) 1613-62; Eng. Puritan statesman: colonial governor of Mass. (1636-37)

Va·nes·sa (və nes'ə) a feminine name

van Eyck (van īk) **1 Hubert** or **Huy·brecht** (hoi'breHt') *c.* 1366-1426; Fl. painter **2 Jan** (yän) died 1441; Fl. painter: brother of Hubert

van Gogh (van gō', -gôkh'; *Du* vän khôkh'), **Vincent** 1853-90; Du. painter

Van Rens·se·laer (van ren'sə lər, -lir'), **Stephen** 1764-1839; U.S. politician & general

van't Hoff (vänt hôf'), **Ja·co·bus Hen·dri·cus** (yä kō'bəs hen drē'kəs) 1852-1911; Du. physical chemist

Van Vleck (van vlek'), **John Has·brouck** (haz'brook) 1899-1980; U.S. physicist

Van·zet·ti (van zet'ē), **Bar·to·lo·me·o** (bär'tō lō mā'ō) 1888-1927; It. anarchist in the U.S.: see SACCO, Nicola

Va·rèse (và rez'; *E* və rāz', -rez'), **Ed·gard** (ed gär') (born *Edgar Victor Achille Charles Varèse*) 1883-1965; U.S. composer, born in France

Var·ro (var'ō), (**Marcus Terentius**) 116-27 B.C.; Rom. scholar & writer

Var·u·na (var'ə nə) ⟦Sans⟧ the Hindu god of the cosmos

Va·sa·ri (vä zä'rē), **Gior·gio** (jôr'jô) 1511-74; It. architect, painter, & biographer of artists

Vash·ti (vash'tē, -tī') ⟦Heb⟧ *Bible* the queen of Ahasuerus of Persia, disowned by him when she slighted his command for her presence at a feast: Esth. 1

Vau·ban (vō bän′), Marquis **de** (də) (*Sébastien Le Prestre*) 1633-1707; Fr. military engineer

Vaughan (vôn) **1** ⟦ < a family name ⟧ a masculine name: also sp. **Vaughn 2** Henry 1622-95; Eng. poet

Vaughan Williams, Ralph 1872-1958; Eng. composer

Veb·len (veb′lən), **Thor·stein** (**Bunde**) (thôr′stīn) 1857-1929; U.S. economist & social scientist

Ve·ga (ve′gä), **Lo·pe de** (lô′pe *the*) (born *Lope Félix de Vega Carpio*) 1562-1635; Sp. dramatist & poet

Ve·láz·quez (ve läth′keth; *E* və las′kes, -kwez), **Die·go Ro·dri·guez de Sil·va y** (dye′gô rô thrē′geth *the* sēl′vä ē) 1599-1660; Sp. painter: also **Ve·lás·quez** (ve läs′keth)

Ven·dôme (vän dōm′), Duc (**Louis Joseph**) **de** (də) 1654-1712; Fr. general: marshal of France

Venerable Bede, the *see* BEDE, Saint

Ve·nus (vē′nəs) ⟦ME < L, lit., love < IE *wenos*, desire < base *wen-*, to strive for, attain > OE *wine*, friend, *winnan*, to win⟧ *Rom. Myth.* the goddess of love and beauty: identified with the Greek Aphrodite

Ve·ra (vir′ə) ⟦ < L *vera*, fem. of *verus*, true ⟧ a feminine name

Ver·cin·get·o·rix (vur′sin jet′ər iks, -get′-) *c.* 72-*c.* 46 B.C.; Gallic chieftain defeated by Julius Caesar

Ver·di (ver′dē), **Giu·sep·pe** (**Fortunino Francisco**) (jōō zep′pe) 1813-1901; It. operatic composer

Ver·gil (vur′jəl) *alt. sp. of* VIRGIL

Ver·laine (ver len′), **Paul** (pôl) 1844-96; Fr. poet

Ver·meer (vər mer′; *E* vər mir′), **Jan** (yän) 1632-75; Du. painter: also called *Jan van der Meer van Delft*

Verne (vurn; *Fr* vern), **Jules** (jōōlz; *Fr* zhül) 1828-1905; Fr. novelist

Ver·non (vur′nən) ⟦ < the surname *Vernon*, prob. after *Vernon*, a town in France ⟧ a masculine name

Ve·ro·ne·se (ve′rô ne′se; *E* ver′ə nēz′), **Pa·o·lo** (pä′ô lô′) (born *Paolo Cagliari*) 1528-88; Venetian painter, born in Verona

Ve·ron·i·ca (və rän′i kə) ⟦ML < Gr *Pherenikē:* see BERNICE⟧ **1** a feminine name **2** Saint woman of Jerusalem who, according to legend, wiped the bleeding face of Jesus on the way to Calvary: her day is July 12

Ver·ra·za·no (ver′rä tsä′nô), **Gio·van·ni da** (jô vän′nē dä) *c.* 1480-*c.* 1527; It. explorer in the service of

France: also sp. **Ver·raz·za′no**

Ver·roc·chio (ver *rôk′kyô*), **An·dre·a del** (än dre′ä del) (born *Andrea di Michele di Francesco di Cioni*) 1435-88; Florentine sculptor and painter

Ver·tum·nus (vər tum′nəs) ⟦ L, altered (infl. by *vertere*, to turn) < *Vortumnus*, of Etr orig. ⟧ *Rom. Myth.* the god of the changing seasons and of growing flowers and fruits, husband of Pomona

Ver·u·lam (ver′yōō ləm), Baron *see* BACON, Francis

Ve·sa·li·us (vi sā′lē əs), **An·dre·as** (an′drē əs) 1514-64; Fl. anatomist in Italy, Spain, etc.

Ves·pa·si·an (ves pā′zhən, -zhē ən) (L. name *Titus Flavius Sabinus Vespasianus*) A.D. 9-79; Rom. emperor (69-79): father of Domitian & Titus

Ves·puc·ci (ves pōōt′chē), **A·me·ri·go** (ä′me rē′gô) (L. name *Americus Vespucius*) 1454-1512; It. navigator & explorer

Ves·ta (ves′tə) ⟦ L, prob. akin to Gr *Hestia*, lit., hearth ⟧ *Rom. Myth.* the goddess of the hearth, identified with the Greek Hestia

Vick·i (vik′ē) a feminine name: var. *Vicky, Vickie*: see VICTORIA

Vi·co (vē′kô), **Gio·van·ni Bat·tis·ta** (jô vän′nē bät tēs′tä) (also called *Giambattista*) 1668-1744; It. philosopher

Vic·tor (vik′tər) ⟦ L *victor*, victor < pp. *vincere*, to conquer < IE base *weik-*, vigorous or hostile display of force ⟧ a masculine name: dim. *Vic*; fem. *Victoria*

Victor Emmanuel II 1820-78; king of Sardinia (1849-61) & 1st king of Italy (1861-78)

Vic·to·ri·a (vik tôr′ē ə) ⟦ L, victory ⟧ **1** a feminine name: dim. *Vicki, Vicky, Vickie*; equiv. Fr. *Victoire*, It. *Vittoria*, Sp. *Vitoria* **2** (born *Alexandrina Victoria*) 1819-1901; queen of Great Britain & Ireland (1837-1901): empress of India (1876-1901): granddaughter of George III

Vi·gny (vē nyē′), **Al·fred Vic·tor Comte de** (àl fred′ vēk tôr′ də) 1797-1863; Fr. poet & man of letters

Vil·la (vē′yä), **Fran·cis·co** (frän sēs′kô) (born *Doroteo Arango*) c. 1877-1923; Mex. revolutionary leader: called *Pancho Villa*

Vil·la-Lo·bos (vē′lä lô′boos; *E* vē′lə lō′bəs), **Hei·tor** (ā tôr′) 1887-1959; Brazilian composer

Vil·lard (vi lärd′), **Oswald Garrison** 1872-1949; U.S. journalist, editor, & writer, born in Germany

Vil·liers (vil′ərz, -yərz), **George** *see* BUCKINGHAM, 1st
Duke of & BUCKINGHAM, 2d Duke of

Vil·lon (vē yōn′), **Fran·çois** (frän swä′) (born *François
de Montcorbier* or *des Loges*) 1431-c. 1463; Fr. poet

Vin·cent (vin′sənt) ⟦LL *Vicentius* < *vincens*, prp. of
vincere, to conquer < IE base *weik-*, vigorous or hostile display of force ⟧ a masculine name: dim. *Vince;*
equiv. Ger. *Vincenz,* It. *Vincenzo,* Sp. *Vicente*

Vincent de Paul (də pôl′), **Saint** (c. 1580-1660); Fr.
priest who founded charitable orders: his day is Sept.
27

Vinci, Leonardo da *see* DA VINCI, Leonardo

Vin·son (vin′sən), **Fred**(erick) **M**(oore) 1890-1953; U.S.
jurist: chief justice of the U.S. (1946-53)

Vi·o·la (vī ō′lə, vē-; vī′ə lə) ⟦< L *viola*, a violet ⟧ a feminine name: dim. *Vi*

Vi·o·let (vī′ə lit) ⟦< ModE *violet* (the flower) < ME <
OFr *violette*, dim. of *viole* < L *viola* < or akin to Gr
ion ⟧ a feminine name: dim. *Vi*

Vir·gil (vur′jəl) ⟦< L *Vergilius*, name of the Roman gens
to which the poet belonged ⟧ (L. name *Publius
Vergilius Maro*) 70-19 B.C.; Rom. poet: author of the
Aeneid

Virgin, the Mary, the mother of Jesus

Vir·gin·ia (vər jin′yə) ⟦L, fem. of *Virginius, Verginius,*
name of a Roman gens ⟧ a feminine name: dim. *Ginny,
Ginie;* equiv. Fr. *Virginie*

Virgin Mary Mary, the mother of Jesus

Virgin Queen *name for* ELIZABETH I

Vis·con·ti (vēs kôn′tē), **Lu·chi·no** (lo͞o kē′nō) (Count
Luchino Visconti, Duke of *Modrone*) 1906-76; It. theater, opera, & film director

Vish·nu (vish′no͞o) ⟦Sans *Visṇu,* lit., prob. all-pervader ⟧
Hinduism the second member of the trinity (Brahma,
Vishnu, and Siva), called "the Preserver" and popularly held to have had several human incarnations,
most important of which is Krishna

Vi·tru·vi·us (vi tro͞o′vē əs) (*Marcus Vitruvius Pollio*) fl.
1st cent. B.C.; Rom. architect & engineer

Vi·val·di (vē väl′dē; *E* vi-), **An·to·nio** (än tô′nyô) 1678-
1741; It. composer

Viv·i·an (viv′ē ən, viv′yən) ⟦L *Vivianus* < *vivus*, alive,
ult. < IE base *gwei-*, to live ⟧ **1** a masculine name:
equiv. Fr. *Vivien* **2** a feminine name: equiv. Fr.

Vivienne **3** *Arthurian Legend* an enchantress, mistress of Merlin: see also LADY OF THE LAKE

Vlad·i·mir I (vlad′ə mir; *Russ* vlä dē′mir) *c.* 956-1015; Russ. ruler & prince of Kiev (980-1015): converted to Christianity (989), which he introduced into Russia: his day is July 15: called *the Great:* also **Saint Vladimir**

Vla·minck (vlá mank′), **Mau·rice de** (mô rēs′ də) 1876-1958; Fr. painter

Vol·ta (vôl′tä), Conte **A·les·san·dro** (ä′les sän′drô) 1745-1827; It. physicist

Vol·taire (väl ter′; *Fr* vôl ter′), (**François Marie Arouet de**) (born *François Marie Arouet*) 1694-1778; Fr. writer and philosopher

von Braun (fôn broun′; *E* vän broun′), **Wern·her** (ver′nər; *E* wur′nər) 1912-77; U.S. rocket engineer, born in Germany

Von Neu·mann (vän noi′mən, -män), **John** 1903-57; U.S. mathematician, born in Hungary

Vor·tum·nus (vôr tum′nəs) *var. of* VERTUMNUS

Vuil·lard (vüē yàr′), (**Jean**) **É·douard** (ā dwàr′) 1868-1940; Fr. painter

Vul·can (vul′kən) ⟦L *Vulcanus, Volcanus* ⟧ *Rom. Myth.* the god of fire and of metalworking: later identified with the Greek Hephaestus

W

Wace (wās, wäs) fl. 12th cent.; Anglo-Norman poet & chronicler: also, prob. erroneously, called **Robert Wace**

Wag·ner (väg′nər), (**Wilhelm**) **Rich·ard** (riH′ärt) 1813-83; Ger. composer

Waite (wāt), **Mor·ri·son Rem·ick** (môr′i sən rem′ik) 1816-88; U.S. jurist: chief justice (1874-88)

Waks·man (waks′mən), **Sel·man A**(braham) (sel′mən) 1888-1973; U.S. microbiologist, born in Russia

Wal·de·mar I (väl′də mär′) 1131-82; king of Denmark (1157-82): called *the Great*

Wald·heim (vält′hīm′), **Kurt** (koort) 1918- ; Austrian diplomat: secretary-general of the United Nations (1972-81): president of Austria (1986-92)

Wal·do (wôl′dō, wäl′-) ⟦OHG < *waldan,* to rule ⟧ a masculine name

Wa·łes·a (vä wen′sä), **Lech** (lekh) 1943- ; Pol. labor leader & politician: president of Poland (1990-)

Wa·ley (wā'lē), **Arthur** (born *Arthur David Schloss*) 1889-1966; Eng. translator of Chin. & Jpn. literature

Wal·lace (wôl'is, wäl'-) ⟦ < the surname *Wallace* < Anglo-Fr *Waleis* or ME *Walisc*, foreign, Welsh ⟧ **1** a masculine name: dim. *Wally* **2 Alfred Russel** 1823-1913; Eng. naturalist **3 Lew(is)** 1827-1905; U.S. general & novelist **4** Sir **William** *c.* 1270-1305; Scot. patriot & leader in struggle against Edward I of England

Wal·len·stein (väl'ən shtīn'; *E* wôl'ən stīn'), **Al·brecht Eu·se·bi·us Wen·zel von** (äl'breHt oɪ zā'bē oos ven' tsəl fôn) 1583-1634; Austrian general in the Thirty Years' War

Wal·ler (wôl'ər, wäl'-), **Edmund** 1606-87; Eng. poet

Wal·pole (wôl'pōl, wäl'-) **1 Horace** 4th Earl of Orford (born *Horatio Walpole*) 1717-97; Eng. writer **2** Sir **Hugh (Seymour)** 1884-1941; Eng. novelist, born in New Zealand **3** Sir **Robert** 1st Earl of Orford 1676-1745; Eng. statesman: prime minister (1721-42): father of Horace

Wal·sing·ham (wôl'siŋ əm), Sir **Francis** *c.* 1532-90; Eng. statesman: secretary of state to Elizabeth I (1573-90)

Wal·ter (wôl'tər; *for 2,* väl'tər) ⟦ NormFr *Waltier* < Frank *Waldheri* < *waldan*, to rule + *heri, hari,* army, host; also < Ger *Walter, Walther* < OHG form of same name ⟧ **1** a masculine name: dim. *Walt, Wally* **2 Bruno** (born *Bruno Walter Schlesinger*) 1876-1962; U.S. orchestra conductor, born in Germany

Walter Mit·ty (mit'ē) *n.* ⟦ < "The Secret Life of *Walter Mitty*," a short story by THURBER ⟧ an ordinary, unassuming person who dreams of being heroic, successful, etc.

Wal·ther von der Vo·gel·wei·de (väl'tər fôn der fō'gəl vī'də) *c.* 1170-*c.* 1230; Ger. minnesinger

Wal·ton (wôlt''n) **1 I·zaak** (ī'zək) 1593-1683; Eng. writer **2** Sir **William (Turner)** 1902-83; Eng. composer

Wan·a·ma·ker (wän'ə mā'kər), **John** 1838-1922; U.S. merchant

Wan·da (wän'də) a feminine name

Wandering Jew in medieval folklore, a Jew condemned to wander the earth restlessly until the second coming of Christ because of his scornful attitude just before the Crucifixion

War·burg (vär'boork'), **Ot·to Hein·rich** (ô'tō hīn'riH)

1883-1970; Ger. biochemist

Ward (wôrd) **1 Ar·te·mus** (ärt'ə məs) (pseud. of *Charles Farrar Browne*) 1834-67; U.S. humorist **2 Barbara** 1914-1981; Eng. writer **3** Mrs. **Humphry** (born *Mary Augusta Arnold*) 1851-1920; Brit. novelist, born in Tasmania

War·hol (wôr'hôl', -hōl'), **An·dy** (an'dē) *c.* 1928-1987; U.S. painter & filmmaker

War·ren (wôr'ən, wär'-) ⟦NormFr *warin* < ? OHG *Warin*, the Varini, a people mentioned by Tacitus⟧ **1** a masculine name **2 Earl** 1891-1974; U.S. jurist: chief justice (1953-69) **3 Robert Penn** 1905-89; U.S. writer & poet: 1st poet laureate of the U.S. (1986-89)

War·wick (wôr'ik, wär'-), Earl of (*Richard Neville*) 1428-71; Eng. statesman & military leader

Wash·ing·ton (wôsh'iŋ tən, wäsh'-) **1 Book·er** T(alia-ferro) (book'ər) 1856-1915; U.S. educator & author **2 George** 1732-99; 1st president of the U.S. (1789-97): commander in chief of the Continental army

Was·ser·mann (väs'ər män'; *E* wäs'ər mən), **Au·gust von** (ou'gōost fōn) 1866-1925; Ger. bacteriologist

Wat·son (wät'sən, wôt'-) **1 James Dewey** 1928- ; U.S. biochemist: helped determine the structure of DNA **2 John B**(roadus) 1878-1958; U.S. psychologist

Wat·son–Watt (wät'sən wät'), Sir **Robert Alexander** 1892-1973; Scot. physicist

Watt (wät), **James** 1736-1819; Scot. engineer & inventor: pioneer in the development of the steam engine

Wat·teau (vȧ tō'; *E* wä tō'), (**Jean**) **An·toine** (än twȧn') Fr. painter

Watts (wäts), **Isaac** 1674-1748; Eng. clergyman & writer of hymns

Waugh (wô), **Eve·lyn** (**Arthur St. John**) (ēv'lin) 1903-66; Eng. novelist

Wa·vell (wā'vəl), **Archibald** (**Percival**) 1st Earl Wavell 1883-1950; Brit. field marshal

Way·land (wā'lənd) *Eng. Folklore, Gmc. Folklore* an invisible smith: also **Wayland** (**the**) **Smith**

Wayne (wān) ⟦< surname *Wayne*⟧ **1** a masculine name **2 Anthony** 1745-96; Am. general in the Revolutionary War: called *Mad Anthony Wayne* **3 John** (born *Marion Michael Morrison*) 1907-79; U.S. film actor

Webb (web) **1 Beatrice** (**Potter**) 1858-1943; Eng. econo-mist & socialist reformer: wife of Sidney James **2**

Sidney (James) 1st Baron Passfield 1859-1947; Eng. economist & socialist reformer

We·ber (vā′bər; *for 4,* web′ər) **1 Carl Ma·ri·a** (Friedrich Ernst) **von** (kärl mä rē′ä fôn) 1786-1826; Ger. composer **2 Ernst Hein·rich** (ernst hīn′riH) 1795-1878; Ger. physiologist & anatomist **3 Max** (mäks) 1864-1920; Ger. sociologist & economist **4 Max** 1881-1961; U.S. painter, born in Russia **5 Wil·helm E·du·ard** (vil′helm′ ā′dōō ärt′) 1804-91; Ger. physicist: brother of Ernst

We·bern (vā′bərn), **An·ton** (von) (än′tôn) 1883-1945; Austrian composer

Web·ster (web′stər) **1** a masculine name **2 Daniel** 1782-1852; U.S. statesman & orator **3 John** *c.* 1580-*c.* 1625; Eng. dramatist **4 Noah** 1758-1843; U.S. lexicographer

We·de·kind (vā′də kint′), **Frank** (fräŋk) 1864-1918; Ger. playwright

Weems (wēmz), **Mason Locke** 1759-1825; U.S. clergyman & writer: called *Parson Weems*

Weil (wīl, vīl; *Fr* ve′y′), **Si·mone** (sē môn′) 1909-43; Fr. philosopher

Weill (wīl; *Ger* vīl), **Kurt** (kurt) 1900-50; U.S. composer, born in Germany

Wein·berg (wīn′burg′), **Steven** 1933- ; U.S. physicist

Weird Sisters the three Fates

Weis·mann (vīs′män), **Au·gust** (ou′goost) 1834-1914; Ger. biologist

Weiz·mann (vīts′män′; *E* wīts′mən), **Cha·im** (khī′im) 1874-1952; Israeli chemist & Zionist leader, born in Russia: 1st president of Israel (1948-52)

Welles (welz), (George) **Orson** 1915-85; U.S. film actor & director

Wel·ling·ton (wel′iŋ tən), 1st Duke of (*Arthur Wellesley*) 1769-1852; Brit. general & statesman, born in Ireland: prime minister (1828-30): called *the Iron Duke*

Wells (welz), **H**(erbert) **G**(eorge) 1866-1946; Eng. novelist & social critic

Wel·ty (wel′tē), **Eu·do·ra** (yōō dôr′ə) 1909- ; U.S. short-story writer & novelist

Wen·ces·laus (wen′səs lôs′) 1361-1419; Holy Roman emperor (1378-1400); as **Wenceslaus IV**, king of Bohemia (1378-1419): Ger. name **Wen·zel** (ven′tsəl)

Wend·y (wen′dē) a feminine name

Wer·fel (ver′fəl), **Franz** (fränts) 1890-1945; Austrian novelist, playwright, & poet, born in Prague

Wes·ley (wes′lē, wez′-) **1** ⟦ < the surname ⟧ a masculine name: dim. *Wes* **2 Charles** 1707-88; Eng. clergyman & hymn writer: brother of John **3 John** 1703-91; Eng. clergyman & evangelist; founder of Methodism

West (west) **1 Benjamin** 1738-1820; Am. painter, in England after 1763 **2 Dame Rebecca** (pseud. of *Cicily Isabel Fairfield*; Mrs. *H. M. Andrews*) 1892-1983; Brit. novelist & critic, born in Ireland

West·ing·house (wes′tiŋ hous′), **George** 1846-1914; U.S. inventor & manufacturer

Whar·ton (hwôrt′'n, wôrt′'n), **Edith** (born *Edith Newbold Jones*) 1862-1937; U.S. novelist

Wheat·ley (hwēt′lē, wēt′-), **Phillis** c. 1753-84; Am. poet, born in Africa & brought to America as a slave

Wheel·er (hwēl′ər, wēl′-), **John Archibald** 1911- ; U.S. physicist

Whip·ple (hwip′əl, wip′-), **George Hoyt** (hoit) 1878-1976; U.S. pathologist

Whis·tler (hwis′lər, wis′-), **James Abbott Mc·Neill** (mək nēl′) 1834-1903; U.S. painter & etcher in England

White (hwīt, wīt) **1 Byron R(aymond)** 1917- ; U.S. jurist: associate justice, U.S. Supreme Court (1962-93) **2 Edward Douglass** 1845-1921; U.S. jurist: chief justice of the U.S. (1910-21) **3 E(lwyn) B(rooks)** 1899-1985; U.S. writer **4 Patrick (Victor Martindale)** 1912-90; Austral. writer **5 Stan·ford** (stan′fərd) 1853-1906; U.S. architect **6 Walter (Francis)** 1893-1955; U.S. author & civil rights leader

White·field (hwīt′fēld′, wīt′-), **George** 1714-70; Eng. Methodist evangelist

White·head (hwīt′hed′, wīt′-), **Alfred North** 1861-1947; Eng. mathematician & philosopher, in the U.S. after 1924

Whit·man (hwīt′mən, wīt′-) **1 Marcus** 1802-47; U.S. pioneer & missionary in the Northwest **2 Walt(er)** 1819-92; U.S. poet

Whit·ney (hwīt′nē, wīt′-), **Eli** 1765-1825; U.S. inventor, esp. of the cotton gin

Whit·ti·er (hwīt′ē ər, wīt′-), **John Green·leaf** (grēn′lēf′) 1807-92; U.S. poet

Whit·ting·ton (hwīt′iŋ tən, wīt′-), **Richard** c. 1358-1423; Eng. merchant: lord mayor of London: associated with various Eng. legends of a Dick Whittington

Whit·tle (hwit′'l), Sir **Frank** 1907- ; Eng. engineer &
pioneer developer of jet propulsion engines

Wick·liffe (wik′lif), **John** alt. sp. of John WYCLIFFE

Wi·du·kind (vē′dōō kint) 8th cent. A.D.; Saxon warrior:
leader of the Saxons against Charlemagne

Wie·land (vē′länt) **1 Chris·toph Mar·tin** (kris′tôf mär′
tēn) 1733-1813; Ger. novelist, poet, & translator **2
Hein·rich (Otto)** (hin′riH) 1877-1957; Ger. chemist

Wie·ner (wē′nər), **Norbert** 1894-1964; U.S. mathematician & pioneer in cybernetics

Wie·sel (wi zel′), **El·ie** (el′ē) 1928- ; U.S. writer, born in
Romania

Wig·gin (wig′in), **Kate Douglas** (born *Kate Smith*) 1856-
1923; U.S. educator & writer of children's novels

Wig·ner (wig′nər), **Eugene Paul** 1902- ; U.S. physicist,
born in Hungary

Wil·ber·force (wil′bər fôrs′), **William** 1759-1833; Eng.
statesman & vigorous opponent of slavery

Wil·bert (wil′bərt) 〖 Ger *Willebert* < OHG *willeo*, will +
beraht, berht, bright 〗 a masculine name

Wil·bur (wil′bər). 〖OE *Wilburh*: prob. a place name <
**Wiligburh,* lit., willow town 〗 a masculine name

Wilde (wīld), **Oscar (Fingal O'Flahertie Wills)** 1854-
1900; Brit. playwright, poet, & novelist, born in Ireland

Wil·der (wil′dər) **1 Laura In·galls** (iŋ′gəlz) (Mrs.
Almanzo Wilder) 1867-1957; U.S. author of children's
books **2 Thorn·ton (Niven)** (thôrnt′'n) 1897-1975; U.S.
novelist & playwright

Wil·fred, Wil·frid (wil′frid) 〖OE *Wilfrith* < *willa,* a
wish, will + *frithu,* peace < Gmc *frithu < IE **pritu-,*
friendship < base **pri-,* to like > Sans *priya-,* dear,
beloved 〗 a masculine name

Wil·helm (vil′helm) a masculine name

Wil·hel·mi·na (wil′hel mē′nə; *Du* vil′hel mē′nä) 〖Ger
Wilhelmine, fem. of *Wilhelm*: see WILLIAM 〗 **1** a feminine name **2** (born *Wilhelmina Helena Pauline
Maria*) 1880-1962; queen of the Netherlands (1890-
1948)

Wilkes (wilks) **1 Charles** 1798-1877; U.S. naval officer
& explorer **2 John** 1727-97; Eng. political reformer

Wil·kins (wil′kinz) **1** Sir **(George) Hubert** 1888-1958;
Austral. polar explorer **2 Maurice H(ugh) F(rederick)**

1916- ; Eng. biophysicist, born in New Zealand: helped determine the structure of DNA **3 Roy** 1901-81; U.S. civil rights leader

Wil·kin·son (wil′kin sən), Sir **Geoffrey** 1921- ; Brit. chemist

Wil·lard (wil′ərd) **1** ‖ < the surname *Willard* ‖ a masculine name **2 Emma** (born *Emma Hart*) 1787-1870; U.S. educator **3 Frances** (**Elizabeth Caroline**) 1839-98; U.S. temperance leader

Wil·liam (wil′yəm) ‖ NormFr *Willaume* < OHG *Willehelm* < *willeo*, will + *helm*, protection < IE base **kel-*, to cover, hide ‖ **1** a masculine name: dim. *Bill, Billy, Liam, Will, Willy:* equiv. Du. *Willem*, Fr. *Guillaume*, Ger. *Wilhelm*, It. *Guglielmo*, Sp. *Guillermo* **2 William I** *c.* 1027-87; duke of Normandy who invaded England & defeated Harold at the Battle of Hastings: king of England (1066-87): called *William the Conqueror* **3 William I** 1533-84; prince of Orange (1544-84) & count of Nassau (1559-84): founder and 1st stadholder (1579-84) of the Netherlands republic: called *William the Silent* **4 William I** 1797-1888; king of Prussia (1861-88) & emperor of Germany (1871-88): son of Frederick William III **5 William II** 1056-1100; king of England (1087-1100): son of William the Conqueror: called *William Rufus* **6 William II** 1859-1941; emperor of Germany & king of Prussia (1888-1918): called *Kaiser Wilhelm* **7 William III** 1650-1702; king of England, Scotland, & Ireland (1689-1702): stadholder of the Netherlands (1672-1702): see MARY II **8 William IV** 1765-1837; king of Great Britain & Ireland (1830-37): son of George III

William of Malmesbury *c.* 1090-*c.* 1143; Eng. historian

Wil·liams (wil′yəmz) **1 Hank** (born *Hiram Williams*) 1923-53; U.S. country singer & composer **2 Ralph Vaughan** *see* VAUGHAN WILLIAMS, Ralph **3 Roger** *c.* 1603-83; Eng. clergyman & colonist in America: founder of R.I. **4 Ten·nes·see** (ten′ə sē′) (born *Thomas Lanier Williams*) 1914-83; U.S. playwright **5 William Car·los** (kär′lōs) 1883-1963; U.S. poet, writer, & physician

William Tell in Swiss legend, a hero in the fight for independence from Austria, forced, on pain of death, to shoot an apple off his son's head with bow and arrow

William the Conqueror *name for* WILLIAM I (duke of Normandy)

Wil·lis (wil'is) ⟦ < the surname *Willis*, prob. < *Willson*, *Wilson* (< *Will's son*) ⟧ a masculine name

Will·stät·ter (vil'shtet'ər), **Richard** (**Martin**) (riH'ärt) 1872-1942; Swiss chemist, born in Germany

Wil·ma (wil'mə) ⟦ Ger, contr. < *Wilhelmina*: see WILLIAM ⟧ a feminine name

Wil·son (wil'sən) **1 Alexander** 1766-1813; Am. ornithologist, born in Scotland **2 Sir Angus** (**Frank Johnstone**) 1913-91; Eng. novelist **3 Charles Thomson Rees** (rēs) 1869-1959; Scot. physicist **4 Edmund** 1895-1972; U.S. writer & critic **5 Sir** (**James**) **Harold** 1916- ; Eng. politician: prime minister (1964-70; 1974-76) **6 Robert Woodrow** 1936- ; U.S. radio astronomer **7** (**Thomas**) **Woodrow** 1856-1924; 28th president of the U.S. (1913-21)

Winck·el·mann (viŋ'kəl män'), **Jo·hann Jo·a·chim** (yō'hän yō'ä khim) 1717-68; Ger. archaeologist & art historian

Win·daus (vin'dous), **A·dolph** (**Otto Rheinhold**) (ä'dôlf) 1876-1959; Ger. chemist

Wind·sor (win'zər) **1** ruling family of Great Britain since 1917, when the name was officially changed from *Saxe-Coburg Gotha* **2 Duke of** (*Edward Albert Christian George Andrew Patrick David*) 1894-1972; king of England, as *Edward VIII* (1936): abdicated: son of George V

Win·fred (win'frid) ⟦ OE *Winfrith* < *wine*, friend + *frithu*, peace: see WILFRED ⟧ a masculine name

Win·i·fred (win'ə frid) ⟦ earlier *Winefred*, *Wynifreed*, altered (infl. by prec.) < Welsh *Gwenfrewi*, lit., white wave ⟧ a feminine name: dim. *Winnie*

Win·nie (win'ē) a feminine name: see EDWINA, WINIFRED

Wins·low (winz'lō), **Edward** 1595-1655; Eng. colonist in America: a founder & governor of Plymouth Colony

Win·throp (win'thrəp) **1 John** 1588-1649; Eng. colonist in America: 1st governor of Massachusetts Bay colony **2 John** 1606-76; governor of Connecticut colony (1657, 1659-76): son of John

Wise (wīz) **1 Stephen Samuel** 1874-1949; U.S. rabbi & Jewish leader, born in Hungary **2 Thomas James** 1859-1937; Eng. bibliophile, editor, & forger

Wis·ter (wis'tər), **Owen** 1860-1938; U.S. novelist

With·er·spoon (wi*th*′ər spoōn′), **John** 1723-94; Am. clergyman & educator, born in Scotland: signer of the Declaration of Independence

Witt·gen·stein (vit′gən shtīn′, -stīn′), **Lud·wig (Josef Johann)** (loōd′vig) 1889-1951; Brit. philosopher, born in Austria

Wit·tig (vit′tiH), **Ge·org** (gā ôrk′) 1897-1987; Ger. chemist

Wode·house (wood′hous), **Sir P(elham) G(renville)** 1881-1975; U.S. novelist & humorist, born in England

Wo·den, Wo·dan (wōd′'n) 〚OE *Woden*, akin to Ger *Wotan* & ON *Odinn* < IE *wōt-*, var. of base *wāt-*, to be mentally excited > L *vates*, prophet, Ger *wut*, rage 〛 the chief deity; identified with the Norse Odin

Wof·fing·ton (wäf′iŋ tən), **Peg** (peg) (born *Margaret Woffington*) c. 1714-60; Ir. actress in England

Wolf (vôlf) **1 Frie·drich Au·gust** (frē′driH ou goōst′) 1759-1824; Ger. classical scholar **2 Hu·go** (hoō′gō) 1860-1903; Austrian composer

Wolfe (woolf) **1 James** 1727-59; Eng. general: defeated the Fr. forces under Montcalm at Quebec (1759) **2 Thomas (Clayton)** 1900-38; U.S. novelist

Wol·fram von Esch·en·bach (vôl′främ fôn esh′ən bäkh′) c. 1170-c. 1220; Ger. epic poet

Woll·stone·craft (wool′stən kraft′), **Mary** (Mrs. *Mary Wollstonecraft Godwin*) 1759-97; Eng. writer & feminist: wife of William Godwin & by him mother of Mary Wollstonecraft Shelley

Wol·sey (wool′zē), **Thomas** c. 1475-1530; Eng. statesman & cardinal: lord chancellor (1515-29) under Henry VIII

Wood (wood) **1 Grant** 1892-1942; U.S. painter **2 Leon·ard** 1860-1927; U.S. general & political administrator

Wood·row (wood′rō) 〚 < the surname *Woodrow* 〛 a masculine name: dim. *Woody*

Wood·ward (wood′wərd), **Robert Burns** 1917-79; U.S. chemist

Woolf (woolf) **1 Leonard (Sidney)** 1880-1969; Eng. publisher & writer **2 Virginia** (born *Adeline Virginia Stephen*) 1882-1941; Eng. novelist & critic: wife of Leonard

Wool·worth (wool′wərth), **F(rank) W(in·field)** 1852-1919; U.S. merchant

Worces·ter (woos′tər), **Joseph Emerson** 1784-1865; U.S.

lexicographer

Words·worth (wʉrdz′wərth), **William** 1770-1850; Eng.
poet: poet laureate (1843-50)

Wren (ren), Sir **Christopher** 1632-1723; Eng. architect

Wright (rīt) **1 Frank Lloyd** 1869-1959; U.S. architect **2
Orville** 1871-1948 U.S. airplane inventor with his
brother Wilbur **3 Richard** 1908-60; U.S. novelist **4
Wilbur** 1867-1912; U.S. airplane inventor

Wul·fi·la (wool′fə lə) *var. of* ULFILAS

Wyatt (wī′ət), Sir **Thomas** *c.* 1503-42; Eng. poet & diplomat

Wych·er·ley (wich′ər lē), **William** *c.* 1640-1716; Eng.
dramatist

Wyc·liffe (or **Wyc·lif**) (wik′lif), **John** *c.* 1330-84; Eng.
religious reformer: made the 1st complete translation
of the Bible into English (from the Vulgate)

Wy·eth (wī′əth) **1 Andrew (Newell)** 1917- ; U.S.
painter: son of Newell **2 N(ewell) C(onvers)** 1882-
1945; U.S. painter & illustrator

X

Xan·thip·pe (zan tip′ē) 5th cent. B.C.; wife of Socrates:
the prototype of the quarrelsome, nagging wife

Xa·vi·er (zā′vē ər, zav′ē-; zāv′yər), Saint **Francis** (1506-
52); Sp. Jesuit missionary: his day is Dec. 3

Xe·noph·a·nes (zi näf′ə nēz′) *c.* 570-*c.* 480 B.C.; Gr.
Eleatic philosopher

Xen·o·phon (zen′ə fən, -fän′) *c.* 430-*c.* 355 B.C.; Gr. historian, essayist, & military leader

Xer·xes I (zʉrk′sēz′) *c.* 519-465 B.C.; king of Persia (486-
465): son of Darius I: called *the Great*

Y

Yah·weh, Yah·we (yä′we, -wā) ⟦Heb, hypothetical
reconstruction of the Tetragrammaton *YHWH*: first
component, *ya, Yahu,* god < older Canaanite name⟧
God: a form of the Hebrew name in the Old Testament: also **Yah·ve** or **Yah·veh** (yä′ve, -vā)

Yah·wist (-wist) the unidentified writer or writers of
certain Old Testament passages in which *Yahweh*
(Jehovah) instead of *Elohim* is used as the name for
God: cf. ELOHIST

Yal·ow (yal′ō), **Ros·a·lyn Suss·man** (räz′ə lin sus′mən) 1921- ; U.S. biochemist

Yang Chen Ning (yäŋ′ chen′ niŋ′) 1922- ; Chin. physicist

Yeats (yāts), **William Butler** 1865-1939; Ir. poet, playwright, & essayist

Yel·tsin (yelt′sin), **Bor·is** (bôr′is) 1931- ; president of Russia (1990-)

Yev·tu·shen·ko (yev′tŏŏ shen′kō), **Yev·ge·ny** (**Aleksandrovich**) (yev gen′ē) 1933- ; Soviet poet

Y·mir (ē′mir′) ⟦ON⟧ *Norse Myth.* the giant from whose body the gods create the world

Yo·lan·da (yō lan′də, -län′-) a feminine name

York (yôrk) ruling family of England (1461-85): founded in 1385 when Edward III's son (*Edmund of Langley*) was created the first Duke of York

Young (yuŋ) **1 Brig·ham** (brig′əm) 1801-77; U.S. Mormon leader **2 Edward** 1683-1765; Eng. poet **3 Thomas** 1773-1829; Eng. physician, physicist, & linguist

Young Pretender *name for* Charles Edward STUART

Yp·si·lan·ti (ip′sə lan′tē; *Gr* ēp′sē län′tē), **Alexander** 1792-1828 and his brother **De·me·tri·os** (də mē′trē əs) 1793-1832; Gr. revolutionary leaders against the Turks

Y·sa·ye (ē zà ē′), **Eu·gène** (ö zhen′) 1858-1931; Belgian violinist, composer, & conductor

Y·seult (i sŏŏlt′) *alt. sp. of* ISEULT (Isolde)

Yu·ka·wa (yŏŏ kä′wä), **Hi·de·ki** (hē′de kē′) 1907-81; Jpn. physicist

Y·vonne (ē vän′) a feminine name: var. *Yvette*

Z

Zach·a·ri·ah (zak′ə rī′ə) ⟦LL(Ec) *Zacharias* < Gr(Ec) < Heb *zecharya*, lit., God remembers < *zachar*, to remember + *ya*, God⟧ a masculine name: dim. *Zach;* var. *Zacharias, Zachary, Zechariah*

Zach·a·ri·as (-əs) **1** a masculine name: see ZACHARIAH **2** *Bible a*) the father of John the Baptist: Luke 1:5 *b*) a man named as a martyr by Jesus: Matt. 23:25

Zach·a·ry (zak′ə rē) a masculine name: see ZACHARIAH

Zang·will (zaŋ′wil′), **Israel** 1864-1926; Eng. novelist & playwright

Zeb·e·dee (zeb′ə dē′) ⟦LL(Ec) *Zebedaeus* < Gr(Ec) *Zebedaios*, prob. < Heb *zevadya*, lit., God has bestowed < *zavad*, to donate, bestow + *ya*, God ⟧ *Bible* father of the disciples James and John: Matt. 4:21

Zeb·u·lun (zeb'yə lən, zə byoo'lən) ⟦ Heb *zevulun* < ? ⟧ *Bible* Jacob's tenth son, whose mother was Leah: Gen. 30:20

Zech·a·ri·ah (zek'ə rī'ə) **1** a masculine name: see ZACHARIAH **2** *Bible* a Hebrew prophet of the 6th cent. B.C. who urged the rebuilding of the Temple

Zee·man (zā'män'), **Pie·ter** (pē'tər) 1865-1943; Du. physicist

Zeng·er (zeŋ'ər, -gər), **John Peter** 1697-1746; Am. journalist & publisher, born in Germany

Ze·no (zē'nō) **1** 5th cent. B.C.; Gr. Eleatic philosopher: also **Zeno of E·le·a** (ē'lē ə) (town in Italy) **2** *c.* 334-*c.* 261 B.C.; Gr. philosopher: founder of Stoicism: also **Zeno of Ci·ti·um** (sish'ē əm) (city in Cyprus)

Ze·no·bi·a (zə nō'bē ə) ⟦ L < Gr *Zēnobia* ⟧ 3d cent. A.D.; queen of Palmyra

Zeph·a·ni·ah (zef'ə nī'ə) ⟦ Heb *tsefanya*, lit., the Lord has hidden < *tsafan*, to hide + *ya*, God ⟧ *Bible* a Hebrew prophet of the 7th cent. B.C.

Zeph·yr (zef'ər) ZEPHYRUS

Zeph·y·rus (zef'ə rəs) ⟦ L < Gr *zephyros*, the west wind ⟧ *Gr. Myth.* the west wind personified as a god

Zeus (zyoos, zoos) ⟦ Gr: for IE base see DEVI ⟧ *Gr. Myth.* the chief deity, son of Cronus and Rhea and husband of Hera: identified with the Roman Jupiter

Zeux·is (zooks'is) fl. 5th cent. B.C.; Gr. painter

Zhao Zi·yang (jou'dzē yäŋ') 1919- ; Chin. Communist leader: prime minister of China (1980-88); general secretary of the Communist Party (1987-89)

Zhou En·lai (jō'en'lī') *Pinyin form of* CHOU EN-LAI

Zhu·kov (zhoo'kôf), **Ge·or·gi K(onstantinovich)** (gyôr'gē) 1896-1974; Soviet marshal

Zieg·feld (zig'feld'), **Flor·enz** (flôr'ənz) 1869-1932; U.S. theatrical producer

Zieg·ler (tsēk'lər), **Karl** (kärl) 1898-1973; Ger. chemist

Zil·pah (zil'pə) ⟦ Heb *zilpa*, akin to *zelef*, a spray, sprinkling ⟧ *Bible* the mother of Gad and Asher: Gen. 30:10-13

Zins·ser (zin'sər), **Hans** 1878-1940; U.S. bacteriologist & writer

Ziṣ·ka (tsis'kä'), **Jo·hann** (yō'hän') *Ger. name of* Jan ŽIŽKA

Žiž·ka (zhish′kä), **Jan** (yän) died 1424; Bohemian general & leader of the Hussites

Zo·e (zō′ē) ⟦ Gr Zōē, lit., life ⟧ a feminine name

Zo·la (zō′lä′, zō lä′; zō′lə), **É·mile** (Édouard Charles Antoine) (ä mēl′) 1840-1902; Fr. novelist

Zo·ro·as·ter (zō′rō as′tər, zôr′ō as′-) c. 6th or 7th cent. B.C.; Pers. religious teacher: founder of Zoroastrianism

Zor·ri·lla (y Moral) (thô rē′lyä), **Jo·sé** (hō se′) 1817-93; Sp. poet & playwright

Zu·lo·a·ga (thōō′lô ä′gä), **Ig·na·cio** (ēg nä′thyô) 1870-1945; Sp. painter

Zur·ba·rán (thōōr′bä rän′), **Fran·cis·co de** (frän thēs′kô the) 1598-1664; Sp. painter

Zweig (tsvīk; zwīg) **1 Ar·nold** (är′nôlt) 1887-1968; Ger. novelist & playwright **2 Ste·fan** (shte′fän′) 1881-1942; Austrian biographer, novelist, & playwright

Zwing·li (zwiŋ′lē, tsviŋ′-), **Ul·rich** (ool′riH′) 1484-1531; Swiss Protestant reformer: also **Hul·dreich Zwingli** (hool′drīH′)

Zwor·y·kin (zwôr′i kin), **Vladimir Kos·ma** (käz′mə) 1889-1982; U.S. engineer & inventor, born in Russia: pioneer in the development of modern TV